KU-689-919

CHURCHILL

WINSTON S. CHURCHILL

THE SECOND WORLD WAR

BOOK IX

CLOSING THE RING
ITALY WON
June 6—November 12, 1943

Illustrations researched and selected
by Roger Jean Ségalat

First published 1952
Fourth Edition 1966

Copyright Cassell and Company Limited
Edito-Service S.A., Geneva, Publishers

13 039 09 R?

MORAL OF THE WORK

IN WAR: RESOLUTION
IN DEFEAT: DEFIANCE
IN VICTORY: MAGNANIMITY
IN PEACE: GOODWILL

PREFACE

In *The Hinge of Fate* I described the decisive change for the better in our fortunes which lighted the winter of 1942 and the spring of 1943. *Closing the Ring* sets forth the year of conflict from June 1943 to June 1944. Aided by the command of the oceans, the mastery of the U-boats, and our ever-growing superiority in the air, the Western Allies were able to conquer Sicily and invade Italy, with the result that Mussolini was overthrown and the Italian nation came over to our side. Hitler and the circle of countries he had occupied was isolated, and, with the immense onslaught of Russia from the east, was completely surrounded. At the same time Japan had been forced on to the defensive and was vainly trying to hold the vast territories she had overrun.

The danger which faced the United Nations was no longer Defeat, but Stalemate. Before them lay the formidable task of invading the two aggressors in their homelands and liberating from their grip the peoples they had struck down. This world-wide problem was faced at the Conferences between Great Britain and the United States at Quebec and Washington in the summer, and at the triple meeting of the main Allies at Teheran in November. There was no difference between us of aim or of resolve to give all to the common cause. Grave divergences of method and of emphasis were inevitable because of the various angles from which the three partners naturally approached the decisions which were required. How agreement was reached upon all the supreme issues is the tale I now have to tell. It carries us to the liberation of Rome and to the eve of the British and American crossing of the Channel and entry into Normandy.

I have followed the method I used in earlier volumes. I do not seek to do more than make a contribution to history from the standpoint of the British Prime Minister and Minister of Defence. In this my directives, telegrams, and minutes, written at the time and not in the after-light, are my stepping-stones. It has been suggested that the answers to many of these documents should also be included. I, on the other hand, have found it necessary in this volume to practise compression and selection in an increasing degree. A final volume is already needed to record and complete the story. I can therefore only make my excuses to any who may feel that their point of view is not fully set forth.

More than seven years have passed since the events here recorded happened. Many international relationships have changed. Deep rifts have opened between former comrades. New and perhaps darker clouds have gathered. Old foes have become friends, and even allies. In this setting some of the sentiments and expressions contained in telegrams, minutes, and reports of Conferences may jar upon the readers in other countries. I can only remind them that these documents have an historical value and that we were then engaged in a fierce and terrible war. When men are fighting for their lives they are not often disposed to be complimentary to those who are trying to kill them. On the other hand, to soften all harsh expressions about the enemy nations of those days would prevent a true picture being presented. Time and Truth are healers.

WINSTON S. CHURCHILL

Chartwell,
    Westerham,
        Kent
September 1, 1951

ACKNOWLEDGMENTS

I MUST again acknowledge the assistance of those who helped me with the previous volumes, namely, Lieutenant-General Sir Henry Pownall, Commodore G. R. G. Allen, Colonel F. W. Deakin, Mr. Denis Kelly, and Mr. C. C. Wood. I have also to thank the very large number of others who have kindly read these pages and commented upon them.

I am obliged to Air Chief Marshal Sir Guy Garrod for his help in presenting the Air aspect.

Lord Ismay has continued to give me his aid, as have my other friends.

I record my obligation to His Majesty's Government for permission to reproduce the text of certain official documents of which the Crown Copyright is legally vested in the Controller of His Majesty's Stationery Office. At the request of His Majesty's Government, on security grounds, I have paraphrased some of the telegrams published in this volume. These changes have not altered in any way the sense or substance of the telegrams.

I am indebted to the Roosevelt Trust for the use they have permitted of the President's telegrams quoted here, and also to others who have allowed their private letters to be published.

TABLE OF CONTENTS

Chapter   *Page*

I   THE COMMAND OF THE SEAS. GUADALCANAL AND
      NEW GUINEA   3

II   THE CONQUEST OF SICILY   23

III   THE FALL OF MUSSOLINI   40

IV   WESTWARD HO! SYNTHETIC HARBOURS   .   .   61

V   THE QUEBEC CONFERENCE: "QUADRANT"   .   .   72

VI   ITALY: THE ARMISTICE   88

VII   THE INVASION OF ITALY. AT THE WHITE HOUSE
      AGAIN   105

VIII   THE BATTLE OF SALERNO. A HOMEWARD VOYAGE   124

IX   A SPELL AT HOME   138

X   TENSIONS WITH GENERAL DE GAULLE   .   .   .   153

XI   THE BROKEN AXIS   166

XII   ISLAND PRIZES LOST   180

XIII   HITLER'S "SECRET WEAPON"   201

XIV   DEADLOCK ON THE THIRD FRONT   214

XV   ARCTIC CONVOYS AGAIN   228

XVI   FOREIGN SECRETARIES' CONFERENCE IN MOSCOW   247

XVII   ADVENT OF THE TRIPLE MEETING. THE HIGH
       COMMANDS   267

APPENDICES:

A.   List of Abbreviations   287

B.   List of Code-Names   288

C.   Prime Minister's Personal Minutes and Telegrams,
       June–October 1943   290

D. Monthly Totals of Shipping Losses, British, Allied, and Neutral, January 1943–May 1944 . . . 321

E. Summary of Order of Battle, German and Italian Divisions, on September 8, 1943 322

INDEX 325

Facsimile showing Mr. Churchill's Minute of May 30, 1942
between 77-78

MAPS AND DIAGRAMS

Cumulative Gains and Losses of Merchant Ships Outside Enemy Control, 1939–45 5

The Rise and Decline of the German U-boat Fleet, 1939–45 9

The Battle of the Atlantic: Merchant Ships Sunk by U-boat 12–14

The South-West Pacific 19

The Conquest of Sicily 27

The Salerno Landing 127

The South Ægean Sea 183

Leros 197

Southern Italy: Operations, September–December 1943 217

Operations in Russia, July-December 1943 . . . 232

BOOK IX

CLOSING THE RING
ITALY WON
June 6—November 12, 1943

THEME OF THE BOOK

HOW

NAZI GERMANY WAS ISOLATED

AND

ASSAILED ON ALL SIDES

CHAPTER I

THE COMMAND OF THE SEAS
GUADALCANAL AND NEW GUINEA

*Maritime Power – The Mediterranean Freed – The Mortal Struggle
with the U-Boats – The Battle of the Atlantic the Dominating Factor
in the War – An Atlantic Convoy Conference Meets – The Decisive
Battle with the U-Boats Fought and Won – Air Cover Protects Our
Convoys – The Climax of April 1943 – A Welcome Respite – New
Weapons – The Schnorkel – Retrospect on the Pacific War – The
Struggle for New Guinea – The Solomon Islands – Guadalcanal – A
Noble Feat of Arms – Our Efforts to Help the United States – The
End of the Japanese Offensive – The Japanese Defeat in New Guinea
– The Turn of the Tide.*

*E*ARLIER volumes have led us to the point where the
aggressors, both in Europe and Asia, had been driven to the
defensive. Stalingrad in February 1943 marked the turn of
the tide in Russia. By May all German and Italian forces in the
African continent had been killed or captured. The American
victories in the Coral Sea and at Midway Island a year before had
stopped Japanese expansion in the Pacific Ocean. Australia and
New Zealand were freed from the threat of invasion. Henceforward in Europe the Axis must expect and await the Anglo-
American assault which had so long been purposed. The tremendous armies of the United States were growing in strength and
quality with every month that passed. But the Western Allies
could never strike home at Hitler's Europe, and thus bring the
war to a decisive end, unless another major favourable change
came to pass. Anglo-American "maritime power", a modern
term expressing the combined strength of naval and air forces

properly woven together, became supreme on and under the surface of the seas and the oceans during 1943. It was not until April and May that the U-boats were beaten and the mastery of the life-lines across the Atlantic was finally won. Without this no amphibious operations on the enormous scale required to liberate Europe would have been possible. Soviet Russia would have been left to face Hitler's whole remaining strength while most of Europe lay in his grip.

In the Mediterranean also the U-boats were mastered. Our armies for the Sicilian and Italian campaigns were assembling and could now be launched across the sea against the under-belly of Hitler's Europe. Besides this the Mediterranean was the main artery in the communications of the British Empire. The extirpation of Axis power in North Africa opened to our convoys the direct route to Egypt, India, and Australia, protected from Gibraltar to Suez by sea and air forces working from the newly won bases along the route. The long haul round the Cape, which had cost us so dear in time, effort, and tonnage, would soon be ended. The saving of an average of forty-five days for each convoy to the Middle East increased magnificently at one stroke the fertility of our shipping.

* * *

The single-handed British struggle against the U-boats, the magnetic mines, and the surface raiders in the first two and a half years of the war has already been described. The long-awaited supreme event of the American alliance which arose from the Japanese attack on Pearl Harbour seemed at first to have increased our perils at sea. In 1940 four million tons of merchant shipping were lost, and more than four million tons in 1941. In 1942, after the United States was our Ally, nearly eight million tons of the augmented mass of Allied shipping had been sunk. Until the end of 1942 the U-boats sank ships faster than the Allies could build them. The foundation of all our hopes and schemes was the immense shipbuilding programme of the United States. During 1943 the curve of new tonnage rose sharply and losses fell. Before the end of that year new tonnage at last surpassed losses at sea from all causes, and the second quarter saw, for the first time, U-boat losses exceed their rate of replacement. The time was presently to come when more U-boats would be

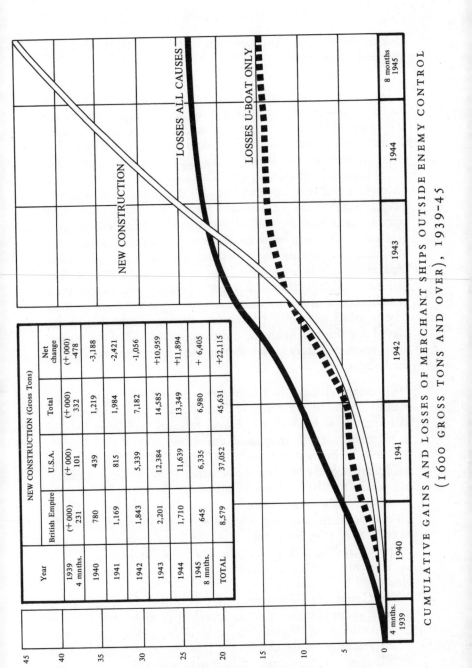

NEW CONSTRUCTION (Gross Tons)				
Year	British Empire	U.S.A.	Total	Net change
1939 4 mnths.	(+ 000) 231	(+ 000) 101	(+ 000) 332	(+ 000) −478
1940	780	439	1,219	−3,188
1941	1,169	815	1,984	−2,421
1942	1,843	5,339	7,182	−1,056
1943	2,201	12,384	14,585	+10,959
1944	1,710	11,639	13,349	+11,894
1945 8 mnths.	645	6,335	6,980	+ 6,405
TOTAL	8,579	37,052	45,631	+22,115

MILLIONS OF GROSS TONS

CUMULATIVE GAINS AND LOSSES OF MERCHANT SHIPS OUTSIDE ENEMY CONTROL
(1600 GROSS TONS AND OVER), 1939–45

sunk in the Atlantic than merchant ships. But before this lay a long and bitter conflict.

* * *

The Battle of the Atlantic was the dominating factor all through the war. Never for one moment could we forget that everything happening elsewhere, on land, at sea, or in the air, depended ultimately on its outcome, and amid all other cares we viewed its changing fortunes day by day with hope or apprehension. The tale of hard and unremitting toil, often under conditions of acute discomfort and frustration and always in the presence of unseen danger, is lighted by incident and drama. But for the individual sailor or airman in the U-boat war there were few moments of exhilarating action to break the monotony of an endless succession of anxious, uneventful days. Vigilance could never be relaxed. Dire crisis might at any moment flash upon the scene with brilliant fortune or glare with mortal tragedy. Many gallant actions and incredible feats of endurance are recorded, but the deeds of those who perished will never be known. Our merchant seamen displayed their highest qualities, and the brotherhood of the sea was never more strikingly shown than in their determination to defeat the U-boat.

* * *

Important changes had been made in our operational commands. Admiral Sir Andrew Cunningham, who had gone to Washington as head of our Naval Mission, had been recalled in October 1942 to command the Allied Navies in "Torch". Admiral Sir Percy Noble, who at Derby House, the Liverpool headquarters of the Western Approaches, had held the commanding post in the Battle of the Atlantic since the beginning of 1941, went to Washington, with his unequalled knowledge of the U-boat problem, and was relieved at Liverpool by Admiral Sir Max Horton, who had commanded the British submarine service with outstanding ability. In February 1943 Air Marshal Slessor became chief of Coastal Command. These arrangements were vindicated by the results.

The Casablanca Conference had proclaimed the defeat of the U-boats as our first objective. In March 1943 an Atlantic Convoy Conference met in Washington, under Admiral King, to pool all Allied resources in the Atlantic. This system did not amount to full unity of command. There was well-knit co-operation

6

at all levels and complete accord at the top, but the two Allies approached the problem with differences of method. The United States had no organisation like our Coastal Command, through which on the British or reception side of the ocean air operations were controlled by a single authority. A high degree of flexibility had been attained. Formations could be rapidly switched from quiet to dangerous areas, and the command was being reinforced largely from American sources. In Washington control was exerted through a number of autonomous subordinate commands called "sea frontiers", each with its allotment of aircraft.

★ ★ ★

After the winter gales, which caused much damage to our escorts, but also checked the U-boat attack, the month of February 1943 had shown an ugly increase in the hostile concentrations in the North Atlantic. In spite of heavy losses, the number of operational U-boats at Admiral Doenitz's disposal at the beginning of the year rose to two hundred and twelve. In March there were over a hundred of them constantly at sea, and the packs in which they hunted could no longer be evaded by skilful routeing. The issue had to be fought out by combined sea and air forces round the convoys themselves. Sinkings throughout the world rose to nearly 700,000 tons in that month.

Amid these stresses a new agreement was reached in Washington whereby Britain and Canada assumed entire responsibility for convoys on the main North Atlantic route to Britain. The decisive battle with the U-boats was now fought and won. Control was vested in two joint naval and air headquarters, one at Liverpool under a British and the other at Halifax under a Canadian admiral. Naval protection in the North Atlantic was henceforward provided by British and Canadian ships, the United States remaining responsible for their convoys to the Mediterranean and their own troop transports. In the air British, Canadian, and United States forces all complied with the day-to-day requirements of the joint commanders at Liverpool and Halifax.

The air gap in the North Atlantic south-east of Greenland was now closed by means of the very-long-range (V.L.R.) Liberator squadrons based in Newfoundland and Iceland. By April a shuttle service provided daylight air-cover along the whole route. The U-boat packs were kept underwater and harried continually, while the air and surface escort of the convoys coped with the attackers. We were now strong enough to form independent flotilla groups to act like cavalry divisions, apart from all escort duties. This I had long desired to see.

*   *   *

It was at this time that the H₂S apparatus, described in Volume IV,* of which a number had been handed over somewhat reluctantly by our Bomber Command to Coastal Command, played a notable part. The Germans had learnt how to detect the comparatively long waves used in our earlier Radar, and to dive before our flyers could attack them. It was many months before they discovered how to detect the very short wave used in our new method. Hitler complained that this single invention was the ruin of the U-boat campaign. This was an exaggeration.

In the Bay of Biscay however the Anglo-American air offensive was soon to make the life of U-boats in transit almost unbearable. The rocket now fired from aircraft was so damaging that the enemy started sending the U-boats through in groups on the surface, fighting off the aircraft with gunfire in daylight. This desperate experiment was vain. In March and April 1943 twenty-seven U-boats were destroyed in the Atlantic alone, more than half by air attack.

In April 1943 we could see the balance turn. Two hundred and thirty-five U-boats, the greatest number the Germans ever achieved, were in action. But their crews were beginning to waver. They could never feel safe. Their attacks, even when conditions were favourable, were no longer pressed home, and during this month our shipping losses in the Atlantic fell by nearly 300,000 tons. In May alone forty U-boats perished in the Atlantic. The German Admiralty watched their charts with strained attention, and at the end of the month Admiral Doenitz recalled the remnants of his fleet from the North Atlantic to rest or to fight in less hazardous waters. By June 1943 the shipping losses fell to the lowest figure since the United States had entered the war. The convoys came through intact, and the Atlantic supply line was safe.

The struggle in these critical months is shown by the table on page 10.

* See Book VII, p. 251.

8

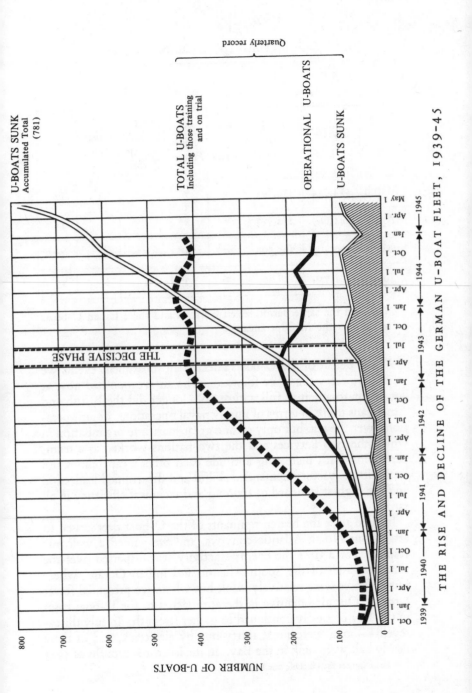

U-BOATS SUNK
Accumulated Total
(781)

Quarterly record

TOTAL U-BOATS
Including those training
and on trial

OPERATIONAL U-BOATS

U-BOATS SUNK

THE DECISIVE PHASE

NUMBER OF U-BOATS

800 — 700 — 600 — 500 — 400 — 300 — 200 — 100 — 0

Oct. 1 | Jan. 1 | Apr. 1 | Jul. 1 | Oct. 1 | Jan. 1 | Apr. 1 | Jul. 1 | Oct. 1 | Jan. 1 | Apr. 1 | Jul. 1 | Oct. 1 | Jan. 1 | Apr. 1 | Jul. 1 | Oct. 1 | Jan. 1 | Apr. 1 | May 1
1939 | 1940 | 1941 | 1942 | 1943 | 1944 | 1945

THE RISE AND DECLINE OF THE GERMAN U-BOAT FLEET, 1939–45

ATLANTIC OCEAN

1943	Allied Shipping sunk		U-boats sunk				
	By U-boat	Total. All Causes	By Naval Forces	By Air Forces	Jointly by Naval and Air Forces	Other Causes	Total
March	514,744	538,695	4	7	—	1	12
April	241,687	252,533	6	8*	1	—	15
May	199,409	205,598	12*	18*	7	3	40
June	21,759	28,269	6	9*	2	—	17

Note.—In the same period seven German and three Italian U-boats were sunk in the Mediterranean.

*   *   *

As the defeat of the U-boats affected all subsequent events we must here carry the story forward. The air weapon had now at last begun to attain its full stature. No longer did the British and Americans think in terms of purely naval operations, or air operations over the sea, but only of one great maritime organisation in which the two Services and the two nations worked as a team, perceiving with increasing aptitude each other's capabilities and limitations. Victory demanded skilful and determined leadership and the highest standard of training and technical efficiency in all ranks.

In June 1943 the beaten remnants of the U-boat fleet ceased to attack our North Atlantic convoys, and we gained a welcome respite. For a time the enemy's activity was dispersed over the remote wastes of the South Atlantic and Indian Oceans, where our defences were relatively weak but where we presented fewer targets. Our air offensive in the approaches to the U-boat bases in the Bay of Biscay continued to gather strength. In July thirty-seven U-boats were sunk, thirty-one by air attack, and of these nearly half were sunk in the Bay. In the last three months of 1943

* These figures each include one Italian.

fifty-three U-boats were destroyed, while we lost only forty-seven merchant ships.

Throughout a stormy autumn the U-boats struggled vainly to regain the ascendancy in the North Atlantic. Our combined sea and air defence was by that time so strong that they suffered heavy losses for small results in every convoy battle. In anti-U-boat warfare the air weapon was now an equal partner with the surface ship. Our convoys were guarded by more numerous and formidable surface escorts than ever before, reinforced with escort carriers giving close and advanced air protection. More than this, we had the means to seek out and destroy the U-boats wherever we could find them. The combination of support groups of carriers and escort vessels, aided by long-range aircraft of Coastal Command, which now included American squadrons, proved decisive. One such group, commanded by Captain F. J. Walker, R.N., our most outstanding U-boat killer, was responsible for the destruction of six U-boats in a single cruise.

The so-called merchant aircraft-carrier, or M.A.C. ship, which came out at this time was an entirely British conception. An ordinary cargo ship or tanker was fitted with a flying deck for naval aircraft. While preserving its mercantile status and carrying cargo it helped to defend the convoy in which it sailed. There were nineteen of these vessels in all, two wearing the Dutch flag, working in the North Atlantic. Together with the catapult-aircraft merchant ships (C.A.M.S.), which had preceded them with a rather different technique, they marked a new departure in naval warfare. The merchant ship had now taken the offensive against the enemy instead of merely defending itself when attacked. The line between the combatant and non-combatant ship, already indistinct, had almost vanished.

The immense United States war production was now reaching its peak. Long-range aircraft and ships of many types, including the escort carriers we so greatly needed, were flowing from American yards and workshops. Many of these, and much special equipment, especially Radar, were placed at our disposal to help our own industry, and American naval and air forces joined in the battle everywhere.

Although in the face of the harsh facts Admiral Doenitz was forced to recoil, he continued to maintain as many U-boats at sea as ever. But their attack was blunted and they seldom attempted

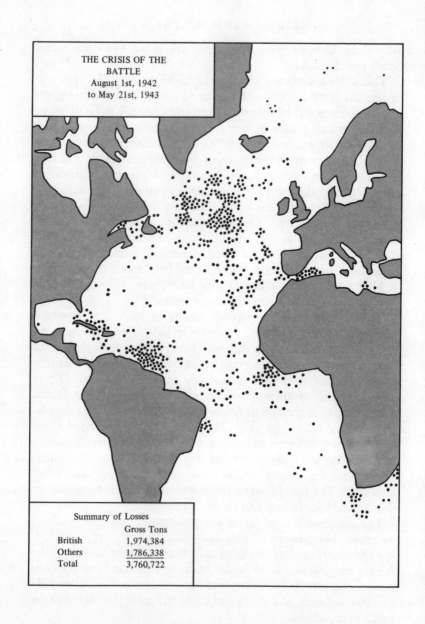

THE CRISIS OF THE
BATTLE
August 1st, 1942
to May 21st, 1943

Summary of Losses	
	Gross Tons
British	1,974,384
Others	1,786,338
Total	3,760,722

THE BATTLE OF THE ATLANTIC
MERCHANT SHIPS   SUNK BY U-BOAT
IN THE ATLANTIC

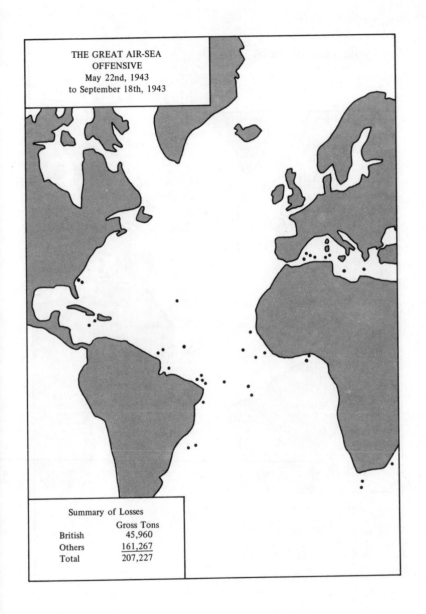

THE GREAT AIR-SEA
OFFENSIVE
May 22nd, 1943
to September 18th, 1943

Summary of Losses

	Gross Tons
British	45,960
Others	161,267
Total	207,227

THE BATTLE OF THE ATLANTIC
MERCHANT SHIPS   SUNK BY U-BOAT
IN THE ATLANTIC

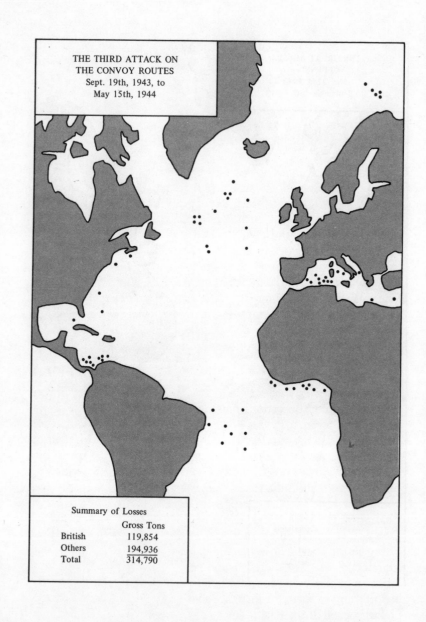

THE THIRD ATTACK ON
THE CONVOY ROUTES
Sept. 19th, 1943, to
May 15th, 1944

Summary of Losses	
	Gross Tons
British	119,854
Others	194,936
Total	314,790

THE BATTLE OF THE ATLANTIC
MERCHANT SHIPS   SUNK BY U-BOAT
IN THE ATLANTIC

to cut through our defences. He did not however despair. On January 20, 1944, he said, "The enemy has succeeded in gaining the advantage in defence. The day will come when I shall offer Churchill a first-rate submarine war. The submarine weapon has not been broken by the setbacks of 1943. On the contrary, it has become stronger. In 1944, which will be a successful but a hard year, we shall smash Britain's supply [line] with a new submarine weapon."

This confidence was not wholly unfounded. At the beginning of 1944 a gigantic effort was being made in Germany to develop a new type of U-boat which could move more quickly underwater and travel much farther. At the same time many of the older boats were withdrawn so that they could be fitted with the "Schnorkel" and work in British coastal waters. This new device enabled them to recharge their batteries while submerged with only a small tube for the intake of air remaining above the surface Their chances of eluding detection from the air were thus improved, and it soon became evident that the Schnorkel-fitted boats were intended to dispute the passage of the English Channel whenever the Allied invasion was launched.

★　★　★

A retrospect is necessary here to remind the reader of the stirring far-flung operations which had changed the whole scene in the Far East in 1942.

While British sea-power was deployed mainly in the Atlantic and the Mediterranean, the United States was bearing almost alone the whole burden of the war against Japan. In the immense ocean spaces from India to the western coast of America itself we could give little support except with slender Australian and New Zealand naval forces. Our depleted Eastern Fleet, now based in East Africa, could do no more for a time than protect our convoys. In the Pacific however the balance had turned. The naval superiority of the United States was re-established, and the Japanese, while trying to consolidate their gains in the East Indies, had nothing to spare for incursions into the Indian Ocean. Much had happened in the Pacific since the Battles of the Coral Sea and Midway Island in the summer of 1942. Admiral Nimitz, with his headquarters at Pearl Harbour, controlled the North, Central, and South Pacific. General MacArthur, who had reached

Australia from the Philippines in March 1942, commanded the South-West Pacific, extending from the China coast to Australia, and including the Philippines, the Bismarck Archipelago, New Guinea, all the east coast of Australia, and the Solomon Islands.

The Imperial Japanese Navy, deeply conscious of defeat in the Central Pacific, turned once more to the South-West. Here, more remote from the main sources of American power, they hoped to renew their triumphant advance. Their first thrust, towards Port Moresby, in New Guinea, having been foiled by the Battle of the Coral Sea, the enemy resolved to attack by land across the Owen Stanley Mountains. Thus began the struggle for New Guinea. Simultaneously they determined to seize the Solomon Islands, a British protectorate.* They already held the small island of Tulagi, and could quickly set about the construction of an air base in the neighbouring island of Guadalcanal. With both Port Moresby and Guadalcanal in their possession they hoped the Coral Sea would become a Japanese lake, bordering upon North-Eastern Australia. From Guadalcanal Japanese airmen could reach out towards other and still more distant island groups along the main line of sea communications between America and New Zealand. American and Australian resistance to these two assaults form an admirable example of bold inter-Service action resting on maritime power.

The Solomon Islands became the objective of both sides, and Admiral King in Washington had long planned their occupation. On July 4, 1942, air reconnaissance disclosed that the enemy were already constructing an airfield on Guadalcanal. Admiral Ghormley, commanding the South Pacific area, without waiting to perfect his plans, struck on August 7 with the 1st Marine Division, already in New Zealand. The uncompleted Japanese air base was quickly captured and the battle for Guadalcanal began. It was to last six months.

$$\star \quad \star \quad \star$$

From their main Fleet base in the Carolines and from Rabaul the Japanese could maintain greatly superior naval and air forces

---

* The British Resident Commissioner and his District Officers and a few residents remained in the Solomons throughout the fighting, concealed and protected by loyal natives. They maintained a coast-watching service with remarkable success and the information which these devoted men contrived to get through by radio was of great help to the American Commanders.

in these waters. The Japanese commander in Rabaul at once sent a strong force of cruisers and destroyers to Guadalcanal. In the early hours of August 9, aided by heavy rain squalls, the Japanese surprised the Allied naval forces guarding the approach to the landing-place and almost annihilated them. In about forty minutes they sank three American heavy cruisers and the Australian cruiser *Canberra*, while receiving themselves only minor damage. Had the Japanese admiral followed up this remarkable success he could have swept through the strait to the eastward and destroyed the American transports, which were still discharging their troops and stores. Like other Japanese commanders before and after him in this war, he missed his opportunity and withdrew.

The American commander could however no longer support the landing. After unloading all that he could he retired, leaving his 17,000 Marines ashore alone on a hostile island without air cover and exposed to reinforced land attack. This was indeed a grim moment. But the United States Marines were undaunted. In spite of ceaseless air attack they held and improved their position, while a supply service by sea was improvised and the captured airfield was brought into use. From this moment fighters and dive-bombers manned by the Marines worked from Guadalcanal itself and gave instant relief.

The Japanese now sought a decision at sea. On August 24 an inconclusive action was fought to the north of the Solomons. Enemy transports approaching Guadalcanal were driven off by air attack. On August 31 the aircraft-carrier *Saratoga* was damaged by a submarine, and a fortnight later the carrier *Wasp*, of Mediterranean repute, was sunk. Both sides built up their strength. Early in October, in another night engagement, a strong force of Japanese cruisers was beaten off, one being sunk; but two enemy battleships bombarded the airfield, and presently landed 4,500 reinforcements at a stroke. Another crisis was at hand.

★   ★   ★

Admiral Nimitz and General MacArthur urged, not unnaturally, that priority should be given to the Pacific theatre at the expense of European operations. They were powerfully supported at Washington by Admiral King. But the descent in North-West Africa ("Torch") was now dominant, and major strategy prevailed. The climax of the battle on land now came. For ten days from October 19, 1942, the Marines in close jungle fighting held all their positions and beat the Japanese to a standstill. In another fleet action, mainly fought by aircraft north of the Solomons, the carrier *Hornet*, which had replaced the *Wasp*, was sunk. The carrier *Enterprise*, the battleship *South Dakota*, and two cruisers were damaged. The Japanese had two carriers disabled.

Admiral Halsey, who had succeeded Admiral Ghormley, and who found himself for the moment without any carriers, now appealed through Admiral Nimitz for one or more British carriers. Although we had little knowledge of American Pacific plans, we realised that an intense crisis had arisen in the Solomons. It was obvious that no carriers could reach the scene for many weeks. I earnestly desired to help in this heroic struggle, but with the main naval responsibility for landing the Anglo-American Army in North-West Africa upon us we could make no immediate proposal. It was not until December that the strain and climax of "Torch" lessened. I then sent the President a full account of our carrier position and made the best offer in our power.

Former Naval Person to President Roosevelt   2 Dec 42

Ever since we received a request for carrier reinforcement for your Pacific Fleet we have been earnestly seeking to meet your wishes. We did not feel able to come to a decision about these very few vital units until we knew how our carriers had fared in the restricted and dangerous waters in which they had to operate for "Torch". The hazards of "Torch" are not yet ended, as our build-up of shore-based aircraft will not enable the withdrawal for some time of the two carriers now employed on "Torch". Knowing however how urgently you require a reinforcement of carriers in the Pacific, we are prepared to take a risk now and come to a decision as to what we can give you.

Our carrier strength consists of four long-endurance armoured fleet carriers. We are prepared to withdraw *Illustrious* from the Eastern Fleet, and give Admiral Somerville the *Unicorn* and an auxiliary carrier. We are also prepared to withdraw *Victorious* from the Home Fleet and to send you both *Victorious* and *Illustrious* if you can allow [your] *Ranger* [a smaller carrier] to join the Home Fleet. In view of the vital importance of the Atlantic communications, the necessity of supporting the North Russian convoys, the possible appearance of *Graf Zeppelin* at the end of the year, and the present condition of *Indomitable* and *Formidable*, we could not release both *Victorious* and *Illustrious* without the addition of *Ranger* to the Home Fleet.

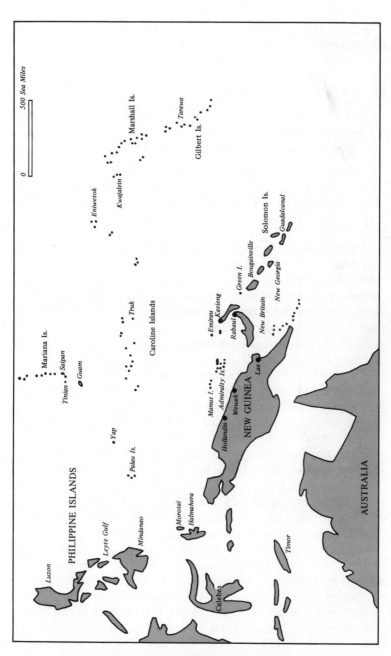

THE SOUTH-WEST PACIFIC

I am much in favour of sending you two carriers rather than one if this can be managed, as this will not only give you increased strength, but would allow the two ships to work as a tactical unit, which would appear to be necessary, as neither ship carries sufficient aircraft to operate singly. I would propose to send Admiral Lyster, who is known to a good many of your officers, in command. Both ships should proceed to Pearl Harbour, arriving about the end of December, to adjust their complement of aircraft. If you are in favour of this exchange Pound will settle details with King.

Admiral King was however unwilling to spare the *Ranger*, and in consequence we could only send the *Victorious*. She left the Home Fleet for Pearl Harbour in December.

★　★　★

Meanwhile in November a series of sea and air fights which eventually proved decisive began around the Solomons, with heavy losses on both sides. On the night of November 13, in a fierce action, two United States cruisers and four destroyers were lost, with both the American admirals engaged. On the Japanese side a battleship and two destroyers were sunk. Eleven Japanese transports, with strong supporting forces, were at the same time moving towards Guadalcanal. In the thirty-six hours of ceaseless fighting which followed a second Japanese battleship, a cruiser, and three destroyers, and above all seven transports filled with troops, were sunk, at the cost to the Americans of only one more destroyer. The Japanese at this point lost confidence in the venture. Ever-increasing American reinforcements began to arrive, and the glorious Marines were relieved by the Army. The conflict continued without pause, but the enemy made no further bid for victory. On January 4, 1943, Imperial Headquarters in Tokyo ordered the evacuation of Guadalcanal, which was accomplished without serious loss. On February 9 Admiral Halsey was able at last to report that the island had been conquered.

This episode marked the end of the Japanese offensive surge. In six major naval engagements and many lesser encounters two American carriers, seven cruisers, and fourteen destroyers had been sunk, besides the Australian cruiser *Canberra*. The Japanese losses were one carrier, two battleships, four cruisers, and eleven destroyers. The loss of life on both sides was severe, on land, at sea, and in the air. "For us who were there," writes an American

eye-witness, whose moving account I have followed, "Guadal-canal is not a name but an emotion, recalling desperate fights in the air, furious night naval battles, frantic work at supply or construction, savage fighting in the sodden jungle, nights broken by screaming bombs and deafening explosions of naval shells."*
Long may the tale be told in the great Republic.

★   ★   ★

The tide of war had also turned in New Guinea. The Japanese overland advance began on July 22, 1942, from the north coast towards Port Moresby, which was guarded by two brigades of the 7th Australian Division back from the Middle East. The Owen Stanley Mountains, rising to over thirteen thousand feet, form the spine of the New Guinea land mass. Through these a foot-track traverses the passes and the virgin jungle. A single Australian Militia battalion fought a stubborn delaying action, and it was not until the second week of September that the five Japanese battalions employed approached Port Moresby. Here, at the Imita Ridge, the enemy advance was stayed.

While all this was in progress 2,000 Japanese Marines landed from the sea and tried on August 26 to take the three air-strips being built near Milne Bay, at the southernmost tip of the great island. After a fortnight's intense fighting along the seashore more than half of the invaders were killed and the rest dispersed. The Japanese were thenceforth thrown on to the defensive in New Guinea. By trying to take both New Guinea and Guadalcanal they had lost their chance of winning either. They now had to retreat over the mountain track under close Australian ground and air pursuit. Disease and hunger took a heavy toll. The American-Australian air-power grew constantly. The United States 32nd Division was flown in. The Japanese convoys carrying reinforcements suffered enormous losses. Ten thousand desperate fighting men, with their backs to the sea, held the final perimeter at Buna. It was not till the third week of January 1943 that the last resistance was overcome. Only a few hundred Japanese survived. More than fifteen thousand had been killed or perished from starvation and disease. By February the south-eastern end of New Guinea, as well as Guadalcanal, was firmly in Allied hands. A Japanese convoy of twelve transports, escorted by ten warships, on its way

* *The Struggle for Guadalcanal,* by S. E. Morison.

to reinforce their important outpost at Lae was detected in the Bismarck Sea. It was attacked from the air on March 2 and 3, and both transports and escort, carrying about fifteen thousand men, were destroyed.

*　*　*

By June 1943, when this volume opens, the prospect in the Pacific was encouraging. The last Japanese thrusts had been hurled back and the enemy was now everywhere on the defensive. They were compelled to reinforce by costly processes the positions they still held in New Guinea, especially the garrisons of Salamaua and Lae, and to build a series of supporting airfields along the coast. The American movement towards the Philippines began to be defined. General MacArthur was working westward along the north coast of New Guinea, and Admiral Halsey was slowly advancing along the island chain of the Solomons towards Rabaul. Behind all towered up the now rapidly rising strength of the United States. The eighteen months which had passed since Pearl Harbour had revealed to the rulers of Japan some of the facts and proportions they had ignored.

CHAPTER II

THE CONQUEST OF SICILY

July and August 1943

Preparations for Invading Sicily – General Alexander's Final Plan – Order of Battle – Concentration of Widespread Forces – Hitler's Conference of May 20 – Our Seizure of Pantelleria Island – Effective Cover Plans – The Appointed Day, July 10 – An Ugly Turn in the Weather – Serious Air Losses – Successful Seaborne Landings – Steady Advance of the British and American Armies – Our Next Strategic Move – My Telegram to Smuts of July 16 – Progress of the Campaign – Eisenhower Declares for the Invasion of Italy – Discussions Between the British and American Chiefs of Staff – General Patton's Fine Advance – Centuripe, Catania, and Messina – Alexander's Report – Sicily Liberated in Thirty-eight Days.

CASABLANCA Conference in January decided to invade Sicily after the capture of Tunis. This great enterprise, known by the code-name "Husky", presented new and formidable problems. Severe resistance had not been expected in the North African landings, but now the still numerous Italian Army might fight desperately in defence of its homeland. In any case it would be stiffened by strong German ground and air forces. The Italian Fleet still possessed six effective modern battleships and might join in the battle.

General Eisenhower considered that Sicily should only be attacked if our purpose was to clear the Mediterranean sea-route. If our real purpose was to invade and defeat Italy he thought that our proper initial objectives were Sardinia and Corsica, "since these islands lie on the flank of the long Italian boot and would force a very much greater dispersion of enemy strength in Italy than the mere occupation of Sicily, which lies off the mountainous

23

toe of the peninsula."[*] This was no doubt a military opinion of high authority, though one I could not share. But political forces play their part, and the capture of Sicily and the direct invasion of Italy were to bring about results of a far more swift and far-reaching character.

The capture of Sicily was an undertaking of the first magnitude. Although eclipsed by events in Normandy, its importance and its difficulties should not be underrated. The landing was based on the experience gained in North Africa, and those who planned "Overlord" learned much from "Husky". In the initial assault nearly 3,000 ships and landing-craft took part, carrying between them 160,000 men, 14,000 vehicles, 600 tanks, and 1,800 guns. These forces had to be collected, trained, equipped, and eventually embarked, with all the vast impedimenta of amphibious warfare, at widely dispersed bases in the Mediterranean, in Great Britain, and in the United States. Detailed planning was required from subordinate commanders whose headquarters were separated by thousands of miles. All these plans had to be welded together by the Supreme Commander at Algiers. Here a special Allied Staff controlled and co-ordinated all preparations. As the plan developed many problems arose which could only be solved by the Combined Chiefs of Staff. Finally the convoys had to be assembled, escorted across the oceans and through the narrow seas, and concentrated in the battle area at the right time.

*　　*　　*

Planning at General Eisenhower's headquarters had begun in February. It now became necessary to appoint his principal subordinates.

In all wars where allies are fighting together the control of strategy usually rests in the main with whoever holds the larger forces. This may be modified by political considerations or the relative war effort in other theatres, but the principle that the more powerful army must rule is sound. For reasons of policy we had hitherto yielded the command and direction of the campaign in North-West Africa to the United States. At the beginning they were preponderant in numbers and influence. In the months that had passed since "Torch" began the arrival of the victorious Eighth Army from the Desert and the building up in Tunisia of

[*] *Crusade in Europe*, p. 176.

the British First Army had given us the proportion there of eleven British divisions to four American. Nevertheless I strictly adhered to the theme that "Torch" was an American expedition, and in every way supported General Eisenhower's position as Supreme Commander. It was however understood in practice that General Alexander as Eisenhower's Deputy had the full operational command. It was in these circumstances that the victory of Tunis was gained and the general picture presented to the American public and to the world as an overriding United States enterprise.

But now we had entered upon a new stage—the invasion of Sicily, and what should follow from it. It was agreed that action against Italy should be decided in the light of the fighting in Sicily. As the Americans became more attracted to this larger adventure, instead of being content for the rest of the year with Sardinia, and while the prospects of another joint campaign unfolded, I felt it necessary that the British should at least be equal partners with our Allies. The proportions of the armies available in July were: British, eight divisions; United States, six. Air: the United States, 55 per cent.; British, 45 per cent. Naval, 80 per cent. British. Besides all this there remained the considerable British armies in the Middle East and in the Eastern Mediterranean, including Libya, which were independently commanded by General Maitland Wilson, from the British headquarters at Cairo. It did not seem too much in these circumstances that we should have at least an equal share of the High Command. And this was willingly conceded by our loyal comrades. We were moreover given the direct conduct of the fighting. Alexander was to command the Fifteenth Army Group, consisting of the Seventh United States and the Eighth British Armies. Air Chief Marshal Tedder commanded the Allied Air Force, and Admiral Cunningham the Allied naval forces. The whole was under the overall command of General Eisenhower.

The British assault was entrusted to General Montgomery and his Eighth Army, while General Patton was nominated to command the United States Seventh Army. The naval collaborators were Admiral Ramsay, who had planned the British landings in "Torch", and Admiral Hewitt, U.S.N., who with General Patton had carried out the Casablanca landing. In the air the chief commanders under Air Chief Marshal Tedder were General

Spaatz, U.S. Army Air Force, and Air Marshal Coningham, while the air operations in conjunction with the Eighth Army were in the hands of Air Vice-Marshal Broadhurst, who had recently added to the fame of the Western Desert Air Force.

The plan and the troops were at first considered only on a tentative basis, as the fighting in Tunisia was still absorbing the attention of commanders and staffs, and it was not until April that we could tell what troops would be fit to take part. The major need was the early capture of ports and airfields to maintain the armies after the landings. Palermo, Catania, and Syracuse were suitable, but Messina, the best port of all, was beyond our reach. There were three main groups of airfields, at the southeast corner of the island, in the Catania plain, and in the western portion of the island.

Air Chief Marshal Tedder argued that we must narrow the attack, capture the south-eastern group of airfields, and seize Catania and Palermo later on. This meant that for some time only the small ports of Syracuse, Augusta, and Licata were likely to be available, and the armies would have to be supplied over the open beaches. This was successful largely because of the new amphibious load-carrier, the American D.U.K.W., and even more the "landing-ship, tank" (L.S.T.). This type of vessel had first been conceived and developed in Britain in 1940. A new design, based on British experience, was thereafter built in large numbers in the United States, and was first used in Sicily. It became the foundation of all our future amphibious operations, and was often their limiting factor.

*   *   *

General Alexander's final plan prescribed a week's preliminary bombardment to neutralise the enemy's Navy and Air. The British Eighth Army, under General Montgomery, was to assault between Cape Murro di Porco and Pozzallo and capture Syracuse and the Pachino airfield. Having established a firm bridgehead and gained touch with the U.S. forces on its left, it was to thrust northwards to Augusta, Catania, and the Gerbini airfields. The U.S. Seventh Army, under General Patton, was to land between Cape Scaramia and Licata, and to capture the latter port and a group of airfields north and east of Gela. It was to protect the flank of the Eighth Army at Ragusa in its forward drive. Strong

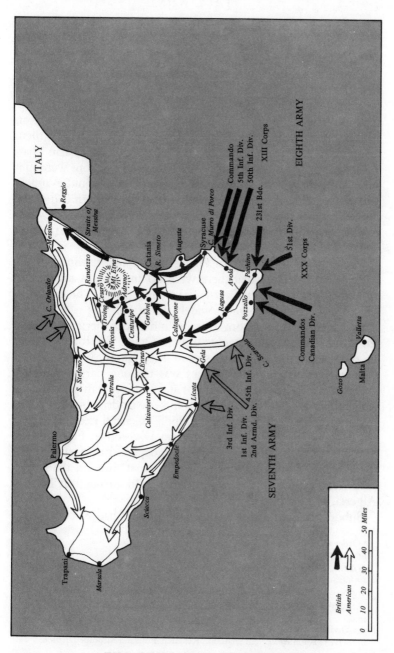

THE CONQUEST OF SICILY

British and U.S. airborne troops were to be dropped by parachute or landed by glider beyond the beach-heads to seize key points and aid the landings.

The Eighth Army comprised seven divisions, with an infantry brigade from the Malta garrison, two armoured brigades, and Commandos. The U.S. Seventh Army had six divisions under its command.* The enemy garrison in Sicily, at first under an Italian general, consisted of two German divisions, one of them armoured, four Italian infantry divisions, and six Italian coast defence divisions of low quality. The German divisions were split up into battle groups, to stiffen their allies and to counter-attack. Misreading our intentions, the enemy held the western end of the island in considerable strength. In the air our superiority was marked. Against more than 4,000 operational aircraft (121 British and 146 U.S. squadrons) the enemy could muster in Sicily, Sardinia, Italy, and Southern France only 1,850 machines.

Provided therefore that there were no mishaps in assembling and landing the troops the prospects seemed good. The naval and military forces were however widely dispersed. The 1st Canadian Division came direct from Britain, and one American division from the United States, staging only at Oran. The forces already in the Mediterranean were spread throughout North Africa. General Dempsey's XIIIth Corps was training partly in Egypt and partly in Syria, and their ships and landing-craft would have to load not only in the Canal area and Alexandria, but at various small ports between Beirut and Tripoli. General Leese's XXXth Corps, composed of the 1st Canadian Division in England, the 51st Division in Tunisia, and the independent 231st Brigade from Malta, would concentrate for the first time on the battle-field. American troops were similarly spread throughout Tunisia, Algeria, and beyond the Atlantic.

Subordinate commanders and Staff officers had to cover great

---

* Order of Battle:

EIGHTH ARMY. Headquarters XIIIth and XXXth Corps.

In the first assault. 1st Canadian, 5th, 50th, 51st Divisions. Part of 1st Airborne Division, 231st Infantry Brigade, 4th and 23rd Armoured Brigades, and three Commandos.

In reserve in North Africa. 78th, 46th Divisions. Remainder of 1st Airborne Division.

U.S. SEVENTH ARMY. Headquarters IInd Corps.

In the first assault. 1st, 3rd, 45th Divisions, 2nd Armoured Division, part of 82nd Airborne Division, 1st Battalion Rangers (Commando).

In reserve in North Africa. 9th Division. Remainder of 82nd Airborne Division.

distances by air to keep in touch with developments in the plan and to supervise the training of their units. Their frequent absence on such missions added to the burdens of the planners. Training exercises afloat were mounted in the United Kingdom and throughout the Mediterranean and the Red Sea. In the Middle East vital craft and equipment had as yet arrived only in token quantities, or not at all. All this material had in the preparatory stages to be taken on trust and included in the plan without trial. In the event nearly all the promises of the supply departments were fulfilled. In spite of anxieties the plan went forward smoothly, and proved a remarkable example of joint Staff work.

★　★　★

On May 20 Hitler held a conference at which Keitel, Rommel, Neurath, the Foreign Secretary, and several others were present. The American translations of the secret records of this and other German conferences are taken from the manuscript in the University of Pennsylvania Library, annotated by Mr. Felix Gilbert. They are a valuable contribution to the story of the war.*

HITLER: You were in Sicily?

NEURATH: Yes, my Fuehrer, I was down there, and I spoke to General Roatta [commander of the Italian Sixth Army in Sicily]. Among other things he told me that he did not have too much confidence in the defence of Sicily. He claimed that he is too weak and that his troops are not properly equipped. Above all, he has only one motorised division; the rest are immobile. Every day the English do their best to shoot up the locomotives of the Sicilian railroads, for they know very well that it is almost impossible to bring up material to replace or repair them, or not possible at all. The impression I gained on the crossing from Giovanni to Messina was that almost all traffic on this short stretch is at a virtual standstill. Of the ferries there—I think there were six—only one remains. This one was being treated as a museum piece; it was said that it was being saved for better purposes.

HITLER: What are the "better purposes"?

NEURATH: Well, my Fuehrer, sometimes the Italians explain, "When the war is over . . ."; others say, "You never know what's going to happen next." The German troops in Sicily have undoubtedly become rather unpopular. That can be explained very easily, because the Sicilians hold the view that we have brought the war to their country. First we have eaten up everything they had, and now we are going to cause the English to come themselves, although—and I must emphasise

* Published in *Hitler Directs his War*, ed. Felix Gilbert.

this—the Sicilian peasant really wouldn't mind that. He thinks that this will end his suffering. The general opinion all over Southern Italy is that the war will be over when the English come, and that the presence of the Germans just delays this.

HITLER: What is the Italian Government doing to counter this attitude?

NEURATH: My Fuehrer, as far as I know the prefects and officials who are still around are not doing much about it. Whenever I directed their attention to it and complained that German soldiers were being cursed in the streets I was told that they didn't know what to do about it, since this represented the popular view. They said, "That's how the people feel. You have made yourselves unpopular; you have requisitioned things and eaten up all our chickens." But I do think that the officials could make more of an effort, and make examples of the more flagrant cases.

HITLER: They won't take action?

NEURATH: It is very difficult. They just won't take action. The Sicilian temperament is different from the North Italian. But on the whole it is very unpleasant to see how they let things slide. The threat to Sicily from the enemy air is extremely strong.

The discussion then turned on the fidelity of General Roatta and other Italian leaders, and the increasingly difficult position of Mussolini. Altogether a very disquieting picture was presented to the Fuehrer.

*　　*　　*

In the channel between Tunisia and Sicily lay the small island of Pantelleria, which served as an enemy base for aircraft and E-boats. In January 1941 we had planned to assault and capture it, but the opportunity passed and it remained a thorn in our side throughout the hardest period of the siege of Malta. Now it became necessary not only to subdue it, but to use it ourselves for our fighter aircraft. Attacks by air and sea began immediately after the fall of Tunis. Bombardment continued until June 8, when unconditional surrender was demanded. This being refused, a landing from the sea was carried out on June 11, supported by heavy naval and air bombardment. Much had been made beforehand of the magnitude and perils of this enterprise. It was entirely successful, with no casualties, except, according to sailors' stories, one soldier bitten by a mule. Over 11,000 prisoners fell into our hands. During the next two days the neighbouring islands of

Lampedusa and Linosa also capitulated. No enemy outpost now remained south of Sicily.

* * *

Intense air attack upon Sicily began on July 3 with the bombing of airfields both there and in Sardinia, which made many unusable. The enemy fighters were thrown on to the defensive, and their long-range bombers forced to withdraw their bases to the Italian mainland. Four of the five train ferries operating across the Straits of Messina were sunk. By the time our convoys were approaching the island air superiority was firmly established, and Axis warships and aircraft made no serious effort to interfere with the seaborne assault. By our cover plans the enemy were kept in doubt until the last moment where our stroke would fall. Our naval movements and military preparations in Egypt suggested an expedition to Greece. Since the fall of Tunis they had sent more planes to the Mediterranean, but the additional squadrons had gone, not to Sicily, but to the Eastern Mediterranean, North-West Italy, and Sardinia. In the critical period while the convoys were approaching their target General Eisenhower established his headquarters in Malta, where communications were excellent. Here he was joined by General Alexander and Admiral Cunningham. Air Marshal Tedder remained near Carthage to control the combined air operations.

July 10 was the appointed day. On the morning of July 9 the great armadas from east and west were converging south of Malta, and it was time for all to steam for the beaches of Sicily. Admiral Cunningham says in his dispatch: "The only incidents which occurred to mar the precision of this remarkable concentration were the loss by U-boat attack of three ships in convoy.* The passage of the convoys was covered most effectively; the majority were not sighted by enemy aircraft."

On my way to Chequers, where I was to await the result, I spent an hour in the Admiralty War Room. The map covered an entire wall, and showed the enormous convoys, escorts, and supporting detachments moving towards their assault beaches. This was the greatest amphibious operation so far attempted in history. But all depended on the weather.

* * *

* A fourth ship was sunk in a convoy from Egypt.

The morning of the 9th was fine, but by noon a fresh and unseasonable north-west wind sprang up. During the afternoon the wind increased, and by evening there was a heavy swell, which would make landings hazardous, particularly on the western beaches in the American sector. The landing-craft convoys plunging northward from Malta and from many African ports between Bizerta and Benghazi were having a rough voyage.

Arrangements had been made for postponing the landing in case of necessity, but a decision would have to be taken not later than noon. Watching anxiously from the Admiralty, the First Sea Lord inquired by signal about the weather conditions. Admiral Cunningham replied at 8 p.m., "Weather not favourable, but operation proceeding." "It was," he says, "manifestly too late for postponement, but considerable anxiety was felt, particularly for the small-craft convoys making up against the sea." They were indeed much delayed and became scattered. Many ships arrived late, but fortunately no great harm resulted. "The wind," says Cunningham, "mercifully eased during the night, and by the morning of the 10th had ceased, leaving only a tiresome swell and surf on the western beaches."

The bad weather helped to give us surprise. Admiral Cunningham continues: "The very efficient cover plan and the deceptive routeing of convoys played their part. In addition the vigilance of the enemy was undoubtedly relaxed owing to the unfavourable phase of the moon. Finally came this wind, dangerously close at the time to making some, if not all, the landings impracticable. These apparently unfavourable factors had actually the effect of making the weary Italians, who had been alert for many nights, turn thankfully in their beds, saying, 'To-night at any rate they can't come.' BUT THEY CAME."

The airborne forces met hard fortune. More than one-third of the gliders carrying our 1st Air Landing Brigade were cast off too early by their American towing aircraft and many of the men they carried were drowned. The rest were scattered over southeastern Sicily, and only twelve gliders arrived at the important bridge which was their aim. Out of eight officers and sixty-five men who seized and held it until help came twelve hours later only nineteen survived. This was a forlorn feat of arms. On the American front the air landings were also too widely dispersed,

War at Sea

1 German mine-layers.

2 A German aircraft and a destroyer coordinating an attack on a British submarine.
3 The sinking of a submarine: an explosive charge hits the submarine as,
damaged, it surfaces.

4 An attack on a British convoy bound for Russia.
5 The British destroyer "Bittern" on fire.

6 Russian motor torpedo boats ready to depart.

but the many small parties creating damage and confusion inland worried the Italian coastal divisions.

The seaborne landings, under continuous fighter protection, were everywhere highly successful. Syracuse and Pachino on the British front, Licata and Gela on the American, were captured. The Eighth Army took Augusta on the 12th. On the American front very heavy counter-attacks were made on the U.S. 1st Division by part of a German armoured division. For a time the position was critical, but after a stiff fight the enemy were beaten off and our Allies pressed on to capture the important airfields east of Gela.

The major effort of the Eighth Army was now directed against the airfields at Catania and Gerbini. Aided by more airborne and seaborne landings of parachute and Commando troops, which captured vital bridges, the Army crossed the river Simeto. But now German troops from farther west reinforced the Italians and progress beyond the river was stopped. On the 16th the left flank of the Eighth Army reached Caltagirone, in close touch with the Americans, who were also pressing westwards along the coast and had taken Porto Empedocle.

Twelve airfields were now in our hands, and by July 18 there were only twenty-five serviceable German aircraft in the island. Eleven hundred planes, more than half of them German, were left behind destroyed or damaged. Our air forces tried hard to stop the passage of troops from the mainland to Messina. They were only partly successful against the heavy anti-aircraft fire.

On July 16 General Alexander ordered the Eighth Army to attack the western side of Mount Etna, and the Seventh Army to seize the roads around Enna and cut the west-east highway at Petralia. The 50th Division could make little progress, and the Germans had brought reinforcements, including six battalions of the redoubtable 1st Parachute Division, from the mainland. On its left we made some ground, but it was clear that a new plan and more troops were needed. There was a lull on the British front till the 78th Division arrived from Tunisia.

*   *   *

Our next strategic move was still in suspense. Should we cross the Straits of Messina and seize the toe of Italy, should we seize the heel at Taranto, or should we land higher up the west coast, in the Gulf of Salerno, and capture Naples? Or, again, must we restrict ourselves to the occupation of Sardinia? In June General Eisenhower had been asked for his opinion. The problem was a difficult one. At the Washington Conference in May ("Trident") we had decided to transfer to India about August much of the assault shipping and certain air forces then allotted to the Sicily attack. Eisenhower had also been warned that after November 1 four American and three British divisions would have to be with-drawn to Britain for the cross-Channel invasion in 1944. On June 30 he proposed that when the capture of Sicily had been completed we should attack either the toe of Italy or Sardinia. If Sardinia were chosen he could probably be ready by October, but he did not expect to be able to invade the mainland of Italy before November, and by then the weather might be too bad for amphibious landings. To justify so late a descent upon Italy there had to be a good prospect of a speedy advance.

The progress made in Sicily clarified the scene. The contrast may be judged from the telegram in which I set the whole position before Smuts on July 16.

16 July 43

In our May talks at Washington we found serious American mis-givings lest we should become deeply involved in the Mediterranean, and a hankering for winding up the campaign there with the capture of Sardinia. This we combated, and as our forces in the Mediterranean far outnumber the American we were able to have the matter left open till after the capture of Sicily. Not being satisfied with this, I requested the President to send General Marshall with me to North Africa, and there upon the spot to convince Eisenhower and others that nothing less than Rome could satisfy the requirements of this year's campaign. We agreed that the decision should be taken when it was seen how the fighting in Sicily went. If it was severe and prolonged, then only Sardinia might be possible. If however our enterprise prospered and Italian resistance was seen not to be formid-able, then we were immediately to invade the Italian mainland.

2. The moment is now approaching when this choice must be made, and I need not tell you I shall make it a capital issue. I believe the President is with me; Eisenhower in his heart is naturally for it. I will in no circumstances allow the powerful British and British-controlled armies in the Mediterranean to stand idle. I am bringing the very fine Polish army from Persia into Syria, where it can also participate.

3. The situation in the Balkans is also most hopeful, and I am send-ing you a report from the Middle East Headquarters showing the

Italian forces on the verge of collapse. Not only must we take Rome and march as far north as possible in Italy, but our right hand must give succour to the Balkan Patriots. In all this there is great hope provided action is taken worthy of the opportunity. I am confident of a good result, and I shall go all lengths to procure the agreement of our Allies. If not, we have ample forces to act by ourselves.

4. When are you coming over here? You know what a warm welcome awaits you and how close is our community of ideas on war. All the above is for your eye alone and of operational secrecy.

★   ★   ★

Meanwhile Allied Air Forces were harrying the enemy communications and airfields in Southern Italy and the port of Naples. On July 19 a strong force of American bombers attacked the railway yards and airport at Rome. Havoc was wrought, and the shock was severe. In Sicily itself the Americans were advancing steadily under the spirited leadership of General Patton. Their 3rd Infantry and 2nd Armoured Divisions were given the task of reducing the western end, where only Italians now remained, while their IInd Corps, comprising the 1st and 45th Divisions, was directed to gain the northern coast and then to thrust eastward along the two main roads towards Messina. Palermo was taken on July 22, and by the end of the month the Americans had reached the line Nicosia–S. Stefano. Their 3rd Division, its task in Western Sicily completed, had been brought in to support the coastal drive, while the 9th Division was brought over from Africa, where, like our 78th, it had been in reserve.

The field was thus disposed for the final battles. These were certain to be severe, since, apart from what remained of the Italian garrison, more than three German divisions were now in action, under a well-tried German commander, General Hube. But the speedy collapse of Italy became probable. There was a marked change of feeling in our circles in Whitehall, and we decided on the bolder plan of a direct attack on the west coast of Italy to seize Naples. Washington agreed, but insisted that no more forces could be provided than those agreed upon at the "Trident" Conference. The Americans held that none of the operations elsewhere, especially "Overlord", should be prejudiced by more vigorous action in the Mediterranean. This reservation was to cause keen anxiety during the landing at Salerno.

General Eisenhower and his principal commanders now agreed that Italy should be the next and immediate target. They still preferred to land first on the toe, because they were short of landing-craft and planes, but for the first time they too began to favour the direct attack on Naples. This was so far from our newly won air bases in Sicily that it would much reduce the fighter cover for the landing. None the less Naples soon became the centre of all thoughts. The chance of quickly crushing Italy seemed to justify delaying operations against Burma, and the Admiralty stopped the assault shipping for India from leaving the Mediterranean.

On July 22 the British Chiefs of Staff urged their American colleagues to plan the direct attack on Naples on the assumption that extra shipping and aircraft-carriers would be available. The Americans took a different view. While agreeing to the attack, they adhered to their original decision that no reinforcements from America should be sent to General Eisenhower for this or any other purpose. He should do the best he could with what he had. Moreover, they insisted that three of his heavy bomber groups should be withdrawn to Britain. Conflict thus arose. The American Chiefs of Staff did not believe that the conquest of Italy would threaten Germany, and they also feared that the Germans would withdraw and that we should find ourselves hitting the air. They did not think there was much to be gained by bombing Southern Germany from airfields in Southern Italy, and they wanted all efforts against Germany to be concentrated on the shortest route across the English Channel, although nothing could happen there for ten months.

The British Chiefs of Staff pointed out that the Washington Conference had expressly stated that the elimination of Italy from the war was one of the prime Allied objects. The attack on Naples, now given the code-name of "Avalanche", was the best means of accomplishing this, and the collapse of Italy would increase enormously the chances of the cross-Channel invasion being not only successful but decisive. Portal, Chief of the Air Staff, emphasised that the full-scale attack on German industry, particularly on factories producing fighters, could only be effective with the help of the Italian airfields. Their possession would therefore be a great contribution to a successful invasion of France. The Americans remained unmoved. However, most of the forces to be employed in "Avalanche" were British, and we resolved to do everything in our power to ensure its success. To overcome the weakness in long-range fighters the Admiralty allotted four escort carriers and a light fleet carrier to support the landing, and the Air Ministry gave General Eisenhower three of our bomber squadrons which had been due for early withdrawal.

While these somewhat sharp discussions were in progress the scene was completely transformed by the fall of Mussolini on July 25. The argument for invading Italy seemed overwhelming. As will be seen, the Germans reacted very quickly, and our invasion, and particularly the attack on Naples, was not greatly eased. "Avalanche" only just succeeded, and it was fortunate that we had provided additional British sea- and air-power. The risks would have been further reduced if the extra shipping which we considered essential to accelerate the build-up after landing there had been accorded. In this we could not carry American opinion with us, and before the operation began many American ships were withdrawn, and some of the British assault shipping was also released to India.

* * *

We must now return to the Sicilian battlefield. On August 3 Alexander telegraphed:

The offensive has opened well. . . . I have just returned from a visit to General Patton, who is in great heart. The Seventh American Army have done a grand job of work and are fighting really well. The Canadians have made a very satisfactory début and are fighting well. Progress may be slow, but the country must be seen to be believed. Only a few mountain roads, which pass through gorges and round cliffs, which are easily defended and more easily demolished.

The brilliant capture of Centuripe by our newly arrived 78th Division marked the last phase. Catania fell on the 5th, and thereafter the whole British line swung forward to the southern and western slopes of Mount Etna. The U.S. 1st Division took Troina on August 6 after a stiff fight, and their 9th Division, passing through the 1st, entered Cesaro on the 8th. Along the north coast the U.S. 45th Division, followed by their 3rd Division, reached Cape Orlando on August 10, with the aid of two small but skilful outflanking amphibious operations. After the capture of Randazzo on the 13th the enemy broke contact all along the front, and, under cover of their strong anti-aircraft defences of the Messina Straits, escaped during the following nights to the mainland. Our armies raced for Messina. Enemy demolitions on the coastal road from Catania slowed up the Eighth Army, and by a narrow margin the prize fell to the Americans, who entered the town on August 16.

General Alexander to Prime Minister   17 Aug 43
    The following facts are of interest:
    Sicily invaded July 10. Messina entered August 16. Island taken in thirty-eight days. Sicily has coastline 600 miles and area 10,000 square miles. Island is heavily fortified with concrete pill-boxes and wire. Axis garrison: Italian, 9 divisions; German, 4 divisions, equalling 13 divisions. Total forces: Italian, 315,000; German, 90,000, making total 405,000 soldiers. Our forces: Seventh Army, 6 divisions, including airborne division; Eighth Army, 7 divisions, including airborne and armoured brigades, making Allied total 13 divisions. . . .
    It can be assumed that all Italian forces in island on July 10 have been destroyed, though a few battered units may have escaped to mainland. It is impossible yet to estimate booty and war material captured. Guns, tanks, rifles, and machine-guns are lying scattered about all over island.
    During whole operation the Air Forces have maintained domination throughout, and their tactical air forces have in consequence concentrated a record proportion of their efforts on support of our armies in the field. Over 1,000 enemy aircraft have been taken on airfields. The Royal Navy have kept our sea-lanes open and supplied us with everything we needed.

And later:

General Alexander to Prime Minister   17 Aug 43
    By 10 a.m. this morning, August 17, 1943, the last German soldier was flung out of Sicily and the whole island is now in our hands.

★   ★   ★

So ended a successful and skilful campaign of thirty-eight days. The enemy, once they had recovered from the initial surprise, had fought stubbornly. The difficulties of the ground were great. The roads were narrow, and cross-country movement was often impossible except for men on foot. On the Eighth Army front the towering mass of Mount Etna blocked the way, and enabled the enemy to watch our moves. As they lay on the low ground

of the Catania plain malaria ran riot among our men. Nevertheless, once we were safely ashore and our Air Forces were operating
from captured airfields the issue was never in doubt. The enemy,
according to General Marshall's report, lost 167,000 men, of
whom 37,000 were Germans. The Allies lost 31,158 killed,
wounded, and missing.

CHAPTER III

THE FALL OF MUSSOLINI

Mussolini in the Toils – A Joint Proclamation to the Italian People – Mussolini Confers with Hitler near Rimini – Arrival of Grandi on the Scene – The Fascist Grand Council Meets, July 24 – Grandi's Motion for the Deposition of Mussolini Carried – The Arrest of Mussolini, July 25 – The End of Twenty-one Years' Dictatorship – Hitler's Unwise Dispersion of Forces – He Receives the News from Italy – My Forecast of November 25, 1942 – Correspondence with Roosevelt on Impending Italian Peace Proposals – My Thoughts on the Fall of Mussolini – The Fate of British Prisoners in Italy – Anglo-American Discussion of Armistice Terms.

MUSSOLINI now had to bear the brunt of the military disasters into which he had, after so many years of rule, led his country. He had exercised almost absolute control and could not cast the burden on the Monarchy, Parliamentary institutions, the Fascist Party, or the General Staff. All fell on him. Now that the feeling that the war was lost spread throughout well-informed circles in Italy the blame fell upon the man who had so imperiously thrust the nation on to the wrong and the losing side. These convictions formed and spread widely during the early months of 1943. The lonely dictator sat at the summit of power, while military defeat and Italian slaughter in Russia, Tunis, and Sicily were the evident prelude to direct invasion.

In vain he made changes among the politicians and generals. In February General Ambrosio had succeeded Cavallero as Chief of the Italian General Staff. Ambrosio, together with the Duke of Acquarone, the Minister of Court, were personal advisers of the King and had the confidence of the Royal circle. For months they had been hoping to overthrow the Duce and put an end to the Fascist régime. But Mussolini still dwelt in the European scene as if he were a principal factor. He was affronted when his new military chief proposed the immediate withdrawal of the Italian divisions from the Balkans. He regarded these forces as the counterpoise to German predominance in Europe. He did not realise that defeats abroad and internal demoralisation had robbed him of his status as Hitler's ally. He cherished the illusion of power and consequence when the reality had gone. Thus he resisted Ambrosio's formidable request. So durable however was the impression of his authority and the fear of his personal action in extremity that there was prolonged hesitation throughout all the forces of Italian society about how to oust him. Who would "bell the cat"? Thus the spring had passed with invasion by a mighty foe, possessing superior power by land, sea, and air, drawing ever nearer.

During July the climax came. Since February the taciturn, cautious-minded, constitutional King had been in contact with Marshal Badoglio, who had been dismissed after the Greek disasters in 1940. He found in him at length a figure to whom he might entrust the conduct of the State. A definite plan was made. It was resolved that Mussolini should be arrested on July 26, and General Ambrosio agreed to find the agents and create the situation for this stroke. The General was aided unwittingly by elements in the Fascist Old Guard, who sought a new revival of the party, by which, in many cases, they would not be the losers. They saw in the summoning of the highest party organ, the Fascist Grand Council, which had not met since 1939, the means of confronting the Duce with an ultimatum. On July 13 they called on Mussolini and induced him to convene a formal session of the Council on July 24. The two movements appear to have been separate and independent, but their close coincidence in date is significant.

* * *

We had at the time no definite knowledge of the inner stresses of Italian politics, but reports of growing demoralisation and unrest had for some time reached Allied headquarters. Strikes and rioting in the Northern Italian cities had followed on our bombing raids. We knew that the food situation in Italy had worsened as rail traffic was disrupted. It seemed that the time had come to launch an appeal to the Italian people upon the Sicily landing. President Roosevelt had proposed a proclamation which seemed to us to assume for the United States a position which was not fair to the British share in the Italian war. On July 5 I cabled him as follows:

The War Cabinet had contemplated a joint declaration to the Italian people in the name of both our countries. Whereas "Torch" was by agreement planned as an American expedition with a British contingent and I have acted as your lieutenant throughout, we consider "Husky" [Sicily] and post-"Husky" as joint undertakings in which we are equal partners. This would certainly seem justified by the proportion of troops, naval forces, shipping, and aircraft involved. I fully accept your dictum that "there should be no senior partner".

2. However, since we have been longer in quarrel or war with Italy than you, and also since a document of this character written by one man in its integrity is better than a joint production, we are ready that you should speak at this juncture to the Italian people on behalf of both our countries and in the interests of the common cause.

3. There are a few amendments which I venture to suggest to you in all the frankness of our friendship. They are of importance, because without them untoward reactions might grow among the British people and their forces that their contribution had not received equal or sufficient recognition. In fact, they are only mentioned once, and all else is either United States or United Nations.

4. The amendments are as follows:

(a) After the words "against whom on December 11, 1941, your Government declared war" insert, "I speak also on behalf of His Britannic Majesty's Government and in their name."

(b) After the words "under the command of General Eisenhower" insert, "and his Deputy General Alexander."

(c) The end of the sentence "The skies over Italy are dominated by the vast air armadas of the United Nations" should read, "of the United States and Great Britain. Italy's sea-coasts are threatened by the greatest accumulation of British and Allied sea-power ever concentrated in the Mediterranean." (I am sure you will see the justice of this, as after all it is the United States and Great Britain who are doing virtually the whole thing.)

5. Finally, we think that the message to the Italian people would seem to come better after an initial success in Sicily has been achieved, because a repulse would make it somewhat inappropriate. It would anyhow be lost to the world in the cannonade, and will hardly get through to the Axis fighting troops in time to influence the crunch.

Roosevelt recognised the justice of our case, and I sent him a revised draft which we felt would be appropriate.

This is a message to the Italian people from the President of the United States of America and the Prime Minister of Great Britain.

At this moment the combined armed forces of the United States and Great Britain, under the command of General Eisenhower and his Deputy General Alexander, are carrying the war deep into the territory of your country. This is the direct consequence of the shameful leadership to which you have been subjected by Mussolini and his Fascist régime. Mussolini carried you into this war as the satellite of a brutal destroyer of peoples and liberties. Mussolini plunged you into a war which he thought Hitler had already won. In spite of Italy's great vulnerability to attack by air and sea, your Fascist leaders sent your sons, your ships, your air forces, to distant battlefields to aid Germany in her attempt to conquer England, Russia, and the world. This association with the designs of Nazi-controlled Germany was unworthy of Italy's ancient traditions of freedom and culture—traditions to which the peoples of America and Great Britain owe so much. Your soldiers have fought, not in the interests of Italy, but for Nazi Germany. They have fought courageously, but they have been betrayed and abandoned by the Germans on the Russian front and on every battlefield in Africa from El Alamein to Cape Bon.

To-day Germany's hopes for world conquest have been blasted on all fronts. The skies over Italy are dominated by the vast air armadas of the United States and Great Britain. Italy's sea-coasts are threatened by the greatest accumulation of British and Allied sea-power ever concentrated in the Mediterranean. The forces now opposed to you are pledged to destroy the power of Nazi Germany, which has ruthlessly been used to inflict slavery, destruction, and death on all those who refuse to recognise the Germans as the master race.

The sole hope for Italy's survival lies in honourable capitulation to the overwhelming power of the military forces of the United Nations. If you continue to tolerate the Fascist régime, which serves the evil power of the Nazis, you must suffer the consequences of your own choice. We take no satisfaction in invading Italian soil and bringing the tragic devastation of war home to the Italian people; but we are determined to destroy the false leaders and their doctrines which have brought Italy to her present position. Every moment that you resist the combined forces of the United Nations—every drop of blood that you sacrifice—can serve only one purpose: to give the Fascist and Nazi leaders a little more time to escape from the inevitable consequences of their own crimes. All your interests and all your traditions have been betrayed by Germany and your own false and corrupt leaders;

it is only by disavowing both that a reconstituted Italy can hope to occupy a respected place in the family of European nations.

The time has now come for you, the Italian people, to consult your own self-respect and your own interests and your own desire for a restoration of national dignity, security, and peace. The time has come for you to decide whether Italians shall die for Mussolini and Hitler—or live for Italy, and for civilisation.

ROOSEVELT
CHURCHILL

Allied aircraft dropped leaflets of this proclamation over Rome and other Italian cities on July 17.

*   *   *

Two days later the Duce, accompanied by General Ambrosio, left by air to meet Hitler at a villa at Feltre, near Rimini. "There was a most beautiful cool and shady park," writes Mussolini in his memoirs, "and a labyrinthine building which some people found almost uncanny. It was like a crossword puzzle frozen into a house." All preparations had been made to entertain the Fuehrer for at least two days, but he left the same afternoon. "The meeting," says Mussolini, "was, as usual, cordial, but the entourage and the attitude of the higher Air Force officers and of the troops was chilly."*

The Fuehrer held forth lengthily upon the need for a supreme effort. The new secret weapons, he said, would be ready for use against England by the winter. Italy must be defended, "so that Sicily may become for the enemy what Stalingrad was for us." †
The Italians must produce both the man-power and the organisation. Germany could not provide the reinforcements and equipment asked for by Italy owing to the pressure on the Russian front.

Ambrosio urged his chief to tell Hitler plainly that Italy could not continue in the war. It is not clear what advantage would have come from this, but the fact that Mussolini seemed almost dumbstruck finally decided Ambrosio and the other Italian generals present that no further leadership could be expected from him.

In the midst of Hitler's discourse on the situation an agitated Italian official entered the room with the news, "At this moment

---

* Mussolini, *Memoirs, 1942-43* (English edition), p. 50.
† Rizzoli, *Hitler e Mussolini: Lettere e Documenti*, p. 173.

Rome is undergoing a violent enemy air bombardment." Apart
from a promise of further German reinforcements for Sicily,
Mussolini returned to Rome without anything to show. As he
approached he flew into a huge black cloud of smoke rising from
hundreds of wagons on fire in the Littorio railway station. He
had an audience of the King, whom he found "frowning and
nervous". "A tense situation," said the King. "We cannot go
on much longer. Sicily has gone west now. The Germans
will double-cross us. The discipline of the troops has broken
down...." Mussolini answered, according to the records, that he
hoped to disengage Italy from the Axis alliance by September 15.
The date shows how far he was out of contact with reality.

The chief actor in the final drama now appeared on the
scene. Dino Grandi, veteran Fascist, former Foreign Minister and
Ambassador to Britain, a man of strong personal determination,
who had hated the Italian declaration of war upon Britain, but
had hitherto submitted to the force of events, arrived in Rome to
take the lead at the meeting of the Grand Council. He called on
his old leader on July 22, and told him brutally that he intended
to propose the formation of a National Government and the
restoration to the King of the supreme command of the armed
forces.

★   ★   ★

At 5 p.m. on the 24th the Grand Council met. Care appears
to have been taken by the Chief of Police that they should not be
disturbed by violence. Mussolini's musketeers, his personal body-
guard, were relieved of their duty to guard the Palazzo Venezia,
which was also filled with armed police. The Duce unfolded
his case, and the Council, who were all dressed in their black
Fascist uniform, took up the discussion. Mussolini ended: "War
is always a party war—a war of the party which desires it; it is
always one man's war—the war of the man who declared it. If
to-day this is called Mussolini's war, the war in 1859 could have
been called Cavour's war. This is the moment to tighten the reins
and assume the necessary responsibility. I shall have no difficulty
in replacing men, in turning the screw, in bringing forces to bear
not yet engaged, in the name of our country, whose territorial
integrity is to-day being violated."

Grandi then moved a resolution calling upon the Crown to
assume more power and upon the King to emerge from obscurity

45

and assume his responsibilities. He delivered what Mussolini describes as "a violent philippic", "the speech of a man who was at last giving vent to a long-cherished rancour." The contacts between members of the Grand Council and the Court became evident. Mussolini's son-in-law, Ciano, supported Grandi. Everyone present was now conscious that a political convulsion impended. The debate continued till midnight, when Scorza, secretary of the Fascist Party, proposed adjourning till next day. But Grandi leaped to his feet, shouting, "No, I am against the proposal. We have started this business and we must finish it this very night!" It was after two o'clock in the morning when the voting took place. "The position of each member of the Grand Council," writes Mussolini, "could be discerned even before the voting. There was a group of traitors who had already negotiated with the Crown, a group of accomplices, and a group of uninformed who probably did not realise the seriousness of the vote, but they voted just the same." Nineteen replied "Yes" to Grandi's motion and seven "No". Two abstained. Mussolini rose. "You have provoked a crisis of the régime. So much the worse. The session is closed." The party secretary was about to give the salute to the Duce when Mussolini checked him with a gesture, saying, "No, you are excused." They all went away in silence. None slept at home.

Meanwhile the arrest of Mussolini was being quietly arranged. The Duke of Acquarone, the Court Minister, sent instructions to Ambrosio, whose deputies and trusted agents in the police and the Carabinieri acted forthwith. The key telephone exchanges, the police headquarters, and the offices of the Ministry of the Interior were quietly and unobtrusively taken over. A small force of military police was posted out of sight near the Royal villa.

Mussolini spent the morning of Sunday, July 25, in his office, and visited some quarters in Rome which had suffered by bombing. He asked to see the King, and was granted an audience at five o'clock. "I thought the King would withdraw his delegation of authority of June 10, 1940, concerning the command of the armed forces, a command which I had for some time past been thinking of relinquishing. I entered the villa therefore with a mind completely free from any forebodings, in a state which, looking back on it, might really be called utterly unsuspecting."

On reaching the Royal abode he noticed that there were every-where reinforcements of Carabinieri. The King, in Marshal's uniform, stood in the doorway. The two men entered the draw-ing-room. The King said, "My dear Duce, it's no longer any good. Italy has gone to bits. Army morale is at rock-bottom. The soldiers don't want to fight any more. . . . The Grand Council's vote is terrific—nineteen votes for Grandi's motion, and among them four holders of the Order of the Annunciation! . . . At this moment you are the most hated man in Italy. You can no longer count on more than one friend. You have one friend left, and I am he. That is why I tell you that you need have no fears for your personal safety, for which I will ensure protection. I have been thinking that the man for the job now is Marshal Badoglio. . . ."

Mussolini replied, "You are taking an extremely grave decision. A crisis at this moment would mean making the people think that peace was in sight, once the man who declared war had been dismissed. The blow to the Army's morale would be serious. The crisis would be considered as a triumph for the Churchill-Stalin set-up, especially for Stalin. I realise the people's hatred. I had no difficulty in recognising it last night in the midst of the Grand Council. One can't govern for such a long time and impose so many sacrifices without provoking resentments. In any case, I wish good luck to the man who takes the situation in hand." The King accompanied Mussolini to the door. "His face," says Mussolini, "was livid and he looked smaller than ever, almost dwarfish. He shook my hand and went in again. I descended the few steps and went towards my car. Suddenly a Carabinieri captain stopped me and said, 'His Majesty has charged me with the protection of your person.' I was continuing towards my car when the captain said to me, pointing to a motor-ambulance standing near by, 'No. We must get in there.' I got into the ambulance, together with my secretary. A lieutenant, three Carabinieri, and two police agents in plain clothes got in as well as the captain, and placed themselves by the door armed with machine-guns. When the door was closed the ambulance drove off at top speed. I still thought that all this was being done, as the King had said, in order to protect my person."

Later that afternoon Badoglio was charged by the King to form a new Cabinet of Service chiefs and civil servants, and in the evening the Marshal broadcast the news to the world. Two days later the Duce was taken on Marshal Badoglio's order to be interned on the island of Ponza.

*　　*　　*

Thus ended Mussolini's twenty-one years' dictatorship in Italy, during which he had raised the Italian people from the Bolshevism into which they might have sunk in 1919 to a position in Europe such as Italy had never held before. A new impulse had been given to the national life. The Italian Empire in North Africa was built. Many important public works in Italy were completed. In 1935 the Duce had by his will-power overcome the League of Nations—"Fifty nations led by one"—and was able to complete his conquest of Abyssinia. His régime was far too costly for the Italian people to bear, but there is no doubt that it appealed during its period of success to very great numbers of Italians. He was, as I had addressed him at the time of the fall of France, "the Italian lawgiver." The alternative to his rule might well have been a Communist Italy, which would have brought perils and misfortunes of a different character both upon the Italian people and Europe. His fatal mistake was the declaration of war on France and Great Britain following Hitler's victories in June 1940. Had he not done this he could well have maintained Italy in a balancing position, courted and rewarded by both sides and deriving an unusual wealth and prosperity from the struggles of other countries. Even when the issue of the war became certain Mussolini would have been welcomed by the Allies. He had much to give to shorten its course. He could have timed his moment to declare war on Hitler with art and care. Instead he took the wrong turning. He never understood the strength of Britain, nor the long-enduring qualities of Island resistance and sea-power. Thus he marched to ruin. His great roads will remain a monument to his personal power and long reign.

*　　*　　*

At this time Hitler made a crowning error in strategy and war direction. The defection of Italy, the victorious advance of Russia, and the evident preparations for a cross-Channel attack by Britain and the United States should have led him to concentrate and develop the most powerful German army as a central reserve. In this way only could he use the high qualities of the German command and fighting troops, and at the same time take full advantage of the central position which he occupied, with its interior lines and remarkable communications. As General von Thoma said while a prisoner of war in our charge, "Our only chance is to create a situation where we can use the Army." Hitler, as I have pointed out in an earlier volume, had in fact made a spider's web and forgotten the spider. He tried to hold everything he had won. Enormous forces were squandered in the Balkans and in Italy which could play no part in the main decisions. A central reserve of thirty or forty divisions of the highest quality and mobility would have enabled him to strike at any one of his opponents advancing upon him and fight a major battle with good prospects of success. He could, for instance, have met the British and Americans at the fortieth or fiftieth day after their landing in Normandy a year later with fresh and greatly superior forces. There was no need to consume his strength in Italy and the Balkans, and the fact that he was induced to do so must be taken as the waste of his last opportunity.

Knowing that these choices were open to him, I wished also to have the options of pressing right-handed in Italy or left-handed across the Channel, or both. The wrong dispositions which he made enabled us to undertake the main direct assault under conditions which offered good prospects and achieved success.

* * *

Hitler had returned from the Feltre meeting convinced that Italy could only be kept in the war by purges in the Fascist Party and increasing pressure by the Germans on the Fascist leaders. Mussolini's sixtieth birthday fell on July 29, and Goering was chosen to pay him an official visit on this occasion. But during the course of July 25 alarming reports from Rome began to come in to Hitler's headquarters. By the evening it was clear that Mussolini had resigned or had been removed, and that Badoglio had been nominated by the King as his successor. It was finally decided that any major operation against the new Italian Government would require withdrawals of more divisions than could be spared from the Eastern Front in the event of the expected Russian offensive. Plans were made to rescue Mussolini, to occupy Rome, and to support Italian Fascism wherever possible. If Badoglio signed an armistice with the Allies, further plans were drawn up for seizing the Italian Fleet and occupying key positions throughout Italy, and for overawing Italian garrisons in the Balkans and in the Ægean.

"We must act," Hitler told his advisers on July 26. "Otherwise the Anglo-Saxons will steal a march on us by occupying the airports. The Fascist Party is at present only stunned, and will recover behind our lines. The Fascist Party is the only one that has the will to fight on our side. We must therefore restore it. All reasons advocating further delays are wrong; thereby we run the danger of losing Italy to the Anglo-Saxons. These are matters which a soldier cannot comprehend. Only a man with political insight can see his way clear."

* * *

We had long pondered over the consequences of an Italian collapse. Eight months before I had written:

POSITION OF ITALY
NOTE FOR THE WAR CABINET BY THE PRIME MINISTER
November 25, 1942

It is in my opinion premature to assume that no internal convulsion in Italy could produce a Government which would make a separate peace. If we increase the severity of our pressure upon Italy . . . the desire, and indeed the imperative need, of getting out of the war will come home to all the Italians, including the rank and file of the Fascist Party. Should Italy feel unable to endure the continued attacks which will be made upon her from the air, and presently, I trust, by amphibious operations, the Italian people will have to choose between, on the one hand, setting up a Government under someone like Grandi to sue for a separate peace, or, on the other, submitting to a German occupation, which would merely aggravate the severity of the war.

2. I do not share the view that it is in our interest that the Germans should occupy and take over Italy. We may not be able to prevent it. It is still my hope that the Italians themselves will prevent it, and we should certainly do what we can to further this move. If there were a revolution in Italy and an Armistice Government came into power it is at least arguable that the German interests would be as well served by standing on the Brenner as by undertaking the detailed defence of Italy against the wishes of its people, and possibly of a Provisional Government.

3. When a nation is thoroughly beaten in war it does all sorts of things which no one would imagine beforehand. The sudden, sullen, universal, simultaneous way in which Bulgaria—Government, Army,

and people alike—cut out in 1918 remains in my memory. Without caring to make any arrangements for their future or for their safety, the troops simply marched out of the lines and dispersed to their homes, and King Ferdinand fled. A Government headed by a peasant leader remained to await the judgment of the victors.

4. Therefore I would not rule out the possibilities of a sudden peace demand being made by Italy, and I agree with the United States policy of trying to separate the Italian people from their Government. The fall of Mussolini, even though precautions may have been taken against it beforehand, might well have a decisive effect upon Italian opinion. The Fascist chapter would be closed. One tale would be finished and another would begin. I consider it would be well to drop leaflets over all Italian towns that are bombed, on the theme, "One man alone is the cause of your sufferings—Mussolini."

5. It is to be observed that we are under no obligations to offer any terms to the vanquished, should they sue for them. That decision must be taken when and if we are offered their surrender, and in the meanwhile we certainly ought not to make promises, as some of the American propaganda leaflets have seemed to do.

The news from Rome now raised these issues, and prompted me to telegraph to the President.

Former Naval Person to President Roosevelt   26 July 43
Changes announced in Italy probably portend peace proposals. Let us consult together so as to take joint action. The present stage may only be transition. But anyhow Hitler will feel very lonely when Mussolini is down and out. No one can be quite sure this may not go further.

The President's message to me crossed this telegram.

President Roosevelt to Prime Minister   26 July 43
By coincidence I was again at Shangri-La this afternoon when the news from Rome came, but this time it seems to be true. If any overtures come we must be certain of the use of all Italian territory and transportation against the Germans in the north *and against the whole Balkan peninsula,** as well as use of airfields of all kinds. It is my thought that we should come as close as possible to unconditional surrender, followed by good treatment of the Italian populace. But I think also that the Head Devil should be surrendered, together with his chief partners in crime. In no event should our officers in the field fix on any general terms without your approval and mine. Let me have your thoughts.

*   *   *

* Author's italics.

51

The results of our joint action would dominate the future course of the war. I spent part of the same day in setting down on paper my reactions to the Italian drama. In the afternoon the War Cabinet met to discuss the new situation, and to consider the draft which I had composed. That evening I sent a copy to the President for his comments.

Former Naval Person to President Roosevelt   26 July 43

I send you my thoughts in the form in which I submitted them to the War Cabinet, obtaining their full approval.

2. I don't think myself that we should be too particular in dealing with any non-Fascist Government, even if it is not all we should like. Now Mussolini is gone I would deal with any non-Fascist Italian Government which can deliver the goods. The goods are set out in my memo. herewith. My colleagues also agreed with this.

THOUGHTS ON THE FALL OF MUSSOLINI
By the Prime Minister

It seems highly probable that the fall of Mussolini will involve the overthrow of the Fascist régime, and that the new Government of the King and Badoglio will seek to negotiate a separate arrangement with the Allies for an armistice. Should this prove to be the case it will be necessary for us to make up our minds first of all upon what we want, and secondly upon the measures and conditions required to gain it for us.

2. At this moment above all others our thoughts must be concentrated upon the supreme aim, namely, the destruction of Hitler, Hitlerism, and Nazi Germany. Every military advantage arising out of the surrender of Italy, should that occur, must be sought for this purpose.

3. The first of these is, in the President's words, "the use of all Italian territory and transportation against the Germans in the north and against the whole Balkan peninsula, as well as use of airfields of all kinds." This must include the surrender to our garrisons of Sardinia, the Dodecanese, and Corfu, as well as of all the naval and air bases on the Italian mainland as soon as they can be taken over.

4. Secondly, and of equal importance, the immediate surrender to the Allies of the Italian Fleet, or at least its effective demobilisation and paralysis, and the disarmament of the Italian air and ground forces to whatever extent we find needful and useful. The surrender of the Fleet will liberate powerful British naval forces for service in the Indian Ocean against Japan, and will be most agreeable to the United States.

5. Also, of equal consequence, the immediate withdrawal from, or surrender of, all Italian forces in Corsica, the Riviera, including Toulon, and the Balkan peninsula—to wit, in Yugoslavia, Albania, and Greece.

6. Another objective of the highest importance, about which there will be passionate feeling in this country, is the immediate liberation of all British prisoners of war in Italian hands, and the prevention, which can in the first instance only be by the Italians, of their being transported northwards to Germany. I regard it as a matter of honour and humanity to get our own flesh and blood back as soon as possible and spare them the measureless horrors of incarceration in Germany during the final stages of the war.

7. The fate of the German troops in Italy, and particularly of those south of Rome, will probably lead to fighting between the Germans and the Italian Army and population. We should demand their surrender, and that any Italian Government with whom we can reach a settlement shall do their utmost to procure this. It may be however that the German divisions will cut their way northwards in spite of anything that the Italian armed forces are capable of doing. We should provoke this conflict as much as possible, and should not hesitate to send troops and air support to assist the Italians in procuring the surrender of the Germans south of Rome.

8. When we see how this process goes we can take a further view about action to be taken north of Rome. We should however try to get possession of points on both the west coast and east coast railways of Italy as far north as we dare. And this is a time to dare.

9. In our struggle with Hitler and the German Army we cannot afford to deny ourselves any assistance that will kill Germans. The fury of the Italian population will now be turned against the German intruders, who have, as they will feel, brought all these miseries upon Italy and then come so scantily and grudgingly to her aid. We should stimulate this process in order that the new, liberated, anti-Fascist Italy shall afford us at the earliest moment a safe and friendly area on which we can base the whole forward air attack upon South and Central Germany.

10. This air attack is a new advantage of the first order, as it brings the whole of the Mediterranean air forces into action from a direction which turns the entire line of air defences in the West, and which furthermore exposes all those centres of war production which have been increasingly developed so as to escape air attack from Great Britain. It will become urgent in the highest degree to get agents, Commandos, and supplies by sea across the Adriatic into Greece, Albania, and Yugoslavia. It must be remembered that there are fifteen German divisions in the Balkan peninsula, of which ten are mobile.

Nevertheless, once we have control of the Italian peninsula and of the Adriatic, and the Italian armies in the Balkans withdraw or lay down their arms, it is by no means unlikely that the Germans will be forced to withdraw northwards to the line of the Save and Danube, thus liberating Greece and other tortured countries.

11. We cannot yet measure the effects of Mussolini's fall and of an Italian capitulation upon Bulgaria, Roumania, and Hungary. They may be profound. In connection with this situation the collapse of Italy should fix the moment for putting the strongest pressure on Turkey to act in accordance with the spirit of the Alliance, and in this Britain and the United States, acting jointly or severally, should if possible be joined or at least supported by Russia.

12. The surrender of, to quote the President, "the Head Devil, together with his chief partners in crime," must be considered an eminent object, and one for which we should strive by all means in our power short of wrecking the immense prospects which have been outlined in earlier paragraphs. It may be however that these criminals will flee into Germany or escape into Switzerland. On the other hand, they may surrender themselves or be surrendered by the Italian Government. Should they fall into our hands, we ought now to decide, in consultation with the United States, and, after agreement with them, with the U.S.S.R., what treatment should be meted out to them. Some may prefer prompt execution without trial except for identification purposes. Others may prefer that they be kept in confinement till the end of the war in Europe and their fate decided together with that of other war criminals. Personally I am fairly indifferent on this matter, provided always that no solid military advantages are sacrificed for the sake of immediate vengeance.

"Your message," replied the President to me on July 30, "expresses generally my thoughts of to-day on the prospects and methods of handling the Italian situation with which we are now confronted." He suggested certain minor changes. These in no way altered the substance of the document, and were readily adjusted. "I have not had time to consult my colleagues," I replied on the 31st, "but I have no doubt whatever that our joint draft as amended expresses in perfect harmony the minds of our two Governments on the broad policy to be pursued. It seems to be a case of 'two hearts that beat as one'."

My paper in a slightly amended form was placed before the War Cabinet on August 2, and approved by them as a draft joint directive from both Governments to' the Combined Chiefs of Staff. I took it with me when I went to Quebec for a final discussion with the President. Its main interest however lies in showing our joint reactions to the news of Mussolini's fall.

* * *

Complex problems now lay before us. We had to consider how to treat the new Italian Government. We had to expect the imminent collapse of Italy as an Axis partner, and to draft in detail the terms of surrender, bearing in mind not only the reactions in Italy itself, but also in Germany. We had to take into account the strategic implications of these events, to plan what to do in areas outside Italy, in the Ægean and in the Balkans, which were still held by Italian forces.

On July 27 the President sent me the draft of a broadcast for General Eisenhower to make to the Italian people. This had been approved by the Joint United States Chiefs of Staff, and contained the following sentence: "Your men will return to their normal life and their productive avocations, and hundreds of thousands of Italian prisoners now in our hands will return to the countless Italian homes who long for them. The ancient liberties and traditions of your country will be restored."

I was not only concerned about the draft of this joint message, but about the fate of our prisoners of war in Italian hands.

Former Naval Person to President Roosevelt   28 July 43

. There are 74,000 British prisoners in Italy, and there are also about 30,000 Yugoslavs and Greeks. We cannot agree to any promise to release "hundreds of thousands of Italian prisoners now in our hands" unless our men and Allied men are saved from the horrors of German captivity and restored to us.

2. Moreover, apart from Italian prisoners taken in Tunis and Sicily, we have at least a quarter of a million Italians captured by Wavell two years ago and parked about the world. We think it is too much to offer the return of such a large plurality of prisoners arising from earlier phases of the war, nor do we think it necessary. We are ready however to agree to all Italian prisoners taken in Tunis and taken or to be taken in Sicily being traded against the British and Allied prisoners mentioned above.

3. Accordingly we suggest that Eisenhower's message at this point should read as follows:

"Your men will return to their normal life and to their productive avocations, and, provided all British and Allied prisoners now in your hands are restored safely to us and not taken away to Germany, the hundreds of thousands of Italian prisoners captured by us in Tunisia and Sicily will return to the countless Italian homes who long for them," etc.

The following day I telegraphed to General Eisenhower:

Prime Minister to General Eisenhower (Algiers)   29 July 43

There are obvious dangers in trying to state armistice terms in an attractive, popular form to the enemy nation. It is far better that all should be cut and dried and that their Government should know our full demands and their maximum expectations. We are sending our alternative draft to your Government, and will no doubt reach agreement with them in plenty of time for any negotiations which you may have to conduct or which we shall be handling.

All our thoughts are now concentrated upon the great battle which Alexander is about to begin under your supreme direction in Eastern Sicily. The destruction of the three German divisions now facing the Fifteenth Army Group, happening at this time of all others, may well produce decisive effects in every quarter.

And to the President:

Former Naval Person to President Roosevelt   29 July 43

I was so glad to hear your voice again [on the telephone] and that you were in such good spirits.

2. I have told Eisenhower that we fully agree to his releasing the proclamation with our amendment inserted about British and Allied prisoners.

3. Discarding etiquette, I have sent a direct message to the King of Italy through Switzerland emphasising our vehement and savage interest in this matter. I am most grateful for your promise to put the screw on through the Pope or any other convenient channel. If the King and Badoglio allow our prisoners and key men to be carried off by the Huns without doing their utmost to stop it, by which I mean using physical force, the feeling here would be such that no negotiations with that Government would stand a chance in public opinion.

4. *Armistice Terms.* The War Cabinet are quite clear that we ought not to broadcast armistice terms to the enemy. It is for their responsible Government to ask formally for an armistice on the basis of our principle of unconditional surrender. Then I suppose envoys would be appointed and a rendezvous fixed. Our version is already in your hands. As you will see, it follows the main lines of Eisenhower's draft, but is more precise and is cast in a form suited to discussion between plenipotentiaries rather than a popular appeal. There are great dangers in trying to dish this sort of dose up with jam for the patient.

5. We also think that the terms should cover civil as well as military requirements, and that it would be much better for them to be settled by envoys appointed by our two Governments than by the general commanding in the field. He can of course deal with any proposals coming from the troops on his immediate front for a local surrender.

6. Finally, all our thoughts are concentrated upon the great battle about to be fought by the British Eighth and United States Seventh Armies against the 65,000 Germans cornered in the Eastern Sicilian tip. The destruction of these men could not come at a better time to influence events, not only in Italy but throughout the world. It is grand to think of our soldiers advancing side by side like brothers and with good prospects of victory ahead.

The President agreed with us that Eisenhower should not broadcast terms for an armistice with the enemy, but urged that in order to avoid unnecessary and possibly costly military action against Italy he should be authorised to state conditions when and if the Italian Government asked him for them. I did not see why such a proposal should necessarily be made to Eisenhower, none of whose forces were in contact with the enemy except in Sicily, and then only with the Germans. It seemed to me more likely that the Italian Government would negotiate through the Vatican, the Turks, or the Swiss. I agreed however that if Eisenhower were suddenly approached by an envoy he should have precise terms, embodying the principle of unconditional surrender, which he could immediately use as the basis for granting an armistice, and after much discussion the following articles were agreed:

1. Immediate cessation of all hostile activity by the Italian armed forces.

2. Italy will use her best endeavours to deny to the Germans facilities that might be used against the United Nations.

3. All prisoners or internees of the United Nations to be immediately turned over to the Allied Commander-in-Chief, and none of these may from the beginning of these negotiations be evacuated to Germany.

4. Immediate transfer of the Italian Fleet and Italian aircraft to such points as may be designated by the Allied Commander-in-Chief, with details of disarmament to be prescribed by him.

5. Agreement that Italian merchant shipping may be requisitioned by the Allied Commander-in-Chief to meet the needs of his military-naval programme.

6. Immediate surrender of Corsica and of all Italian territory, both

islands and mainland, to the Allies, for such use as operational bases and other purposes as the Allies may see fit.

7. Immediate guarantee of the free use by the Allies of all airfields and naval ports in Italian territory, regardless of the rate of evacuation of the Italian territory by the German forces. These ports and fields to be protected by Italian armed forces until this function is taken over by the Allies.

8. Immediate withdrawal to Italy of Italian armed forces from all participation in the current war, from whatever areas in which they may now be engaged.

9. Guarantee by the Italian Government that if necessary it will employ all its available armed forces to ensure prompt and exact compliance with all the provisions of this armistice.

10. The Commander-in-Chief of the Allied forces reserves to himself the right to take any measure which in his opinion may be necessary for the protection of the interests of the Allied forces or for the prosecution of the war, and the Italian Government binds itself to take such administrative or other action as the Commander-in-Chief may require, and in particular the Commander-in-Chief will establish Allied military government over such parts of Italian territory as he may deem necessary in the military interests of the Allied nations.

11. The Commander-in-Chief of the Allied forces will have a full right to impose measures of disarmament, demobilisation, and demilitarisation.

On July 31 I telegraphed to the President:

. . . So much for the immediate emergency. We hope however that you will also urgently have our Instrument of Surrender* examined, so that we reach full agreement on it. There are several points in this not dealt with in the emergency terms, and it is couched in a precise, formal, and legal vein, on which much thought has been bestowed here. We are rather puzzled to know why you never refer to this document, as it seems to us to be in fact only a more careful and comprehensive version of the emergency armistice terms. We should be very grateful if you would let us know how you feel about it. We ought certainly to have it, or something like it, ready as soon as possible.

The President agreed, but said that he needed further advice from the American Chiefs of Staff and the State Department. We thought it was essential that any statement made to the Italian people should be agreed formally both by the Americans and our-

* Not printed.

selves and not merely put out by Allied Headquarters at Algiers, and anyhow it was very much better for the generals to go on with the military operations and to keep the armistice terms till they were asked for.

★   ★   ★

Upon our attitude to the new Italian Government of Badoglio depended the speed with which the Italians would probably approach us for peace terms.

We gave much thought to this matter, which was already being observed in the Press on both sides of the Atlantic.

President Roosevelt to Prime Minister   30 July 43

There are some contentious people here who are getting ready to make a row if we seem to recognise the House of Savoy or Badoglio. They are the same element which made such a fuss over North Africa.

I told the Press to-day that we have to treat with any person or persons in Italy who can best give us, first, disarmament, and, second, assurance against chaos, and I think also that you and I after an armistice comes could say something about self-determination in Italy at the proper time.

Former Naval Person to President Roosevelt   31 July 43

My position is that once Mussolini and the Fascists are gone I will deal with any Italian authority which can deliver the goods. I am not in the least afraid for this purpose of seeming to recognise the House of Savoy or Badoglio, provided they are the ones who can make the Italians do what we need for our war purposes. Those purposes would certainly be hindered by chaos, Bolshevisation, or civil war. We have no right to lay undue burdens on our troops. It may well be that after the armistice terms have been accepted both the King and Badoglio will sink under the odium of surrender and that the Crown Prince and a new Prime Minister may be chosen.

I should deprecate any pronouncement about self-determination at the present time, beyond what is implicit in the Atlantic Charter. I agree with you that we must be very careful not to throw everything into the melting-pot.

Prime Minister to Foreign Secretary   31 July 43

Many things in life are settled by the two-stage method. For instance, a man is not prevented from saying, "Will you marry me darling?" because he has not got the marriage contract, drawn up by the family solicitors, in his pocket. Personally I think the terms which Eisenhower may now offer are much more likely to be understood by an envoy, and thus be capable of immediate acceptance, than the legal verbiage of the Instrument of Surrender, and they will look much better if published. If we get emergency terms it means that the Italians will have given themselves up to us, lock, stock, and barrel. There would be nothing improper in our requiring them to hand over the pull-through and other cleaning materials afterwards.

President Roosevelt to Prime Minister   3 Aug 43
I have read Instrument of Surrender, and while the language seems on the whole good I seriously doubt advisability of using it at all. After all, the terms of surrender already approved and sent to Eisenhower ought to be all that is necessary. Why tie his hands by an instrument that may be over-sufficient or insufficient? Why not let him act to meet situations as they arise?

All this awaited our impending Conference at Quebec.

CHAPTER IV

WESTWARD HO!
SYNTHETIC HARBOURS

On Board the "Queen Mary" – Brigadier Wingate – The Plan for "Overlord" – The Combined Operations Organisation – The Work of "Cossac" – Where to Strike? – The Need of Harbours and Piers – The Birth of the "Mulberries" – The Plan is Unfolded – A Majestic Project – Floating Breakwaters – Vision of a Floating Airfield – Three Dominating Assumptions About "Overlord" – Mountbatten Given the Supreme Command in Burma – My Note of August 7 on Operations in the Far Eastern Theatre.

P ROSPECTS of victory in Sicily, the Italian situation, and the progress of the war made me feel the need in July for a new meeting with the President and for another Anglo-American Conference. It was Roosevelt who suggested that Quebec should be the scene. Mr. Mackenzie King welcomed the proposal, and nothing could have been more agreeable to us. No more fitting or splendid setting for a meeting of those who guided the war policy of the Western world could have been chosen at this cardinal moment than the ancient citadel of Quebec, at the gateway of Canada, overlooking the mighty St. Lawrence River. The President, while gladly accepting Canadian hospitality, did not feel it possible that Canada should be formally a member of the Conference, as he apprehended similar demands by Brazil and other American partners in the United Nations. We also had to think of the claims of Australia and the other Dominions. This delicate question was solved and surmounted by the broad-minded outlook of the Canadian Prime Minister and Government. I for my part was determined that we and the United States should have the Conference to ourselves, in view of all the vital business we had in common. A triple meeting of the heads of the three major Powers was a main object of the future; now it must be for Britain and the United States alone. We assigned to it the name "Quadrant".

I left London for the Clyde, where the *Queen Mary* awaited us, on the night of August 4, in a train which carried the very heavy staffs we needed. We were, I suppose, over two hundred, besides about fifty Royal Marine orderlies. The scope of the Conference comprised not only the Mediterranean campaign, now at its first climax, but even more the preparations for the cross-Channel design of 1944, the whole conduct of the war in the Indian theatre, and our share in the struggle against Japan. For the Channel crossing we took with us three officers sent by Lieut.-General F. E. Morgan, Chief of Staff to the Supreme Allied Commander, yet to be finally chosen, who with his combined Anglo-American staff had completed our joint outline plan. As the whole of our affairs in the Indian and Far Eastern theatres were under examination I brought with me General Wavell's Director of Military Operations, who had flown specially from India.

I took also with me a young Brigadier named Wingate, who had already made his mark as a leader of irregulars in Abyssinia, and had greatly distinguished himself in the jungle fighting in Burma. These new brilliant exploits won him in some circles of the Army in which he served the title of "the Clive of Burma". I had heard much of all this, and knew also how the Zionists had sought him as a future Commander-in-Chief of any Israelite army that might be formed. I had him summoned home in order that I might have a look at him before I left for Quebec. I was about to dine alone on the night of August 4 at Downing Street when the news that he had arrived by air and was actually in the house was brought me. I immediately asked him to join me at dinner. We had not talked for half an hour before I felt myself in the presence of a man of the highest quality. He plunged at once into his theme of how the Japanese could be mastered in jungle warfare by long-range penetration groups landed by air behind the enemy lines. This interested me greatly. I wished to hear much more about it, and also to let him tell his tale to the Chiefs of Staff.

I decided at once to take him with me on the voyage. I told

him our train would leave at ten. It was then nearly nine. Wingate had arrived just as he was after three days' flight from the actual front, and with no clothes but what he stood up in. He was of course quite ready to go, but expressed regret that he would not be able to see his wife, who was in Scotland and had not even heard of his arrival. However, the resources of my Private Office were equal to the occasion. Mrs. Wingate was aroused at her home by the police and taken to Edinburgh in order to join our train on its way through and to go with us to Quebec. She had no idea of what it was all about until, in the early hours of the morning, she actually met her husband on a platform at Waverley Station. They had a very happy voyage together.

As I knew how much the President liked meeting young, heroic figures, I had also invited Wing-Commander Guy Gibson, fresh from leading the attack which had destroyed the Möhne and Eder Dams. These supplied the industries of the Ruhr, and fed a wide area of fields, rivers, and canals. A special type of mine had been invented for their destruction, but it had to be dropped at night from a height of no more than sixty feet. After months of continuous and concentrated practice sixteen Lancasters of No. 617 Squadron of the Royal Air Force attacked on the night of May 16. Half were lost, but Gibson had stayed to the end, circling under fierce fire over the target to direct his squadron. He now wore a remarkable set of decorations—the Victoria Cross, a Distinguished Service Order and bar, and a Distinguished Flying Cross and bar—but no other ribbons. This was unique.

My wife came with me, and my daughter Mary, now a subaltern in an anti-aircraft battery, was my aide-de-camp. We sailed on August 5, this time for Halifax, in Nova Scotia, instead of New York.

* * *

The *Queen Mary* drove on through the waves, and we lived in the utmost comfort on board her, with a diet of pre-war times. As usual on these voyages, we worked all day long. Our large cipher staff, with attendant cruisers to dispatch outgoing messages, kept us in touch with events from hour to hour. Each day I studied with the Chiefs of Staff the various aspects of the problems we were to discuss with our American friends. The most important of these was of course "Overlord".

I had reserved the interlude which a five days' voyage presented for the consideration of our long-wrought plans for this supreme operation of crossing the Channel. Study on an ever-expanding scale had gone forward since the struggles on the coasts of Norway and France in 1940, and we had learned much about amphibious war. The Combined Operations Organisation, which I had then set up under my friend Admiral of the Fleet Sir Roger Keyes, had played an all-important part and created a new technique. Small-scale raids by the Commandos paved the way for greater things, and not only gave us confidence and experience, but showed the world that although beset on all sides we were not content with passive defence. The Americans, still neutral, had observed this new trend, and later developed it in their own way on a vast scale.

In October 1941 Admiral Keyes was succeeded by Captain Lord Louis Mountbatten. We were still hard-pressed, and our only ally, Russia, seemed near to defeat. Nevertheless I had resolved to prepare for an invasion of the Continent when the tide should turn. First we had to increase the intensity and scope of our raids, and then translate all this experience into something much more massive. To mount a successful invasion from the United Kingdom new engines of war must be contrived and developed, the three fighting Services must be trained to plan and fight as one team, supported by the industry of the nation, and the whole island converted into an armed camp for launching the greatest seaborne assault of all time.

When Mountbatten visited me at Chequers before taking up his new duties I told him, according to his account, "You are to plan for the offensive. In your headquarters you will never think defensively." This governed his actions. To provide him with the necessary authority for his task he had been made a member of the Chiefs of Staff Committee, with the acting rank of Vice-Admiral and equivalent honorary rank in the other Services. As Minister of Defence I retained personal responsibility for his head-quarters, and thus he reported direct to me whenever necessary. At Vaagsö in Norway, at Bruneval, at St. Nazaire and elsewhere, the Commandos played a steadily increasing part in our affairs. Our raids culminated in the costly attack on Dieppe in August 1942. When thereafter we passed to major Anglo-American offensives we applied our lessons to the North African landings and to our amphibious descents in the Mediterranean. In all these Mountbatten's organisation took a prominent and indispensable part.

In May 1942 a body known as "the Combined Commanders" had been appointed to grip the problem. It included the Commanders-in-Chief at home, Mountbatten, and later General Eisenhower, commanding the United States forces in Britain. At the Casablanca Conference in January 1943 it was decided to set up an Allied Inter-Service Staff under a British officer to prepare a definite plan for "Overlord". This group began its task in London, under Lieut.-General F. E. Morgan, with the short title of "Cossac".*

The first question was where a landing in force could best be made. There were several options: the Dutch or Belgian coast; the Pas de Calais; between the mouths of the Somme and the Seine; Normandy; Brittany. Each of these had its own advantages and disadvantages, which had to be weighed up under a whole set of different headings and varying, sometimes uncertain, factors. Of these the principal were beaches; weather and tides; sites for constructing airfields; length of voyage; near-by ports that could be captured; the nature of the hinterland for subsequent operations; provision of cover by home-based aircraft; enemy dispositions, their minefields and defences.

The choice narrowed to the Pas de Calais or Normandy. The former gave us the best air cover, but here the defences were the most formidable, and although it promised a shorter sea voyage this advantage was only apparent. While Dover and Folkestone are much closer to Calais and Boulogne than the Isle of Wight is to Normandy, their harbours were far too small to support an invasion. Most of our ships would have had to sail from ports along the whole south coast of England and from the Thames estuary, and so cross a lot of salt water in any case. General Morgan and his advisers recommended the Normandy coast, which from the first had been advocated by Mountbatten. There can be no doubt now that this decision was sound. Normandy gave us the greatest hope. The defences were not so strong as in the Pas de Calais. The seas and the beaches were on the whole suitable, and were to some extent sheltered from the westerly gales by the Cotentin peninsula. The hinterland favoured the

* Chief of Staff, Supreme Allied Commander.

65

rapid deployment of large forces, and was sufficiently remote from the main strength of the enemy. The port of Cherbourg could be isolated and captured early in the operation. Brest could be outflanked and taken later.

All the coast between Havre and Cherbourg was of course defended with concrete forts and pill-boxes, but as there was no harbour capable of sustaining a large army in this fifty-mile half-moon of sandy beaches it was thought that the Germans would not assemble large forces in immediate support of the sea-front. Their High Command had no doubt said to themselves, "This is a good sector for raids up to ten or twenty thousand men, but unless Cherbourg is taken in working order no army in any way equal to the task of an invasion can be landed or supplied. It is a coast for a raid, but not for wider operations." If only there were harbours which could nourish great armies, here was the front on which to strike.

* * *

Of course, as the reader will have seen, I was well abreast of all the thought about landing-craft and tank landing-craft. I had also long been a partisan of piers with their heads floating out in the sea. Much work had since been done on them, following a minute which in the course of our discussions I had issued as long ago as May 30, 1942.

Prime Minister to Chief of Combined Operations
They *must* float up and down with the tide. The anchor problem must be mastered. The ships must have a side-flap cut in them, and a drawbridge long enough to overreach the moorings of the piers. Let me have the best solution worked out. Don't argue the matter. The difficulties will argue for themselves.*

Thought later moved to the creation of a large area of sheltered water protected by a breakwater based on blockships brought to the scene by their own power and then sunk in a prearranged position. This idea originated with Commodore J. Hughes-Hallett in June 1943, while he was serving as Naval Chief of Staff in General Morgan's organisation. Imagination, contrivance, and experiment had been ceaseless, and now in August 1943 there was a complete project for making two full-scale temporary harbours

* See facsimile, between pp. 77-78.

which could be towed over and brought into action within a few days of the original landing. These synthetic harbours were called "Mulberries", a code-name which certainly did not reveal their character or purpose.

*   *   *   *   *

One morning on our voyage, at my request, Brigadier K. G. McLean, with two other officers from General Morgan's staff, came to me as I lay in my bed in the spacious cabin, and, after they had set up a large-scale map, explained in a tense and cogent tale the plan which had been prepared for the cross-Channel descent upon France. The reader is perhaps familiar with all the arguments of 1941 and 1942 upon this burning question in all its variants, but this was the first time that I had heard the whole coherent plan presented in precise detail both of numbers and tonnage as the result of prolonged study by officers of both nations.

Further discussions on succeeding days led into more technical detail. The Channel tides have a play of more than twenty feet, with corresponding scours along the beaches. The weather is always uncertain, and winds and gales may whip up in a few hours irresistible forces against frail human structures. The fools or knaves who had chalked "Second Front Now" on our walls for the past two years had not had their minds burdened by such problems. I had long pondered upon them.

It must be remembered that in the "Mulberry" harbours we had a multiple problem to face. The whole project involved the construction in Britain of great masses of special equipment, amounting in the aggregate to over a million tons of steel and concrete. This work, undertaken with the highest priority, would impinge heavily on our already hard-pressed engineering and ship-repairing industries. All this equipment would have to be transported by sea to the scene of action, and there erected with the utmost expedition in the face of enemy attack and the vagaries of the weather.

The whole project was majestic. On the beaches themselves would be the great piers, with their seaward ends afloat and sheltered. At these piers coasters and landing-craft would be able to discharge at all states of the tide. To protect them against the wanton winds and waves breakwaters would be spread in a great arc to seaward, enclosing a large area of sheltered water. Thus sheltered, deep-draught ships could lie at anchor and discharge, and all types of landing-craft could ply freely to and from the beaches. These breakwaters would be composed of sunken concrete structures known as "Phoenix" and blockships known as "Gooseberries". In my second volume I have described the similar structures which I thought might in the First World War have been used to create artificial harbours in the Heligoland Bight.* Now they were to form a principal part of the great plan.

* * *

This was the scheme of the "Mulberry" harbour, but even so it was not enough. There would not be room for all the ships we needed. Many would have to discharge outside. To shield these and the very numerous naval vessels engaged an additional scheme of *floating* breakwaters was proposed. For this purpose several devices were being considered, among them one to create a barrier to wave action by means of a continuous screen of air bubbles discharged from pipes laid on the sea-bed. It was hoped that this screen would break up and absorb the rhythm of the waves. Another device, known as a "Lilo", consisted of partially inflated air bags carrying submerged curtains of concrete. These would be moored in line to seaward of the "Phoenix" and enclose a considerable additional area of water. Neither of these ideas reached fruition, but eventually a device called the "Bombardon" was adopted, embodying some of the features of the "Lilo". It was a cruciform steel structure about 200 feet long and 25 feet high, with all but the top arm of the cross submerged. In the event this device was of doubtful value, as we shall see in due course.

I was very well satisfied with the prospect of having the whole of this story presented to the President with my full support. At least it would convince the American authorities that we were not insincere about "Overlord" and had not grudged thought or time in preparation. I arranged to assemble in Quebec the best experts in such matters from London and Washington. Together they could pool resources and find the best answers to the many technical problems.

I was now convinced of the enormous advantages of attacking the Havre-Cherbourg sector, provided these unexpected harbours

* See Book III, Chapter XII.

The Sicily Landings

7 Sicily: the invasion fleet.
8 Infantry reach the beaches after debarking from landing craft.

9 Light equipment and shells pass from hand to hand.

10-11 Heavy equipment being landed.

could be brought into being from the first and thus render possible the landing and sustained advance of armies of a million rising to two million men, with all their immense modern equipment and impedimenta. This would mean being able to unload at least 12,000 tons a day.

* * *

There was another associated problem on which my mind dwelt, namely, the maintenance of fighting air superiority over the battle area. If we could create a floating airfield we could refuel our fighter aircraft within striking distance of the landing points, and thus multiply our air-power on the spot at the decisive moment. Among the numerous devices discussed during this busy voyage was one called "Habakkuk". This project was conceived by a Mr. Pyke on Mountbatten's staff. His idea was to form a structure of ice, large enough to serve as a runway for aircraft. It would be of ship-like construction, displacing a million tons, self-propelled at slow speed, with its own anti-aircraft defence, with workshops and repair facilities, and with a surprisingly small refrigerating plant for preserving its own existence. It had been found that by adding a proportion of wood pulp in various forms to ordinary sea ice the mixture lost the brittle qualities associated with ice and became extremely tough. This substance, called Pykrete, after its inventor, seemed to offer great possibilities not only for our needs in North-West Europe, but also elsewhere. It was found that as the ice melted the fibrous content quickly formed a furry outer surface which acted as an insulator and greatly retarded the melting process. Much development work was eventually done on this idea, particularly in Canada, but for various reasons it never had any success.

* * *

Three dominating assumptions were made both by the framers of the plan and the British Chiefs of Staff. With these I was in entire agreement, and, as will be seen later, they were approved by the Americans and accepted by the Russians.

1. That there must be a substantial reduction in the strength of the German fighter aircraft in North-West Europe before the assault took place.

2. That there should be not more than twelve mobile German

divisions in Northern France at the time the operation was launched, and that it must not be possible for the Germans to build up more than fifteen divisions in the succeeding two months.

3. That the problem of beach maintenance of large forces in the tidal waters of the English Channel over a prolonged period must be overcome. To ensure this it was essential that we should be able to construct at least two effective synthetic harbours.

* * *

I also had many discussions with the Chiefs of Staff on our affairs in the Indian and Far Eastern theatres. We had none too good a tale to tell. A division had advanced at the end of 1942 down the Arakan coast of Burma to recapture the port of Akyab. Though strengthened until a complete corps was engaged, under the command of General Irwin, the operation had failed, and our troops were forced back over the Indian frontier.

Although there was much to be said in explanation, I felt that the whole question of the British High Command against Japan must come under review. New methods and new men were needed. I had long felt that it was a bad arrangement for the Commander-in-Chief India to command the operations in Burma in addition to his other far-reaching responsibilities. It seemed to me that the vigorous prosecution of large-scale operations against the Japanese in South-East Asia necessitated the creation of a separate Supreme Allied Command. The Chiefs of Staff were in complete agreement, and prepared a memorandum on these lines for discussion with their American colleagues in Quebec. There remained the question of the commander of this new theatre, and we were in no doubt that he should be British. Of the various names that were put forward, I was sure in my own mind that Admiral Mountbatten had superior qualifications for this great command, and I determined to make this proposal to the President at the first opportunity. The appointment of an officer of the substantive rank of Captain R.N. to the Supreme Command of one of the main theatres of the war was an unusual step; but, having carefully prepared the ground beforehand, I was not surprised when the President cordially agreed.

* * *

I produced for the Chiefs of Staff Committee a note on plans and policies, from which the following is an extract:

7 Aug 43

Before we meet the Americans we must settle upon:

(a) The general plan for the South-East Asia Command and the Supreme Commander, and

(b) Positive proposals for attacking the enemy, and proving our zeal in this theatre of war, which by its failures and sluggishness is in a measure under reasonable reproach.

I feel that we ought to let Brigadier Wingate tell his story and furnish the United States Chiefs of Staff with copies of his report, and thus convince them that we mean business in this sector of the South-East Asia front. Obviously the Arakan force should lie up against the enemy and engage him. But the amphibious operations against Akyab ought to be stopped now, not only in the interests of the Mediterranean campaign, which should be paramount, but also because it is in itself a faulty and unsound operation. It seeks to strike the enemy where he is best prepared. It lays itself open to serious counter-measures by him. It achieves no major strategic purpose.

* * *

It is astonishing how quickly a voyage can pass if one has enough to do to occupy every waking minute. I had looked forward to an interval of rest and a change from the perpetual clatter of the war. But as we approached our destination the holiday seemed to be over before it had begun.

CHAPTER V

THE QUEBEC CONFERENCE:
"QUADRANT"

*Arrival at Halifax – My Telegram to the King, August 11 – Visit
to Hyde Park – My Memorandum of August 17 – The "Quadrant"
Conference Opens, August 19 – The Chiefs of Staff Report Upon
"Overlord" – I Propose an American Commander – Strategy in Italy
– A Supreme Commander for South-East Asia – Major Strategy
Against Japan – Proposed British Contribution Against Sumatra –
My Telegram to Mr. Attlee, August 22 – British Claims to Share
in the Main Attack on Japan – An Amusing Incident – Mountbatten
Appointed to S.E. Asia – My Telegram to Mr. Attlee of August 25 –
My Liaison Officers with General MacArthur and Generalissimo
Chiang Kai-shek – Eisenhower Prepares for the Invasion of Italy –
Need to Take Naples – Disquieting Estimates of British Reinforcements
– I Give Instructions for a Large Increase.*

HALIFAX was reached on August 9. The great ship drew
in to the landing jetty and we went straight to our train.
In spite of all precautions about secrecy, large crowds were
assembled. As my wife and I sat in our saloon at the end of the
train the people gathered round and gave us welcome. Before
we started I made them sing *The Maple Leaf* and *O Canada!* I
feared they did not know *Rule, Britannia*, though I am sure they
would have enjoyed it if we had had a band. After about twenty
minutes of hand-shakings, photographs, and autographs we left
for Quebec.

Two days later I telegraphed to the King:

Prime Minister to His Majesty the King   11 Aug 43
    With humble duty.

    1. The Citadel is in every way delightful, and ideally suited to the
purpose. Arrangements for the President are perfect. He has the

upper floor, and ramps are fitted everywhere for his convenience. I am most grateful to Your Majesty for arranging this. I have telegraphed to the Governor-General thanking him for the trouble he has taken and for his kindly welcome.

2. The holding of this Conference in Canada, and especially at Quebec, is most timely, as there is a lot of fretfulness here, which I believe will soon be removed. I meet the Canadian Cabinet this morning and the Quebec Cabinet this afternoon, and start thereafter for Hyde Park.

3. I presume Your Majesty will already have seen the question that I put to the Deputy Prime Minister and Foreign Secretary about Mountbatten. I have not yet heard from them, but I am increasingly inclined to suggest this solution to the President. Brigadier Wingate made a deep impression on all during the voyage, and I look for a new turn being given to the campaign in Upper Burma.

4. Your Majesty will also have noticed that I have heard from the Great Bear, and that we are on speaking, or at least growling, terms again.

I also telegraphed to the President.

Former Naval Person to President Roosevelt 11 Aug 43
I have just arrived, after a most swift and agreeable journey, on which it has been possible to work continuously. The Warden family* are looking forward keenly to their visit to Hyde Park, where we propose to arrive the afternoon of the 12th. Are we right in thinking we should all bring our thinnest clothes?

My wife was forced to rest in the Citadel, but next day Mary and I travelled to Hyde Park. We visited Niagara Falls on the way. The reporters asked me what I thought of them, and gave the following account of our talk: " 'I saw them before you were born. I came here first in 1900.' 'Do they look the same?' 'Well,' I replied, 'the principle seems the same. The water still keeps falling over.' " We were the President's guests till August 14. It was so hot that I got up one night because I was unable to sleep and hardly to breathe, and went outside to sit on a bluff overlooking the Hudson River. Here I watched the dawn.

*   *

In these same August days I prepared a general statement upon the whole of our war policy. The greater part of it concerned operations in Burma and the Indian Ocean and their reactions

---

* My code-name was "Colonel Warden".

upon the war against Japan. These will be described later. The paper is dated August 17. The immediate point on which my mind was focused was to procure the invasion of Italy as the natural consequence and exploitation of our victory in Sicily and Mussolini's fall.

Should Naples be captured [Operation "Avalanche"] in the near future we shall have a first-rate port in Italy, and other harbours, like Brindisi and Taranto, will fall into our possession thereafter. If by November our front can be established as far north as the Leghorn–Ancona line the landing-craft in the Mediterranean will have played their part. A detachment would be required from the landing fleet for amphibious turning movements such as we have seen in Sicily, for minor descents across the Adriatic, and for operations such as "Accolade" [the capture of Rhodes and other islands in the Ægean]. The disappearance of the Italian Fleet as a factor should enable a great diminution in naval strength in the Mediterranean to be made, just as the use of first-class harbours supersedes the need of landing-craft. There should therefore be during the late autumn the power to move landing-craft and assault ships back for "Overlord", and also to send a sufficient detachment through the Suez Canal to the Indian theatre. I repeat however that the *maximum* number for which landing-craft should be supplied in a single flight is 30,000 men.

Although I have frequently spoken of the line of the Po or of the Alps as being desirable objectives for us this year in Italy, it is not possible to see so far at present. A very great advantage will have been gained if we stop at the Leghorn–Ancona line. We should thus avoid the danger which General Wilson has pointed out of the immense broadening of the front which will take place as soon as that line has been passed. The estimate which has been given me of twenty-two divisions was presumably formed for this broad front. What is the estimate needed to hold the Leghorn–Ancona line? If we cannot have the best there are very good second bests. From such a position we could by air supply a fomented rising in Savoy and the French Alps, to which the young men of France would be able to rally, and at the same time with our right hand we could act across the Adriatic to stimulate the Patriot activities in the Balkan peninsula. It may be necessary for us to accept these limitations in order that the integrity of Operation "Overlord" shall not be marred.

* * *

On August 17 the President and Harry Hopkins reached Quebec, and Eden and Brendan Bracken flew in from England. As the delegations gathered further news of Italian peace moves came out to us, and it was under the impression of Italy's approaching surrender that our talks were held. The Chiefs of Staff had been at work with their American colleagues in the Citadel since August 14, and had drafted a comprehensive progress report on the future strategy of the war for 1943–44. In fact "Quadrant" was a series of technical Staff conferences, the results of which were surveyed in two meetings between the President and myself and our Service chiefs.

The first plenary session was held on August 19. Highest strategic priority "as a prerequisite to 'Overlord'" was given to the combined bomber offensive against Germany. The lengthy discussions upon Operation "Overlord" were then summarised in the light of the combined planning in London by General Morgan. The Chiefs of Staff now reported as follows:

OPERATION "OVERLORD"

(a) This operation will be the primary United States-British ground and air effort against the Axis in Europe. (Target date, May 1, 1944.) After securing adequate Channel ports, exploitation will be directed towards securing areas that will facilitate both ground and air operations against the enemy. Following the establishment of strong Allied forces in France, operations designed to strike at the heart of Germany and to destroy her military forces will be undertaken.

(b) Balanced ground and air force to be built up for "Overlord", and there will be continuous planning for and maintenance of those forces available in the United Kingdom in readiness to take advantage of any situation permitting an opportunistic cross-Channel move into France.

(c) As between Operation "Overlord" and operations in the Mediterranean, where there is a shortage of resources available resources will be distributed and employed with the main object of ensuring the success of "Overlord". Operations in the Mediterranean theatre will be carried out with the forces allotted at "Trident" [the previous Conference at Washington in May], except in so far as these may be varied by decision of the Combined Chiefs of Staff.

We have approved the outline plan of General Morgan for Operation "Overlord", and have authorised him to proceed with the detailed planning and with full preparations.

These paragraphs produced some discussion at our meeting. I pointed out that the success of "Overlord" depended on certain conditions being fulfilled in regard to relative strength. I emphasised that I strongly favoured "Overlord" in 1944, though I had not been in favour of "Sledgehammer" in 1942 or "Round-up" in 1943. The objections which I had to the cross-Channel operation were however now removed. I thought that every effort should be made to add at least 25 per cent. to the first assault. This would mean finding more landing-craft. There were still nine months to go, and much could be done in that time. The beaches selected were good, and it would be better if at the same time a landing were to be made on the inside beaches of the Cotentin peninsula. "Above all," I said, "the initial lodgment must be strong."

As the United States had the African command, it had been earlier agreed between the President and me that the commander of "Overlord" should be British, and I proposed for this purpose, with the President's agreement, General Brooke, the Chief of the Imperial General Staff, who, it may be remembered, had commanded a corps in the decisive battle on the road to Dunkirk, with both Alexander and Montgomery as his subordinates. I had informed General Brooke of this intention *early in 1943*. This operation was to begin with equal British and American forces, and as it was to be based on Great Britain it seemed right to make such an arrangement. However, as the year advanced and the immense plan of the invasion began to take shape I became increasingly impressed with the very great preponderance of American troops that would be employed after the original landing with equal numbers had been successful, and now at Quebec I myself took the initiative of proposing to the President that an American commander should be appointed for the expedition to France. He was gratified at this suggestion, and I dare say his mind had been moving that way. We therefore agreed that an American officer should command "Overlord" and that the Mediterranean should be entrusted to a British commander, the actual date of the change being dependent upon the progress of the war. In August 1943 I informed General Brooke, who had my entire confidence, of this change, and of the reasons for it. He bore the great disappointment with soldierly dignity.

$$\ast \quad \ast \quad \ast$$

As to Italy, the Chiefs of Staff proposed that there should be three phases in our future operations. First, we should drive Italy out of the war and establish airfields near Rome, and if possible farther north. I pointed out that I wanted it definitely understood that I was not committed to an advance beyond the Ancona–Pisa line. Second, we should seize Sardinia and Corsica, and then press hard against the Germans in the north of the peninsula to stop them joining in the fight against "Overlord". There was also "Anvil", a projected landing in Southern France in the neighbourhood of Toulon and Marseilles and an advance northwards up the Rhone valley. This was to lead to much controversy later on. Recommendations were made about supplying Balkan and French guerrillas by air, intensifying the war against the U-boats, and making more use of the Azores as a naval and air base.

* * *

On the major question of the South-East Asia Command the original proposals of the British Chiefs of Staff had been considered. The plan of a Supreme Commander found favour, and the following recommendations were made:

(a) That the Combined Chiefs of Staff will exercise a general jurisdiction over strategy for the South-East theatre and the allocation of American and British resources of all kinds between the China theatre and the South-East Asia Command.

(b) That the British Chiefs of Staff will exercise jurisdiction over all matters pertaining to operations, and will be the channel through which all instructions to the Supreme Commander are passed.

* * *

There was a spirited argument at our first plenary meeting on the whole question of Far Eastern strategy, on which the work of the Chiefs of Staff was to centre in the following days. Japan's island empire must be crushed mainly by the application of maritime power. No army could be engaged without first winning control of Japanese waters. How could the air weapon be used? Opinions diverged sharply. There were some close to the President who advocated making the main assault through Burma into China. They argued that ports and air bases in China would be indispensable for intensive and sustained air attacks against the mainland of Japan. Although politically attractive in American eyes, this idea ignored the impossibility of deploying large armies, most of which would have to be found by Britain, in the jungles of Burma, and also the presence of very strong Japanese forces in China operating on interior lines of

SECRET

Piers for Use on Beaches

CONDITIONS OF BEACH

Average gradient is 1 in 200 and beaches are open to the south west.

CONDITIONS OF TIDE

2. Range of spring tides is 30 feet and the strength of the tide parallel to the beach is 4 knots at springs.

SCAFFOLDING PIERS

3. A pier to be of use for unloading ships of 20 foot draught would have to be 1 mile in length and 40 foot in height at the seaward end. The present type of scaffolding pier does not exceed 20 foot in height. It is doubtful whether a pier of these large dimensions could be made with scaffolding, but in any case the amount of material required would be prohibitive.

4. A pontoon pier would have to be similar in length.

All floating piers suffer from the disadvantage of having to be securely moored with heavy anchors. Even then they are most vulnerable and will not stand up to a gale of wind. The strength of the tide is so great that the moorings will have to be very large. If large pontoons were moored, 20 yards apart, at least 200 anchors would be required. The sea-ward end of a floating pier must be particularly well moored and the mooring chains form an obstacle to ships coming alongside. Owing to the poor ratio between the weight of a floating pontoons and the weight they can carry, and to their vulnerability to sea wind and tide, they are not favoured in comparison with scaffolding piers on open beaches.

C.W.G.
or depth

They must float up & brace w the tide.
The anchor problem must be mastered. The ships must have a self-flap that in turn cut a Sandhedge. Let me know to overcome the unsurmting of the pier. Don't argue the matter. The difficulties will argue for themselves.
WSC 30.5.42

FACSIMILE OF MR. CHURCHILL'S MINUTE OF MAY 30, 1942

communication, and above all the relatively minor contribution which could be made to such an undertaking by the expanding sea-power of the United States.

Alternatively we could make a direct attack by sea against Japan's island barrier in the Central and South Pacific. The burden of this would fall mainly on the Navy and the maritime air forces. Such a thrust would be aimed first at the Philippines, which to all Americans offered an attractive goal. With the Philippines once more in American hands Japan would be isolated from many of her chief sources of supply and the garrisons in the outlying islands of the Dutch East Indies would be cut off from all hope of rescue. They would eventually wither and die without the need for costly fighting.

From the Philippines the encirclement of the Japanese homeland could begin. New bases on the China coast, in Formosa, and in the small islands south of Japan might all be necessary, but once these were obtained the full-scale invasion of Japan became practicable. The bold sweep of this conception was the more attractive in that it rested squarely on the might of American sea-power. Very large naval forces would be needed, but only in the final phase would great armies be required, and by then Hitler would be overthrown and the main strength of Britain and the United States could be hurled against Japan.

I was anxious to state my views on this occasion before the remaining meetings of the Chiefs of Staff. The British planners were proposing in the coming winter to extend the operations of Wingate's forces into Northern Burma, and I was convinced that this should be supplemented by the seizure of the tip of Sumatra. I said at the meeting that I was convinced that "the attack on Sumatra was a great strategic blow which should be struck in 1944. This operation, 'Culverin,' would be the 'Torch' of the Indian Ocean. In my opinion it would not be beyond the compass of our resources. We should be striking and seizing a point of our own against which the Japanese would have to beat themselves if they wished to end the severe drain which would be imposed on their shipping by our air action from Sumatra." The President seemed to think that such an operation would be heading away from the main direction of our advance towards Japan. I pointed out that the alternative would be to waste the entire year, with nothing to show for it but the minor port of Akyab and the future right to toil through the swamps and jungles of Burma, about the suggested reconquest of which I was very dubious. I emphasised the value of the Sumatra project, which I compared, in its promise of decisive consequences, with the Dardanelles operation of 1915. The idea of trying to tie up all our amphibious resources in the Indian Ocean in 1943–44 in order to retake Akyab seemed to me not to be right.

The next day I minuted:

Prime Minister to General Ismay, for C.O.S. Committee   20 Aug 43
We are not yet agreed among ourselves about the policy to be pursued in Akyab, "Culverin," etc., and in my opinion the whole matter has been insufficiently studied. I am still studying it myself. In the meanwhile it is not possible to come to any decision with the Americans in the matter. I hope the Chiefs of Staff will beware of creating a situation where I shall certainly have to refuse to bear any responsibility for a decision which is taken on their level. This would entail the whole matter being referred to the War Cabinet at home after our return. I remain absolutely where I was at the last Conference, and where we all were, that a campaign through Rangoon up the Irrawaddy to Mandalay and beyond would be most detrimental and disadvantageous to us. The capture of Akyab without such a campaign is only an act of waste and folly. . . .

The situation I wish to have at this time next year is that we are masters of "Culverin", that Wingate is in touch with the Chinese in Yunnan, that the communications in Upper Burma have been improved as far as possible, and that we have a free option where to strike next amphibiously, having regard to the reactions from the enemy, which by then will have been apparent.

Two days later I telegraphed home:

Prime Minister (Quebec) to Deputy Prime Minister   22 Aug 43
The President and General Marshall are very keen on Mountbatten's appointment, which it is certain the United States Government will cordially accept. Our Chiefs of Staff concur. There is no doubt of the need of a young and vigorous mind in this lethargic and stagnant Indian scene. I have no doubts whatsoever that it is my duty to make this proposal formally and to submit Mountbatten's name to the King. Mountbatten and Wingate, working together, have thrown a great deal of new light upon future plans. It is essential that, following upon this Conference, an announcement should be made in a few days. I hope my colleagues will feel this is the best course to take.

2. We have also cleared up to our satisfaction the difficulties about

the South-East Asia Command. Broad strategic plans and major assignments of forces and supplies will be decided by the Combined Chiefs of Staff, subject to the approval of their respective Governments. But all operational control will be vested in the British Chiefs of Staff, acting under His Majesty's Government, and all orders will go through them.

3. We have not been able to reach a final conclusion about the extent to which the floods will have delayed the proposed operations in North Burma, nor have we yet given sufficient detailed study to the first stage of Operation "Culverin" to decide whether that should be given priority in amphibious operations during 1944. At least another month's intense study is required. The discussions however have been most friendly, and there is no doubt that the United States Chiefs of Staff are gratified at the constructive interest which we have shown in war plans against Japan in 1944. Soong arrives on Monday, but will in principle be told no more than what is contained in my immediately following.

4. General Marshall has consented to my being represented on General MacArthur's staff by a British liaison officer of General's rank. This will enable us to follow much more closely than hitherto what is happening in that theatre. I discussed this matter with Dr. Evatt when he was in London. He said he was all for it, and I am now telegraphing to Curtin about it, pointing out that this will bring us more closely into touch with the war in the Pacific.

5. Eden and Hull are locked in lengthy discussions. Hull remains completely obdurate about not using the word "recognition" in respect of the French Committee. We have therefore agreed that they shall publish their document, and we ours and the Canadians theirs, after communicating with Russia and others concerned. Eden has this matter in hand. I have pointed out in the plainest terms to the President that they will certainly have a bad Press, but he says he would rather have a sheet anchor out against the machinations of de Gaulle. Our position is of course different, for we are doing no more for the Committee by our formula than we did for de Gaulle when he was alone and quite uncontrolled by others.

★   ★   ★

The Staff discussion upon the share we were to have in the major assault upon Japan became heated and led to an amusing incident. Each of the joint Staffs had behind them a considerable group of twelve to twenty high Staff officers, a quivering audience, silent, with gleaming eyes. Presently the chairman said, "I think we had better discuss this without our Staffs being present," upon which the group of high Staff officers filed out into a waiting-room. The quarrel was duly settled, as usual, and Mountbatten, whose position as Chief of Combined Operations gave him a seat on the British Chiefs of Staff Committee, seized this opportunity to ask the chairman if he might give a demonstration of the special mixture of ice which his scientists had found. This was called Pykrete.* On receiving permission one of his Staff wheeled in on a large dumb-waiter two blocks of ice about three feet high, one common or garden ice, the other Pykrete. He invited the strongest man present to chop each block of ice in half with a special chopper he had brought. All present voted General Arnold into the job of "strong man". He took off his coat, rolled up his sleeves, and swung the chopper, splitting the ordinary ice with one blow. He turned round, smiling, and, clasping his hands, seized the chopper again and advanced upon the block of Pykrete. He swung the chopper, and as he brought it down let go with a cry of pain, for the Pykrete had suffered little damage and his elbows had been badly jarred.

Mountbatten then capped matters by drawing a pistol from his pocket to demonstrate the strength of Pykrete against gunfire. He first fired at the ordinary ice, which was shattered. He then fired at the Pykrete, which was so strong that the bullet ricochetted, narrowly missing Portal.

The waiting officers outside, who had been worried enough by the sound of the blows and the scream of pain from General Arnold, were horrified at the revolver shots, one of them crying out, "My God! They've now started shooting!"

But who in war will not have his laugh amid the skulls?—and here was one.

*   *   *

Actually the dispute between the British and American Chiefs of Staff was on the issue that Britain demanded a full and fair place in the war against Japan from the moment when Germany was beaten. She demanded a share of the airfields, a share of the bases for the Royal Navy, a proper assignment of duties to whatever divisions she could transport to the Far East after the Hitler business was finished. In the end the Americans gave way. My friends on the Chiefs of Staff Committee had been pressed by me

* The special substance for use in the Habakkuk project, and named after its inventor, Mr. Pyke. See p. 69.

to fight this point, not indeed to pistols, but to the utmost limit, because at this stage in the war what I most feared was that American critics would say, "England, having taken all she could from us to help her beat Hitler, stands out of the war against Japan and will leave us in the lurch." However, at the Quebec Conference this impression was effectively removed.

*　　*　　*

On the late afternoon of August 23 we had our second plenary meeting to discuss the draft of the final report of the Combined Chiefs of Staff. This document reiterated the points raised in their first report as amended after our discussion on them, and in addition set out in detail proposed operational arrangements in the Far East. No decision was reached in the report on the actual operations to be undertaken, though it was decided that the main effort should be put into offensive operations with the object of "establishing land communications with China and improving and securing the air route". In the "overall strategic concept" of the Japan war plans were to be made to bring about the defeat of Japan within twelve months after the collapse of Germany. I said I was glad to see that this was to be our target rather than planning on the basis of a prolonged war of attrition.

Finally, the general principle of a separate South-East Asia Command, which I had proposed to the President before the Conference, was accepted. I said that I was anxious to make a public announcement about this as soon as possible. This would also help to show how much of the discussions at "Quadrant" had been concerned with the war against Japan, and thus set forth sufficient reasons why Russia had not been included in the deliberations. It was generally agreed by those present that we should do this.

*　　*　　*

I now told the Viceroy of the decision to set up a South-East Asia Command, with Mountbatten as Supreme Commander.

Prime Minister to Viceroy of India　　　　　　　　　　　　24 Aug 43

We have now formed and set up the South-East Asia Command, separate from the command in India, which was foreshadowed by me at the time of Field-Marshal Wavell's appointment to the Viceroyalty. There are great advantages in having under a British commander a combined command similar to that which exists in North Africa. We have had some discussions with the Americans in the weeks that have passed upon the person of the commander. After a great deal of consideration I decided to propose Lord Louis Mountbatten, now Chief of Combined Operations, for this very important post. Mountbatten has unique qualifications, in that he is intimately acquainted with all three branches of the Services, and also with amphibious operations. He has served for nearly a year and a half on the Chiefs of Staff Committee, and thus knows the whole of our war story from the centre. I regard this as of great importance on account of the extremely varied character of the South-East Asia front by land and sea. Mountbatten is a fine organiser and a man of great energy and daring. His appointment has been cordially welcomed by the President and by the American Chiefs of Staff, and was hailed with delight by Soong on behalf of the Generalissimo. I am therefore, with the approval of the Cabinet, making the necessary submissions to the King, and send this message to you for your information, as it is important that the announcement should emerge out of the present Conference. It will be made public to-morrow, August 25.

Next day I sent the following telegram to my colleagues at home:

Prime Minister to Deputy Prime Minister and   25 Aug 43
War Cabinet only
 Everything here has gone off well. We have secured a settlement of a number of hitherto intractable questions—*e.g.*, the South-East Asia Command, "Tube Alloys," and French Committee recognition. On this last we all had an awful time with Hull, who has at last gone off in a pretty sulky mood, especially with the Foreign Secretary, who bore the brunt. Unanimous agreement is expressed in a masterly report by the Combined Chiefs of Staff, which the President and I have both approved. All differences have been smoothed away, except that the question of the exact form of our amphibious activities in the Bay of Bengal has been left over for further study. I think however it is settling itself as I wished. There is no doubt that Mackenzie King and the Canadian Government are delighted and feel themselves thoroughly "on the map".
 2. The black spot at the present time is the increasing bearishness of Soviet Russia. You will have seen the telegram received from Stalin about the Italian overtures. He has absolutely no ground for complaint, as we have done no more than hand the Italian representative the severe directions expressing unconditional surrender which had already received the cordial approval of the Soviet Government, and have immediately reported all these matters to him.
 3. The President was very much offended at the tone of this message.

He gave directions to the effect that the new Soviet Chargé d'Affaires was to be told he was away in the country and would not be back for some days. Stalin has of course studiously ignored our offer to make a further long and hazardous journey in order to bring about a tripartite meeting. In spite of all this I do not think his manifestations of ill-temper and bad manners are preparatory to a separate peace with Germany, as the hatreds between the two races have now become a sanitary cordon in themselves. It is disheartening to make so little progress with these people, but I am sure my colleagues will not feel that I myself or our Government as a whole have been wanting in any way in patience and in loyalty.

4. I am feeling rather tired, as the work at the Conference has been very heavy and many large and difficult questions have weighed upon us. I hope my colleagues will think it proper for me to take two or three days' rest at one of these mountain camps before I broadcast on Sunday and proceed to Washington. I am also planning to broadcast when taking a degree at Harvard University on September 3, and to return home immediately thereafter. It is only in the event of some unexpected development in Italy or elsewhere which would make it desirable for me and the President to be close together that I should prolong my stay. In any case, I shall be back in good time before the meeting of Parliament. The Foreign Secretary returns by air on Saturday, and is sending Cadogan with me to Washington.

I decided to have two liaison officers, one with MacArthur and the other with Chiang Kai-shek. When I got home I sent for Generals Lumsden and Carton de Wiart to come to Chequers, and offered them these appointments, to the great delight of both. Lumsden was one of our most distinguished and accomplished officers, who at the very beginning of the war, in the first contact with the enemy, had brought the armoured car back into popularity. He soon gained General MacArthur's confidence, and proved a valuable liaison officer. He was killed in January 1945. A Japanese suicide bomber attacked the battleship *New Mexico* during the bombardment of Lingayen Gulf. On the bridge stood Admiral Fraser, the British commander, and General Lumsden. By pure chance the first moved to the opposite side to get a better view. A minute later the suicide bomber struck. All at Lumsden's end of the bridge were killed. His death was a loss to his country and to me personally.

* * *

We must now return to the Italian scene. Contrary to our

earlier hopes, the bulk of the Germans successfully withdrew across the Straits of Messina. On August 10 General Eisenhower had held a meeting of his commanders to select from a variety of proposals the means by which the campaign should be carried into Italy. He had to take special account of the enemy dispositions of that time. Eight of the sixteen German divisions in Italy were in the north under Rommel, two were near Rome, and six were farther south under Kesselring. These powerful forces might be reinforced from twenty German divisions which had been withdrawn from the Russian front to refit in France. Nothing we might gather for a long time could equal the strength which the Germans could put in the field, but the British and Americans had command of sea and air, and also the initiative. The assault upon which all minds were now set was a daring enterprise. It was hoped to gain the ports of Naples and Taranto, whose combined facilities were proportioned to the scale of the armies we must use. The early capture of airfields was a prime aim. Those near Rome were as yet beyond our reach, but there was an important group at Foggia adaptable for heavy bombers, and our tactical air forces sought others in the heel of Italy and at Montecorvino, near Salerno.

General Eisenhower decided to begin the assault in early September by an attack across the Straits of Messina, with subsidiary descents on the Calabrian coast. This would be the prelude to the capture of Naples (Operation "Avalanche") by a British and an American army corps landing on the good beaches in the Gulf of Salerno. This was at the extreme range of fighter cover from the captured Sicilian airfields. As soon as possible after the landings the Allied forces would drive north to capture Naples.

The Combined Chiefs of Staff advised the President and me to accept this plan, and to authorise the seizure of Sardinia and Corsica in second priority. We did so with alacrity; indeed, it was exactly what I had hoped and striven for. Later it was proposed to land an airborne division to capture the airfields south of Rome. This also we accepted. The circumstances in which this feature was cancelled are recounted in a later chapter.

★   ★   ★

What I regarded as highly satisfactory decisions had thus been obtained and all was moving forward. But towards the end of

August a British officer arrived at Quebec from General Eisenhower's headquarters with very disconcerting news. He stated that by December 1 six divisions would have crossed the Straits of Messina and passed through Calabria, and another six would have landed at Salerno. I at once protested against this alarming under-estimate of our resources.

Prime Minister to General Alexander   26 Aug 43

General Whiteley, who has been here, has told us the dates and scales of "Baytown" and "Avalanche" respectively.★ This has filled me with the greatest concern, and I hope you will be able to reassure me. Assuming that our landings are successful and that we are not defeated in the subsequent battles, I cannot understand why two and a half months or more will be required to get ashore, or why it should be necessary, once we have obtained an effective port and bridgehead at "Avalanche", to march all the "Baytown" divisions through Calabria instead of sending some at least of them round by sea.

2. Moreover, the rate of build-up to twelve divisions on the mainland by December 1 seems to me to open dangers of the gravest kind. First, no effective help can come to enable the Italians in Rome to turn against the Germans, and the dangers of a German Quisling Government being installed, or alternatively sheer anarchy supervening, will be aggravated and prolonged. Secondly, if your rate of build-up is no more than twelve divisions by December 1, and these only in the Naples area, what is to prevent the Germans in the same time from bringing far larger forces against them? They are at present said to have sixteen divisions in the Italian peninsula. I am not myself convinced that these are in fact complete divisions. On the contrary, it would seem likely that they are the leading elements and headquarters in several cases. But if the liberation of Rome and the gaining of the important political and military advantages following therefrom are to be delayed for more than three months from now no one can measure the consequences.

3. I am most anxious to hear from you before I leave America, as the President was also much distressed by the date mentioned, and if it is really the kind of time-table that is being worked to it would be better for us to face the worst in consultation. I hope however that you will chase these clouds away.

I addressed myself to this administrative failure as soon as I got home. The measures to re-form our armoured divisions which I had asked for on August 2, and which had been pursued

★ "Baytown": the attack across the Straits of Messina. "Avalanche": the attack on Naples (Salerno).

by General Brooke, were already producing results, and the pessimistic estimates of which General Whiteley had been the bearer were soon overcome. The British 1st Armoured Division was re-equipped and became again a magnificent fighting force. Two Polish divisions, the New Zealand Division, and the 4th British-Indian Division were brought to the highest pitch and transported to Italy. The extraordinary prowess of the United States engineers transformed the port of Naples from ruin into a first-class harbour. In the early days of October a hundred thousand men were added to General Alexander's army. Had this not been achieved a disaster might easily have occurred, for the Germans were arriving in strength.

CHAPTER VI

ITALY: THE ARMISTICE

Italian Peace Overtures – My Telegram to the President of August 5 – Final Meeting between Italian and German Chiefs – Badoglio's Problem – My Telegrams to Mr. Eden of August 7 and 9 – And His Reply – Italian Plenipotentiary from Badoglio Arrives in Spain – I Report to the President, August 16 – Our Joint Telegram to General Eisenhower – Discussions in Lisbon between General Castellano and General Bedell Smith – Congratulations to General Alexander – General Zanussi Arrives – An Ultimatum to the Italian Envoys – Joint Report by the President and Me to Stalin – Signature of the Armistice Terms by General Castellano near Syracuse – The British Eighth Army Crosses the Straits of Messina, September 3 – Italian Fears of German Occupation of Rome – Eisenhower Resolves to Launch "Avalanche" as Planned – Announcement of the Armistice at 6 p.m., September 8 – The Germans Encircle Rome – The King Escapes to Brindisi – Imperative Need to Occupy the Italian Bases in the Eastern Mediterranean – The Italian Fleet Fights its Way Through to Surrender at Malta – Mussolini Rescued by Hitler's Orders, September 12 – The Hundred Days – Italy Becomes a Main Battleground.

DETAILED plans had already been made between the British and United States Governments about the probable surrender by Italy. The drafting of armistice terms was begun before the end of July, and on August 3 I circulated the documents to the War Cabinet "in case of an approach being made to us by Italy". We wished to have time to deal by political or diplomatic channels rather than through Allied Force Head-quarters. On this same day the first peace overtures from Rome were made. Our Ambassador in Lisbon informed the Foreign Office that the new Counsellor of the Italian Legation there, who had just arrived from Rome, wished to see him, and hinted that he bore a message from the Badoglio Government. This Italian diplomat was Ciano's former *chef de cabinet*, the Marquis D'Ayeta. He had American relations, and was an acquaintance of Sumner Welles. His mission to Lisbon had been planned under Badoglio's instructions by the new Italian Foreign Secretary, Guariglia. On the following day D'Ayeta was invited to the British Embassy. He made no reference to an armistice, but explained that, although the King and Badoglio wanted peace, they had to make a pretence of continuing the fight in order to avoid a German *coup d'état* in Italy. It was clear from what he said that Guariglia was particularly concerned to explain away to the Allies a meeting in Northern Italy with Ribbentrop which he was about to fulfil in order to soften German suspicions.

I immediately informed the President of this Italian approach.

Former Naval Person to President Roosevelt   5 Aug 43

The following story has been told to British Ambassador Campbell at Lisbon by a newly arrived Italian Counsellor. . . . I send it to you for what it is worth, which is substantial. Ambassador Campbell was instructed to make no comment. It certainly seems to give inside information. Though I am starting now for Quebec, Anthony will be here, and you can communicate both with him and me.

The King and the Army leaders had been preparing a *coup d'état*, but this was precipitated, probably by a few days only, by the action of the Fascist Grand Council. Fascism in Italy is extinct. Every vestige has been swept away. Italy turned Red overnight. In Turin and Milan there were Communist demonstrations which had to be put down by armed force. Twenty years of Fascism has obliterated the middle class. There is nothing between the King, with the Patriots who have rallied round him, who have complete control, and rampant Bolshevism. The Germans have an armoured division just outside Rome, and will march in if there is any sign of Italian weakening. There are ten thousand scattered about inside Rome, mostly with machine-guns. If we bomb Rome again there will be a popular rising, and the Germans will then march in and slaughter everybody. They have actually threatened the use of gas. As many Italian troops as possible have been concentrated round Rome, but they have no stomach for fighting. They have practically no weapons, and are no match for even one well-equipped German division.

In these circumstances the King and Badoglio, whose first thought was to make peace, have no alternative but to put up a show of going on with the fight. Guariglia is to meet Ribbentrop perhaps to-morrow, as a result of which there will be a communiqué stating in plainer terms than hitherto that Italy is still the active ally of Germany. But this will be only pretence. The whole country is only longing for peace, and above all to be rid of the Germans, who are universally execrated.

If we cannot attack Germany immediately through the Balkans, thus causing German withdrawal from Italy, the sooner we land in Italy the better. The Germans however are resolved to defend it line by line. When we land in Italy we shall find little opposition, and perhaps even active co-operation, on the part of the Italians.

D'Ayeta never from start to finish made any mention of peace terms, and his whole story, as you will have observed, was no more than a plea that we should save Italy from the Germans as well as from herself, and do it as quickly as possible.

He expressed the hope that we would not heap abuse on the King and Badoglio, which would precipitate the blood-bath, although a little of this would help them to keep up the pretence *vis-à-vis* the Germans.

* * *

The desire of all the Italian personalities involved was for peace with the Allies, and the Italian High Command were already eager to fight against the Germans. Guariglia and the Italian Foreign Office hoped by time and caution to achieve the turn-over without incurring German wrath and revenge. Thus, although we could not measure the forces at work, we came in contact with two Italian representatives. So did the Germans. On August 6 Guariglia and General Ambrosio met Ribbentrop and Keitel on the frontier. The military discussions were acrimonious. Ambrosio requested the return home of the Italian divisions in France and the Balkans. Keitel, on the contrary, during the meeting ordered the German units poised at the border posts to enter Italy. Meanwhile Foreign Secretary Guariglia conducted a bland and meaningless conversation with Ribbentrop in the hopes of postponing a German onslaught.

* * *

On August 6 another Italian diplomat, Signor Berio, approached our diplomatic representative in Tangier. His instructions were direct from Badoglio. Again a plea for time was made, but on this occasion a genuine desire to treat was expressed, and Berio was authorised to open negotiations.

I was on my way by sea to the Quebec Conference when this news reached me, together with Mr. Eden's comments. The

Foreign Secretary wrote: "We are entitled to regard it as an offer by the Badoglio Government to negotiate on terms. . . . Should we not then reply that, as is well known, we insist on unconditional surrender, and the Badoglio Government must as a first step notify us that Italy surrenders unconditionally? Subsequently, at a later stage, if the Badoglio Government was to do this, we should then inform them of the terms on which we should be prepared to cease hostilities against Italy."

On receiving this message I minuted in red ink in the margin, "Don't miss the bus"; and again, "If they surrender immediately we should be prepared to accord conditions as acts of grace and not as a bargain." I then sent the following reply, dated August 7, to the Foreign Secretary:

Prime Minister to Foreign Secretary   7 Aug 43

We agree with the course you have taken. Badoglio admits he is going to double-cross someone, but his interests and the mood of the Italian people make it more likely Hitler will be the one to be tricked. Allowance should be made for the difficulties of his position. Meanwhile the war should be carried forward against Italy in every way that the Americans will allow.

And again, on the day of my arrival in Canada:

Prime Minister to Foreign Secretary   9 Aug 43

Badoglio must state that he is prepared to place himself unreservedly in the hands of the Allied Governments, who have already made it plain that they desire Italy to have a respectable place in the New Europe.

Reference should also be made to General Eisenhower's offer of the return of Italian prisoners of war taken in Tunisia and Sicily, provided Allied prisoners are speedily set free.

2. The object of the above is to convey to the Italian Government the feeling that, while they have to make the formal act of submission, our desire is to treat them with consideration, so far as military exigencies allow. Merely harping on "unconditional surrender" with no prospect of mercy held out even as an act of grace may well lead to no surrender at all. The expression "honourable capitulation" has also been officially used by the President, and I do not think it should be omitted from the language we are now to use.

3. We have just arrived [at Halifax], after a most pleasant voyage filled with fruitful discussions.

I passed to the President Mr. Eden's reply.

Former Naval Person (Quebec) to President Roosevelt   12 Aug 43

Eden suggests that our Tangier representative replies to Badoglio's emissary Berio as follows:

Badoglio must understand that we cannot negotiate, but require unconditional surrender, which means that Italian Government should place themselves in hands of Allied Governments, who will then state their terms. These will provide for an honourable capitulation.

The instructions will continue:

Badoglio's emissary should be reminded at the same time that the Prime Minister and President have already stated that we desire that in due course Italy should occupy a respected place in New Europe, when peace has been re-established, and that General Eisenhower has announced that Italian prisoners taken in Tunisia and Sicily will be released provided all British and Allied prisoners now in Italian hands are released.

This is simply made up of our existing declarations. If you approve it in principle please cable at once direct to Eden at the Foreign Office, as I shall be on the move. If text does not meet your view we can discuss it on arrival. I think the Italian envoy ought to have an answer as soon as possible.

The President telegraphed to Mr. Eden approving this language, and the Italian envoy at Tangier was so informed.

These tentative approaches by the Italian Government were now superseded by the appearance in Spain of a plenipotentiary from the Italian High Command. On August 15 General Castellano, Chief of Staff to General Ambrosio, called on Sir Samuel Hoare at the British Embassy in Madrid. Castellano said that he was instructed by Marshal Badoglio to say that as soon as the Allies landed on the Italian mainland the Italian Government was prepared to join them against Germany. If the Allies accepted the proposal Castellano would immediately give detailed information about German troop dispositions. I at once passed this new information to the President.

Former Naval Person (Quebec) tó President Roosevelt   16 Aug 43

I send you herewith four telegrams I have received from London about a renewed approach by Badoglio. The following is the kind of answer which I suggest should be made:

"We note the statement of Italian envoy: 'We are not in a position to make any terms. We will accept unconditional surrender provided we can join as allies in fighting the Germans.' We, the Allies, for our part cannot make any bargain about Italy changing sides, nor can we make plans in common at this stage. If however serious fighting breaks out between the Italian Army and German intruders a new situation would be created. The Italians know quite well that British and United States Governments do not seek to deny Italy her respected place in Europe. The Italian Government should therefore resist the Germans to the best of their ability as soon as possible, pending arrival of Anglo-American armies. In particular they should stop further invasion of Italy by German troops by blowing up bridges and tunnels and tearing up railway lines and roads in north of Italy, and thus cutting communications of German troops in south of Italy. Effective action of this kind would be regarded by victorious Allies as valuable service, and would render further co-operation possible against the common foe. There is no doubt of the ability of Italian Government and people to destroy and paralyse the German communications, and action of this kind would be proof of their sincerity. Another proof would be the safeguarding of British and Allied prisoners from being taken away to Germany. In any case where this is attempted by Germans, and Italian Government have not the power to resist, the prisoners should be set free and succoured by Italian people. A further vital service which Italian Government certainly has it in its power to render to the Allies is to sail Italian warships to any ports in Allied occupation.

"Fourthly, the furnishing by the Italian Government of any information of German dispositions, and any assistance given by Italian troops and people to the disembarkations of Allies when they take place, especially if accompanied by fighting between Italians and Germans, would be favourably recognised. Fifthly, any co-operation between Italian troops in the Balkan peninsula and the various Patriot forces in the field, taking the form of resistance to the Germans and leading to bloodshed, would be favourably viewed.

"Thus, by taking action against the common enemy, the Italian Government, Army, and people could without any bargain facilitate a more friendly relationship with United Nations. In particular we state that if Allied troops arrive at any point where they find Italians fighting Germans we shall aid Italians to our utmost."

Eden should be here to-morrow, and we can discuss the whole position together. I send you this budget in order that you may see way my mind is working.

The Chiefs of Staff are considering the practical steps and timings required to make an Italian turn-over effective.

* * *

The President and I agreed that Eisenhower should send General Bedell Smith and the British General Strong, head of his Intelligence Staff, to Lisbon to open negotiations there with the Italian emissary. They took with them the final military terms of surrender, which had now been thrashed out in our "Quadrant" Conference at Quebec.

The President and Prime Minister to General Eisenhower   18 Aug 43

The President and the Prime Minister having approved, the Combined Chiefs of Staff direct you to send at once to Lisbon two Staff officers, one United States and one British. They should report upon arrival to the British Ambassador. They should take with them the agreed armistice terms, which have already been sent to you. Acting on instructions, the British Ambassador in Lisbon will have arranged a meeting with General Castellano. Your Staff officers will be present at this meeting.

2. At this meeting a communication to General Castellano will be made on the following lines:

The unconditional surrender of Italy is accepted on the terms stated in the document to be handed to him. (He should then be given the armistice terms for Italy already agreed and previously sent to you. He should be told that these do *not* include political, economic, or financial terms, which will be communicated later by other means.)

These terms do *not* visualise the active assistance of Italy in fighting the Germans. The extent to which the terms will be modified in favour of Italy will depend on how far the Italian Government and people do in fact aid the United Nations against Germany during the remainder of the war. The United Nations however state without reservation that wherever Italian forces or Italians fight Germans or destroy German property or hamper German movement they will be given all possible support by the forces of the United Nations. Meanwhile, provided information about the enemy is immediately and regularly supplied, Allied bombing will so far as possible be directed upon targets which affect the movements and operations of German forces.

The cessation of hostilities between the United Nations and Italy will take effect from a date and hour to be notified by General Eisenhower.

Italian Government must undertake to proclaim the armistice immediately it is announced by General Eisenhower, and to order their forces and people from that hour to collaborate with the Allies and to resist the Germans.

The Italian Government must, at the hour of the armistice, order that all United Nations prisoners in danger of capture by the Germans shall be immediately released.

The Italian Government must, at the hour of the armistice, order the Italian Fleet and as much of their merchant shipping as possible to put to sea for Allied ports. As many military aircraft as possible shall fly to Allied bases. Any ships or aircraft in danger of capture by the Germans must be destroyed.

3. General Castellano should be told that meanwhile there is a good deal that Badoglio can do without the Germans becoming aware of what is afoot. The precise character and extent of his action must be left to his judgment, but the following are the general lines which should be suggested to him:

General passive resistance throughout the country, if this order can be conveyed to local authorities without the Germans knowing. . . .

Germans must not be allowed to take over Italian coast defences.

Make arrangements to be put in force at the proper time for Italian formations in the Balkans to march to the coast, with a view to their being taken off to Italy by United Nations.

On August 19 the parties met at the British Embassy in the Portuguese capital. Castellano was told that General Eisenhower would accept the Italian Government's unconditional surrender on the terms now handed to him. It is difficult to make hard-cut military negotiations fit in with flexible diplomacy. The Italian envoy general at Lisbon was placed in a hopeless position. The purpose of his visit, as he emphasised, was to discuss how Italy could take the field against Germany. Bedell Smith had to reply that he could only discuss unconditional surrender.

These talks coincided with the final conquest of Sicily. On the same day I telegraphed to General Alexander:

Prime Minister (Quebec) to General Alexander   19 Aug 43
(Middle East)

I am overjoyed at this new, brilliantly executed achievement. I congratulate you most heartily upon all you have done. I will shortly send you a telegram for publication to your troops of the Fifteenth Army Group, but I think it better that the President and the King should send their compliments to Eisenhower first, and I am so advising.

2. You are no doubt informed of General Castellano's approaches to us and the answer we have sent from here. Our greatest danger is that the Germans should enter Rome and set up a Quisling-Fascist Government under, say, Farinacci. Scarcely less unpleasant would be the whole of Italy sliding into anarchy. I doubt if the Badoglio Government can hold their double-faced position until the present date fixed for "Avalanche", so that anything that can be done to shorten this period without endangering military success will be most helpful.

General Alexander to Prime Minister (Quebec) 20 Aug 43
Many thanks for your kind message, which I value very highly.
Everything possible is being done to put on "Avalanche" at the earliest
possible date. We realise here very clearly that every hour gives enemy
more time to prepare and organise against us.

*   *   *

The discussions in Lisbon with General Castellano continued
throughout the night of August 19. The Italian general drew out
on a map the dispositions of both the German and Italian forces in
Italy after he had realised that there would be no yielding by
Bedell Smith upon the question of terms. After a suitable delay
in order to cover up his visit to Portugal, Castellano returned to
Rome bearing the military terms of surrender, and also a wireless
set and Allied codes in order to remain in contact with Allied
Force Headquarters in Algiers.

Yet another Italian emissary, General Zanussi, appeared on
August 26 in Lisbon. He was the principal assistant to the chief of
the Italian General Staff, and was accompanied by General Carton
de Wiart, V.C., who had been released from a British prisoner-of-
war camp to act as intermediary to this mission. The purpose of
this latest visitor was far from clear. Perhaps Badoglio feared that
Castellano had given too much away and wanted to be clear what
he was doing. Carton de Wiart had been told that "one dove had
been sent out, but as it had not returned another was being dispatched". Zanussi had instructions from Badoglio to try to reach
London and press for an Allied landing north of Rome.

As discussions had already begun with Castellano, it was
decided to send Zanussi to General Eisenhower's headquarters.
Before he left however an incident of chivalry took place. The
Italian general wished to return to Rome to report on the failure
of his mission. He discussed the matter with his English companion, who quietly said that he was of course prepared to
accompany him. Zanussi describes in his own words Carton de
Wiart's remarks. "I am a prisoner of war. I have been released to
accompany you on a mission to London. Since the mission has
not taken place and you are returning to Italy I shall take my
place again at the side of my comrades." The Italian replied that
he would not hear of such a plan. He knew that all had been done
that was possible to get him to England, and he would go and
see General Eisenhower as suggested. Carton de Wiart should

96

therefore consider himself free. It was an Anglo-Italian episode which may well be remembered by both nations.

The latest Italian emissary was therefore sent to Algiers, where he gave further information about the movements of the Germans in Italy.

On August 31 General Bedell Smith, accompanied by General Zanussi, met Castellano in Sicily, as had been arranged. Castellano explained that if the Italian Government were a free agent they would accept and announce the armistice terms as the Allies desired. They were however under the control of the Germans. Since the Lisbon meeting the Germans had sent more troops into Italy, and the whole country was virtually under German occupation. It was therefore impossible for the armistice to be announced at the time required by the Allies—*i.e.*, before the main Allied landing in Italy, details of which Castellano was most anxious to learn. The Italians wanted to be quite sure that these landings would be strong enough to guarantee the security of the King and Government in Rome.

It was clear that the Italian. Government were particularly anxious that we should make a landing north of Rome to protect them against the German divisions near the city. Castellano talked in terms of fifteen Allied divisions taking part in such an operation. General Bedell Smith made it clear that he was not prepared to continue the talks on the basis that the armistice should be announced *after* the main Allied landings, and refused to give him any information on the strength of the impending Allied operations. Castellano thereupon asked to be allowed to consult his Government again. He was told that the terms were final and the time-limit had already expired, but that in view of the present discussion the Allies were willing to wait until midnight of September 1-2, by which time a firm acceptance or refusal must be given. That evening Castellano returned to Rome.

The Allied High Command perceived that the Italian Government was rapidly losing its nerve and would not have the courage to sign an armistice unless convinced of the overwhelming strength of the Anglo-American attack upon the mainland of Italy. General Eisenhower therefore proposed to General Castellano that an airborne force should be landed near Rome. This would depend upon a guarantee by Badoglio's Government that "the armistice is signed and announced as desired by the Allies; that the Italians will seize and hold the necessary airfields and stop all anti-aircraft fire; that the Italian divisions in the Rome area will take action against the Germans".

The President and I, now together in the White House, sent the following telegram to Eisenhower: "We highly approve your decision to go on with 'Avalanche' and to land an airborne division near Rome on the conditions indicated. We fully recognise military considerations must be dominant at this juncture." The War Cabinet met in London on the same day and endorsed this view.

★　★　★

We reported to Stalin the development of the Italian situation.

Prime Minister and President Roosevelt to Premier Stalin　　　2 Sept 43

We have received from General Castellano statement that the Italians accept and that he is coming to sign, but we do not know for certain whether this refers to short military terms, which you have already seen, or to more comprehensive and complete terms in regard to which your readiness to sign was specifically indicated.

2. The military situation there is at once critical and hopeful. Our invasion of the mainland is beginning almost immediately, and the heavy blow called "Avalanche" will be struck in the next week or so. The difficulty of the Italian Government and people in extricating themselves from Hitler's clutches may make a still more daring enterprise necessary, for General Eisenhower will need as much Italian help as he can get. The Italian acceptance of the terms is largely based on the fact that we shall send an airborne division to Rome to enable them to hold off the Germans, who have gathered Panzer strength in that vicinity, and who may replace the Badoglio Government with a Quisling Administration, probably under Farinacci. Matters are moving so fast there that we think General Eisenhower should have discretion not to delay settlement with the Italians for the sake of the difference between the short and long terms. It is clear that short terms are included in long terms, that they proceed on basis of unconditional surrender, placing the interpretation in hands of Allied C.-in-C.

3. We are therefore assuming that you expect General Eisenhower to sign short terms on your behalf if that be necessary to avoid the further journeying of General Castellano to Rome and consequent delay and uncertainty affecting military operations. We are of course anxious that Italian unconditional surrender be to Soviet as well as to

Great Britain and United States. The date of surrender announcement must of course be fitted in with the military stroke.

★ ★ ★

General Castellano returned to Sicily, formally authorised by his Government to sign the military terms of surrender. On September 3 in an olive grove near Syracuse the act was performed. I received this news in a telegram from General Alexander.

General Alexander to Prime Minister   3 Sept 43
The short armistice terms were signed this afternoon, on the fourth anniversary of the war, between General Bedell Smith, representing General Eisenhower, and General Castellano, representing Marshal Badoglio, duly authorised to do so.

Castellano is remaining here near my headquarters, and we are starting military talks this evening to arrange best assistance which Italian forces can contribute to our operations.

Before dawn on September 3 the British Eighth Army had crossed the Straits of Messina to enter the Italian mainland.

Prime Minister to Premier Stalin   5 Sept 43
General Castellano, after a long struggle, signed the short terms on September 3, and he is now working out with Generals Eisenhower and Alexander the best way to bring them into force. This will certainly lead to immediate fighting between Italian and German forces, and we are going to help the Italians at every possible point as effectively and speedily as we can. The next week will show a startling development. The invasion of the toe has been successful and is being pressed, and Operation "Avalanche" and the airborne venture are both imminent. Though I believe we shall get ashore at "Avalanche" in strong force, I cannot foresee what will happen in Rome or throughout Italy. The dominant aim should be to kill Germans and make Italians kill Germans on the largest scale possible in this theatre.

I am staying over this side of the Atlantic till this business clears itself. Meanwhile accept my warmest congratulations on your new set of victories and penetrations on your main front.

It now remained to co-ordinate the terms of the Italian surrender with our military strategy. The American General Taylor, of the 82nd Airborne Division, was sent to Rome on September 7. His secret mission was to arrange with the Italian General Staff for the airfields around the capital to be seized during the night of the 9th. But the situation had radically

99

changed since Castellano had asked for Allied protection. The Germans had powerful forces at hand, and appeared to be in possession of the airfields. The Italian Army was demoralised and short of ammunition. Divided counsels seethed round Badoglio. Taylor demanded to see him. Everything hung in the balance. The Italian leaders now feared that any announcement of the surrender, which had already been signed, would lead to the immediate German occupation of Rome and the end of the Badoglio Government. At two o'clock on the morning of September 8 General Taylor saw Badoglio, who, since the airfields were lost, begged for delay in broadcasting the armistice terms. He had in fact already telegraphed to Algiers that the security of the Rome airfields could not be guaranteed. The air descent was therefore cancelled.

Eisenhower now had to make a quick decision. The attack on Salerno was due to be launched within less than twenty-four hours. He therefore telegraphed to the Combined Chiefs of Staff:

8 Sept 43

I have just completed a conference with the principal commanders, and have determined *not* to accept the Italian change of attitude. We intend to proceed in accordance with plan for the announcement of the armistice, and with subsequent propaganda and other measures. Marshal Badoglio is being informed through our direct link that this instrument entered into by his accredited representative with presumed good faith on both sides is considered valid and binding, and that we will *not* recognise any deviation from our original agreement.

After consultation the President and I sent the following reply:

8 Sept 43

It is the view of the President and the Prime Minister that, the agreement having been signed, you should make such public announcement regarding it as would facilitate your military operations.

Accordingly at 6 p.m. General Eisenhower broadcast the announcement of the armistice, followed by the text of the declaration, which Marshal Badoglio himself announced about an hour later from Rome. The surrender of Italy had been completed.

*   *   *

During the night of September 8–9 German forces began the encirclement of Rome. Badoglio and the Royal Family installed themselves in a state of siege in the building of the Ministry of War. There were hasty discussions in an atmosphere of mounting tension and panic. In the small hours a convoy of five vehicles passed through the eastern gates of Rome on the road to the Adriatic port of Pescara. Here two corvettes took on board the party, which contained the Italian Royal Family, together with Badoglio and his Government and senior officials. They reached Brindisi in the early morning of September 10, when the essential services of an anti-Fascist Italian Government were rapidly set up on territory occupied by Allied forces.

After the departure of the fugitives the veteran Marshal Caviglia, the victor of Vittorio Veneto in the First World War, arrived in Rome to take upon himself the responsibility of negotiating with the German forces closing in round the city. Scattered fighting was already taking place at the gates. Certain regular units of the Italian Army and Partisan bands of Roman citizens engaged the Germans on the outskirts.

On September 11 opposition ceased with the signature of a military truce, and the Nazi divisions were free to move through the city.

*   *   *

The surrender had been pressed on Marshal Badoglio in order not to upset the timing of the Allied landings in the heel and in the Rome area. The essential steps were completed in the formal signature of the armistice terms, but there were other fruits to be gathered in this dread harvest: the Italian Fleet must be safely transferred to Allied ports; there were many Italian divisions in South-Eastern Europe whose equipment would be valuable to the Allies in the continued struggle against Nazi Germany; there were still more important Italian bases in the Eastern Mediterranean. It was essential that these islands should not fall into hostile hands.

I was acutely aware of this particular danger.

Prime Minister to General Wilson (Middle East)   13 Sept 43
The capture of Rhodes by you at this time with Italian aid would be a fine contribution to the general war. Let me know what are your plans for this. Can you not improvise the necessary garrison out of the forces in the Middle East? What is your total ration strength?

This is a time to think of Clive and Peterborough and of Rooke's men taking Gibraltar.

101

Lest it should be thought that I pressed this mood unduly, I cite the final summary of the Combined Chiefs of Staff of our decisions recorded at Washington.

EASTERN MEDITERRANEAN

The Combined Chiefs of Staff have taken note of the action which the Commander-in-Chief Middle East is taking in respect of Rhodes and other islands in the Dodecanese. They approve this action, and are considering what further can be done.

I was soon to revert to these matters.

* * *

Meanwhile, after dark on September 8, in accordance with Allied instructions, the main body of the Italian Fleet left Genoa and Spezia on a daring voyage of surrender to Malta, unprotected either by Allied or Italian aircraft. Next morning when steaming down the west coast of Sardinia it was attacked by German aircraft from bases in France. The flagship *Roma* was hit, and blew up with heavy loss of life, including the Commander-in-Chief, Admiral Bergamini. The battleship *Italia* was also damaged. Leaving some light craft to rescue survivors, the rest of the Fleet continued its painful journey. On the morning of the 10th they were met at sea by British forces, including the *Warspite* and *Valiant*, which had so often sought them before under different circumstances, and were escorted to Malta. A squadron from Taranto, including two battleships, had also sailed on the 9th, and, after passing at sea the British force on its way to occupy that port, reached Malta the following day without incident.

On the morning of the 11th Admiral Cunningham informed the Admiralty that "the Italian battle fleet now lies at anchor under the guns of the fortress of Malta".

* * *

I was anxious that we should treat the Italian Navy well. To Cunningham I cabled on September 10: "Should the Italian Fleet arrive in our ports after having scrupulously fulfilled armistice conditions and sustained the revengeful attack of German bombers, I hope you will consult General Eisenhower in order that they shall be received in kindly and generous manner. I feel sure this will be in accordance with your sentiments." And later in the day: "Films should be taken if possible of surrender of

Italian Fleet, their courteous reception by the British, and kindly treatment of wounded, etc."

The splendid prize of the whole Fleet of what had been a victorious Power of the first rank thus fell into our hands. It must be made to play its part on our side.

Prime Minister to Admiral Cunningham (Algiers)　　　　　12 Sept 43

At the earliest possible moment you should report on the ammunition of all natures of guns and torpedoes in the Italian Fleet, beginning with the most important units, showing how much on board, any taken at Taranto, etc., and estimates of quantities and exact specifications for manufacture. Without waiting for the whole story to be complete, send at once to Admiralty for transmission to United States through proper channels requirements for the principal and most modern units. I can probably arrange for speedy manufacture here.

With the collapse of the Fascist régime every region of Italy was in a ferment of political speculation. The organisation of resistance to the Germans fell by default into the hands of an underground Committee of Liberation in Rome, and linked with the mounting activity of Partisan bands which now began activities throughout the peninsula. The members of this committee were politicians driven from power by Mussolini in the early 1920s or representatives of groups hostile to Fascist rule. Over all hung the menace of a recrudescence of the hard core of Fascism in the hour of defeat. The Germans certainly did their best to promote it.

* * *

Mussolini had been interned after July 26 on the island of Ponza, and later at La Maddalena, off the coast of Sardinia. Fearing a German *coup de main*, Badoglio had at the end of August moved his former master to a small mountain resort high in the Abruzzi, in Central Italy. In the haste of the flight from Rome no precise instructions were given to the police agents and Carabinieri guarding the fallen Dictator. On the morning of Sunday, September 12, ninety German parachutists landed by glider near the hotel where Mussolini was confined. He was removed, without casualties, in a light German aircraft, and carried to yet another meeting in Munich with Hitler.

The rescue of Mussolini enabled the Germans to set up in the north a rival Government to Badoglio's. A skeleton Fascist régime was established on the shores of Lake Garda, and it was here that was played out the drama of Mussolini's Hundred Days. The Germans clamped down their military occupation upon the regions lying north of Rome; a skeleton Administration of uncertain allegiance sat in Rome, now open to the movements of the German Army; at Brindisi the King and Badoglio set up a rump Government under the eyes of an Allied Commission and with no effective authority beyond the boundaries of the administrative building of the town. As our armies advanced from the toe of the peninsula Allied military government took over the task of controlling the liberated regions.

Italy was now to pass through the most tragic time in her history and to become the battle-ground of some of the fiercest fighting in the war.

CHAPTER VII

THE INVASION OF ITALY
AT THE WHITE HOUSE AGAIN

Angling in the Lake of the Snows – My Broadcast from Quebec – Growing Canadian Share in the War – The Second and Third Fronts – The Campaign in Africa and Italy – Mountbatten, a "Complete Triphibian" – I Join the President in Washington – A Degree at Harvard – Importance of the Combined Chiefs of Staff Committee – General Smuts' Criticisms of the Plans and Progress of the War – He Offers an Alternative Plan – My Reply – He Suggests Postponing "Overlord" – I Dismiss this Idea – Invasion of the Toe of Italy – Resignation of Admiral Pound through Ill-health – Our Conference of September 9 at the White House – My Memorandum to the President – Wide Agreement in Principle Between Us All – I Preside at Another Plenary Meeting in the White House – An Event in Anglo-American History.

T
HE Quebec Conference ended on August 24, and our notable colleagues departed and dispersed. They flew off in every direction like the fragments of a shell. After all the study and argument there was a general desire for a few days' rest. One of my Canadian friends, Colonel Clarke, who had been attached to me by the Dominion Government during the proceedings, owned a ranch about seventy-five miles away amid the mountains and pine forests from which the newspapers get their pulp to guide us on life's journey. Here lay the Lake of the Snows, an enormous dammed-up expanse of water reported to be full of the largest trout. Brooke and Portal were ardent and expert anglers, and a plan had been made among other plans at the Conference for them to see what they could do. I promised to join them later if I could, but I had undertaken to deliver a broadcast on the 31st, and this

hung overhead like a vulture in the sky. I remained for a few days in the Citadel, pacing the ramparts for an hour each afternoon, and brooding over the glorious panorama of the St. Lawrence and all the tales of Wolfe and Quebec. I had promised to drive through the city, and I had a lovely welcome from all its people. I attended a meeting of the Canadian Cabinet, and told them all that they did not already know about the Conference and the war. I had the honour to be sworn a Privy Counsellor of the Dominion Cabinet. This compliment was paid me at the instance of my old friend of forty years' standing and trusted colleague, Mr. Mackenzie King.

There was so much to say and not to say in the broadcast that I could not think of anything, so my mind turned constantly to the Lake of the Snows, of which glittering reports had already come in from those who were there. I thought I might combine fishing by day with preparing the broadcast after dark. I resolved to take Colonel Clarke at his word, and set out with my wife by car. I had noticed that Admiral Pound had not gone with the other two Chiefs of Staff to the lake, and I suggested that he should come with us now. His Staff officer said that he had a lot of cleaning up to do after the Conference. I had been surprised by the subdued part he had taken in the far-ranging naval discussions, but when he said he could not come fishing I had a fear that all was not well. We had worked together in the closest comradeship from the first days of the war. I knew his worth and courage. I also knew that at home he would get up at four or five in the morning for a few hours' fishing before returning to the Admiralty whenever he saw the slightest chance. However, he kept to his quarters and I did not see him before starting.

We had a wonderful all-day drive up the river valley, and after sleeping at a rest-house on the way my wife and I reached the spacious log cabin on the lake. Brooke and Portal were leaving the next day. It was just as well. They had caught a hundred fish apiece each day, and had only to continue at this rate to lower the level of the lake appreciably. My wife and I sallied forth in separate boats for several hours, and though we are neither of us experts we certainly caught a lot of fine fish. We were sometimes given rods with three separate hooks, and once I caught three fish at the same time. I do not know whether this was fair. We did not run at all short of fresh trout at the excellent meals. The President had wanted to come himself, but other duties claimed him. My aide-de-camp, Mary, had been invited to address an important gathering of American W.A.C.s at Ogle-thorpe, and was flown off accordingly. The President sent me the following:

President to Colonel Warden   27 Aug 43
Wednesday the first is all right in every way [for Washington]. If Subaltern [Mary] wants to go to Oglethorpe it would give her more time in Washington if she were to come down a day or two ahead. I hope Lady Warden is getting a real rest, and that you are also. Also I hope you have gone to One Lake.* Be sure to have big ones weighed and verified by Mackenzie King.

I sent the biggest fish I caught to him at Hyde Park. The broad-cast made progress, but original composition is more exhausting than either arguing or fishing.

*   *   *

We returned to Quebec for the night of the 29th. I attended another meeting of the Canadian Cabinet, and at the right time on the 31st, before leaving for Washington, I spoke to the Canadian people and to the Allied world. A few quotations are pertinent to this account.

The contribution which Canada has made to the combined effort of the British Commonwealth and Empire in these tremendous times has deeply touched the heart of the Mother Country and of all the other members of our widespread family of States and races.
From the darkest days the Canadian Army, growing stronger year by year, has played an indispensable part in guarding our British home-land from invasion. Now it is fighting with distinction in wider and ever-widening fields. The Empire Air Training Organisation, which has been a wonderful success, has found its seat in Canada, and has welcomed the flower of the manhood of Great Britain, of Australia, and New Zealand to her spacious flying-fields and to comradeship with her own gallant sons.
Canada has become in the course of this war an important seafaring nation, building many scores of warships and merchant ships, some of them thousands of miles from salt water, and sending them forth

* During the Quebec Conference the President invited me to come for an afternoon's fishing with him in a lake to which he had been recommended. We had a very pleasant luncheon, but I only caught one small fish and he none. He therefore called the lake "One Lake".

manned by hardy Canadian seamen to guard the Atlantic convoys and our vital life-line across the ocean. The munitions industries of Canada have played a most important part in our war economy. Last, but not least, Canada has relieved Great Britain of what would otherwise have been a debt for these munitions of no less than two thousand million dollars.

All this of course was dictated by no law. It came from no treaty or formal obligation. It sprang in perfect freedom from sentiment and tradition and a generous resolve to serve the future of mankind. I am glad to pay my tribute on behalf of the people of Great Britain to the great Dominion, and to pay it from Canadian soil. I only wish indeed that my other duties, which are exacting, allowed me to travel still farther afield and tell Australians, New Zealanders, and South Africans to their faces how we feel towards them for all they have done, and are resolved to do. . . .

We have heard a lot of talk in the last two years about establishing what is called a Second Front in Northern France against Germany. Anyone can see how desirable that immense operation of war would be. It is quite natural that the Russians, bearing the main weight of the German armies on their front, should urge us ceaselessly to undertake this task, and should in no way conceal their complaints, and even reproaches, that we have not done it before. I do not blame them at all for what they say. They fight so well, and they have inflicted such enormous injury upon the military strength of Germany, that nothing they could say in honest criticism of our strategy or the part we have so far been able to take in the war would be taken amiss by us, or weaken our admiration for their own martial prowess and achievement. We once had a fine front in France, but it was torn to pieces by the concentrated might of Hitler; and it is easier to have a front pulled down than it is to build it up again. I look forward to the day when British and American liberating armies will cross the Channel in full force and come to close quarters with the German invaders of France. . . . Personally, I always think of the Third Front as well as the Second Front. I have always thought that the Western democracies should be like a boxer who fights with two hands and not one.

I believe that the great flanking movement into North Africa, made under the authority of President Roosevelt and of His Majesty's Government, for whom I am a principal agent, will be regarded in the after-time as quite a good thing to do in all the circumstances. Certainly it has reaped rich and substantial results. Africa is cleared. All German and Italian armies in Africa have been annihilated, and at least half a million prisoners are in our hands. In a brilliant campaign of thirty-eight days Sicily, which was defended by over 400,000 Axis

12 Troops at work making landing-areas on the sand.
13 The arrival of the Highland Division.

14 Officers go from one ship to another by the hazardous means of a breeches-bouy.
15 Maybe the enemy is just behind the wave.

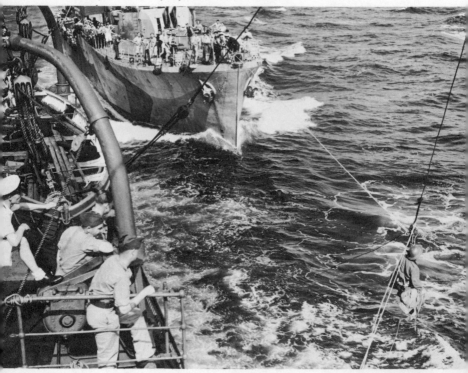

16 Street fighting in Acireale on road to Messina.
17 The victors of the deserts fighting in different conditions: the invasion of a
   mountainous region.

18 Devasted streets in Pantelleria.

troops, has been conquered. Mussolini has been overthrown. The war impulse of Italy has been destroyed, and that unhappy country is paying a terrible penalty for allowing itself to be misled by false and criminal guides. How much easier it is to join bad companions than to shake them off! A large number of German troops have lately been drawn away from France in order to hold down the Italian people, in order to make Italy a battleground, and to keep the war as distant and as long as possible from German soil. By far the greater part of the German Air Force has been drawn off from the Russian front, and indeed is being engaged and worn down with ever-growing intensity, by night and day, by British and American and Canadian airmen. More than all this, we have established a strategic initiative and potential, both from the Atlantic and from the Mediterranean, of which the enemy can neither measure the weight nor foresee the hour of application.

To judge by the latest news from the Russian battle-fronts, Marshal Stalin is certainly not wasting his time. The entire British Empire sends him our salutes in this brilliant summer campaign, and on the victories of Orel, Kharkov, and Taganrog, by which so much Russian soil has been redeemed and so many hundreds of thousands of its invaders wiped out.

I gave the fullest prominence to Mountbatten's appointment.

A Supreme Commander of the South-East Asia front has been chosen, and his name has been acclaimed by British, American, and Chinese opinion. He will act in constant association with Generalissimo Chiang Kai-shek. It is true that Lord Louis Mountbatten is only forty-three. It is not often under modern conditions and in established military professions that a man gets so great a chance so early. But if an officer, having devoted his life to the military art, does not know about war at forty-three he is not likely to learn much more about it later on. As Chief of Combined Operations Lord Louis has shown rare powers of organisation and resourcefulness. He is what—pedants notwithstanding—I will venture to call a "complete triphibian"—that is to say, a creature equally at home in three elements, earth, air, and water, and also well accustomed to fire. We all wish the new command and its commander full success in their novel, varied, and certainly most difficult task.

*   *   *

I left Quebec by train, and arrived at the White House on September 1. Throughout the talks at Quebec events had been marching forward in Italy. The President and I, as has been recorded elsewhere, had directed during these critical days the course of the secret armistice talks with the Badoglio Government, and had also been following anxiously and closely the military arrangement for a landing on Italian soil. I deliberately prolonged my stay in the United States in order to be in close contact with our American friends at this critical moment in Italian affairs. On the day of my arrival in Washington the first definite and official news was received that Badoglio had agreed to accept the surrender terms proposed by the Allies. The strategic arrangements debated at "Quadrant" had of course been considered in the light of the possible Italian collapse, and this aspect was our main concern in these days.

While in Washington I attended several American Cabinets or their equivalent and was in close touch with leading American personalities. Poor Hopkins at this time was very ill and had to retire for a complete rest to the naval hospital. The President was very anxious for me to keep a longstanding appointment and receive an honorary degree at Harvard. It was to be an occasion for a public declaration to the world of Anglo-American unity and amity. On September 6 I delivered my speech. The following extract may be printed here.

To the youth of America, as to the youth of Britain, I say, "You cannot stop." There is no halting-place at this point. We have now reached a stage in the journey where there can be no pause. We must go on. It must be world anarchy or world order. Throughout all this ordeal and struggle which is characteristic of our age you will find in the British Commonwealth and Empire good comrades to whom you are united by other ties besides those of State policy and public need. To a large extent they are the ties of blood and history. Naturally I, a child of both worlds, am conscious of these.

Law, language, literature—these are considerable factors. Common conceptions of what is right and decent, a marked regard for fair play, especially to the weak and poor, a stern sentiment of impartial justice, and above all the love of personal freedom, or, as Kipling put it, "Leave to live by no man's leave underneath the law"—these are common conceptions on both sides of the ocean among the English-speaking peoples. We hold to these conceptions as strongly as you do.

We do not war primarily with races as such. Tyranny is our foe. Whatever trappings or disguise it wears, whatever language it speaks, be it external or internal, we must for ever be on our guard, ever mobilised, ever vigilant, always ready to spring at its throat. In all this we march together. Not only do we march and strive shoulder to shoulder at this moment under the fire of the enemy on the fields of war or in the air, but also in those realms of thought which are consecrated to the rights and the dignity of man.

I spoke about our Combined Staffs.

At the present time we have in continual vigorous action the British and United States Combined Chiefs of Staff Committee, which works immediately under the President and myself as representative of the British War Cabinet. This Committee, with its elaborate organisation of Staff officers of every grade, disposes of all our resources, and in practice uses British and American troops, ships, aircraft, and munitions just as if they were the resources of a single State or nation. I would not say there are never divergences of view among these high professional authorities. It would be unnatural if there were not. That is why it is necessary to have plenary meetings of principals every two or three months. All these men now know each other. They trust each other. They like each other, and most of them have been at work together for a long time. When they meet they thrash things out with great candour and plain, blunt speech, but after a few days the President and I find ourselves furnished with sincere and united advice.

This is a wonderful system. There was nothing like it in the last war. There never has been anything like it between two allies. It is reproduced in an even more tightly knit form at General Eisenhower's headquarters in the Mediterranean, where everything is completely intermingled and soldiers are ordered into battle by the Supreme Commander or his Deputy, General Alexander, without the slightest regard to whether they are British, American, or Canadian, but simply in accordance with the fighting need.

Now in my opinion it would be a most foolish and improvident act on the part of our two Governments, or either of them, to break up this smooth-running and immensely powerful machinery the moment the war is over. For our own safety, as well as for the security of the rest of the world, we are bound to keep it working and in running order after the war—probably for a good many years, not only until we have set up some world arrangement to keep the peace, but until we know that it is an arrangement which will really give us that protection we must have from danger and aggression, a protection we have already had to seek across two vast world wars.

Alas, unwisdom has already prevailed!

* * *

I had, as usual, had an official summary of the Conference sent to the Dominion Prime Ministers. Field-Marshal Smuts was disappointed by the scale on which our plans were based, and also by their apparent leisurely time-table. I always, as the reader knows, found great comfort in feeling that our minds were in step. The cables that passed between us throw a true and intimate light upon the main issues of the war at this milestone. It was no burden to me but a relief to dictate from my general body of knowledge acquired at the summit full explanations to one I knew so well.

General Smuts to Prime Minister   31 Aug 43
For your private ear I should like to voice my personal misgivings about the progress of the war. If you don't agree with me please forget my grouse. But if in any way you share my feeling you will take your own initiative in the matter.

While our Middle East campaign was conducted with conspicuous vigour from El Alamein to the end in Tunisia, I sense a slackening and tardiness in operations since then. It took us several months between Tunisia and the Sicilian landing, and there is now another strange pause after Sicily at a stage in our affairs when the urgency is very great. To compare the Anglo-American effort, with all our vast resources, with that of Russia during the same period is to raise uncomfortable questions which must occur to many others. Our comparative performance on land is insignificant and its speed very unsatisfactory. There is much and constant boasting of our production effort, especially of the colossal American production. And after almost two years of war the American fighting forces must be enormous. But still, the Russians account for the vast bulk of the German Army on land. Shipping and other troubles account for this difference in part, but that is not the whole story. I have the uncomfortable feeling that the scale and speed of our land operations leaves much to be desired. Our Navy is acting up to its usual high standard, and our Air Force is magnificent. But almost all the honours on land go to the Russians, and deservedly so, considering the scale and speed of their fighting and the magnificence of their strategy on a vast front.

Surely our performance can be bettered and the comparison with Russia rendered less unflattering to us. To the ordinary man it must appear that it is Russia who is winning the war. If this impression continues what will be our post-war world position compared with that of Russia? A tremendous shift in our world status may follow, and will leave Russia the diplomatic master of the world. This is both unnecessary and undesirable, and would have especially bad reactions for the British Commonwealth. Unless we emerge from the war on terms of equality our position will be both uncomfortable and dangerous. . . . I do not yet know what was being planned at Quebec, and assume the best programmes have been worked out and approved. But what about the rate of their execution? There is grave danger in delay, in tardiness of performance on our part.

General Smuts to Prime Minister   3 Sept 43

After sending my previous message criticising our war progress I must frankly express my disappointment with this Quebec plan as being an inadequate programme for the fifth year of the war, and especially after the enormous change that has taken place in our war fortunes recently. This plan has only added to my misgivings and fears for the future. It does no justice to the real strength of our position, and may gravely affect public morale as well as future relations with Russia. We are capable of a much greater effort, and should face the position with greater boldness.

In effect, the plan merely proposes to continue and increase the present bombing and anti-U-boat campaigns, to take Sardinia and Corsica and the South of Italy and bomb northwards from there. We are then to fight our way northwards through Italy over difficult mountainous terrain in a campaign which may take much time before we reach Northern Italy and the main German defence position. Next spring we shall cross the Channel in force if the air and military situation in France is favourable, and we may invade France from the south if only as a diversion. We leave the Balkans to the guerrillas, with air encouragement from us.

So much for the West. In the East we do some island-hopping which may bring us up against the enemy's main base in the Carolines some time towards the end of next year. The resources of the Dutch East Indies we leave meanwhile to the enemy while we make efforts to open the Burma route and assist China as much as possible by air. Some undefined amphibious operations against Burma are also indicated.

Bombing appears to me the only serious part of this plan. All the rest is still on a small scale, similar to what we have been doing for the last couple of years. Surely this would not be a serious effort for this stage of the war nor a proper use of our greatly improved war position. If by the end of 1944 we have done no better than merely nibble at the enemy's main positions we may experience a dangerous revulsion of opinion, and rightly so. It would compare most unfavourably with the grand effort and achievement of Russia, who may conclude that her suspicions of us are justified.

In the absence of inner Staff information, it is difficult for me to suggest alternative plans, but I feel convinced that we can and should do much more and better than the Quebec plan, which would unduly drag out and prolong the war, with all the attendant risks and possibilities I have indicated in my former message. The bombing policy, the anti-U-boat campaign, and the large-scale attack across the Channel I approve. But in the Mediterranean we should take Sardinia and Corsica and immediately attack in North Italy without fighting our way all up the peninsula. We should immediately take Southern Italy and move on to the Adriatic, and from a suitable point there launch a real attack on the Balkans and set its resurgent forces going. This will bring Turkey into the picture and carry our Fleet into the Black Sea, where we shall join hands with Russia, supply her, and enable her to attack Hitler's fortress itself from the east and south-east. With the vast change in the war situation on the Russian front I do not think this too ambitious a programme to work to. . . .

After consideration I replied to Smuts.

Prime Minister to Field-Marshal Smuts   5 Sept 43
   Your two telegrams.
   1. The invasion of the toe of Italy now begun is of course only the prelude to a far heavier attack which is imminent, and will, if successful, produce consequences of a far-reaching character. We hope presently to open a heavy front across Italy as far north as we can get. Such a front will absorb about twenty divisions from the Mediterranean, and may require reinforcement if selected for counter-attack by the enemy.
   2. I have always been most anxious to come into the Balkans, which are already doing so well.* We shall have to see how the fighting in Italy develops before committing ourselves beyond Commandos, agents, and supplies, but the whole place is aflame, and with the defection of the twenty-four Italian divisions scattered in the Balkans, who have ceased to fight and now only try to get home, it may well be that the Germans will be forced to retire to the line of the Save and the Danube. . . .
   3. I think it better not to demand entry into the war by Turkey at this present time, as the forces with which we should have to fight are more usefully employed in the Central Mediterranean. The question may be put to Turkey later in the year.
   4. In spite of these serious needs and projects in the Mediterranean, which strain our resources to the full, we have to find seven divisions from that theatre from November on for the build-up of Operation

---

* This sentence appears inconsistent with my general policy as so often expressed in these volumes. I did not mean "come into the Balkans" with an army.

"Overlord" in the spring of 1944. For this purpose every personnel ship which can be gathered, apart from those used by the United States in the Pacific, is being employed in the ceaseless transportation of American troops and air forces. None of our ships have been idle this year, and yet there are so far only two American divisions in England. It is not physically possible to make a larger concentration by the date mentioned. We shall be able to match the American expedition with a nearly equal force of British divisions, but after the initial assault the build-up must be entirely American, as I am completely at the end of man-power resources, and even now have to ask the Americans to interrupt the movement of field troops in order to send over some thousands of engineers to help make the installations and establishments required for the gathering of their transatlantic army.

5. These projects in Europe, together with the air offensive and the sea war, completely absorb all our resources of man-power and of ship-power. This fact must be faced. There is no comparison between our conditions and those prevailing in Russia, where the whole strength of a nation of nearly two hundred millions, less war losses, long organised into a vast national army, is deployed on a two-thousand-miles land front. This again is a fact which must be faced.

6. I think it inevitable that Russia will be the greatest land Power in the world after this war, which will have rid her of the two military Powers, Japan and Germany, who in our lifetime have inflicted upon her such heavy defeats. I hope however that the "fraternal association" of the British Commonwealth and the United States, together with sea- and air-power, may put us on good terms and in a friendly balance with Russia at least for the period of rebuilding. Farther than that I cannot see with mortal eye, and I am not as yet fully informed about the celestial telescopes.

7. In the East we British have no shortage of forces, but the same difficulty of coming into action as the United States in the Atlantic and also in the Pacific. The shipping stringency rules all oversea and amphibious action, and, for the rest, in Burma there are the jungles, the mountains, and the fact that more than half the year is swamped by the monsoon. However, a vigorous campaign has been set on foot. I brought young Wingate to Quebec, and he is being raised from a Brigadier to a Corps Commander, with powerful jungle forces adapted to the purpose being formed with the utmost speed for an attack in the first month of next year. The appointment of Mountbatten heralds an amphibious operation of novelty and far-reaching scope which I am pressing with all possible energy, the details of which I will unfold to you when we meet.

8. Believe me, my dear friend, I am not at all vexed at your two

telegrams of criticism. I am confident that if we were together for two or three days I could remove such of your anxieties as are not inherent inexorable facts. Night and day I press for greater speed in action and less cumbrousness in organisation. I am waiting this side of the Atlantic pending the Italian *coup* and its repercussions, but I expect to be home when Parliament meets, and hope to find you at least approaching our shores.

Smuts was to some extent reassured by this full statement. "Your telegram," he said, "has come as a great relief. It makes clear that Italian expedition of twenty divisions would cover whole peninsula and constitute another real front." But he added a day later:

9 Sept 43

I suggest that our victories in Mediterranean should be followed up in Italy and Balkans instead of our now adopting a cross-Channel plan, which means switching on to a new theatre requiring very large forces and involving grave risks unless much more air softening has taken place. Preparations for Channel plan should be slowed down or put into temporary cold storage while bombing campaign is intensified to prepare for eventual military knock-out.

This last suggestion required immediate correction from me if our two minds were to continue to work harmoniously on the problem from independent angles. Smuts alone and far from Washington could not know the atmosphere and proportions which governed our collective thought.

Prime Minister to Field-Marshal Smuts   11 Sept 43

There can be no question whatever of breaking arrangements we have made with United States for "Overlord". The extra shipping available in consequence of U-boat warfare slackening and of Italian windfalls will probably enable us to increase build-up of "Avalanche" [the expedition to Italy]. I hope you will realise that British loyalty to "Overlord" is keystone of arch of Anglo-American co-operation. Personally I think enough forces exist for both hands to be played, and I believe this to be the right strategy.

* * *

Meanwhile the invasion of Italy had begun. At dawn on September 3 the 5th British and 1st Canadian Divisions of the Eighth Army crossed the Straits of Messina.* Practically no opposition was encountered. Reggio was speedily taken, and the

* See map, p. 217.

advance began along the narrow and hilly roads of Calabria. "The Germans," cabled Alexander on September 6, "are fighting their rearguard action more by demolitions than by fire. . . . While in Reggio this morning there was not a warning sound to be heard or a hostile plane to be seen. On the contrary, on this lovely summer day naval craft of all types were plying backwards and forwards between Sicily and the mainland, carrying men, stores, and munitions. In its lively setting it was more like a regatta in peace-time than a serious operation of war."

In a few days the divisions of the Eighth Army had reached Locri and Rosarno, while an infantry brigade, landed by sea at Pizzo, found only the tail of the retreating Germans. There was little fighting, but the advance was severely delayed by the physical difficulties of the country, demolitions carried out by the enemy, and his small but skilfully handled rearguards.

Prime Minister to General Alexander   7 Sept 43

Many thanks for your telegrams about operations in the toe of Italy. Please tell me exactly what the move of airborne division to seize Rome involves, and where it fits into your programme. We are all fully in favour of the bold policy proposed, although we have to take details on trust.

2. I am also deeply interested in your mention of Taranto. About when do you propose doing this?

3. I am still very much concerned about build-up after "Avalanche". Surely if you can get the port of Naples into working order you should be able to push in two divisions a week. Let me know the order in which you propose to bring our army into Italy. When do the New Zealanders, Poles, 4th Indian and 1st Armoured and other really high-class divisions come into action? It seems you will have to hold a front at least as large as that in final stages of Tunis—*i.e.*, about a hundred and seventy miles—and one never can tell if, given time, Germans may not bring a real punch to bear upon that front.

4. I am waiting here with the President to judge results of "Avalanche", and thereafter returning home. I hope however to come out to you in the first half of October, and General Marshall will come from America. I shall have some important things to tell you then.

Alexander replied that the Italian Government's being unable to announce the armistice had forced him to make certain changes. The 82nd U.S. Airborne Division could not be flown in to the Rome area, as no arrangement for its reception had been made by the Italians and the Germans were thought to be in occupation of the airfields. "Avalanche" would go in as planned, except that no airborne forces would take part. About 3,000 soldiers of the 1st Airborne Division had sailed in naval ships for Taranto, and should arrive there on September 9. It was impossible to say what reception they would receive. By opening the port of Taranto early he hoped to increase the build-up into Italy.

At the same time our efforts to seize Rhodes and other islands in the Ægean began. Later chapters will tell the tale.

* * *

In the White House the President and I sat talking after dinner in his study, and Admiral Pound came to see us upon a naval point. The President asked him several questions about the general aspects of the war, and I was pained to see that my trusted naval friend had lost the outstanding matter-of-fact precision which characterised him. Both the President and I were sure he was very ill. Next morning Pound came to see me in my big bed-sitting-room and said abruptly, "Prime Minister, I have come to resign. I have had a stroke and my right side is largely paralysed. I thought it would pass off, but it gets worse every day and I am no longer fit for duty." I at once accepted the First Sea Lord's resignation, and expressed my profound sympathy for his breakdown in health. I told him he was relieved at that moment from all responsibility, and urged him to rest for a few days and then come home with me in the *Renown*. He was completely master of himself, and his whole manner was instinct with dignity. As soon as he left the room I cabled to the Admiralty placing Vice-Admiral Syfret in responsible charge from that moment pending the appointment of a new First Sea Lord.

* * *

On September 9 we held a formal conference with the President at the White House. The C.I.G.S. and the C.A.S. had flown back to London some days before, and I was accompanied by Field-Marshal Dill, Ismay, and the three representatives of the British Chiefs of Staff in Washington. The President brought with him Leahy, Marshall, King, and Arnold. A number of telegrams about the Italian Fleet coming over to us made an agreeable introduction. I expressed the hope that the Italian Fleet would be treated with respect by the Allies wherever it might arrive.

In preparation for this meeting I had prepared a memorandum to the President, which I had submitted to him earlier in the day. He asked me to read it out, and thought it would make a basis for our discussion.

9 Sept 43

It would surely be convenient before we separate to have a plenary meeting of the Combined Chiefs of Staff in order to take stock of the new world situation which will arise on the assumption that the present battle for Naples and Rome is successful and that the Germans retreat to the line of the Apennines or the Po.

2. Assuming we get the Italian Fleet, we gain not only that Fleet, but the British Fleet, which has hitherto contained it. This very heavy addition to our naval power should be used at the earliest possible moment to intensify the war against Japan. I have asked the First Sea Lord to discuss with Admiral King the movement of a powerful British battle squadron, with cruisers and ancillaries, to the Indian Ocean via the Panama Canal and the Pacific. We need a strong Eastern Fleet based on Colombo during the amphibious operations next year. I should be very glad if it were found possible for this fleet to serve under the American Pacific Command and put in at least four months of useful fighting in the Pacific before taking up its Indian Ocean station. We cannot afford to have idle ships. I do not know however how the arrival of such reinforcements would enable the various tasks assigned to United States forces in the Pacific to be augmented. Apart from strategy, from the standpoint of high policy His Majesty's Government would desire to participate in the Pacific war in order to give such measure of assistance as is in their power not only to their American Allies, but on account of the obligations to Australia and New Zealand. Such a movement of our ships to and through the Pacific would undoubtedly exercise a demoralising effect upon Japan, who must now be conscious of the very great addition of naval weight thrust against her, and besides this it would surely give satisfaction in the United States as being a proof positive of British resolve to take an active and vigorous part to the end in the war against Japan.

3. The public must be gradually led to realise what we and our Combined Staffs have so fully in mind, namely, the conversion of Italy into an active agent against Germany. Although we could not recognise Italy as an ally in the full sense, we have agreed she is to be allowed to work her passage, and that useful service against the enemy will not only be aided but recompensed. Should fighting break out between Italians and Germans the public prejudices will very rapidly depart, and in a fortnight or so matters may be ripe, if we can so

direct events, for an Italian declaration of war against Germany. The question of the Italian flag flying from Italian ships, and even some arrangement of Italians manning those vessels under British or American control, requires consideration. The whole problem of handling and getting the utmost use out of the Italian Navy requires review now on a high level.

4. On the overall assumption of a decisive victory in the Naples area, we are, I presume, agreed to march northwards up the Italian peninsula until we come up against the main German positions. If the Italians are everywhere favourable and their Army comes over to help, the deployment of at least a dozen Italian divisions will be of great advantage in holding the front across Italy and in permitting relief of Allied forces. If, after the Battle of Naples is over, we are not seriously resisted south of the main German line, we ought not to be long getting up against it with light forces, and I should hope that by the end of the year at the latest we should be confronting it in full strength. If sooner, then better. There can be no question of whittling down "Overlord". We must not forget at this juncture our agreement to begin moving the seven divisions away in succession from the beginning of November. All the more important is it to bring Italian divisions into the line, and our State policy should be adapted to procure this end.

5. I have been contemplating the 1944 campaign in the light of these new possibilities, and I remain strongly convinced that we should be very chary of advancing northward beyond the narrow part of the Italian peninsula. Of course, if the Germans retreat to the Alps another situation is presented, but, failing that, it would seem beyond our strength, having regard to the requirements of "Overlord", to broaden out into the plains of Lombardy. We have also to consider that the Germans, working on interior lines, may perhaps bring a heavier force to bear upon our front in Italy than we shall have there at the end of the year. The possibility of a strong German counterattack cannot be excluded. I should like it to be considered whether we should not, when we come up against the main German position, construct a strong fortified line of our own, properly sited in depth. Italian military labour could be used on a large scale for this purpose. Italian troops could naturally take part in defending the line. Thus by the spring we should be able in this theatre either to make an offensive if the enemy were weak, and anyhow to threaten one, or, on the other hand, stand on the defensive, using our air-power, which will in the meanwhile have been built up, from behind our fortified line, and divert a portion of our troops for action elsewhere, either to the west or to the east. I hope this may be studied.

6. We are both of us acutely conscious of the great importance of the Balkan situation. We should make sure that the Mediterranean High Command, absorbed in its present battle, does not overlook the needs of the Patriot forces there. The problem of the Italian forces requires immediate study. The orders of the C.-in-C. Middle East, General Wilson, published to-day, are well conceived for the moment, but we require to see more clearly exactly what is intended. On the assumption that the Italians can be drawn into the war against Germany, far-reaching possibilities seem to be open. There is surely no need for us to work from the bottom of the Balkans upwards. If we can get an agreement between the Patriots and the Italian troops it should be possible to open quite soon one or more good ports on the Dalmatian coast, enabling munitions and supplies to be sent in by ship and all forces that will obey our orders to be raised to good fighting condition. The German situation in all this theatre will become most precarious, especially from the point of view of supplies. When the defensive line across Northern Italy has been completed it may be possible to spare some of our own forces assigned to the Mediterranean theatre to emphasise a movement north and north-eastward from the Dalmatian ports. For the moment the utmost efforts should be put forth to organise the attack upon the Germans throughout the Balkan peninsula and to supply agents, arms, and good direction.

7. Lastly, the question of islands is now ripe for consideration. Sardinia, I imagine, will come over immediately, though we may have to send some help to the Italians in procuring the disarmament of any German units there. In Corsica the Germans have perhaps already been overcome, but surely here is the place for a French expedition. Even if only one division could be sent by the French National Committee, the island could probably be quickly liberated, and there is little doubt that its manhood would enable at least another division or two to be raised locally. General Wilson's telegram about the operations against Rhodes and other islands in the Dodecanese is all right so far as it goes, but I am not satisfied that sufficient use is being made under the present conditions of the forces in the Middle East. I am making an immediate inquiry into the exact location of all troops above battalion strength, hoping that improvised expeditionary forces and garrisons may be provided for various minor ventures.

8. We must expect far-reaching reactions in Bulgaria, Roumania, and Hungary, and these again may produce a movement from the Turk without our having to make any request or incur any obligation. All this again requires military and political consideration on the high level, and I feel that we should do well to take a preliminary survey this afternoon if you are agreeable.

There was wide agreement in principle between us all along the lines set forth in the above note, and the Staffs concerted the necessary action in the days that followed.

*   *   *

The next day the President left Washington for his home at Hyde Park. He asked me to use the White House not only as a residence but for any conference I might wish to hold, either with the British Empire representatives who had gathered in Washington or with the United States war chiefs, and not to hesitate to call another plenary meeting should I deem it necessary. I availed myself fully of these generous facilities. Accordingly, as there was a general desire to take stock of the rapid movement of events in Italy and of the progress of the fierce and critical battle for Naples, I convened another meeting at the White House on September 11, at which I presided myself. The United States were represented by Admiral Leahy, General Marshall, Admiral King, General Arnold, Harry Hopkins, Averell Harriman, and Lew Douglas. I brought with me Dill and Ismay, and our three representatives on the Combined Chiefs of Staff.

All current matters were discussed. General Marshall reported the conditions in the Naples area, and the rapid reinforcement of the German divisions. General Arnold mentioned that we had now nearly three thousand operative aircraft engaged over Italy, which, he said, was more than the whole German Air Force on all fronts. I directed attention to the lamentable proposals for building up our forces on the mainland. I had been, I said, horrified to see the figure of only twelve divisions to be achieved by December 1. It was vitally important to accelerate the growth of the army in Italy by every possible division. Even the arrival of one division a fortnight earlier might make a serious difference. General Marshall entirely agreed and said that everything should be done.

He then told us about the brilliantly successful air landings by the United States Air Force in the South Pacific theatre. As a result of their descent in the Markham valley, combined with seaborne attack, the garrison of eight to ten thousand Japanese had been virtually isolated. American troops were pounding Salamaua and were close to Lae. Airfields should soon be in our possession from which the enemy airfields could be made untenable. This in turn would change the whole sea situation. The Japanese position in New Britain might soon be desperate. There were also signs of Japanese evacuation from the Solomons.

It was an honour to me to preside over this conference of the Combined Chiefs of Staff and of American and British authorities in the Council Room of the White House, and it seemed to be an event in Anglo-American history.

CHAPTER VIII

THE BATTLE OF SALERNO
A HOMEWARD VOYAGE

Anglo-American Descent Upon Salerno – Stubborn German Resistance – Taranto Seized – Alexander on the Spot – The Navy Lends a Hand – Congratulations from Stalin – We Embark on the "Renown" – Progress of the Battle: Alexander's Reports – The Victory Gained – My Message to Eisenhower – Mary's Adventure – Naples Taken – My Telegram to Eisenhower of September 25, and His Reply – Interchanges with the Commanders – A Pause to Consolidate.

ON the night of September 8 Alexander sent me his "Zip" message. As the Allied armada approached the Salerno beaches that evening they heard the announcement from the British broadcast of the Italian surrender. To men keyed up for battle the news came as a shock, which for the moment relaxed the tension and had an unfortunate psychological effect. Many thought that on the morrow their task would be a walk-over. Officers at once strove to correct any such impression, pointing out that whatever the Italians might do there would certainly be strong resistance from German forces. There was a sense of anticlimax. Nevertheless, as Admiral Cunningham remarked, to have withheld the existence of the armistice would have been a breach of faith with the Italian people.

Covered by a strong British fleet, the assault convoys entered the Gulf of Salerno with only minor air attack. The enemy was aware of their approach, but he could not tell until the last moment where the blow would fall.

The landing of the Fifth Army, commanded by General Clark, began before dawn. The assault was delivered by the VIth U.S.

Corps and the British Xth Corps, with British Commandos and U.S. Rangers on the northern flank. The convoys had been sighted at sea, and General Eisenhower's broadcast of the previous evening caused the German troops in the neighbourhood to act immediately. Disarming the Italians, they took over the whole defence themselves, and made good use of the advantage which modern weapons give to the defence in the early stages of a landing. Our men were met by well-aimed fire as they waded ashore, and they suffered heavily. It was difficult to provide proper air cover for them, as many of our fighters were operating at extreme range from Sicily, but these were reinforced by carrier-borne aircraft.

Once across the beaches the VIth U.S. Corps made good progress, and by the night of the 11th had advanced as much as ten miles, with their right flank bent back to the sea. The British corps met stiffer opposition. They succeeded in taking Salerno and Battipaglia. The Montecorvino airfield also fell into our hands, but as it remained under enemy fire it could not provide the sorely needed refuelling ground for our fighters. The Germans reacted very quickly. Their troops opposing the Eighth Army, which was toiling its way up the toe of Italy, were brought at all speed to the new battle. From the north came the greater part of three divisions, from the east a regiment of parachutists.* Our own reinforcement was much slower, as shipping, especially small craft, was scarce. The German Air Force, though weakened by their losses in Sicily, made an intense effort, and their new radio-controlled and glider bombs caused losses to our shipping. All the resources of the Allied Air were turned on to hamper the approach of enemy reinforcements and blast their concentrations. Warships steamed into Salerno Bay to give the support of their heaviest guns. The Eighth Army was spurred on by Montgomery to gain contact with the hard-pressed Fifth. All this helped, and in the opinion of a highly placed German officer the eclipse of the Luftwaffe and the lack of any defence against naval bombardment were decisive.

*   *   *

While the Salerno battle was raging a remarkable stroke was made upon Taranto, for which not only Alexander, but Admiral

* The order of battle of the German and Italian divisions on September 8 is set out in Appendix E (p. 322).

Cunningham, on whom fell the brunt of execution, deserve the highest credit for well-run risks. This first-class port was capable of serving a whole army. The Italian surrender which now broke upon us seemed to Alexander to justify daring. There were no transport aircraft to lift the British 1st Airborne Division, nor any ordinary shipping to carry it by sea. Six thousand of these picked men were embarked on British warships, and on September 9, the day of the landing on Salerno beaches, the Royal Navy steamed boldly into Taranto harbour and deposited the troops ashore, unopposed. One of our cruisers which struck a mine and sank was our only naval loss.*

* * *

It had been planned that I and those of our party who had not already flown to England should go home by sea, and the *Renown* awaited us at Halifax. I broke the train journey to say good-bye to the President, and was thus with him at Hyde Park when the Battle of Salerno began. I resumed my train journey on the night of the 12th, to reach Halifax on the morning of the 14th. The various reports which reached me on the journey, as well as the newspapers, made me deeply anxious. Evidently a most critical and protracted struggle was in progress. My concern was all the greater because I had always strongly pressed for this seaborne landing, and felt a special responsibility for its success. Surprise, violence, and speed are the essence of all amphibious landings. After the first twenty-four hours the advantage of sea-power in striking where you will may well have vanished. Where there were ten men there are soon ten thousand. My mind travelled back over the years. I thought of General Stopford waiting nearly three days on the beach at Suvla Bay in 1915 while Mustafa Kemal marched two Turkish divisions from the lines at Bulair to the hitherto undefended battlefield. I had had a more recent experience when General Auchinleck had remained at his headquarters in Cairo surveying orthodoxly from the summit and centre the wide and varied sphere of his command, while the battle, on which everything turned, was being decided against him in the desert. I had the greatest confidence in Alexander, but all the same I passed a painful day while our train rumbled for-

* I have in my home the Union Jack, the gift of General Alexander, that was hoisted at Taranto, and was one of the first Allied flags to be flown in Europe since our expulsion from France.

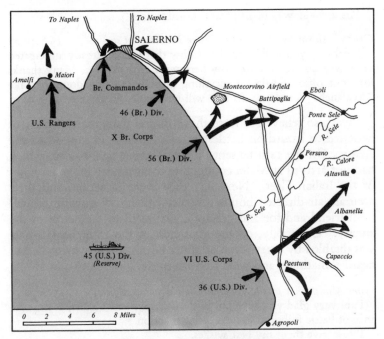

THE SALERNO LANDING

ward through the pleasant lands of Nova Scotia. At length I wrote out the following message for Alexander, feeling sure he would not resent it. It was not sent till after I had sailed.

Prime Minister to General Alexander   14 Sept 43

I hope you are watching above all the Battle of "Avalanche", which dominates everything. None of the commanders engaged has fought a large-scale battle before. The Battle of Suvla Bay was lost because Ian Hamilton was advised by his C.G.S. to remain at a remote central point where he would know everything. Had he been on the spot he could have saved the show. At this distance and with time-lags I cannot pretend to judge, but I feel it my duty to set before you this experience of mine from the past.

2. *Nothing* should be denied which will nourish the decisive battle for Naples.

3. Ask for anything you want, and I will make allocation of necessary supplies, with highest priority irrespective of every other consideration.

His answer was prompt and comforting.

General Alexander (Salerno) to Prime Minister (at sea)   15 Sept 43
I feel sure you will be glad to know that I have already anticipated your wise advice and am now here with Fifth Army. Many thanks for your offer of help. Everything possible is being done to make "Avalanche" a success. Its fate will be decided in the next few days.

I was also relieved to learn that Admiral Cunningham had not hesitated to hazard his battleships close inshore in support of the Army. On the 14th he sent up the *Warspite* and *Valiant*, which had just arrived at Malta conducting to surrender the main body of the Italian Fleet. Next day they were in action, and their accurate air-directed bombardment with heavy guns impressed both friend and foe and greatly contributed to the defeat of the enemy. Unhappily, on the afternoon of the 16th the *Warspite* was disabled by a new type of glider bomb, about which we had heard something, and were to learn more.

Prime Minister (at sea) to Admiral Cunningham (Algiers)   15 Sept 43
I am very glad you have put in the *Warspite* and *Valiant*, as importance of battle fully justifies exceptional action.
Please give them my best wishes.

The following also came in:

Premier Stalin to President Franklin D. Roosevelt   14 Sept 43
and to Prime Minister Churchill
I congratulate you on new successes, and especially on the landing at Naples. There is no doubt that the successful landing at Naples and break between Italy and Germany will deal one more blow upon Hitlerite Germany and will considerably facilitate the actions of the Soviet armies at the Soviet-German front. For the time being the offensive of the Soviet troops is successfully developing. I think that we shall be in a position to achieve more successes within the next two-three weeks. It is possible that we shall have recaptured Novorossisk within the next few days.

It was a relief to board the *Renown*. The splendid ship lay alongside the quay. Admiral Pound was already on board, having come through direct from Washington. He bore himself as erect as ever, and no one looking at him would have dreamed that he was stricken. I invited him to join us at my table on the homeward voyage, but he said he would prefer to take his meals in his cabin with his staff officer. Within half an hour we sailed, and for the next six days we zigzagged our way across the ocean.

* * *

All the time the Battle at Salerno went on. The telegrams flowed in. Alexander was kind enough to keep me fully informed, and his vivid messages can be read in their relation to the whole event.

General Alexander to Prime Minister (at sea) 16 Sept 43
I have just returned from an extensive tour of the Fifth Army front. I saw both corps commanders, all division commanders, and several front line brigades. Although I am not entirely happy about the situation, I am happier than I was twenty-four hours ago, for following reasons:

The Germans have not put in a serious attack since night 13th. This has given us time to improve our position somewhat, rest for very exhausted troops, and get some reinforcements of men and material in. Eighth Army are also drawing nearer. I have also been able to cheer them up and issue certain directions, of which the following are most important. Hold what we have gained, at all costs consolidating key positions by digging, wiring, and mining. Reorganise scattered and mixed units and formations. Form local reserves and as strong a mobile reserve as possible. Inform troops of rapid approach of Eighth Army and flow of reinforcements now arriving day and night. Present weakness is [due to] following. Germans have been able concentrate strong forces quicker than we have been able to build up sufficient forces to hold what had been gained in first rush. Germans hold most of the dominating features and overlook us on to the beach. Our troops are tired. There is very little depth anywhere; we have temporarily lost the initiative. Last night our Air dropped a parachute battalion behind enemy lines in Avellino area. Air flew in 1,600 men of the 82nd Division last night. I have arranged with the Navy to bring 1,500 British infantry reinforcements from Philippeville in cruisers; these should be here in under forty-eight hours. I have speeded up arrival 3rd U.S. Division, which will start landing on 18th.

First elements of 7th Armoured Division arrive to-night, but will take few days to disembark and concentrate. One infantry brigade also arrives to-night. We have just completed three landing strips, and Spitfires are now operating from Salerno and neighbourhood.

The whole of the air forces are concentrated on this battle area. We shall regain the initiative and start to gain key points as soon as we are strong enough to do so. God's blessing on our enterprise and a little luck will ensure success to our arms.

Prime Minister (at sea) to General Alexander 16 Sept 43

My feeling about "Avalanche" is expressed in Foch's maxim, *Cramponnez partout*. The Navy are quite right to throw their heavy ships in, for this is a battle of far-reaching significance. My feeling is you are going to win.

Prime Minister to General Alexander 17 Sept 43

I am very glad to feel you have taken a personal grip of "Avalanche" position. I had, as you know, been worried about rate of "Avalanche" build-up. It is great news that Montgomery expects to bring Eighth Army into action on 17th.

2. It is right to use the battleships in the inshore squadron in view of favourable naval balances.

3. Every good wish. Please continue to keep me informed. I am in mid-ocean, but can receive fully at all hours.

For three critical days the issue hung in the balance. Battipaglia was lost, but the 56th Division, though weakened by heavy losses, succeeded in stopping a further drive from there to the sea. On the front of the VIth U.S. Corps the enemy, taking advantage of the thinly held gap between that corps and the British, turned in from the north, crossed the river Sele, and threatened to reach the landing beaches behind the Americans. They were stopped only just in time by the defence of the American batteries. The Allied line was held by the narrowest of margins. The 45th U.S. Division, which had been held in reserve on board their ships, was now in full action on the VIth Corps front. Reinforcements were beginning to arrive. Our 7th Armoured Division and the 82nd U.S. Airborne Division came in by sea and air. After six days of bitter fighting, in which we suffered moments of grave hazard, the Germans failed to throw us back into the sea. On the 15th Kesselring realised he could not succeed. Pivoting his right on the high ground above Salerno, he began to swing his whole line back. Next day the Fifth and Eighth Armies joined hands. We had won.

* * *

General Alexander to Prime Minister (at sea) 18 Sept 43

The general situation continues to improve, and the initiative is passing to us. There have been several strongish attacks against Xth British Corps in north, but all these have been repulsed. On VIth Corps front Americans are on offensive, and fighting is still going on in Altavilla. As you know, Fifth Army and Eighth Army patrols have joined hands. 7th Armoured Division are getting ashore well. 1,500 infantry reinforcements for Xth Corps arrived last night. American reinforcement of about 1,600 due to arrive in a day or two. 3rd U.S. Division starts disembarking to-morrow evening. The build-up of ammunition and supplies is satisfactory. Eighth Army are advancing on Aluetta and Potenza, but up to writing I have not received [any] report as to the location of their spearheads. 1st British Airborne Division, in Taranto area, are active, and have joined hands with the Canadians, but are too weak to do more than harass the Germans. 78th Infantry Division is due to start unloading at Taranto on September 22, and 8th Indian Division at Brindisi on September 23. My immediate aim is to build up three strong fighting groups: Fifth U.S. Army in Salerno area, Eighth Army in centre, British Vth Corps under Eighth Army in Taranto area. From these firm bases we shall advance northwards, and I have issued a directive to the following effect. Fifth Army to pivot on hills north-west of Salerno and secure the heights about Avellino. Eighth Army to secure Potenza area. Next objectives will be Fifth Army to secure port Naples, Eighth Army the airfields in Foggia area. I do not wish to mislead you by being over-optimistic, but I am satisfied that we now have the situation in hand, and will be able to carry out our future operations according to plan.

As we reached the Clyde decisive news arrived from Alexander.

General Alexander to Prime Minister   19 Sept 43
I can say with full confidence that the whole situation has changed in our favour and that the initiative has passed to us. . . .
I am rejoining my main H.Q. at Syracuse to-morrow.

On September 21 I sent my congratulations to General Eisenhower, and asked him to convey my compliments to General Clark.

Prime Minister to General Eisenhower (Algiers)   21 Sept 43
I congratulate you on the victorious landing and deployment northwards of our armies. As the Duke of Wellington said of the Battle of Waterloo, "It was a damned close-run thing," but your policy of running risks has been vindicated. If you think fit, send a message from me on to Clark, who from all I hear has done wonders. We certainly do work together in a way never before seen among allies.
2. It does seem to me most desirable, if you could manage it, to push more French troops into Corsica and to put a substantial detachment of British or American troops into Sardinia. As we now have good harbours for disembarkation they need not be combat-loaded, but their presence will animate the Italian troops and the French and local Patriots.

3. We are backing you up all we can about working with the Italian Government, and I am pretty sure all will go as you wish it.

4. Field-Marshal Smuts will be in Cairo Monday, September 27, staying with Casey, and will be in your theatre about four days later on his way here. He possesses my entire confidence, and everything can be discussed with him with the utmost freedom. He will stay some months in London, taking up his full duties as a member of the British War Cabinet. He will carry great weight here with public opinion. I shall be grateful if he is treated with the utmost consideration. He is a magnificent man and one of my most cherished friends.

*　　*　　*

Our six-day voyage would have been less pleasant if I had known what was happening to some of my children. Randolph had been in Malta recruiting volunteers for the 2nd Special Air Service Regiment in the early days of September. Here he met Brigadier Laycock, who was a great friend of his and mine. Laycock, who knew what was going to happen, said, "There is going to be a show for the Commandos. Would you like to come?" So Randolph went with him, and was closely engaged throughout the battle.

Mary had an adventure of a different kind. The *Renown* was slanting across a fairly rough sea when one of the officers suggested a walk on the quarterdeck. This, as he should have known, was forbidden on account of the zigzags, which made it impossible to calculate how waves would come aboard. Mary was leaning over the taffrail with her companion when the ship changed course. "Oh, look," she said, "there's a lovely wave coming towards us!" "Cling on!" cried the officer, who realised the danger. In one second the deluge swept them both head over heels across the deck to the starboard scuppers, and but for the fact that Mary came against an upright of the rails she would have gone overboard. The commander saw what had happened from behind the after-turret, and was about to order a "Man overboard" buoy to be dropped, when the recovery heel of the ship sent most of the water that had come on board pouring back the other way, and Mary on the return journey managed to clutch the anchor cables. The poor officer went to and fro in the same excursion. They were dragged, dripping, into safety. The officer was much scolded. Mary changed her clothes, and all this was concealed from me until we landed.

Another event of a more agreeable character also occurred in my personal circle. Among the party of a dozen Wrens who had come with us was a most beautiful girl. Leslie Rowan, my private secretary, wooed and won her in these few days at sea. But this was kept hidden from all by the parties concerned. They are now happily married.

On our arrival I received the following:

President Roosevelt to Prime Minister   20 Sept 43
Delighted you are all safely home, and I hope you had a smooth run. All is quiet here. Congress has been here for a week, and it is still quiet. My best to all three of you.

★   ★   ★

Once the Battle of Salerno had been won Naples and the Foggia airfields lay before us. The British Xth Corps, with the United States VIth Corps on their right, drove back the enemy's rear-guards around Vesuvius, marched past the ruins of Pompeii and Herculaneum, and entered Naples. An immense effort was now concentrated upon opening the harbour, which had been subjected to every form of destruction at experienced hands. Nevertheless this work, in which the Americans excelled, was so effective that within a fortnight 5,000 tons of supplies a day could be handled. The two airfields near the city were soon brought into use, and gave welcome relief to our fighter squadrons, hitherto acting from improvised landing strips. Meanwhile on the east coast the 1st Airborne Division had patrolled as far as Gioja and Bari by September 15. The 78th Division and an armoured brigade landed behind them, and, with the Vth Corps headquarters, joined the Eighth Army. Six Royal Air Force squadrons began to act from the Gioja airfield at the same time. The enemy evacuated the Foggia airfields on September 25. Termoli was taken by Commandos landed from the sea, who, with the help of reinforcements, held out against fierce counter-attacks.

★   ★   ★

A few days after my return I sent General Eisenhower a telegram which should be borne in mind in reading all my messages and memoranda of the autumn and winter. The second paragraph sought to establish the proportion of effort, especially where bottle-necks were concerned, which should be devoted to our various enterprises. These proportions should not be overlooked by those who wish to understand the controversies with which a later chapter deals. War presents the problem of the correct employment of available means, and cannot often be epitomised as "One thing at a time".

Prime Minister to General Eisenhower (Algiers)   25 Sept 43

As I have been pressing for action in several directions, I feel I ought to place before you the priorities which I assign in my own mind to these several desirable objectives.

2. Four-fifths of our effort should be the build-up of Italy. One-tenth should be our making sure of Corsica (which will soon finish) and in the Adriatic. The remaining tenth should be concentrated on Rhodes. This of course applies to the limiting factors only. These, I presume, are mainly landing-craft and assault shipping, with light naval craft.

3. I send this as a rough guide to my thought only because I do not want you to feel I am pressing for everything in all directions without understanding how grim are your limitations.

General Eisenhower to Prime Minister   26 Sept 43

We are examining resources carefully to give Mid-East necessary support in this project, and feel sure that we can meet minimum requirements of Mid-East.

When Montgomery can get the bulk of his forces forward to support the right of the Fifth Army things will begin to move more rapidly on the Naples front. As is always the case following the early stages of a combined operation, we have been badly stretched both tactically and administratively. We are working hard to improve the situation and you will have good news before long.

Eisenhower's answer did not refer as specifically as I had hoped to what I deemed the all-important part of my message, namely, the small proportion of troops required for subsidiary enterprises.

*   *   *

I continued my interchanges with Alexander and Montgomery.

Prime Minister to General Alexander   25 Sept 43

I quite understand that the Eighth Army has to pull up its tail.

2. I like the idea of an advance on a broad front which the enemy will have difficulty in stemming, but I suppose you will also help yourself forward with minor amphibious scoops.

3. You will see that I have announced in Parliament that the Italian campaign is the "Third Front". The Second Front is here in Great Britain, in potential but not yet engaged. This form of statement

should be adhered to, as it is less disagreeable to the Russians and avoids arguing with them as to whether the Italian campaign is the Second Front or not.

Naples was entered by the Anglo-American Fifth Army on October 1.

Prime Minister to General Eisenhower (Algiers)   2 Oct 43

I rejoice with you at the brilliant turn our affairs in the Mediterranean have taken, and that Sardinia and Corsica have fallen as mere incidents in the campaign. Every good wish for the future.

Prime Minister to General Alexander (Italy)   2 Oct 43

I consider that the advance of the Eighth Army on the eastern flank is of enormous value.

I note that Montgomery will soon have to halt to bring up supplies, but I trust this does not mean that his patrols and light forces will not keep in touch with the enemy's rearguards. Everything in our Intelligence goes to show that the enemy's object is to gain time and retire northwards without serious losses. He has not in any case the strength to make a front against the forces you are now deploying. I consider that this favourable position is due to your master-stroke in seizing Taranto, with its unequalled harbour facilities, and beg you to accept my most sincere compliments upon it.

I have studied the plan you have sent home by your officer, and note that you have already accomplished the first and second phases of it. I hope the third phase will be accomplished by the end of the month or thereabouts, and that we shall meet in Rome.

General Alexander to Prime Minister   3 Oct 43

I am most grateful for your kind message, and I appreciate your praise so much. . . . Once I can get R.A.F. properly established and our administrative set-up working as it should, then all will be straight sailing.

I have now established my headquarters at Bari, where I am near the battle-front and within easy reach of my two Army Commanders and my main bases. Air Marshal Coningham is of course with me.

To sum up, all will be well, and the German will be harassed and continuous pressure applied to his rearguards all the time by light mobile forces and air forces when we cannot reach him with our main bodies.

Prime Minister to General Montgomery (Italy)   2 Oct 43

I am delighted to see the Eighth Army striding on so splendidly. Many congratulations on all you have done. I daresay you remember what I said to you that day in Tripoli about where we might meet.

Thank you for your kind message. We have advanced a long way and very quickly. It had to be done in order to come to the help of Fifth Army, but it has been a very great strain on my administration, which had to be switched from the toe to the heel during the operations and which is now stretched to the limit. When I have got the lateral Termoli–Campobasso I will have to halt my main bodies for a short period and operate in advance of that lateral only with light forces while I get my administration on a sound basis during the period of the halt. But light forces directed in sensitive areas can be very effective, and by this means I will retain the initiative and gain ground. After the halt I will advance with my whole strength on Pescara and Ancona. I shall look forward to meeting you in Rome.

★ ★ ★

A pause was now enforced upon both our armies. North of Naples the Fifth Army met strong resistance along the river Volturno, which needed time and supplies to overcome. In the Eighth Army's advance up the toe of Italy General Montgomery had deliberately taken every administrative risk in order to reach the Salerno battlefield. His base had now to be moved from the toe at Reggio to the heel at Taranto and Bari. Until this was accomplished the Eighth Army had reached the end of its tether. Moreover, the capture of Foggia enabled a start to be made in occupying its airfields with heavy bombers. This was a massive task, requiring the carriage of many thousand tons of stores, and could be effected only by degrees. In mid-October the Germans had nineteen divisions in Italy, and the Allies the equivalent of thirteen. Large reinforcements and much consolidation were required to hold our rapid and brilliant conquests. All this put a strain on our shipping.

September had been indeed a fruitful month. Anglo-American inter-Service co-operation by land, sea, and air had reached a new record. The commander of the German Tenth Army in Italy has since stated that the harmonious co-operation between our Army, Air, and Naval forces under one supreme command was regarded by the Germans with envy. The Italian Fleet was in our hands; their Air Force and Army, though prevented by the Germans from joining us in useful numbers, were no longer ranged against us. The enemy had been defeated in pitched battle and our armies had bitten three hundred miles off Italy's boot. Behind them lay captured airfields and ports, ample, when developed, for our needs. Sardinia, so long thrust forward in Staff argument as the alternative to the assault on Italy, fell into our hands for nothing, as a mere bonus, on September 19, and Corsica was taken by French troops a fortnight later. The Italian enterprise, to launch which we had struggled so hard, had been vindicated beyond the hopes even of its most ardent and persistent advocates.

Great credit is due to General Eisenhower for his support of this brief and spirited campaign. Although the execution fell to Alexander, the Supreme Commander had really taken the British view of the strategy, and had been prepared to accept the ultimate responsibility for an enterprise the risks of which had been needlessly sharpened by his own military chiefs in their rigid adherence to the plans for Burma, and by their stern and strict priorities for "Overlord", which were carried in the secondary ranks to a veritable pedantry. There can be no doubt at all that Italy was the greatest prize open to us at this stage, and that a more generous provision for it could have been made without causing any delay to the main cross-Channel plan of 1944.

CHAPTER IX

A SPELL AT HOME

Report on the War to Parliament – Complaints of Delay – Agitations for a Second Front – Appraisal of the Action of the Italian Government – Application of Similar Principles to Germany – Nazi Tyranny and Prussian Militarism the Target – Warning about the Pilotless Aircraft Bombardment – Need to Rally the Italian Nation – Death of the Chancellor of the Exchequer, Sir Kingsley Wood – Sir John Anderson Succeeds Him – Death of Admiral Pound – The Anglo-Portuguese Treaty of 1373 and the Azores – Position in the Coal-mining Industry – The Rebuilding of the House of Commons – Two Essential Features of an Effective Chamber – My Memorandum on the Transition from War to Peace – Plans for the Transition Period – Appointment of Lord Woolton as Minister of Reconstruction.

DURING the homeward voyage I prepared a speech for Parliament upon my return. I was well aware of the criticism I should have to meet, and that the increasing success of the war would only make the disaffected elements in the House and in the Press feel more free to speak their minds.

On September 21, two days after landing, I accordingly made a report to the House of Commons, which occupied no less than two and a half hours. To avoid the Members tailing off for luncheon I asked for an hour's adjournment, which was accorded.

*　　*　　*

The first complaint was that much time had been lost in making the attack upon Naples by futile negotiations with the Italian Government. To this I could see I had a good answer.

I have seen it said that forty days of precious time were lost in these negotiations, and that in consequence British and American blood was needlessly shed around Salerno. This criticism is as ill-founded in fact as it is wounding to those who are bereaved. The time of our main attack upon Italy was fixed without the slightest reference to the attitude of the Italian Government, and the actual provisional date of the operation was settled long before any negotiations with them had taken place, and even before the fall of Mussolini. That date depended upon the time necessary to disengage our landing-craft from the beaches of Southern Sicily, across which up to the first week in August the major part of our armies actually engaged there had to be supplied from day to day. These landing-craft had then to be taken back to Africa. Those that had been damaged—and they were many—had to be repaired, and then reloaded with all their ammunition, etc., in the most exact and complex order before there could be any question of carrying out another amphibious operation.

I suppose it is realised that these matters have to be arranged in the most extraordinary detail. Every landing vessel or combat ship is packed in the exact order in which the troops landing from it will require the supplies when they land, so far as can be foreseen. Every lorry indeed is packed with precisely the articles which each unit will require when that lorry comes. Some of the lorries swim out to the ships and swim back. They are all packed exactly in series, with the things which have priority at the top and so on, so that nothing is left to chance that can be helped. Only in this way can these extraordinary operations be carried out in the face of the vast modern fire-power which a few men can bring to bear. The condition and preparation of the landing-craft were the sole but decisive limiting factors. It had nothing to do with "wasting time over the negotiations", nothing to do with the Foreign Office holding back the generals while they worried about this clause or that clause and so forth. There was never one moment's pause in the process of carrying out the military operations, and everything else had to fit in with that main-line traffic.

When I hear people talking in an airy way of throwing modern armies ashore here and there as if they were bales of goods to be dumped on a beach and forgotten I really marvel at the lack of knowledge which still prevails of the conditions of modern war. . . .

I must say, if I may make a momentary digression, that this class of criticism which I read in the newspapers when I arrived on Sunday morning reminds me of the simple tale about the sailor who jumped into a dock, I think it was at Plymouth, to rescue a small boy from drowning. About a week later this sailor was accosted by a woman, who asked, "Are you the man who picked my son out of the dock the other night?" The sailor replied modestly, "That is true, ma'am." "Ah," said the woman, "you are the man I am looking for. Where is his cap?"   ★   ★   ★

The second complaint was about the Second Front, for which the Communist elements and some others were steadily pressing.

I now tried to speak to the German High Command as well as the House of Commons, and at the same time to mislead the first and instruct the second.

I call this front we have opened, first in Africa, next in Sicily, and now in Italy, the Third Front. The Second Front, which already exists potentially and which is rapidly gathering weight, has not yet been engaged, but it is here, holding forces on its line. No one can tell—and certainly I am not going to hint—the moment when it will be engaged. But the Second Front exists, and is a main preoccupation already of the enemy. It has not yet opened or been thrown into play, but the time will come. At the right time this front will be thrown open, and the mass invasion from the West, in combination with the invasion from the South, will begin.

It is·quite impossible for those who do not know the facts and figures of the American assembly in Britain, or of our own powerful expeditionary armies now preparing here, who do not know the dispositions of the enemy on the various fronts, who cannot measure his reserves and resources and his power to transfer large forces from one front to another over the vast railway system of Europe, who do not know the state and dimensions of our Fleet and landing-craft of all kinds, to pronounce a useful opinion upon this operation.

[Here one of our two Communist Members interjected, "Does that apply to Marshal Stalin?"]

We should not in a matter of this kind take advice from British Communists, because we know that they stood aside and cared nothing for our fortunes in our time of mortal peril. Any advice that we take will be from friends and Allies who are all joined together in the common cause of winning the victory. The House may be absolutely certain that His Majesty's present Government will never be swayed or overborne by any uninstructed agitation, however natural, or any pressure, however well-meant, in matters of this kind. We shall not be forced or cajoled into undertaking vast operations of war against our better judgment in order to gain political unanimity or a cheer from any quarter. The bloodiest portion—make no mistake about it —of this war for Great Britain and the United States lies ahead of us. Neither the House nor the Government will shrink from that ordeal. We shall not grudge any sacrifice for the common cause.

* * *

The most difficult issue was the decision the President and I had taken, of which I was, as the reader has seen, a strong partisan, to deal with the King and Marshal Badoglio and recognise and treat them as co-belligerents. The same passions were aroused on this occasion in the same kind of people as on the Admiral Darlan affair the year before. I felt however on even stronger ground in this case.

We may pause for a moment to survey and appraise the act of the Italian Government, endorsed and acclaimed as it was by the Italian nation. Herr Hitler has left us in no doubt that he considers the conduct of Italy treacherous and base in the extreme—and he is a good judge in such matters. Others may hold that the act of treachery and in-gratitude took place when the Fascist confederacy, headed by Musso-lini, used its arbitrary power to strike for material gain at falling France and so became the enemy of the British Empire, which had for so many years cherished the cause of Italian liberty. There was the crime. Though it cannot be undone, and though nations which allow their rights and liberties to be subverted by tyrants must suffer heavy penalties for those tyrants' crimes, yet I cannot view the Italian action at this juncture as other than natural and human. May it prove to be the first of a series of acts of self-redemption.

The Italian people have already suffered terribly. Their manhood has been cast away in Africa and Russia, their soldiers have been deserted in the field, their wealth has been squandered, their empire has been irretrievably lost. Now their own beautiful homeland must become a battlefield for German rearguards. Even more suffering lies ahead. They are to be pillaged and terrorised in Hitler's fury and revenge. Nevertheless, as the armies of the British Empire and the United States march forward in Italy the Italian people will be rescued from their state of servitude and degradation, and be enabled in due course to regain their rightful place among the free democracies of the modern world.

I cannot touch upon this matter of Italy without exposing myself to the question, which I shall be most properly asked, "Would you apply this line of argument to the German people?" I say, "The case is different." Twice within our lifetime, and three times counting that of our fathers, they have plunged the world into their wars of expansion and aggression. They combine in the most deadly manner the qualities of the warrior and the slave. They do not value freedom themselves, and the spectacle of it in others is hateful to them. When-ever they become strong they seek their prey, and they will follow with an iron discipline anyone who will lead them to it. The core of Germany is Prussia. There is the source of the recurring pestilence. But we do not war with races as such. We war against tyranny, and we seek to preserve ourselves from destruction. I am convinced that the British, American, and Russian peoples, who have suffered measureless waste, peril, and bloodshed twice in a quarter of a century through the Teutonic urge for domination, will this time take steps to put it beyond the power of Prussia or of all Germany to come at them again with pent-up vengeance and long-nurtured plans. Nazi tyranny and Prussian militarism are the two main elements in German life which must be absolutely destroyed. They must be rooted out if Europe and the world are to be spared a third and still more frightful conflict.

The controversies about whether Burke was right or wrong when he said "I do not know the method of drawing up an indictment against a whole people" seem to me to be sterile and academic. Here are two obvious and practical targets for us to fire at—Nazi tyranny and Prussian militarism. Let us aim every gun and let us set every man who will march in motion against them. We must not add needlessly to the weight of our task or the burden that our soldiers bear. Satellite States, suborned or overawed, may perhaps, if they can help to shorten the war, be allowed to work their passage home. But the twin root of all our evils, Nazi tyranny and Prussian militarism, must be extirpated. Until this is achieved there are no sacrifices that we will not make and no lengths in violence to which we will not go. I will add this. Having, at the end of my life, acquired some influence on affairs, I wish to make it clear that I would not needlessly prolong this war for a single day; and my hope is that if and when British people are called by victory to share in the august responsibilities of shaping the future we shall show the same poise and temper as we did in the hour of our mortal peril.

$$\star \qquad \star \qquad \star$$

I had thought it right in the course of my speech to give at this time a serious and precise warning about the attack which was impending upon us by pilotless aircraft or rockets. It is always prudent to be on record publicly as having given warning long before the event. This is more particularly true when its scale and gravity cannot be measured.

We must not in any circumstances allow these favourable tendencies to weaken our efforts or lead us to suppose that our dangers are past or that the war is coming to an end. On the contrary, we must expect that the terrible foe we are smiting so heavily will make frenzied efforts to retaliate. The speeches of the German leaders, from Hitler downwards, contain mysterious allusions to new methods and new weapons which will presently be tried against us. It would of course be natural for the enemy to spread such rumours in order to encourage his own people, but there is probably more in it than that. For example, we now have experience of a new type of aerial bomb which the enemy has begun to use in attacks on our shipping, when at close quarters with the coast. This bomb, which may be described as a sort of rocket-assisted glider, is released from a considerable height, and is then apparently guided towards its target by the parent aircraft. It may be that the Germans are developing other weapons on novel lines with which they may hope to do us damage and to compensate to some extent for the injury which they are daily receiving from us. I can only assure the House that unceasing vigilance and the most intense study of which we are capable are given to the possibilities.

★ ★ ★

I also outlined my thought upon the political state of Italy, and upon the now cruel reality of civil war spreading in that unhappy country.

The escape of Mussolini to Germany, his rescue by paratroops, and his attempts to form a Quisling Government which, with German bayonets, will try to re-fix the Fascist yoke on the necks of the Italian people, raise of course the issue of Italian civil war. It is necessary in the general interest as well as in that of Italy that all surviving forces of Italian national life should be rallied together around their lawful Government, and that the King and Marshal Badoglio should be supported by whatever Liberal and Left Wing elements are capable of making head against the Fascist-Quisling combination, and thus of creating conditions which will help to drive this villainous combination from Italian soil, or, better still, annihilate it on the spot. We are coming to the rescue and liberation of Italy. [A Member interjected, "You will not get the Italian people to rise behind the banner of turncoats."] I think the hon. gentleman may be not thinking quite sufficiently of the importance of diminishing the burden which our soldiers have to bear. . . . The Government certainly intend to pursue a policy of engaging all the forces they can to make head against the Germans and drive them out of Italy. We are not going to be put off that action by any fear that perhaps we should not have complete unanimity on the subject. Parliament does not rest on unanimity; democratic assemblies do not act on unanimity. They act by majorities. That is the way they act. I wish to make it perfectly clear that we are endeavouring to rally the strongest forces together in Italy to make head against the Germans and the Mussolini-Quisling-Fascist combination.

My final words were somewhat unceremonious, but true:

The best method of acquiring flexibility is to have three or four plans for all the probable contingencies, all worked out with the utmost detail. Then it is much easier to switch from one to the other as and where the cat jumps.

These arguments convinced the House and there was no effective challenge.

★ ★ ★

On the same day that I finished this lengthy speech I and my colleagues suffered a very heavy and unexpected loss in the sudden death of the Chancellor of the Exchequer. I did not hear the news till I awoke on the morning of the 22nd. Kingsley Wood had become in later years a close personal friend of mine. After he went to the Air Ministry in 1938 we worked for the same objects. I gave him my full support, and undoubtedly he made an invaluable contribution to the readiness of the Royal Air Force to meet the mortal trial of 1940. He had been Chancellor of the Exchequer from the time I was called upon to form the National Government, and his record was a very fine one. His third Budget, balanced at five and three-quarter thousand millions, conformed to all the soundest principles of war-time finance. Half was raised by taxation. Our rate of borrowing was incredibly low. Instead of the slogan "Security and 6 per cent." of the First World War, we succeeded in borrowing enormous sums in the fifth year of this war at an average rate of 2 per cent. The cost of living had not risen by more than 30 per cent. over the pre-war level. The "Pay as you earn" principle had occupied the closing weeks of Kingsley Wood's life, and on the very day that he died he was looking forward to making a statement to the House on the subject. He had given effect, with high efficiency, to the request I made to him in 1940 to provide compensation for those whose homes and businesses were destroyed in the Blitz, by the elaborate insurance scheme which he devised. I spent the few hours that remained before the House met in preparing a tribute to him, which is on record.

In Sir John Anderson, at this time Lord President of the Council and chairman of our most important Cabinet Committee, and our chief representative on "Tube Alloys",★ I found a worthy successor. John Anderson had been Chairman of the Board of Inland Revenue, and also head of the Home Office for

★ Atom Bomb Research and Development.

ten years, but he had a far wider outlook than can be gained from any department. In the Irish troubles he had risked his life continually with the utmost composure, and this bearing was repeated when as Governor of Bengal an attempt was made to assassinate him. He had an acute and powerful mind, a firm spirit, and long experience of widely varied responsibilities. His appointment was announced on September 24.

*   *   *

Except for a few chats on the deck, I had seen little of Sir Dudley Pound on our homeward voyage, as he kept to his cabin. On the train journey to London he sent me a letter formally resigning his office of First Sea Lord, of the burden of which I had relieved him when his illness became pronounced in Washington. The question of his successor required careful consideration. Admiral Sir Andrew Cunningham was an obvious choice, proposed by the First Lord, Mr. Alexander, on account of the reputation which he had won in all the fighting in the Mediterranean. Could he, on the other hand, be spared from this scene at a time when so much was going forward and all operations expanding? In Admiral Fraser, then commanding the Home Fleet, we had an officer of the highest seagoing reputation, who had also long experience of Admiralty administration and staff work. It was to him I first offered the post. The Admiral said that of course he would serve wherever he was sent, but that he thought Andrew Cunningham was the right man. "I believe I have the confidence of my own fleet," he said. "Cunningham has that of the whole Navy." He asked me to weigh the matter longer. I replied that his attitude was most becoming, and after further thought and consultation I took him at his word and decided to face the serious change in the Mediterranean fighting command. Admiral Andrew Cunningham was therefore chosen. His second-in-command, Admiral John Cunningham, took his place. The changes were announced to the public and the Service, who knew nothing of Pound's illness, on October 4, when I published the following letter to Sir Dudley Pound:

I am sorry indeed that you have felt it necessary to lay down your charge on account of your health, and that our four years' work together in this war must come to an end. No one knows better than I the quality of your contribution at the Admiralty and on the Chiefs of Staff Committee to the safety of the country and the success of our arms. Your vast and precise knowledge of the sea war in all its aspects, your fortitude in times of anxiety and misfortune, your resourcefulness and readiness to run the risks without which victory can never be won, have combined to make your tenure as First Sea Lord memorable in the records of the Royal Navy.

You leave us at a moment when the control of the Mediterranean is virtually within our grasp, when the Italian Fleet has made its surrender in Malta harbour, and when, above all, the U-boat peril has been broken in a degree never before seen in this war. These results have been of measureless value to your country, and your notable share in them sheds lustre on your name.

Pound lived for little more than a fortnight. He became completely paralysed by another more severe stroke. The last time I saw him, though his mind was as good as ever, he could neither speak nor move the greater part of his body. When I shook his left hand on parting he gripped me with a most surprising strength. He had been a true comrade to me, both at the Admiralty and on the Chiefs of Staff Committee. He died on October 21, Trafalgar Day.

Admiral Fraser went back to his fleet at Scapa. At the end of the year he had the distinction of fighting in his own flagship and sinking the *Scharnhorst* in a direct encounter. This was a naval episode of high honour and importance. When I next saw him in London I reminded him of the famous lines:

> Not once or twice in our rough island-story
> The path of duty was the way to glory.

The Admiral seemed all the more pleased because, as I judged, he had never heard the quotation before. I hoped he thought I had made it up myself on purpose.

* * *

I have not burdened this account with the lengthy correspondence with the United States and Portugal which led to our agreement about the use by British and American flotillas and air forces of the extremely important key islands of the Azores. Everything was settled in a satisfactory manner, so that on October 12 I could report our conclusions to Parliament. "I have an announcement" I said, "to make to the House arising out of the treaty signed between this country and Portugal in the year

The Battle of Italy

19 The landings South of Rome.
20 Under enemy fire.

21 Fording a river under fire.
22 British soldiers crouching in a bomb crater before the assault; burning fuel
   stores can be seen in front of them.

23 In the villages, each house contains an enemy soldier.
24 German soldiers at the Nettuno front.

25 German prisoners.
26 American prisoners.

1373 between His Majesty King Edward III and King Ferdinand and Queen Eleanor of Portugal." I spoke in a level voice, and made a pause to allow the House to take in the date, 1373. As this soaked in there was something like a gasp. I do not suppose any such continuity of relations between two Powers has ever been, or will ever be, set forth in the ordinary day-to-day work of British diplomacy.

"This treaty," I went on,

was reinforced in various forms by treaties of 1386, 1643, 1654, 1660, 1661, 1703, and 1815, and in a secret declaration of 1899. In more modern times the validity of the Old Treaties was recognised in the Treaties of Arbitration concluded with Portugal in 1904 and 1914. Article I of the treaty of 1373 runs as follows:

"In the first place we settle and covenant that there shall be from this day forward . . . true, faithful, constant, mutual, and perpetual friendships, unions, alliances, and deeds of sincere affection, and that as true and faithful friends we shall henceforth, reciprocally, be friends to friends and enemies to enemies, and shall assist, maintain, and uphold each other mutually, by sea and by land, against all men that may live or die."

This engagement has lasted now for nearly six hundred years, and is without parallel in world history. I have now to announce its latest application. At the outset of the war the Portuguese Government, in full agreement with His Majesty's Government in the United Kingdom, adopted a policy of neutrality with a view to preventing the war spreading into the Iberian peninsula. The Portuguese Government have repeatedly stated, most recently in Dr. Salazar's speech of April 27, that the above policy is in no way inconsistent with the Anglo-Portuguese Alliance, which was reaffirmed by the Portuguese Government in the early days of the war.

His Majesty's Government in the United Kingdom, basing themselves upon this ancient alliance, have now requested the Portuguese Government to accord them certain facilities in the Azores which will enable better protection to be provided for merchant shipping in the Atlantic. The Portuguese Government have agreed to grant this request, and arrangements, which enter into force immediately, have been concluded between the two Governments regarding (1) the conditions governing the use of the above facilities by His Majesty's Government in the United Kingdom and (2) British assistance in furnishing essential material and supplies to the Portuguese armed forces and the maintenance of the Portuguese national economy. The agreement concerning the use of facilities in the Azores is of a

ITALY WON

temporary nature only, and in no way prejudices the maintenance of Portuguese sovereignty over Portuguese territory.

* * *

The next day I had to make a long speech to the House on the coal-mining situation, which was affected by the vital need of coal and the claims of the fighting forces for man-power, and also by the underlying threat of the nationalisation of the coal-mines, which was a suspended issue between the parties. There had been a lot of rumblings on this point, and I was concerned only with the maintenance of national unity.

I thought it might help if I reminded the House at the outset of this discussion of the general foundations upon which we stand at the present time. We have a National Coalition Government, which came together to try to pull the nation out of the forlorn and sombre plight into which the action, or inaction, of all political parties over a long period of years had landed it. I stand very well placed in that matter, having been out for eleven years. What holds us together is the prosecution of the war. No Socialist or Liberal or Labour man has been in any way asked to give up his convictions. That would be indecent and improper. We are held together by something outside, which rivets all our attention. The principle that we work on is, "Everything for the war, whether controversial or not, and nothing controversial that is not bona fide needed for the war." That is our position.

We must also be careful that a pretext is not made of war needs to introduce far-reaching social or political changes by a side-wind. Take the question of nationalising the coal-mines. Those words do not terrify me at all. I advocated nationalisation of the railways after the last war, but I am bound to say that I was a bit affected by the experience of the national control of the railways after the war, which led to the public getting a very bad service, to the shareholders having very unsatisfactory returns, and to one of the most vicious and hazardous strikes with which I have ever been concerned. However, as I say, the principle of nationalisation is accepted by all, provided proper compensation is paid. The argument proceeds not on moral grounds, but on whether in fact we could make a more fertile business for the nation as a whole by nationalisation than by relying on private enterprise and competition. It would raise a lot of difference of opinion and be a tremendous business to nationalise the coal-mines, and unless it could be proved to the conviction of the House and of the country and to the satisfaction of the responsible Ministers that that was the only way in which we could win the war we should not be justified

148

in embarking upon it without a General Election. It would be very
difficult to have a General Election at the present time. . . .

I am told and can well realise that anxiety exists among the miners
about what is to happen to them and their industry after the war.
They had a very grim experience after the last war, which went on
biting away at them for a long period and greatly affected the whole
conception that they had of mining as a means of getting their living.
I know that there is anxiety. We can all lie awake thinking of the
nightmares that we are going to suffer after the war is over, and everyone has his perplexities and anxieties about that time. But I for one,
being an optimist, do not think peace is going to be so bad as war, and
I hope we shall not try to make it as bad. After the last war, which I
lived through in a responsible position, nearly everyone behaved as
badly as they could, and the country was at times almost uncontrol-
lable. We have profited a great deal in this war by the experience of
the last. We make war much better than we did, owing to previous
experience. We are also going to try to profit to the full by the hard
experience of what happened in the last peace. I am casting no reflection on the Government of that day when I say that, armed with their
dear-bought experience, we shall make the transition from war to
peace in a more orderly and disciplined fashion than we did last time.

But the miners are worried about their future. His Majesty's
Government give the assurance to them that the present system of
control, plus any improvements that may be made to it, will be
continued after the war until Parliament shall decide upon the future
structure of the industry. That means either that there will be a settlement by agreement between the great parties, or that there will be a
General Election at which the people will be free to choose between
political doctrines and political leaders. But anyhow, until all that is
over there will be no decisive change in the present structure of the
coal industry, or any removal of the many guarantees for the continuity of employment and wages and limitation of profits which are
embodied in it. I am so anxious that we should all be together in this.

This statement eased the tension which existed, and I am glad
to-day to read it over again.

*   *   *

Finally, on October 28 there was the rebuilding of the House
of Commons to consider. One unlucky bomb had blown to
fragments the Chamber in which I had passed so much of my life.
I was determined to have it rebuilt at the earliest moment that
our struggle would allow. I had the power at this moment
to shape things in a way that would last. Supported by my

colleagues, mostly old Parliamentarians, and with Mr. Attlee's cordial aid, I sought to re-establish for what may well be a long period the two great principles on which the British House of Commons stands in its physical aspect. The first is that it must be oblong, and not semicircular, and the second that it must only be big enough to give seats to about two-thirds of its Members. As this argument has long surprised foreigners, I record it here.

There are two main characteristics of the House of Commons which will command the approval and the support of reflective and experienced Members. The first is that its shape should be oblong and not semicircular. Here is a very potent factor in our political life. The semicircular assembly, which appeals to political theorists, enables every individual or every group to move round the centre, adopting various shades of pink according as the weather changes. I am a convinced supporter of the party system in preference to the group system. I have seen many earnest and ardent Parliaments destroyed by the group system. The party system is much favoured by the oblong form of chamber. It is easy for an individual to move through those insensible gradations from Left to Right, but the act of crossing the Floor is one which requires serious consideration. I am well informed on this matter, for I have accomplished that difficult process, not only once, but twice. Logic is a poor guide compared with custom. Logic, which has created in so many countries semicircular assemblies with buildings that give to every member not only a seat to sit in, but often a desk to write at, with a lid to bang, has proved fatal to Parliamentary government as we know it here in its home and in the land of its birth.

The second characteristic of a chamber formed on the lines of the House of Commons is that it should *not* be big enough to contain all its members at once without overcrowding, and that there should be no question of every member having a separate seat reserved for him. The reason for this has long been a puzzle to uninstructed outsiders, and has frequently excited the curiosity and even the criticism of new Members. Yet it is not so difficult to understand if you look at it from a practical point of view. If the House is big enough to contain all its members nine-tenths of its debates will be conducted in the depressing atmosphere of an almost empty or half-empty chamber. The essence of good House of Commons speaking is the conversational style, the facility for quick, informal interruptions and interchanges. Harangues from a rostrum would be a bad substitute for the conversational style in which so much of our business is done. But the conversational style requires a fairly small space, and there should be on great occasions a sense of crowd and urgency. There should be a sense of the importance of much that is said, and a sense that great matters are being decided, there and then, by the House.

This anyhow was settled as I wished.

★ ★ ★

During these busy days I thought it right, now that our ultimate victory appeared certain, to dwell upon what would descend upon us at the same time as victory. This chapter may well close with the two notes I wrote to my colleagues upon these problems, already looming ahead.

WAR—TRANSITION—PEACE

MEMORANDUM BY THE PRIME MINISTER AND MINISTER OF DEFENCE

19 Oct 43

It is the duty of His Majesty's Government to prepare for the tasks which will fall upon us at the end of the war. The urgent needs are:

- (a) A sound scheme of demobilisation, having regard to the undoubted need of our keeping considerable garrisons in enemy-occupied territory.
- (b) The provision of food for our island on a scale better than the war-time rations.
- (c) The resumption of the export trade and the restoration of our Mercantile Marine.
- (d) The general turn-over of industry from war to peace.

   And, above all,

- (e) The provision during a transition period of employment for all able-bodied persons seeking it, and especially for the ex-Service-men.

Any decisions which are needed for the supreme objects of *food* and *employment* in the years immediately after the war must be taken now, whether they involve legislation and whether they are controversial or not.

2. Much work has already been done on these lines by the departments and committees concerned. We must be careful not to have these urgent practical duties confused and overlaid by party politics or held up by endless discussions about long-term schemes for building a new world order, etc.

3. There are in fact three stages, namely,

- (i) War,
- (ii) Transition, and
- (iii) Peace and freedom.

The present Government and Parliament are fully entitled to make all necessary preparations for the transition period, and we should be held severely accountable if found in default. As early as possible in the transition period (for which all preparations will have been made) a General Election must be held, in order that the electors may express their will upon the form that is to be given to our post-war and post-transition society.

4. We do not know whether this election will be fought on an agreed programme by the parties now composing the Coalition Government or whether the leader of the majority in the present House of Commons will be forced to place his own programme before the electors. In either case it is probable that a Four Years Plan will be announced, which, apart from carrying out the enormous administrative measures required in the transition period, will also comprise a series of large decisions on progress and reform which will, from one angle or the other, shape the post-war and post-transition period. There will therefore be no lack of work for the new Parliament.

5. In the meanwhile there are a number of important policies, such as education, social insurance, the rebuilding of our shattered dwellings and cities, on which there is or may be found a wide measure of general agreement. These steps must be brought to a high degree of preparation now during the war, any necessary preliminary legislation being passed, so that they are ready to come into force in the early days of the transition period.

6. It is impossible to tell how long the war against Japan will out-last the war against Germany. It would perhaps be safe, as a working basis, to make the transition period last for two years after the defeat of Germany, or four years from January 1, 1944, whichever period shall end the sooner.

★   ★   ★

A month later I decided upon the appointment of a Minister of Reconstruction, whose office would be the focal point for all plans for the transitional period. Lord Woolton's conduct of the Food Ministry had gained widespread satisfaction and general confidence. He seemed in every way equipped with the qualities and experience to concert and stimulate the activities of the many departments concerned. He took up his duties on November 12.

CHAPTER X

TENSIONS WITH GENERAL DE GAULLE

*Upsurge of the de Gaullist Movement – French Committee of National
Liberation Set Up – The Question of Recognition of the Committee –
President Roosevelt on the Situation – My Memorandum of July 13 –
I Try to Persuade the President to Accord Limited Recognition – He
Suggests Instead a Formula of Co-operation – We Debate the Position
at Quebec – Qualified Recognition is Given – The Struggle for Power
Between de Gaulle and Giraud Continues – Formation of a Free French
Consultative Assembly – De Gaulle Becomes Sole President of the
French National Committee – Violent Action in Syria – A Year of
Disappointing Relationships with the Free French.*

URING the summer of 1943 the relations of the British
Government with de Gaulle deteriorated. We had made
great efforts to bring together Frenchmen of all parties at
Algiers, and I had constantly pressed the Americans to accept
General de Gaulle as a leading figure in the political arrangements which we were both trying to facilitate. In the strained
atmosphere which pervaded French affairs after the signature of
the Clark-Darlan agreements and the appearance of Giraud de
Gaulle became more than ever intractable. His position had
strengthened in recent weeks. He had many supporters in
Tunisia, which was now in Allied hands. News from Metropolitan France, together with the creation of the clandestine Central
Committee there, showed the extent of his prestige and an upsurge of the de Gaullist movement. It was in these circumstances
that Giraud agreed to meet his rival in North Africa.

On May 30 de Gaulle arrived in Algiers, and sharp and sulky
negotiations were begun with the object of setting up a united
Provisional Committee to administer the affairs of Fighting
France. Wrangling centred round three main issues: Giraud's

assumption of supreme civil and military authority; de Gaulle's determination to affirm formally the sovereignty of Fighting France—a step which would violate the letter of the agreements which Darlan had made with General Mark Clark in November 1942; and the question of the former Vichy administrators now in key offices in North Africa, particularly Noguès, Peyrouton, and Boisson. The last-named was a special target. De Gaulle had never forgiven him for the events of 1940 at Dakar.

Tension mounted in Algiers as these bitter discussions were prolonged. On the afternoon of June 3 however agreement was reached, and a French Committee of National Liberation was set up, which included Giraud and de Gaulle, Generals Catroux and Georges, and certain members of the Gaullist Committee from London, which had been dissolved when de Gaulle left for North Africa. The former Vichy governors were excluded from the new body, which was now to be the central provisional administration of Fighting France and her Empire until the end of the war.

* * *

The reader will recall that I was in North Africa with General Marshall for conferences with General Eisenhower during these talks on the future of France, and just before my departure I had invited the new Committee to luncheon. When I got back to London I received a telegram from the President voicing his anxiety. "I want to give you," he said on June 5, "the thought that North Africa is in last analysis under British-American military rule, and that for this reason Eisenhower can be used on what you and I want. The bride evidently forgets that there is still a war in progress over here. We receive only the bride's publicity. What is the matter with our British-American information services? Best of luck in getting rid of our mutual headache."

I sent to the President in reply my impressions of Algiers.

Former Naval Person to President Roosevelt   6 June 43

We had the whole French Committee to luncheon on Friday (June 4), and everybody seemed most friendly. General Georges, whom I got out of France a month ago, and who is a personal friend of mine, is a great support to Giraud. If de Gaulle should prove violent or unreasonable he will be in a minority of five to two, and possibly completely isolated. The Committee is therefore a body with collective authority with which in my opinion we can safely work.

2. I consider that the formation of this Committee brings to an end my official connection with de Gaulle as leader of the Fighting French, which was set out in the letters exchanged with him in 1940 and certain other documents of later date, and I propose, in so far as is necessary, to transfer these relationships, financial and otherwise, to the Committee as a whole. While I consider the Committee is a safe repository for arms and supplies, I feel that we should see how they conduct their business and themselves before deciding what degree of recognition we should give them as representing France. Macmillan and Murphy are working in the closest accord, and will keep Eisenhower, with whom the supreme and ultimate power rests, fully informed.

3. I should be strongly opposed to Boisson being dismissed from his post.

★   ★   ★

But the wrangling did not cease. De Gaulle would not accept Giraud as Supreme Commander of the French forces. Giraud was anxious to keep the French Army of North Africa intact and clear of Free French influences. This attitude of de Gaulle on the question of military command exacerbated American dislike and distrust of him.

The President again telegraphed to me:

President Roosevelt to Prime Minister   10 June 43
I have just received the following message from Murphy:
"I was told this afternoon by Giraud that de Gaulle during this morning's session of the French Committee finally brought into the open his wish to act as Commissioner for National Defence, having the attributes of a Minister of War in the ordinary Cabinet set-up. He also demanded the command of French forces not actively engaged in operations, which is contrary to what he has told Eisenhower, Macmillan, and me with respect to his intentions. Giraud absolutely refused to yield command of French forces. He insisted that General Georges be appointed Commissioner for National Defence. A compromise proposal submitted by Catroux very much favoured de Gaulle's proposition. Giraud told me of his determination to retire if the Committee outvoted him on this question, and to inform the British and American Governments and the French people of the injustice caused by de Gaulle's ambition. I have asked Giraud to delay any such action until there has been an opportunity to discuss this question with several members of the Committee."

Macmillan had reported to me in the same sense. I was only anxious that a straightforward agreement should be reached.

Prime Minister to Mr. Harold Macmillan (Algiers)　　　　11 June 43

There can be no question of our giving recognition until we know what it is we have to recognise. See St. Matthew, chapter vii, verse 16: "Ye shall know them by their fruits. Do men gather grapes of thorns, or figs of thistles?" Indeed, the whole chapter is instructive.

You are quite right to play for time and let de Gaulle have every chance to come to his senses and realise the forces around him. We play fair with him if he plays fair with us and with France.

The President was less patient.

President Roosevelt to Prime Minister　　　　17 June 43

The following is a paraphrase of a cable I have to-day sent to General Eisenhower:

"The position of this Government is that during our military occupation of North Africa we will not tolerate the control of the French Army by any agency which is not subject to the Allied Supreme Commander's direction. We must have someone whom we completely and wholly trust. We would under no circumstances continue the arming of a force without being completely confident in their willingness to co-operate in our military operations. We are not interested moreover in the formation of any Government or Committee which presumes in any way to indicate that, until such time as the French people select a Government for themselves, it will govern in France. When we get into France the Allies will have a civil Government plan that is completely in consonance with French sovereignty. Lastly, it must be absolutely clear that in North and West Africa we have a military occupation, and therefore without your full approval no independent civil decision can be made. . . ."

*　　*　　*

These telegrams from the President revealed such a mounting hostility to de Gaulle's actions in Algiers that I feared for the whole future of Allied relations with the Free French. The Americans reached the point where they might refuse to recognise any provisional administrative body if they thought that de Gaulle would be the dominating influence which would affect the future of France after the war. It was essential to allay American fears on the military question and at the same time to keep in being the new Provisional Committee.

Former Naval Person to President Roosevelt 18 June 43

... I am not in favour at this moment of breaking up the Committee of Seven or forbidding it to meet. I should prefer that General Eisenhower should take your instructions as his directive, and that Murphy and Macmillan should work towards its fulfilment by whatever means they find most appropriate. His Majesty's Government will associate themselves with this policy.

The Committee will then be confronted with a choice of either accepting our decision by a majority or placing themselves in definite opposition to the two rescuing Powers. If, as seems probable, they accept the decision by a majority, it will be for de Gaulle to decide whether he and other dissentients will submit or resign. If de Gaulle resigns he will put himself in the wrong with public opinion, and the necessary measures must be taken to prevent him from creating a disturbance. If he submits we shall probably have further trouble in the future, but this will be better than our sweeping away a Committee on which many hopes are founded among the United Nations as well as in France. We should prescribe the conditions essential for the safety of our forces and place the onus on de Gaulle. At any rate, it would be wise to try this first.

★　　★　　★

The American attitude to the French political scene in North Africa was in part dominated by military necessity. The background to the dispute over de Gaulle was the preparation of the Sicily landings. The quarrels over the French High Command, provoked by de Gaulle, had come at the critical moment. Whatever past arrangements had existed between the British Government and de Gaulle, they could not be allowed to impair our relations with the United States.

On July 13 I had written a paper for my colleagues summarising these developments in American policy towards France, in which I stated:

It has for a good many months past been our object to bring about a union between the French elements cultivated by the Americans in North-West Africa and the French National Committee in London, and particularly between Generals Giraud and de Gaulle. I could, I think, have made a good arrangement at Casablanca, but, as my colleagues know, this was frustrated by the preposterous conduct of General de Gaulle. Since then the President has armed General Giraud's troops in North Africa on a very considerable scale, and he is now much concerned about the demeanour and control of this army.

157

Meanwhile the de Gaullist organs in London and at Brazzaville, with their backers in the British and American Press, have ceaselessly criticised American policy, and there is no doubt that not only Mr. Hull but the President have become bitterly antagonised thereby.

For all these reasons we have hoped that the personality of de Gaulle should be merged first in the National Committee in London, and, now that juncture has been effected with the Algiers elements, in the Committee of National Liberation. After some crises and spasms this Committee is gradually acquiring a collective character, especially now that the civilian elements are increasing and asserting themselves. The lines of cleavage are no longer defined by the partisans of Giraud or of de Gaulle. These healthy tendencies should be allowed to develop, and if it should become clear in the course of the next few months that de Gaulle and his faction are not the masters of the Liberation Committee, and that he himself has settled down to honest teamwork within its ranks, it might be possible to procure from the President some kind of recognition of the Committee. This result will not however be easily or swiftly obtained, and we have to consider what our course should be in the meanwhile.

When the Liberation Committee was formed I made haste to transfer to it the engagements previously made with General de Gaulle. This process must continue, as otherwise we should have no one to deal with about finance, propaganda, Syria and other French possessions, and the control of the French armed forces. The Foreign Secretary has pointed out to me that we passed an Act of Parliament investing de Gaulle with powers of discipline over the Free French forces in British territory, and certainly these powers must now be vested in the new Committee. There is no objection to dealing with the Committee in its collective capacity as the *de facto* authority. Transacting necessary business with them can only do them good, and, if they are worthy of their responsibilities, will add to their strength.

In a certain sense this implies recognition of the Committee, but it will only be making unnecessary trouble with the United States to emphasise this point or do anything of a *de jure* character at the present stage. We should avoid the use of the word "recognition", and avoid also anything in the nature of a splash or a gesture, while at the same time working with them, for what they are worth, from day to day. It is the duty of the Committee and also in their interest to regain or build up the wounded confidence of the Rescuing Powers, and in particular the estranged United States Government. If we were to take any step of formally recognising the Committee at this juncture, this would give the very greatest offence in Washington. It would draw upon the Administration there the hostile criticism of all who are attempting to oust the President at next year's election. The whole course of the war depends upon our cordial relations with the American Government and President, and we owe it to our troops in the field not to make their task harder by taking any step which would lead to a serious decline in the present very remarkable co-operation. Even if Soviet Russia recognises de Gaulle on account of his recent flirtations with Communist elements, we should still be wise to measure our course by that of the United States. Indeed, in this case it would be still more important not to leave them isolated and give the appearance of working with Russia against them. . . .

I have repeatedly stated that it is in the major interests of Great Britain to have a strong France after the war, and I should not hesitate to sustain this view. I am afraid lest the anti-de Gaullism of the Washington Government may harden into a definite anti-France feeling. If however de Gaulle is gradually merged and submerged into the Committee, and the Committee comports itself in a reasonable and loyal manner, this dangerous tendency on the part of the United States may be deflected and assuaged.

There is no harm in the French Committee coming to feel that we should like to put them into better relations with the United States. It may still be possible to gain for France and the French Empire a recognised place in the councils of the Allies, if the healthy and helpful processes I have noted are allowed to take their course, and if we act with patience, and above all with a sense of proportion, in these vexatious matters.

★   ★   ★

Opinion in our Cabinet circle moved steadily towards some form of recognition, and I sent a further telegram to the President.

Former Naval Person to President Roosevelt   21 July 43

I am under considerable pressure from the Foreign Office, from my Cabinet colleagues, and also from the force of circumstances, to "recognise" the Committee of National Liberation in Algiers. What does recognition mean? One can recognise a man as an Emperor or as a grocer. Recognition is meaningless without a defining formula. Until de Gaulle went to North-West Africa and the new Committee was formed all our relations were with him and his Committee. I stated to Parliament on June 8 that "The formation of this Committee with its collective responsibility supersedes the situation created by the correspondence between General de Gaulle and myself in 1940. Our dealings, financial and otherwise, will henceforward be with the Committee as a whole". I was glad to do this because I would rather deal with the Committee collectively than with de Gaulle alone. I had in fact for many months been working to induce or compel de Gaulle to "Put himself in commission". This seemed to be largely achieved by the new arrangement. Macmillan tells us repeatedly that the Committee is acquiring a collective authority and that de Gaulle is by no means its master. He tells us further that if the Committee breaks down, as it may do if left utterly without support, de Gaulle will become once again the sole personality in control of everything except the powers exercised by Giraud under the armed force of the United States in North-West Africa and Dakar. He strongly recommends a measure of recognition. He reports that Eisenhower and Murphy both agree with this. . . .

I am therefore reaching the point where it may be necessary for me to take this step so far as Great Britain and the Anglo-French interests set out above are concerned. If I do, Russia will certainly recognise [them], and I fear lest this might be embarrassing to you.

I do hope therefore that you will let me know (a) whether you could subscribe to our formula or something like it, or (b) whether you would mind if His Majesty's Government took that step separately themselves. There is no doubt whatever in my mind that the former would be far the better. There are a lot of good men on the Committee—Catroux, Massigli, Monnet, Georges, and of course Giraud, who arrived here yesterday. He will certainly raise all this and bring it to a head.

But it was clear that the Americans were not prepared to recognise the Algiers Committee as now constituted. Giraud was now in the United States negotiating for the supply of arms and equipment for the French army in North Africa. His presence there did not smooth the temper of the de Gaullists.

On July 22 I received a long and important telegram from the President setting forth the considered view of his Government on French affairs.

President Roosevelt to Prime Minister   22 July 43
Various sources continue, though with less pressure, to ask recognition of the existing French Committee of National Liberation. Some people want to recognise it as the organisation acting for French interests in all French territory, including France. Other people want to recognise it as acting for French interests only in former French Empire. Most, not all, are willing to accept the Committee's authority, subject to the military requirements of the British and American forces.

We have been saying, first, that the military requirements are and will be paramount to all civil matters; second, that the French Committee of National Liberation has only begun to function, and should give further and more satisfactory evidence of the complete and genuine unity of the Committee. This unity must eliminate hitherto French political or factional controversies designed to promote either group antagonisms or individual aspirations, and demonstrate a real purpose to unify itself and, behind it, all Frenchmen in support of the co-operative efforts of the United Nations in the prosecution of the war against the Axis Powers, having in mind its single cause of the liberation of France and the success of the United Nations.

The French Committee was supposedly conceived on the principle of collective responsibility of individual Frenchmen for the prosecution of the war, and our relations with it should be kept on this basis, it being understood that as to matters of a military character the two Governments will deal directly with the French Commander-in-Chief of the French forces. French political questions must be left to solution by the people of France when they have been freed from the present domination of the enemy. . . .

This Government is most anxious to join with you and the other United Nations to move along the line of limited acceptance of the Committee, subject always to military requirements, but we should make it clear that the plain conditions of French unity must be properly met.

I do not think we should at any time use the word "recognition", because this would be distorted to imply that we recognise the Committee as the Government of France as soon as we land on French soil. Perhaps the word "acceptance" of the Committee's local civil authority in various colonies on a temporary basis comes nearer to expressing my thought. We must however retain the right and continue the present practice of dealing directly with local French officials in the colonies whenever military advantage to the Allied cause so dictates. Martinique is an illustrative example.

Giraud's visit here was very successful. We kept it on a purely military basis, and we are starting immediately to send additional equipment for his army with every North African convoy. . . .

Roosevelt ended by suggesting a joint formula based on "co-operation with" instead of "recognition of" the French Committee.

I replied to the President's telegram of July 22:

Former Naval Person to President Roosevelt   3 Aug 43
I thought first that your proposed formula was rather chilling and would not end the agitation there is for recognition in both our countries. Meanwhile events have moved in our favour. The

Committee have felt acutely being ignored while the whole Italian problem is open. De Gaulle, I feel, is now more enclosed in the general body of the Committee. The arrangements for command also seem more satisfactory to us than the previous deadlock.

2. I have therefore asked the Foreign Office to suggest a certain modification in your formula designed to bring our two views into harmony. . . . If we cannot agree we will talk it over.

The Quebec Conference already described was now imminent. Meanwhile we had reached a deadlock.

President Roosevelt to Prime Minister   4 Aug 43
I earnestly hope that nothing will be done in the matter of recognition of the Committee of National Liberation until we have an opportunity to talk it over together.

★ ★ ★

It was only after stubborn talks that I was able to persuade the Americans to make a declaration in general terms supporting the political arrangements which had already taken shape in North Africa.

Prime Minister (Quebec) to Mr. Macmillan (Algiers)   25 Aug 43
After prolonged discussions of a laborious character we reached what I trust will be considered a series of satisfactory solutions about recognition. We thought it better that we should all express our thought in our own words rather than persevere in a joint declaration by the United States and United Kingdom.

2. In my opinion the President and Mr. Hull have gone a long way to meet our desires. You should tell my friends on the Committee that I am sure the right course for them is to welcome the American declaration in most cordial terms, and not to draw invidious distinctions between any of the forms in which recognition is accorded. On the contrary, the more pleasure they show at the American declaration the more value it will have for them. This is a moment when a friendly attitude towards the United States would be singularly helpful to the interests of France. If, on the other hand, newspaper or radio polemics and reproaches are indulged in the only effect will be to rouse new flames of resentment in the State Department.

★ ★ ★

The announcement of the recognition of the French National Committee on the following day marked the end of a period, and though the French leaders were not brought into the armistice negotiations with Italy, nor into the Mediterranean Commission which was subsequently set up to deal with Italian affairs, they were now on formal terms with the Allies as the representatives of France.

*   *   *

The struggle for power between de Gaulle and Giraud went on unabated as the weeks passed, and frequent clashes took place over both civil and military appointments. The fault did not lie always with de Gaulle, and there were unnecessary incidents over the liberation of Corsica, where Free French elements on the island had occupied Ajaccio on the night of September 9. Giraud ordered a French expedition to Corsica two days later, and the unfortunate disputes between his military commander and the de Gaullist leaders on the spot still further worsened relations. The liberation of the island, from the military point of view, was slowly but successfully accomplished.

Prime Minister to Mr. Harold Macmillan (Algiers)   3 Oct 43
If you think well, you should give the following message from me to Generals Giraud and de Gaulle:
"Many congratulations on the successful progress of your troops in Corsica. I look forward intensely to this famous island soon being liberated and restored to France."

The occupation of the island by French forces was completed on the following day.

*   *   *

Plans for summoning a provisional Consultative Assembly to broaden the basis of French administration advanced during the month of October. Giraud's position steadily weakened. The only support he possessed lay in certain Army circles who valued American goodwill, and in his rôle of co-President of the National Committee this was fast disappearing. De Gaulle showed himself incomparably the more powerful personality. On November 3 the Assembly met for the first time in Algiers. French political life was crystallising into an embryo Government for the future. On November 8, one year exactly after the North African landings, Giraud resigned from the National Committee, but remained Commander-in-Chief of the French forces. I was disturbed at the possible consequences of these events. It was essential for the future unity of France that some balance of power between these divergent elements should be reached.

I therefore telegraphed to the President:

Prime Minister to President Roosevelt   10 Nov 43
I am not at all content with the changes in the French National
Committee which leave de Gaulle sole President. The body we
recognised was of a totally different character, the essence being the
co-Presidency of Giraud and de Gaulle. I suggest we maintain an
attitude of complete reserve until we can discuss the position together.

I hoped on my way through to Cairo to the Teheran Conference to bring the rival Generals together myself at a review of
the new French Army.

Prime Minister to Mr. Macmillan (Algiers)   2 Nov 43
In case I am able to find a few days in Africa between now and
Christmas, I should like to see something of the new French Army.
You might ascertain discreetly from both Generals de Gaulle and
Giraud whether this would be agreeable to them. We might have an
afternoon parade, spend the night somewhere, and see some exercises
in the morning. In these circumstances I should like to be the guest of
the French National Committee. It occurred to me they might take
this as a compliment, which it is intended to be. I cannot fix dates at
the present time, for many obvious reasons.

★   ★   ★

My intention was frustrated by the rough and tragic behaviour
of the Free French Administration in Syria. The formal independence of Syria and the Lebanon had been proclaimed by the Free
French at the end of 1941. We had recognised these republics,
and Sir Edward Spears had been sent as British Minister in
February 1942. Throughout the year however no progress was
made. Changes of Ministry took place in both countries, but no
elections were held. Anti-French antagonisms grew. Provisional
Governments were appointed in March 1943. The elections in
July and August resulted in an overwhelming Nationalist expression in both republics. The majorities demanded the complete
revision of the mandatory constitution. The weakness of the
Free French Administration led the local politicians, who had
little faith in French promises of after-war independence, to strike.
On October 7 the Lebanese Government proposed to abolish the
French position in the republic. A month later the Free French
Committee in Algiers challenged the right of the Lebanese to act
in this one-sided manner. M. Helleu, General Catroux's deputy,

returned from Algiers to give orders for the arrest of the Lebanese President and most of the Ministers, thereby provoking disturbances, which led to bloodshed, particularly at Beirut. The British Cabinet was disturbed by these events.

The action taken by the French stultified the agreements we had made with the French, and also with the Syrians and Lebanese. It was contrary to the Atlantic Charter and much else that we had declared. It seemed that the situation would be distorted throughout the whole of the Middle East and the Arab world, and also everywhere people would say, "What kind of a France is this which, while itself subjugated by the enemy, seeks to subjugate others?"

Accordingly I felt that the British and United States Governments should react strongly together. Already the character of the body we had recognised at Quebec had been totally altered by de Gaulle's complete assumption of power. But the outbreaks in the Levant were of a different character, and afforded full justification, with the support of world public opinion, for bringing the issue with de Gaulle to a head. I thought that the kidnapped Lebanese President and Ministers should be set at liberty and permitted to resume their full function, and that the Lebanon Assembly should meet again as soon as conditions of law and order could be guaranteed. If de Gaulle refused to do this at once, we should withdraw our recognition from the French National Committee and stop the process of arming the French troops in North Africa.

I was forced to give instructions to General Wilson to be prepared if necessary to take over control of the Lebanon and to re-establish order with British troops. Happily this was not necessary. General Catroux had arrived from Algiers on November 16 to act as mediator, and on November 22 the French authorities released the politicians under arrest, and protracted negotiations began for the ultimate independence of Syria and the Lebanon.

These incidents left their mark upon our relations with the Free French Committee and with General de Gaulle. The result of our year of effort to bring about a united policy founded upon a true sense of comradeship between the United States, Britain, and the Free French leaders had been disappointing.

CHAPTER XI

THE BROKEN AXIS

Autumn 1943

Civil War in Italy – Need to Sustain the King and the Badoglio Government – I Put the Case to the President – We Agree on Policy – Mussolini Meets Hitler, September 14 – Hitler on the Duce – The Republic of Salo – Fate of the Italian Forces in the Balkans and Ægean – I Explain the Situation to Stalin – Marshal Badoglio Signs the Long-Term Surrender Agreement at Malta – Declaration about Italian Co-belligerency by the President, Stalin, and Me – Count Sforza Comes on the Scene – Use of Italian Man-power and Shipping – Italy Declares War on Germany, October 13 – A Fragile Situation.

MUSSOLINI'S bid for a Fascist revival plunged Italy into the horrors of civil war. In the weeks following the September armistice officers and men of the Italian Army stationed in German-occupied Northern Italy and Patriots from the towns and countryside began to form Partisan units and to operate against the Germans and against their compatriots who still adhered to the Duce. Contacts were made with the Allied armies south of Rome and with the Badoglio Government. In these months the network of Italian resistance to the German occupation was created in a cruel atmosphere of civil strife, assassinations, and executions. The insurgent movement in Central and Northern Italy here as elsewhere in occupied Europe convulsed all classes of the people.

Not the least of their achievements was the succour and support given to our prisoners of war trapped by the armistice in camps in Northern Italy. Out of about eighty thousand of these men, conspicuously clothed in battle dress, and in the main with little knowledge of the language or geography of the country, at least ten thousand, mostly helped by the local population with civilian clothes, were guided to safety, thanks to the risks taken by members of the Italian Resistance and the simple people of the countryside.

* * *

From the moment when the armistice was signed and when the Italian Fleet loyally and courageously joined the Allies I felt myself bound to work with the King of Italy and Marshal Badoglio, at least until Rome was occupied by the Allies and we could construct a really broad-based Italian Government for the prosecution of the war jointly with us. I was sure that King Victor Emmanuel and Badoglio would be able to do more for what had now become the common cause than any Italian Government formed from the exiles or opponents of the Fascist régime. The surrender of the Italian Fleet was solid proof of their authority. On the other hand, there were the usual arguments against having anything to do with those who had worked with or helped Mussolini, and immediately there grew up an endless series of intrigues among the six or seven Leftish parties in Rome to get rid of the King and Badoglio and take the power themselves. Considering the critical nature of the battle and the supreme importance of getting Italy to fight with a good heart on our side, I resisted these movements whenever they came to my notice. In this I was supported by Marshal Stalin, who followed the Russian maxim, "You may always walk with the Devil till you get to the end of the bridge."

* * *

After considering proposals from Macmillan at Algiers, and from General Eisenhower, I telegraphed to the President asking for his comments.

Prime Minister to President Roosevelt   21 Sept 43
. . . I and my colleagues in the War Cabinet have come to the following conclusions:
It is vital to build up the authority of the King and the Brindisi Administration as a Government and have unity of command throughout Italy. . . . Despite Badoglio's broadcast to-night we still feel it is essential that the King should go to the microphone at Bari, tell the Italian people he is there, and proclaim that Badoglio is carrying on the legitimate Government of Italy under his authority. This is needed

not only for the Italian people, but for the Italian representatives and garrisons abroad.

The King and Badoglio should be told that they must build up the broadest-based anti-Fascist coalition Government possible. Any healthy elements that can deliver some goods should be rallied in this crisis. These points should be made plain in the King's broadcast. It would be very useful if Count Sforza and the professors who claim to represent the six parties were willing to join in the common effort. It must however be clearly understood that none of these provisional arrangements, dictated by war needs, will stand in the way of the free choice by the Italian people of the form of democratic government which they prefer.

The question of giving the Badoglio Government an Allied status does not come into our immediate programme. Co-belligerency is good enough. On this footing we should work for the gradual conversion of Italy into an effective national force against Germany, but, as we have said, she must work her passage. Useful service against the enemy will be recognised by us in the adjustment and working of the armistice terms. In return we expect Badoglio to continue to work for the Allies on the basis of the armistice. Our principle will be payment by results. Badoglio should be free to declare war on Germany, and by so doing he would at once become, though not an ally, a co-belligerent.

Badoglio can be told that it is no part of our plan to install Allied military government everywhere. If he will co-operate we are ready to hand over territory to his Government as quickly as it is free from the enemy. This offer applies to the historic mainland of Italy, Sicily, and Sardinia. The dealings of the United Nations with the Italian Government in territories which they are allowed to administer will be carried out through a Control Commission.

It would make it much easier for us if the full instrument of surrender, even though somewhat superseded, could now be signed. It is true that many of the clauses could not be operated by the Brindisi Administration in their present situation. But as we go up the peninsula and turn over territory to the Italian Government these questions will become real. We do not want to put ourselves in the position of having to haggle over every requirement with the Government. The longer we leave it the more difficult it becomes to get the instrument signed, so I hope Eisenhower will get Badoglio's signature to it as soon as possible on the basis suggested in the Foreign Secretary's telegrams.

This programme should be put to the King and Badoglio at once. The first essential is that the King should make the public announcement suggested. This should not surely await final refinements of policy.

This crossed the following telegram from the President:

President Roosevelt to Prime Minister   21 Sept 43

I will send the following message to General Eisenhower immediately upon your concurrence:

"In view of the existing situation in Italy the earliest practicable action is important.

"1. You will withhold long-term armistice provisions pending further instructions.

"2. On the basis of military necessity, you are empowered to make recommendations from time to time to lighten the provisions of the military armistice in order to enable the Italians, within the limit of their capacities, to wage war against Germany.

"3. On condition that it declares war on Germany, the present Government of Italy should be permitted, subject to the provisions of paragraph 4 hereunder, to carry on as the Government of Italy, and as such should be treated as a co-belligerent in the war against Germany; such relationship to be based on the clear understanding that it is not in any way to prejudice the untrammelled right of the people of Italy to decide on the form of government they will eventually have, and that no final form of government of Italy will be decided upon until the Germans are evicted from Italian territory.

"4. The Allied Military Government and the appropriate functions contemplated for the Armistice Control Commission will be merged as promptly as practicable into an Allied Commission under the Allied Commander-in-Chief, which shall be empowered to furnish guidance and instructions from time to time to the Badoglio Government on military, political, and administrative matters.

"5. You will encourage in all practicable ways the vigorous use, under your direction, of the Italian armed forces against Germany."

Our two messages did not seem to me to conflict on any important point, except the question of withholding the long terms of surrender. On this I deferred to the President, and we agreed that his telegram should be sent to General Eisenhower as a directive from both of us.

★   ★   ★

On September 14 Mussolini met Hitler for the first time since his "liberation". During the succeeding days the two men debated how to extend the life of Italian Fascism in those parts of

Italy still occupied by the German troops. On the 15th the Duce announced that he had reassumed the leadership of Fascism and that a new Republican-Fascist Party, purged and uplifted from traitorous elements, would rebuild a faithful Government in the North. For a moment it seemed that the old system, now dressed up in a pseudo-revolutionary garb, might flare again into life. But the results disappointed the Germans. Goebbels's comment at this time is revealing.

The Duce has not drawn the moral conclusions from Italy's catastrophe which the Fuehrer had expected. He was naturally overjoyed to see the Fuehrer and to be fully at liberty again. But the Fuehrer expected that the first thing the Duce would do would be to wreak full vengeance on his betrayers. He gave no such indication, however, which showed his real limitations. He is not a revolutionary like the Fuehrer or Stalin. He is so bound to his own Italian people that he lacks the broad qualities of a world-wide revolutionary and insurrectionist.*

But there was to be no turning back. Mussolini's half-hearted "Hundred Days" began. At the end of September he set up his headquarters on the shores of Lake Garda. This pitiful shadow Government is known as the "Republic of Salo". Here the squalid tragedy was played out. The dictator and lawgiver of Italy for more than twenty years dwelt with his mistress in the hands of his German masters, ruled by their will, and cut off from the outside world by carefully chosen German guards and doctors.

The Italian surrender caught their armies in the Balkans completely unawares, and many troops were trapped in desperate positions between local guerrilla forces and the vengeful Germans. There were savage reprisals. The Italian garrison of Corfu, over seven thousand strong, was almost annihilated by their former allies. The Italian troops of the island of Cephalonia held out until September 22. Many of the survivors were shot, and the rest deported. Some of the garrisons of the Ægean islands managed to escape in small parties to Egypt. In Albania, on the Dalmatian coast, and inside Yugoslavia a number of detachments joined the Partisans. More often they were taken off to forced labour and their officers shot. In Montenegro the greater part of two Italian divisions were formed by Tito into the "Garibaldi Divisions", which suffered heavy losses by the end of the war. In the Balkans and Ægean the Italian armies lost nearly forty thousand men after

* *The Goebbels Diaries*, p. 378.

the announcement of the armistice on September 8, not including those who died in deportation camps.

* * *

I explained the situation and our policy to Stalin.

Prime Minister to Premier Stalin 21 Sept 43

Now that Mussolini has been set up by the Germans as the head of a so-called Republican-Fascist Government, it is essential to counter this move by doing all we can to strengthen the authority of the King and Badoglio, who signed the armistice with us, and have since faithfully carried it out to the best of their ability and surrendered the bulk of their Fleet. Besides, for military reasons we must mobilise and concentrate all the forces in Italy which are anxious to fight or at least obstruct the Germans. These are already active.

I propose therefore to advise the King to appeal on the wireless to the Italian people to rally round the Badoglio Government, and to announce his intention to build up a broad-based, anti-Fascist coalition Government, it being understood that nothing shall be done to prevent the Italian people from settling what form of democratic Government they will have after the war.

It should also be said that useful service by the Italian Government, Army, and people against the enemy will be recognised in the adjustment and working of the armistice; but that, while the Italian Government is free to declare war on Germany, this will not make Italy an ally, but only a co-belligerent.

I want at the same time to insist on the signing of the comprehensive armistice terms, which are still outstanding, even though some of those terms cannot be enforced at the present time. Against this Badoglio would be told that the Allied Governments intend to hand over the historic mainland of Italy, Sicily, and Sardinia to the administration of the Italian Government under the Allied Control Commission as they are freed from the enemy.

I am putting these proposals also to President Roosevelt, and I hope that I may count on your approval. As you will readily understand, the matter is vitally urgent for military reasons. For instance, the Italians have already driven the Germans out of Sardinia, and there are many islands and key points which they still hold and which we may get.

He replied as follows:

Premier Stalin to Premier Churchill 22 Sept 43

I received your message of September 21.

I agree with your proposal concerning the appeal by radio of the Italian King to the Italian people; but I consider it entirely necessary that in the appeal of the King it should be clearly stated that Italy, which capitulated to Great Britain, the United States, and the Soviet Union, will fight against Germany together with Great Britain, the United States, and the Soviet Union.

2. I also agree with your proposal about the necessity of signing comprehensive armistice terms. In regard to your reservation that certain of these terms cannot be put into force at the present moment, I understand this reservation only in the sense that these terms cannot be realised now on the territory which so far is held by the Germans. In any case, I should like to receive confirmation or the necessary explanation from you on that point.

I asked the President what he thought of this, and said that I considered that the long-term provisions of surrender might well be dealt with by the Armistice Commission which we were setting up in Italy. I later sent him the following:

Former Naval Person to President Roosevelt   24 Sept 43
Macmillan now tells me that he is confident that Badoglio's signature can be obtained to the whole set of terms within the next few days, and that the longer we leave it the more haggling there will be. It may be some time before the new Commission can give their views, and I should myself feel happier if we clinched the matter now. This might save us a good deal of trouble later on.

At Eisenhower's suggestion we have made the preamble less harsh. We also provided that the armistice of September 3 will remain operative.

Prime Minister to President Roosevelt   25 Sept 43
I have not answered Uncle Joe's telegram in favour of backing up the King of Italy, and also his remarks about the comprehensive terms, because I do not know what line you are taking with him. You will no doubt have received my telegram. Macmillan reports that there will be no difficulty in getting Badoglio to sign.

The President replied:

President Roosevelt to Prime Minister   25 Sept 43
I go along with your thought about the long set of terms if signature can be obtained quickly, and I am so advising Eisenhower.

*   *   *

Other political complications occurred.

Prime Minister to Mr. Macmillan (Algiers)   25 Sept 43
Astonishment was caused here at a broadcast from the Bari radio in the name of "the King of Italy and Albania and Emperor of Ethiopia"

I need scarcely say that any repetition of follies like that will bring our whole policy into discredit here. How would the King like to be sent back to his Empire in Ethiopia to be crowned?

. . . I presume we are going to see the King's speech before he lets it off, or if there is no time for this that you will anyhow vet it. The reference to the Soviet is of capital importance, as Stalin's support for our policy of using the Italian Government is invaluable.

On September 28 Marshal Badoglio left Brindisi in an Italian cruiser to sign the long-term surrender at Malta. He was received with ceremony on board the battleship *Nelson* by General Eisenhower and his Chief of Staff, General Bedell Smith, Lord Gort, and General Alexander. Badoglio hoped to be spared the clause on unconditional surrender, but the Allied commanders insisted that this was a formal meeting to sign documents presented by the Allied Governments which would admit of no discussion.

After the signatures had been appended Badoglio had a short discussion with General Eisenhower about declaring war on Germany, which the Italian Marshal wished to do. The day ended with a visit to the units of the Italian Fleet anchored in Malta harbour.

Prime Minister to President Roosevelt   28 Sept 43

We agree that the long-term surrender document should be kept secret for the present. I have no doubt U.J. will concur, but it would be well if you told him our views, speaking for both of us.

We think it would be a mistake to talk about making Rome an open city, as it may hamper our forward movement, and will anyway not bind the enemy.

★ ★ ★

The situation was at first bewildering for our troops on the spot. The Italians had been their enemies for more than three years. By joining the United Nations they had in the space of a few weeks acquired a new status, and some of them assumed a new attitude. Requisitioning was no longer possible. Accommodation was denied to British troops, and food refused to officers without Italian ration cards. British military currency was treated with suspicion. Senior officers who had held the rank of Military Governor now became mere liaison officers with the Italians, from whom they could request but no longer compel the facilities which they needed. Much of this was the growing pains of the new régime in Italy, and was presently rectified by high authority,

173

but some Italian civilians were ready to take the fullest advantage of the changes which had occurred. The President and General Eisenhower felt that a public declaration was needed in order to explain "co-belligerent" status to the Italians, and indeed to the world. I welcomed this.

Prime Minister to President Roosevelt   30 Sept 43

I agree that we should make a joint announcement, but would it not be a good chance of getting U.J. in too? It is clear now that he does accept the Italians as co-belligerents. It is true that we may lose a few days in communicating with Moscow, but this delay seems relatively unimportant compared with the value of Russian participation.

If you agree, would you put it to Stalin in the form that we wish an announcement of the kind made; will he join with us in making it, or would he prefer us to go ahead without him? Of course, we should consider any drafting alterations he might wish to propose.

I myself would like to see several changes, and my immediately following telegram embodies these. If you see no objection to them, would you, if you agree to approach Stalin, put the text to him in this form?

The text of the declaration which I drafted read as follows:

"The Governments of Great Britain, the United States, and the Soviet Union acknowledge the position of the Royal Italian Government as stated by Marshal Badoglio, and accept the active co-operation of the Italian nation and armed forces as a co-belligerent in the war against Germany. The military events since September 8 and the brutal maltreatment by the Germans of the Italian population, culminating in the Italian declaration of war against Germany, have in fact made Italy a co-belligerent, and the American, British, and Soviet Governments will continue to work with the Italian Government on that basis. The three Governments acknowledge the Italian Government's pledge to submit to the will of the Italian people after the Germans have been driven from Italy, and it is understood that nothing can detract from the absolute and untrammelled right of the people of Italy by constitutional means to decide on the democratic form of government they will eventually have.

"The relationship of co-belligerency between the Government of Italy and the United Nations Governments cannot of itself affect the terms recently signed, which retain their full force and can only be adjusted by agreement between the Allied Govern-

27 Sir Winston Churchill reviews the Highlanders.

28 The Quebec Conference: front row: Mackenzie King, Roosevelt and Churchill; back row: Admirals and Generals Arnold, Portal, Brooke, King, Dill, Pound, Leahy.
29 Nikita Khruchev as an officer of the Red Army.

30 Sir Winston and Lady Churchill aboard the "Queen Mary".
31 Sir Winston at Whitehall making his "V" for victory sign to the crowd.

32 The German General, Guderian.

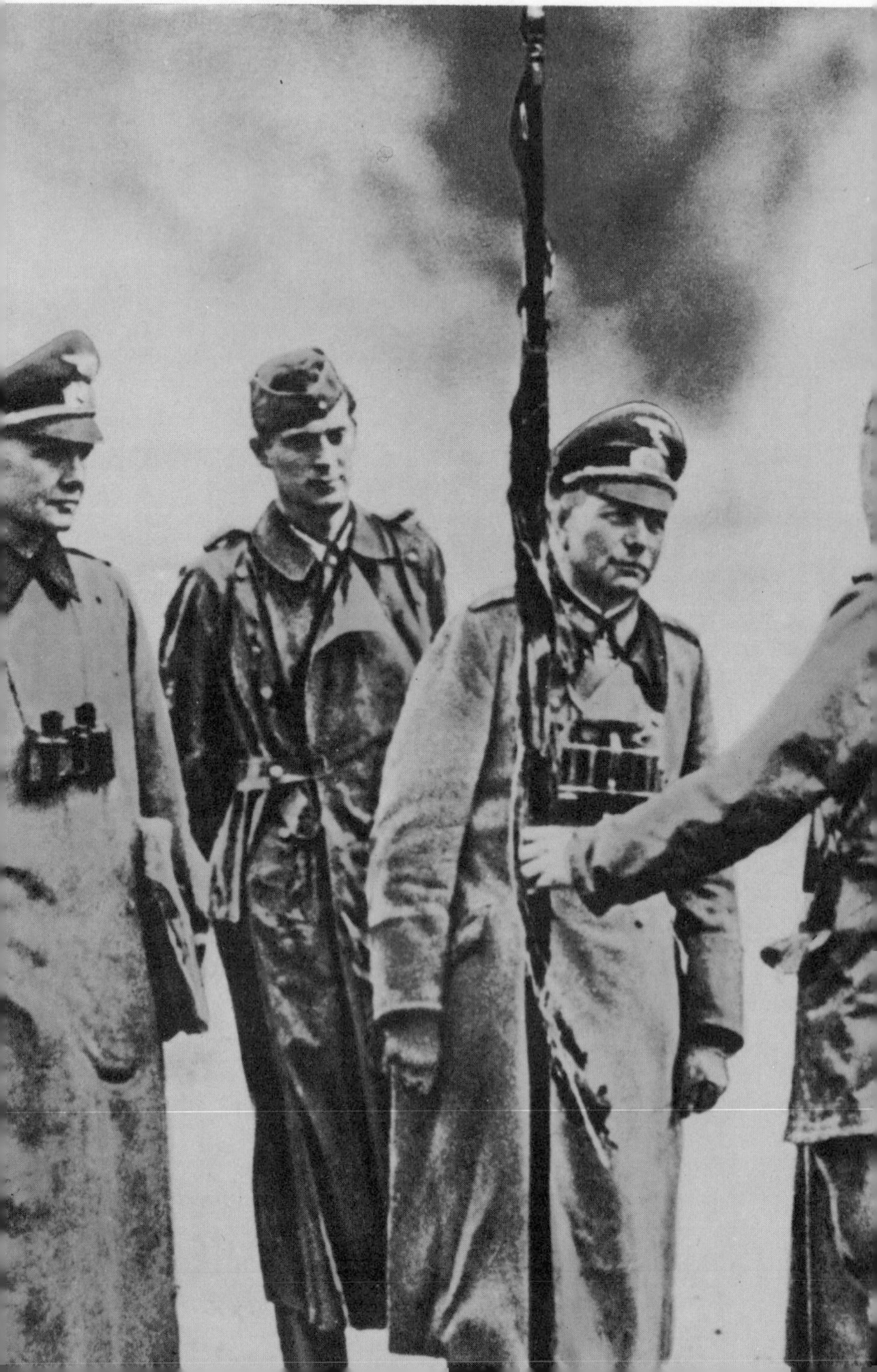

ments in the light of the assistance which the Italian Government may be able to afford to the United Nations' cause."

This was approved by both the President and Stalin.

* * *

Count Sforza now entered the Italian scene. Before the Fascist revolution he had been Foreign Minister and Ambassador in Paris. During Mussolini's régime he had been an exile. He had become an outstanding figure among Italians in America. He had declared himself in favour of bringing Italy into the war on the side of the Allies, and had in a letter which he had recently written to a high State Department official expressed his willingness to work with Badoglio. As the situation sharpened he saw his opportunity to gain the chief power in Italy, and was convinced of his right to it. He commanded a good deal of American support, and some of the American-Italian vote. The President hoped it might be possible to bring him into the new system of government without upsetting the King and Badoglio, upon whom our military thought about the Italian campaign was based.

President Roosevelt to Prime Minister   30 Sept 43

Referring to your telegram in regard to Sforza playing with the team, his public speech was, to say the least, not complimentary to the King of Italy. I find however in a recording of his September 26 speech the following extracts, which indicate that he may be useful to our war effort:

"With the present leaders of Italy, if they behave well, if they wage war well, our duty is to go to war, all of us, and to oust the Germans out of Italy.

"I say so out of my only main desire to do a thing which helps victory. We may rally round any Government which enjoys the confidence of the Allies if this Government for the time being proves that it is able to wage a war and to oust the Germans out of Italy.

"If I had to proclaim a republic to-morrow I would say, 'No. First of all we must oust the Germans out of Italy. This is what the Italians want; but when Italy is free the Italians will decide.'"

Former Naval Person to President Roosevelt   1 Oct 43

Your telegram about Sforza. He seems to be saying all sorts of things, many very different to what he wrote in his letter. He really should make up his mind whether he is going to try to help the Royal Badoglio Government or try to discredit it. We ought to know where we are before we build him up. Would it not be a good thing for you

175

to route him to Italy via the United Kingdom and let us give him further friendly treatment here? I don't see much use in having him go to Italy merely to undermine whatever small fighting head against Fascism and the Germans Eisenhower has been able to produce out of the Italians.

President Roosevelt to Prime Minister   2 Oct 43

Your telegram in regard to Sforza. I am informed that he, with his son, expects to arrive by airplane at Prestwick, October 3, en route to Marrakesh.

I hope you can effectively indoctrinate him during his stop in U.K. I am this date sending the following to Eisenhower:

"Inform Badoglio that it is the view of this Government that Grandi's presence in Badoglio Government at this time would not be acceptable. Even though Grandi was perhaps the chief figure in deposition of Mussolini, he had been so closely associated with Fascism that to place him now in Brindisi Government would cause much adverse comment and misinterpretation. First accretions to Badoglio Government should be men of unequivocal liberal and democratic principle. It is only through the use of such men in responsible positions that this Government can feel justified in supporting the present Italian Government.

"Germany has already taken active belligerent steps against Italy, and the chief strength of Badoglio's Government is its announced determination to rid Italy by force of the German invader. An immediate declaration of war by the Italian Government on Germany is necessary if Italy is to be given the status of a co-belligerent."

I had a long conversation with Count Sforza on his way through London, and believed we had reached an agreement whereby he was to work loyally with the King and Badoglio until we were in a position, following on the capture of Rome at the earliest moment, to form a broad-based non-Fascist Government. I thus steadily held to our charted course. We intended to sustain the monarchy until the liberation of Italy, to bring an Italian Government in on our side in the struggle against Germany, to strengthen that Government by adding representative and resisting elements, and to associate the Russians with our immediate arrangements about Italian affairs.

★   ★   ★

While these exchanges went on I pressed for the fullest use of Italian man-power and shipping.

Prime Minister to Foreign Secretary   26 Sept 43

Ought we not to make a convention with the Italian Government in respect of the use of Italian prisoners of war and man-power? We cannot allow these large numbers of Italians to be freed from discipline and control and left at large in Britain or North Africa. There is no means of repatriating them without straining our shipping. Meanwhile we need their man-power. We cannot have the operations in Africa cumbered up with heavy masses of prisoners to guard. Our 1st Armoured Division has been virtually destroyed by being used as mere guards to prisoners.

There is empty shipping coming back from Africa to the United Kingdom.. We should ask that the process of shipping prisoners to the United Kingdom should continue pending some new arrangement with the Italian Government. I am quite prepared to consider a change of status for the Italians, provided they continue to do the same work as now and that the discipline is effective.

Prime Minister to First Lord, V.C.N.S., and Admiral   2 Oct 43
Cunningham

We cannot afford to allow units of the Italian Navy to remain idle, whether at Alexandria or elsewhere. My present idea is that we suggest to the Americans that the *Littorios* go to the United States to be fitted for the Pacific warfare and to be used there by them. I would also suggest to the President that after the war these ships be ceded to us, because, first, we have had the main part of the war against them; secondly, we have had heavy losses in capital units; and, thirdly, we have discontinued building capital units in order to further current short-term operations. I am sure such proposals will be received in a most friendly spirit. I should like your advice about all this, and also of course about the structure and value of these ships.

2. With regard to cruisers and other vessels, they must all be put to the highest use. We cannot have valuable ships lolling about in the Mediterranean harbours. The most valuable and modern should be brought into service and our older ones laid up. The older Italian battleships may also have a part to play in the inshore bombarding squadrons, which will certainly be required, though only for short periods, during 1944, both in the Channel and the Indian Ocean.

★ ★ ★

Former Naval Person to President Roosevelt   4 Oct 43

Now that U.J. has come in with us about the Italian declaration it appears of the highest importance to compel the King to declare war as soon as possible. This is, as I know, your view. I suggest that instructions be given to Eisenhower to put the fullest pressure upon him. There should be no nonsense about waiting until Rome is taken. It seems to us high time that the Italians began to work their passage. If you are in agreement, pray give the necessary orders without further reference to us.

The President acted promptly.

President Roosevelt to Prime Minister   8 Oct 43
On October 5 I informed Eisenhower as follows:
"The President and Prime Minister are in agreement that the King of Italy declare war on Germany as soon as possible. There appears to be no necessity for waiting until Rome is occupied. You will therefore put pressure on the Italian Government for an early declaration of war without waiting for further successes."

Accordingly on October 13 the Royal Italian Government declared war on Germany.

* * *

Prime Minister to Mr. Macmillan (Algiers)   23 Oct 43
. . . Our policy is to broaden the base and increase the Leftward emphasis of the Italian Government. We have very little information here about the personalities who are already available. You will be watching all this, and should keep me fully informed.

I am clear that any reconstruction of the Italian Government had better wait until we are in Rome. In Rome lie the title-deeds of Italy and of the Roman Catholic Church. Badoglio and the King reinstated there will have a far better chance of rallying such elements of Italian strength as exist. There is the place for us to make our deal and for them to issue their prospectus.

In the meanwhile be careful that nothing is done to make the King and Badoglio weaker than they are. On the contrary, we must hold them up and carry them forward with our armies. Meanwhile all search for strengthening elements can continue.

Prime Minister to President Roosevelt   6 Nov 43
All my information goes to show that we should lose a lot in breaking up the present King-Badoglio show. Victor Emmanuel is nothing to us, but his combination with Badoglio did in fact deliver the Italian Fleet, which is rendering very useful service now, and this same combination is at this moment holding the loyalties of a very large part of the unhappy Italian Army and people, and of course of Italian diplomatic representatives everywhere. Why should we add to the burden of our British and United States soldiers on the march to Rome by weakening any of those aids? We ought not, in my personal opinion,

to countenance a change in the Badoglio-King régime till we are seated in Rome and a really broad-based Italian Government can be formed.

I understand Eisenhower in the main inclines to this view. Surely we should stick to what we have got till we are sure we can get something better, and this can only be ascertained when we have Rome in our possession.

Such was the fragile state of Italian affairs when I set out for Cairo and Teheran.

CHAPTER XII

ISLAND PRIZES LOST

Rhodes, Key to the Eastern Mediterranean – The Command of the Ægean Within Our Reach – General Wilson's Plans Disrupted – Major Lord Jellicoe's Exploit – Seizure of Rhodes, Leros, and Cos Approved by the Combined Chiefs of Staff – The German Grip on Rhodes – Hitler's Concern About the Ægean – The Germans Retake Cos – Imperative Need to Attack Rhodes – My Telegram to the President of October 7 – His Disappointing Reply – My Further Appeals, October 8 – Washington Obdurate – The Question Nevertheless Left Open – News of Hitler's Decision to Fight South of Rome Fatal to the Project – Wilson's Report of October 10 – I Submit with Grief – My Telegram of October 10 to the President – The Fate of Our Leros Garrison – The Germans Attack, November 12 – A Bitter Blow – Pedantic Denials in the Minor Sphere.

THE surrender of Italy gave us the chance of gaining important prizes in the Ægean at very small cost and effort. The Italian garrisons obeyed the orders of the King and Marshal Badoglio, and would come over to our side if we could reach them before they were overawed and disarmed by the Germans in the islands. These were much inferior in numbers, but it is probable that for some time past they had been suspicious of their allies' fidelity and had their plans laid. Rhodes, Leros, and Cos were island fortresses which had long been for us strategic objectives of a high order in the secondary sphere. Rhodes was the key to the group, because it had good airfields from which our own air forces could operate in defence of any other islands we might occupy and complete our naval control of these waters. Moreover, the British air forces in Egypt and Cyrenaica could defend Egypt just as well, or even better, if some of them moved forward to Rhodes. It seemed to me a rebuff to fortune not to pick up these treasures. The command of the Ægean by air and by sea was within our reach. The effect of this might be decisive upon Turkey, at that time deeply moved by the Italian collapse. If we could use the Ægean and the Dardanelles the naval short-cut to Russia was established. There would be no more need for the perilous and costly Arctic convoys, or the long and wearisome supply line through the Persian Gulf.

I felt from the beginning we must be ready to take advantage of any Italian landslide or German round-up.

Prime Minister to General Ismay, for C.O.S. Committee   2 Aug 43

Here is a business of great consequence, to be thrust forward by every means. Should the Italian troops in Crete and Rhodes resist the Germans and a deadlock ensue, we must help the Italians at the earliest moment, engaging thereby also the support of the populations.

2. The Middle East should be informed to-day that all supplies to Turkey may be stopped for the emergency, and that they should prepare expeditionary forces, not necessarily in divisional formations, to profit by the chances that may offer.

3. This is no time for conventional establishments, but rather for using whatever fighting elements there are. Can anything be done to find at least a modicum of assault shipping without compromising the main operation against Italy? It does not follow that troops can only be landed from armoured landing-craft. Provided they are to be helped by friends on shore, a different situation arises. Surely caiques and ships' boats can be used between ship and shore?

I hope the Staffs will be able to stimulate action, which may gain immense prizes at little cost, though not at little risk.

Plans and preparations for the capture of Rhodes had been perfected in the Middle East Command over several months. In August the 8th Indian Division had been trained and rehearsed in the operation, and was made ready to sail on September 1. But on August 26, in pursuance of a minor decision at the Washington Conference in the previous May, the command received the orders of the Combined Chiefs of Staff to dispatch to India, for an operation against the coast of Burma, the shipping that could have taken the 8th Indian Division to Rhodes. The division itself was put under orders to join the Allied forces in the Central Mediterranean.

★   ★   ★

When the tremendous events of the Italian surrender occurred my mind turned to the Ægean islands, so long the object of strategic desire. On September 9 I had cabled from Washington to General Wilson, Commander-in-Chief of the Middle East, "This is the time to play high. Improvise and dare." General Wilson was eager for swift action, but his command had been stripped. He had only available the 234th Brigade, formerly part of the hard-tried garrison of Malta, and no shipping other than what could be scraped up from local resources. The trained assault shipping recently taken from him was not beyond superior control, but the American pressure to disperse our shipping from the Mediterranean, either westwards for the preparations for a still remote "Overlord" or to the Indian theatre, was very strong. Agreements made before the Italian collapse and appropriate to a totally different situation were rigorously invoked, at least at the secondary level. Thus Wilson's well-conceived plans for rapid action in the Dodecanese were harshly upset. Thereafter we were condemned to try our best with insufficient forces to occupy and hold islands of invaluable strategic and political importance.

The Special Air Service Regiment, which had been formed by Lieut.-Colonel David Stirling, D.S.O., and which had already carried out a series of daring and successful raids on enemy airfields, two and three hundred miles behind the enemy lines, had recently been extending its activities beyond the Desert. On the night of September 9 Major Lord Jellicoe, son of the Admiral, who was a leading figure in this daring unit, landed by parachute in Rhodes to try to procure the surrender of the island. If we could gain a port and an airfield the quick dispatch of a few British troops might encourage the Italians to dominate the Germans, whom they far outnumbered. But the Germans were stubborn and stiff, and the Italians yielded themselves to their authority. Jellicoe had to leave hurriedly. Thereafter the capture of Rhodes, held by 6,000 Germans, required forces greater than were available to the Middle East Command.

The occupation of Rhodes, Leros, and Cos was specifically approved by the Combined Chiefs of Staff in their final summary of the Quebec decisions on September 10.* Wilson had sent with great promptitude small parties by sea and air to a number of other islands, and on September 14 reported as follows:

* See Chapter VI, p. 102.

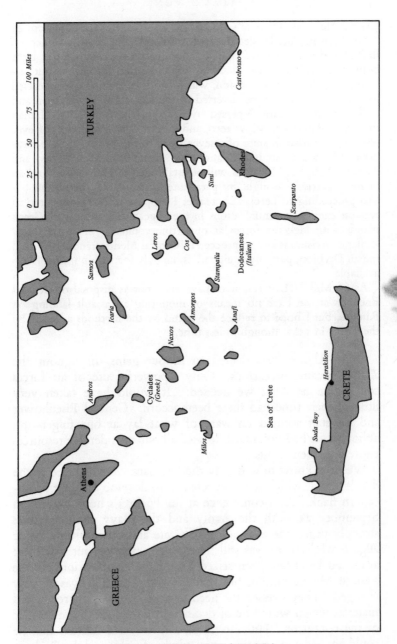

THE SOUTH ÆGEAN SEA

General Maitland Wilson to C.I.G.S.   14 Sept 43

Situation in Rhodes deteriorated too rapidly for us to take action. Italians surrendered town and harbour [to the Germans] after light bombing. Only an assault landing was thereafter practicable, but unfortunately 8th Indian Division, which had been trained and rehearsed for this operation, is now diverted to the Central Mediterranean and its ships and craft are dispersed by order of the Admiralty. Italian morale in Rhodes is below zero, and indicates little intention of ever resisting Germans in spite of asseverations to the contrary. We have occupied Castelrosso island, and have missions in Cos, Leros, and Samos. A flight of Spitfires will be established in Cos to-day, and an infantry garrison to-night by parachute. An infantry detachment is also proceeding to Leros. Thereafter I propose to carry out piratical war on enemy communications in the Ægean and to occupy Greek islands with Hellenic forces as opportunity offers. Since the New Zealand Division is also to proceed to Central Mediterranean, the 10th Indian Division, partially equipped, is the only formation immediately available.

As all Middle East resources have been put at disposal of General Eisenhower we have no means of mounting an assault landing on Rhodes, but I hope to reduce the island by the methods adopted by the Turks in 1522, though in less time.

Once Rhodes was denied to us our gains throughout the Ægean became precarious. Only a powerful use of air forces could give us what we needed. It would have taken very little of their time had there been accord. General Eisenhower and his staff seemed unaware of what lay at our finger-tips, although we had voluntarily placed all our considerable resources entirely in their hands.

We now know how deeply the Germans were alarmed at the deadly threat which they expected us to develop on their southeastern flank. At a conference at the Fuehrer's headquarters on September 24 both the Army and the Navy representatives strongly urged the evacuation of Crete and other islands in the Ægean while there was still time. They pointed out that these advanced bases had been seized for offensive operations in the Eastern Mediterranean, but that now the situation was entirely changed. They stressed the need to avoid the loss of troops and material which would be of decisive importance for the defence of the continent. Hitler overruled them. He insisted that he could not order evacuation, particularly of Crete and the Dodecanese, because of the political repercussions which would follow. He said, "The attitude of our allies in the south-east and Turkey's attitude is determined solely by their confidence in our strength. Abandonment of the islands would create a most unfavourable impression." In this decision to fight for the Ægean islands he was justified by events. He gained large profits in a subsidiary theatre at small cost to the main strategic position. In the Balkans he was wrong. In the Ægean he was right.

★   ★   ★

We rightly made no attempt to occupy Crete, where the considerable German garrison rapidly disarmed the Italians and took charge, but for a time our affairs prospered in the outlying small islands. Troop movements by sea and air began on September 15. The Royal Navy lent a helping hand with destroyers and submarines. For the rest, small coasting vessels, sailing ships, launches, were all pressed into service, and by the end of the month Cos, Leros, and Samos were occupied by a battalion each, and detachments occupied a number of other islands. Italian garrisons, where encountered, were friendly enough, but their vaunted coast and anti-aircraft defences were found to be in poor shape, and the transport of our own heavier weapons and vehicles was hardly possible with the shipping at our disposal.

Apart from Rhodes, the island of Cos was strategically the most important. It alone had an airfield from which our fighter aircraft could operate. This was rapidly brought into use and twenty-four Bofors guns landed for its defence. Naturally it became the objective of the first enemy counter-attack, and from September 18 onwards the target of increasing air raids. Our reconnaissance reported an enemy convoy approaching, and at dawn on October 3 German parachutists descended on the central airfield and overwhelmed the solitary company defending it. The rest of the battalion, in the north of the island, where the enemy landed, was cut off. Clearly a single battalion, all we could spare, could do little on an island thirty miles long to ward off such a double blow. The island fell. The Navy had done their best, without success, to intercept the convoy on its way to Cos, but owing to an unlucky event all but three destroyers had been for the moment drawn away. As part of the main naval concentration at Malta, which was not especially urgent, two of our battleships had been ordered thither at this moment, and needed all the remainder to escort them.

* * *

On September 22 Wilson reported his minimum and modest needs for an attack on Rhodes about October 20. Using the 10th Indian Division and part of an armoured brigade, he required only naval escorts and bombarding forces, three L.S.T.s, a few M.T. ships, a hospital ship, and enough transport aircraft to lift one parachute battalion. I was greatly troubled at our inability to support the Ægean operations, and on September 25 I cabled to General Eisenhower:

You will have seen the telegrams from the Commander-in-Chief Middle East about Rhodes. Rhodes is the key both to the Eastern Mediterranean and the Ægean. It will be a great disaster if the Germans are able to consolidate there. The requirements which the Middle East ask for are small. I should be most grateful if you would let me know how the matter stands. I have not yet raised it with Washington.*

The small aids needed seemed very little to ask from our American friends in order to gain the prize of Rhodes and thus retain Leros and retake Cos. The concessions which they had made to my unceasing pressure during the last three months had been rewarded by astounding success. Surely I was entitled to the very small aid which I required to supplement the British forces which were available for action in the Ægean, or had, with the approval of the Combined Chiefs of Staff, already been sent to dangerous positions. The landing-craft for a single division, a few days' assistance from the main Allied Air Force, and Rhodes would be ours. The Germans, who had now regripped the situation, had moved many of their planes to the Ægean to frustrate the very purpose which I had in mind.

* * *

I laid the issue before the President in its full scope.

Former Naval Person to President Roosevelt   7 Oct 43

I am much concerned about the situation developing in the Eastern Mediterranean. On the collapse of Italy we pushed small detachments from Egypt into several of the Greek islands, especially Cos, which has a landing ground, and Leros, which is a fortified Italian naval base

* See also my telegram to him of the same date, Chapter VIII, p. 134.

with powerful permanent batteries. We ran this risk in the hope that the Italian garrisons which welcomed us would take part in the defence. This hope appears vain, and Cos has already fallen, except for some of our troops fighting in the mountains. Leros may well share its fate. Our enterprises against Rhodes have not yet succeeded.

2. I believe it will be found that the Italian and Balkan peninsulas are militarily and politically united, and that really it is one theatre with which we have to deal. It may indeed not be possible to conduct a successful Italian campaign ignoring what happens in the Ægean. The Germans evidently attach the utmost importance to this Eastern sphere, and have not hesitated to divert a large part of their straitened Air Force to maintain themselves there. They have to apprehend desertion by Hungary and Roumania and a violent schism in Bulgaria. At any moment Turkey may lean her weight against them. We can all see how adverse to the enemy are the conditions in Greece and Yugoslavia. When we remember what brilliant results have followed from the political reactions in Italy induced by our military efforts should we not be short-sighted to ignore the possibility of a similar and even greater landslide in some or all of the countries I have mentioned? If we were able to provoke such reactions and profit by them our joint task in Italy would be greatly lightened.

3. I have never wished to send an army into the Balkans, but only by agents, supplies, and Commandos to stimulate the intense guerrilla prevailing there. This may yield results measureless in their conse-quence at very small cost to main operations. What I ask for is the capture of Rhodes and the other islands of the Dodecanese, and the movement northward of our Middle Eastern air forces and their establishment in these islands and possibly on the Turkish shore, which last might well be obtained, thus forcing a diversion on the enemy far greater than that required of us. It would also offer the opportunity of engaging the enemy's waning air-power and wearing it down in a new region. This air-power is all one, and the more continually it can be fought the better.

4. Rhodes is the key to all this. I do not feel the present plan of taking it is good enough. It will require and is worth at least up to a first-class division, which can of course be replaced by static troops once the place is ours. Leros, which for the moment we hold so precariously, is an important naval fortress, and once we are ensconced in this area air and light naval forces would have a most fruitful part to play. The policy should certainly not be pursued unless done with vigour and celerity, requiring the best troops and adequate means. In this way the diversion from the main theatre would only be temporary, while the results may well be of profound and lasting importance.

5. I beg you to consider this and not let it be brushed aside and all these possibilities lost to us in the critical months that lie ahead. Even if landing-craft and assault ships on the scale of a division were withheld from the build-up of "Overlord" for a few weeks without altering the zero date it would be worth while. I feel we may easily throw away an immense but fleeting opportunity. If you think well, would you very kindly let General Marshall see this telegram before any decision is taken by the Combined Chiefs of Staff.

I was pained to receive from the President a telegram which he had sent to Eisenhower which practically amounted to the refusal of all help and left me, already committed, with his and the American Chiefs of Staff's approval, to face the impending blow. The negative forces which hitherto had been so narrowly overcome had indeed resumed their control.

President Roosevelt to Prime Minister   8 Oct 43
I do not want to force on Eisenhower diversions which limit the prospects for the early successful development of the Italian operations to a secure line north of Rome.
I am opposed to any diversion which will in Eisenhower's opinion jeopardise the security of his current situation in Italy, the build-up of which is exceedingly slow, considering the well-known characteristics of his opponent, who enjoys a marked superiority in ground troops and Panzer divisions.
It is my opinion that no diversion of forces or equipment should prejudice "Overlord" as planned.
The American Chiefs of Staff agree.
I am transmitting a copy of this message to Eisenhower.

I noticed in particular the sentence "It is my opinion that no diversion of forces or equipment should prejudice 'Overlord' as planned". To pretend that the delay of six weeks in the return of nine landing-craft for "Overlord" out of over five hundred involved, which would in any case have had six months in hand, would compromise the main operation of May 1944 was to reject all sense of proportion. I therefore resolved to make a further earnest appeal to the President. Looking back upon the far-reaching favourable results which had followed from my journey with General Marshall to Algiers in June, from which the whole of our good fortune had sprung, I thought I might ask for the same procedure, and I made all preparations to fly at once to Tunis.

Prime Minister to President Roosevelt   8 Oct 43

I earnestly pray that my views may receive some consideration from you at this critical juncture, remembering how fruitful our concerted action has been in the past and how important it is for the future.

2. I am sure that the omission to take Rhodes at this stage and the ignoring of the whole position in the Eastern Mediterranean would constitute a cardinal error in strategy. I am convinced also that if we were round the table together this operation could be fitted into our plan without detriment either to the advance in Italy, of which, as you know, I have always been an advocate, or to the build-up of "Overlord", which I am prepared faithfully to support.

3. May I remind you of my anxiety at Quebec when we were informed that the build-up in Italy could not exceed twelve divisions ashore by December 1? There are now by October 9 over fifteen divisions ashore, of which about twelve are in action. We know that the enemy is withdrawing to the north, fighting rearguard actions and carrying off booty; we cannot yet tell whether it is in October or November that we can occupy Rome, but it is certain that we shall not come in contact with the main German forces at the top of the leg of Italy till December, or even later, and we certainly have control of the rate of advance.

4. There is therefore plenty of time to provide a division for the conquest of Rhodes and restore it to the battle-front in Italy before we reach the German fortified line.

5. We must find some means of resolving these difficulties and making sure of what is the right thing to do. I am willing to proceed to Eisenhower's headquarters with the British Chiefs of Staff immediately, if you will send General Marshall, or your personal representative, to meet me there, and we can then submit the results of a searching discussion to you and your Chiefs of Staff. We can be there Sunday afternoon [Oct. 10].

And later in the day:

8 Oct 43

I should have added that my estimate of the effect on "Overlord" to which I referred is limited to a delay of about six weeks in sending home nine landing-craft which were to have started from the Mediterranean this month, nearly six months before they would actually be needed for "Overlord". There ought, I think, to be some elasticity and a reasonable latitude in the handling of our joint affairs.

2. The Quebec decision to send four landing ships with the craft they carry from the Eastern Mediterranean to the Bay of Bengal also for training purposes has turned out ill. This decision should have been reviewed in the light of the new circumstances opened by the

surrender of Italy. Unhappily this was not done, and in consequence the Middle East was stripped bare [of landing-craft] at a moment when great prizes could be cheaply secured.

It is important to note the date of these two telegrams, October 8. On that day our information fully justified the belief that the enemy were withdrawing under cover of rearguards towards or beyond Rome. It was not till a day or two afterwards that we began to apprehend that their intention was to stand and fight south of the city. Though that produced a new situation it did not in itself involve any immediate peril to our forces in Italy.

President Roosevelt to Prime Minister   9 Oct 43

I have received your [telegrams of October 8] and given careful personal consideration to the points you make. I have given careful thought to them, and so has the Staff. I am concerned about the possibility of our armies suffering a reverse by the action of an enemy with superior forces except by air, under a commander of proved audacity and resourcefulness. This applies especially to the absolute safety to the line we hope to gain in Italy.

With a full understanding of your difficulties in the Eastern Mediterranean, my thought in sending [my previous telegram] was that no diversion of force from Italy should be made that would jeopardise the security of the Allied armies in Italy, and that no action toward any minor objective should prejudice the success of "Overlord".

We have almost all the facts now at our disposal on which to judge the commitments probably involved in the Rhodes operation. As I see it, it is not merely the capture of Rhodes, but it must mean of necessity, and it must be apparent to the Germans, that we intend to go farther. Otherwise Rhodes will be under the guns of both Cos and Crete.

I was in accord with obtaining whatever hold we could in the Dodecanese without heavy commitments, but the present picture involves not only a well-organised, determined operation, but a necessary follow-through. This in turn involves the necessity of drawing for the means, largely shipping and air, not ground troops, from some other source, which inevitably must be Italy, "Overlord," or possibly Mountbatten's amphibious operation. The problem then is, are we to enter into a Balkan campaign, starting with the southern tip, or is there more to be gained, and with security, by pushing rapidly to the agreed upon position north of Rome? It appears to me that a greater Allied threat against the Balkans is implied in this than by a necessarily precarious amphibious operation against Rhodes, with a lack evident to the enemy of the necessary means for the follow-through. Strategically, if we get the Ægean islands, I ask myself where do we go from there? and, *vice versa*, where would the Germans go if for some time they retained possession of the islands?

As to the meeting you propose for Sunday [10th] in Africa, this would be in effect another meeting of the Combined Chiefs of Staff, necessarily involving only a partial representation and in which I cannot participate. Frankly, I am not in sympathy with this procedure under the circumstances. It seems to me the issue under discussion can best be adjusted by us through our C.O.S. set-up in better perspective than by the method you propose. We have most of the facts, and will soon have the results of the conference scheduled for to-morrow in Tunis.

★   ★   ★

Mr. Roosevelt's reply quenched my last hopes. All I could now do was to ask that the President's original negative message should not prevent a free discussion of the issue at the conference of Commanders-in-Chief. This was accorded for what it was worth.

Prime Minister to General Wilson   9 Oct 43
You should press most strongly at the conference for further support for "Accolade" [Rhodes]. I do not believe the forces at present assigned to it are sufficient, and if you are left to take a setback it would be bad. It is clear that the key to the strategic situation in the next month in the Mediterranean is expressed in the two words "Storm Rhodes". Do not therefore undertake this on the cheap. Demand what is necessary, and consult with Alexander. I am doing all I can.

Prime Minister to President Roosevelt   9 Oct 43
Thank you very much for your kindness in giving so much of your time and thought to the views which I ventured to set before you. At your wish, and as you cannot send General Marshall, I have cancelled my journey, which I told Harry on the telephone I would never undertake without your blessing.

2. I agree with the end of your telegram of to-day, namely, that we should await the result of the conference scheduled for to-day in Tunis, which can then be considered and adjusted by us through the Combined C.O.S. Committee.

3. I am afraid however that your telegram of October 8 to me, a copy of which was sent to Eisenhower, will be taken as an order from you and as closing the subject finally. This I should find it very hard to accept. I hope therefore that you will make it clear that the conference is free to examine the whole question in all its bearings, and should report their conclusions to you and me through Combined Chiefs of Staff. I ask that the conference shall give full, free, patient,

and unprejudiced consideration to the whole question after they have heard the Middle East point of view put forward by its representatives.

4. At the present time General Wilson is preparing to attack Rhodes on the 23rd, with forces from his own command, or which have been assigned to him by General Eisenhower. He thinks these forces are sufficient, but I am doubtful whether they are not cut too fine.

The question, to my mind, therefore is whether he should have this modest reinforcement or whether the operation should be cancelled.

5. Cancellation will involve loss of Leros, even if they can hold out so long, and the complete abandonment by us of any foothold in the Ægean, which will become a frozen area, with most unfortunate political and psychological reactions in that part of the world instead of great advantages.

6. I fully agree with all you say about the paramount importance of the build-up in Italy, and I have given every proof of my zeal in this matter by stripping the British Middle Eastern Command of everything which can facilitate General Eisenhower's operations, in which we also have so great a stake.

To this the President replied:

President Roosevelt to Prime Minister   9 Oct 43
The following message has been sent to Eisenhower:
"The Prime Minister in a message to the President expresses the fear that the repetition to you of the President's message of October 8 to the Prime Minister would be taken as an order from the President and as closing the subject finally. The Prime Minister desires that it be made clear to you that the conference scheduled for to-day in Tunis is free to examine the whole question in all its bearings and should report their (your and General Wilson's) conclusions to the President and the Prime Minister through the Combined Chiefs of Staff. The Prime Minister asks that the conference shall give full, free, patient, and unprejudiced consideration to the whole question after having heard the Middle East point of view put forward by its representatives.

"The President directs that the foregoing desire expressed by the Prime Minister be accepted for your guidance."

At the critical moment of the conference information was received that Hitler had decided to reinforce his army in Italy and fight a main battle south of Rome. This tipped the scales against the small reinforcement required for the attack on Rhodes. Wilson reported:

General Wilson to Prime Minister   10 Oct 43
I received your message before conference at Tunis yesterday. I

also had a talk with Cunningham and Alexander. I agree that our Rhodes plan as it stood was on such a scale as to incur risk of failure. It might have been worked at the moment of the armistice, but unfortunately some days earlier our shipping resources had been removed and the fleeting opportunity found us powerless to act.

2. Since then conditions have changed to the extent that an assault of a single brigade group followed up by one other brigade four days later would risk having both flights defeated in detail if bad weather intervened. If the forces which at yesterday's conference we all agreed are now necessary were to be made available this would be at the expense of "Overlord" in landing-craft and of Alexander's offensive in ships, landing-craft, and aircraft. The conditions in Italy also having changed materially, according to latest information received yesterday, I could but agree that Alexander's operations ought to have the whole of the available resources.

3. This morning John Cunningham, Linnell, and I reviewed the situation in the Ægean on the assumption that Rhodes would not take place till a later date. We came to the conclusion that the holding of Leros and Samos is not impossible, although their maintenance is going to be difficult, and will depend on continued Turkish co-operation. I am going to talk to Eden about this when he arrives on Tuesday. In any case, the problem of evacuation of the garrison would be one of extreme difficulty, and we hope it may never arise. Our tenancy in the Ægean has hitherto caused the enemy to divert considerable forces in attempts to turn us out.

I replied at once:

Prime Minister to General Wilson   10 Oct 43
Cling on if you possibly can. It will be a splendid achievement. Talk it over with Eden and see what help you can get from the Turk.* If after everything has been done you are forced to quit I will support you, but victory is the prize.

Although I could understand how, in the altered situation, the opinion of the generals engaged in our Italian campaign had been affected, I remained—and remain—in my heart unconvinced that the capture of Rhodes could not have been fitted in. Nevertheless with one of the sharpest pangs I suffered in the war I submitted. If one has to submit it is wasteful not to do so with the best grace possible. When so many grave issues were pending I could not risk any jar in my personal relations with the President. I therefore took advantage of the news from Italy to accept what

* Mr. Eden was on his way to the Foreign Secretaries' Conference at Moscow.

I thought, and think, to have been an improvident decision, and sent him the following telegram, which, although the first paragraph is also recorded elsewhere, I now give in full:

Former Naval Person to President Roosevelt   10 Oct 43
I have now read General Eisenhower's report of the meeting. The German intention to reinforce immediately the south of Italy and to fight a battle before Rome is what General Eisenhower rightly calls "a drastic change within the last forty-eight hours". I agree that we must now look forward to very heavy fighting before Rome is reached instead of merely pushing back rearguards. I therefore agree with the conclusions of the conference that we cannot count on any comparative lull in which Rhodes might be taken, and that we must concentrate all important forces available on the battle, leaving the question of Rhodes, etc., to be reconsidered, as General Eisenhower suggests, after the winter line north of Rome has been successfully occupied.

2. I have now to face the situation in the Ægean. Even if we had decided to attack Rhodes on the 23rd, Leros might well have fallen before that date. I have asked Eden to examine with General Wilson and Admiral Cunningham whether with resources still belonging to the Middle East anything can be done to regain Cos, on the basis that Turkey lets us use the landing grounds close by. If nothing can be worked out on these lines, and unless we have luck to-night or to-morrow night in destroying one of the assaulting convoys, the fate of Leros is sealed.

3. I propose therefore to tell General Wilson that he is free, if he judges the position hopeless, to order the garrison to evacuate by night, taking with them all Italian officers and as many other Italians as possible and destroying the guns and defences. The Italians cannot be relied upon to fight, and we have only 1,200 men, quite insufficient to man even a small portion of the necessary batteries, let alone the perimeter. Internment in Turkey is not strict, and may not last long; or they may get out along the Turkish coast.

4. I will not waste words in explaining how painful this decision is to me.

★   ★   ★

To Alexander I said:
                                                            10 Oct 43
You should now try to save what we can from the wreck. . . . If there is no hope and nothing can be done you should consider with General Wilson whether the garrison of Leros should not be evacuated to Turkey, or perhaps wangled along the coast after blowing up the batteries. Efforts must also be made to withdraw the Long-Range

Desert Groups who are on other islands. This would be much better than their being taken prisoners of war and the Italian officers executed.

And to General Wilson:

14 Oct 43

I am very pleased with the way in which you used such poor bits and pieces as were left you. *Nil desperandum.*

★　　★　　★

Nothing was gained by all the over-caution. The capture of Rome proved to be eight months distant. Twenty times the quantity of shipping that would have helped to take Rhodes in a fortnight were employed throughout the autumn and winter to move the Anglo-American heavy bomber bases from Africa to Italy. Rhodes remained a thorn in our side. Turkey, witnessing the extraordinary inertia of the Allies near her shores, became much less forthcoming, and denied us her airfields.

The American Staff had enforced their view; the price had now to be paid by the British. Although we strove to maintain our position in Leros the fate of our small force there was virtually sealed. Having voluntarily placed at Eisenhower's disposal all our best fighting forces, ground and air, far beyond anything agreed at Washington in May or Quebec in August, and having by strenuous exertions strengthened the Army in Italy beyond the plans and expectations of its Supreme Headquarters, we had now to see what could be done with what remained. Severe bombing attacks on Leros and Samos were clearly the prelude to a German enterprise. The Leros garrison was brought up to the strength of a brigade—three fine battalions of British infantry who had undergone the whole siege and famine of Malta* and were still regaining their physical weight and strength.

On the day that Cos fell the Admiralty had ordered strong naval reinforcements, including five cruisers, to the Ægean from Malta. General Eisenhower also dispatched two groups of long-range fighters to the Middle East as a temporary measure. There they soon made their presence felt. On October 7 an enemy convoy carrying reinforcements to Cos was destroyed by naval and air action. Some days later the Navy sank two more transports. However, on the 11th the long-range fighters were withdrawn. Thereafter the Navy once more faced conditions similar

* 4th Bn. the Buffs, 2nd Bn. Royal Irish Fusiliers, 1st Bn. King's Own.

to those which had existed in the battle for Crete two years
before. The enemy had air mastery, and it was only by night
that our ships could operate without crippling loss.

★   ★   ★

The withdrawal of the fighters sealed the fate of Leros. The
enemy could continue to build up his forces without serious
interference, using dispersed groups of small craft. We now
know that the enemy faced a critical situation in shipping. The
delay in attacking Leros was due mainly to his fears about an
Allied attack in the Adriatic. On October 27 we heard that 4,000
German Alpine troops and many landing-craft had reached the
Piræus, apparently destined for Leros, and early in November
reports of landing-craft movements portended an attack. Concealed from our destroyers at night amid the islands, moving in
small groups by day, under their strong fighter protection, the
German troops and aircraft gathered. Our own naval and air
forces were unable to interfere with their stealthy approach.

The garrison was alert, but too few. The island of Leros is
divided by two narrow necks of land into three hilly sectors, to
each of which one of our battalions was allotted. Early on
November 12 German troops came ashore at the extreme north-
east of the island, and also in the bay south-east of Leros town.
The attack on the town was at first repulsed, but that afternoon
six hundred parachutists dropped on the neck between Alinda
and Gurna Bays and cut the defence in two. Previous reports
had stated that the island was unsuited for paratroop landings and
the descent was a surprise. Very strong efforts were made to
recapture the neck. In the last stages the garrison of Samos, the
2nd Royal West Kents, had been dispatched to Leros, but all was
over. They fell themselves a prey. With little air support of their
own and heavily attacked by enemy aircraft, the battalions fought
on till the evening of November 16, when, exhausted, they could
fight no more. Thus this fine brigade of troops fell into enemy
power. General Wilson reported:

General Wilson to Prime Minister   17 Nov 43
   Leros has fallen, after a very gallant struggle against overwhelming
air attack. It was a near thing between success and failure. Very little
was needed to turn the scale in our favour and to bring off a triumph.
Instead we have suffered a reverse of which the consequences are only

196

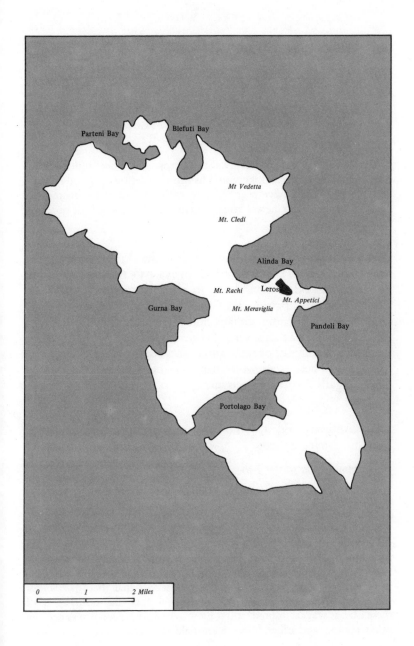

LEROS

too easy to foresee. . . . When we took the risk in September it was with our eyes open, and all would have been well if we had been able to take Rhodes. Some day I trust it will be our turn to carry out an operation with the scales weighted in our favour from the start.

I had read the telegrams as they came in day after day during my voyage to Cairo with deep feelings.* I now replied:

Prime Minister to General Wilson   18 Nov 43
Thank you for your messages about Leros. I approve your conduct of the operations there. Like you, I feel this is a serious loss and reverse, and like you I feel I have been fighting with my hands tied behind my back. I hope to have better arrangements made as a result of our next Conference.

* * *

With the loss of Leros all our hopes in the Ægean were for the time being ended. We tried at once to evacuate the small garrisons in Samos and other islands, and to rescue survivors from Leros. Over a thousand British and Greek troops were brought off, as well as many friendly Italians and German prisoners, but our naval losses were again severe. Six destroyers and two submarines were sunk by aircraft or mine and four cruisers and four destroyers damaged. These trials were shared by the Greek Navy, which played a gallant part throughout.

* * *

To Anthony Eden, who had now returned home from Moscow, I telegraphed:

Prime Minister (at sea) to Foreign Secretary   21 Nov 43
Leros is a bitter blow to me. Should it be raised in Parliament, I recommend the following line:
One may ask, should such operation ever have been undertaken without the assurance of air superiority? Have we not failed to learn the lessons of Crete, etc.? Have we not restored the Stukas to a fleeting moment of their old triumphs? The answer is that these are very proper questions to ask, but it would not be advisable to answer them in detail. All that can be said at the moment is that there is none of these arguments which was not foreseen before the occupation of these islands was attempted, and if they were disregarded it was because other reasons and other hopes were held to predominate over them.

* I was on my way to the Cairo–Teheran Conference, which is recounted later. (See Book X.)

If we are never going to proceed on anything but certainties we must certainly face the prospect of a prolonged war.

No attempts should be made to minimise the poignancy of the loss of the Dodecanese, which we had a chance of getting so easily and at so little cost and which we have now lost after heavy expenditure. You should also stress the tremendous effort made by the Germans, their withdrawal of almost half their air forces from Italy, where they were already outmatched, and the assistance given to our troops thereby.

3. Don't forget that we probably drowned the best part of two thousand Germans on the way, which, together with those killed in action, is at any rate an offset to our three thousand prisoners. It may well be that the Germans have paid much more than life for life, including prisoners, in this struggle. None the less it is just to say that it is our first really grievous reverse since Tobruk, 1942. I hope however that there will be no need to make heavy weather over this at all.

★   ★   ★

I have recounted the painful episodes of Rhodes and Leros in all their details. They constitute, happily on a small scale, the most acute difference I ever had with General Eisenhower. For many months, in the face of endless resistances, I had cleared the way for his successful campaign in Italy. Instead of only gaining Sardinia, we had established a large group of armies on the Italian mainland. Corsica was a bonus in our hands. We had drawn an important part of the German reserves away from other theatres. The Italian people and Government had come over to our side. Italy had declared war on Germany. Their Fleet was added to our own. Mussolini was a fugitive. The liberation of Rome seemed not far distant. Nineteen German divisions, abandoned by their Italian comrades, lay scattered throughout the Balkans, in which we had not used a thousand officers and men. The date for "Overlord" had not been decisively affected.

I had been instrumental in finding from the British and Imperial forces in Egypt four first-class divisions over and above those which, according to General Whiteley's report, the North-West African Supreme Headquarters had deemed possible. Not only had we aided General Eisenhower's Anglo-American Staff upon their victorious career, but we had furnished them with substantial unexpected resources, without which disaster might well have occurred. I was grieved that the small requests I had made for strategic purposes almost as high as those already achieved should have been so obdurately resisted and rejected. Of course, when you are winning a war almost everything that happens can be claimed to be right and wise. It would however have been easy, but for pedantic denials in the minor sphere, to have added the control of the Ægean, and very likely the accession of Turkey, to all the fruits of the Italian campaign.

CHAPTER XIII

HITLER'S "SECRET WEAPON"

General Ismay's Minute of April 15, 1943 – Mr. Sandys' Appointment – Reports on Peenemünde – Decision of the Defence Committee to Attack Peenemünde – Hitler's Sanguine Hopes – Warning of Rockets and Pilotless Aircraft – Difference of Opinion About Their Relative Importance – Successful Attack on Peenemünde, August 17 – Prolonged Delay Caused to the Germans Thereby – Far-reaching Consequences – Arrival of the Pilotless Aircraft – Report by Dr. R. V. Jones – The "Ski Sites" – My Telegram to President Roosevelt, October 25 – His Reply – Sir Stafford Cripps' Report – Our Timely Measures of Defence.

*S*EVERAL years before the war the Germans had begun the development of rockets and pilotless aircraft, and had built an experimental station to carry out this work on the Baltic coast at Peenemünde. This activity was of course a closely guarded secret. Nevertheless they were not able entirely to conceal what was going on, and already in the autumn of 1939 references to long-range weapons of various kinds began to appear in our Intelligence reports. During the early years of the war rumours on this subject and scraps of information, often contradictory, reached us from various quarters. In the spring of 1943 the position was reviewed by the Chiefs of Staff, as a result of which on April 15 General Ismay sent me the following minute:

Prime Minister
The Chiefs of Staff feel that you should be made aware of reports of German experiments with long-range rockets. The fact that five reports have been received since the end of 1942 indicates a foundation of fact even if details are inaccurate.
The Chiefs of Staff are of the opinion that no time should be lost in

establishing the facts, and, if the evidence proves reliable, in devising counter-measures. They feel this is a case where investigation directed by one man who could call on such scientific and Intelligence advisers as might be appropriate would give the best and quickest results. They therefore suggest that you should appoint an individual who should be charged with the task forthwith. They suggest for your consideration the name of Mr. Duncan Sandys, who, they think, would be very suitable if he could be made available.

In addition, the Chiefs of Staff propose to warn the Minister of Home Security of the possibility of such an attack, and of what is proposed. It is not considered desirable to inform the public at this stage, when the evidence is so intangible.

The Chiefs of Staff ask for your approval to the proposals above.

Mr. Sandys had served in an anti-aircraft unit in Norway in the early days of the war. Later he had suffered crippling disablement to both his feet in a motor accident when commanding the first experimental rocket regiment. He had joined the Government in July 1941 as Financial Secretary at the War Office, and afterwards as Under-Secretary at the Ministry of Supply. In both these offices he had had considerable responsibility for the general direction of weapon development, and had consequently been brought into close contact with the Chiefs of Staff Committee. As he was my son-in-law I was naturally glad that the Chiefs of Staff should wish to give him this important work, though I had in no way suggested it.

A month later he presented his first report, which was circulated to the War Cabinet. The following extract gives the main points.

I have reviewed the evidence regarding German long-range rocket development. In order to supplement this, I asked that an air reconnaissance should be undertaken of the area around Peenemünde, on the Baltic coast of Germany, where, judging from the reports, it seemed probable that rocket development was proceeding. This flight has been made, and the photographs obtained have provided further important information.

It would appear that the Germans have for some time past been trying to develop a heavy rocket capable of bombarding an area from a very long range. This work has probably been proceeding side by side with the development of jet-propelled aircraft and airborne rocket torpedoes. Very little information is available about the progress of this development. However, such scanty evidence as exists suggests that it may be far advanced. London, in view of its size, is much the most likely target.

An intensive effort should be made to obtain further information on this subject from agents on the Continent, from prisoners of war, and by air reconnaissance.

The experimental establishments and factories which appear most likely to be connected with the development and production of this weapon in Germany and German-occupied territory, together with any suspicious works in the coastal region of North-West France, should be subjected to bombing attack. A preliminary list of suggested targets is being sent to the Air Staff.

On June 4 Air Marshal Evill, Vice-Chief of the Air Staff, issued instructions enabling Sandys to deal directly with the Intelligence branches concerned about obtaining further information from agents and prisoners of war, and requested him to make recommendations for air reconnaissance and to notify the Air Staff of the conclusions drawn therefrom. All possible methods of tracing the trajectory of such projectiles and of locating the firing-point were examined. Civil Defence and security measures were set on foot.

On June 11 Mr. Sandys sent a minute to the Air Staff asking that reconnaissance flights should be made at regular intervals over the Peenemünde area and that air photographs should be obtained of all territory in Northern France within 130 miles of London. He also recommended that the experimental station at Peenemünde should be bombed. In his next report he stressed the importance of making the attack without delay.

The latest air reconnaissance photographs provide evidence that the Germans are pressing on as quickly as possible with the development of the long-range rocket at the experimental establishment at Peenemünde, and that frequent firings are taking place. There are also signs that the light anti-aircraft defences at Peenemünde are being further strengthened.

In these circumstances it is desirable that the projected bombing attack upon this establishment should be proceeded with as soon as possible.

On June 28 Sandys reported that aerial photographs of Peenemünde showed large rockets alongside the firing-point. They might have a range of about 90 to 130 miles.

In spite of all efforts to prevent them, the Germans may, without being detected, succeed in emplacing a number of projectors in Northern France and in launching a rocket attack upon London. In that event it would be necessary to locate with the utmost speed the sites from which the rockets were being fired, in order that these might be put out of action by immediate bombing attack.

With the equipment already available at existing Radar stations it should be possible to observe the rockets during flight and to determine the points from which they have been fired, to within a circle of ten miles radius. This performance can be considerably improved by fitting certain ancillary apparatus. The construction of this ancillary apparatus has already been put in hand. The first equipment is now in process of being installed at Rye. The remainder will be completed within two to three months. Special instructions have been issued to the five most suitable stations (Swingate, Rye, Pevensey, Poling, and Ventnor), and the necessary training of operators has begun.

On June 29 the Defence Committee, having been kept fully informed since April, decided:

That the most searching and rigorous examination of the area in Northern France within a radius of 130 miles of London should be organised and maintained, no step being neglected to make this as efficient and thorough as possible.

That the attack on the experimental station at Peenemünde should take the form of the heaviest possible night attack by Bomber Command on the first occasion when conditions are suitable.

That as far as possible plans should be prepared for immediate air attack on rocket firing-points in Northern France as soon as these are located.

* * *

Hitler was meanwhile intent upon the plan. Accompanied by some of his principal adherents of Cabinet level, he inspected Peenemünde about the beginning of June 1943. We were at this time better informed about rocket missiles than about pilotless aircraft. Both methods were in full preparation on a large scale, and Peenemünde was the summit of all research and experiment. No decisive progress had been made by the Germans towards the atomic bomb. "Heavy water" gave little encouragement, but in pilotless aircraft and the rockets Hitler and his advisers saw a means of delivering a new and possibly decisive attack upon England and the rupturing of the Anglo-American plans for a major cross-Channel return to the Continent. The Fuehrer was comforted by all he learned at Peenemünde, and he hurled the utmost German effort into this new and perhaps last hope.

About June 10 he told his assembled military leaders that the Germans had only to hold out. By the end of 1943 London would be levelled to the ground and Britain forced to capitulate. October 20 was fixed as zero day for rocket attacks to begin. It is said that Hitler personally ordered the construction of 30,000 rockets for that day. This, if true, shows the absurd ideas on which he lived. The German Minister of Munitions, Dr. Speer, said that each V2* required about as many man-hours to make as six fighters. Hitler's demand was therefore for the equivalent of 180,000 fighters to be made in four months. This was ridiculous; but the production of both weapons was given first priority and 1,500 skilled workers were transferred from anti-aircraft and artillery production to the task.

On July 9 Mr. Sandys reported that in addition to their plans for a rocket attack on London there was also evidence that the Germans intended to use pilotless aircraft and very long-range guns. Two excavations of a suspicious character had been detected—at Watten, near St. Omer, and at Bruneval, near Fécamp. Special instructions were therefore issued to the selected Radar stations in South-East England to watch for rocket-firing. Plans were also made by the Home Office, not for any wholesale evacuation of London, but for the removal when the time came of a hundred thousand persons in priority classes, such as school-children and pregnant mothers, at the rate of ten thousand a day. Thirty thousand Morrison table shelters were moved into London, bringing the reserve in the Metropolis up to about fifty thousand.

On July 19 our reports stated:

Work of an unexplained nature, including railway sidings, turn-tables, buildings, and concrete erections, is proceeding in North-West France. At most of these places construction is going ahead at a con-siderable pace, particularly in the case of Watten, where great activity is developing. Some attempt is being made to camouflage this work, and in one case the arrival of anti-aircraft guns has been observed.

When all these facts and reports were brought before the Defence Committee many differences of opinion arose concern-ing them. Among the scientists and technical officers opinions varied deeply and sharply on the question whether the new form

* Our name for the rocket. Pilotless aircraft were called V1.

of attack on the Island would be by rocket bombs or by pilot-less aircraft. At first the rocket was favourite, but its backers weakened their case by what turned out to be vastly exaggerated estimates of the size and destructive power of the missile. Con-fronted with these, those responsible for home security faced the possibility not only of evacuating children, expectant mothers, and other selected persons from London, but even a wholesale evacuation of the capital itself.

The Minister for Home Security was profoundly disquieted by the reports he studied, and always presented the danger in its most serious aspect. It was certainly his special duty to make sure that the danger was not underrated. Lord Cherwell, on the other hand, did not believe that even if giant rockets could be made it would pay the Germans to make them. As he had maintained from the very beginning, he insisted that they would get far better results at much smaller cost by using pilotless aircraft. Even if they used rockets with warheads of ten or twenty tons, as had been forecast, but which he did not believe was possible, he did not think the destruction in Britain would approach the figures which were produced. Listening to the discussions, which were frequent over many months, between him and Mr. Herbert Morrison, it might have seemed at times that the two protago-nists were divided as to whether the attack by self-propelled weapons would be annihilating or comparatively unimportant. Actually the issue, as is usual, was not in the realm of "Yes or No", but in that of "More or Less".

Lord Cherwell's minutes show very clearly that his views on the possible scale of attack were on the whole right and that the most alarmist estimates were wrong.

*   *   *

These discussions caused no delay or indecision in our actions. An attack on Peenemünde was difficult, but imperative, and on the night of August 17 Air Marshal Harris, Chief of Bomber Command, struck with 571 heavy bombers. The buildings were scattered along a narrow strip of coast and protected by a smoke-screen. They could neither be reached by radio-navigation beams from the United Kingdom nor sufficiently identified by the apparatus carried in our planes. It was therefore necessary to bomb by moonlight, although the German night fighters were close at hand and it was too far to send our own. The crews were ordered to bomb from 8,000 feet, much below their usual height, and were told by Air Marshal Harris that if the operation failed on the first night it would have to be repeated on the next night, and on all suitable nights thereafter, regardless of casualties and regardless of the fact that the enemy would obviously do everything possible to increase his defences after the first attack. At the same time everything was done to guide our airmen and deceive the foe. Pathfinders flew ahead to mark the route and the straggling installations, and a master bomber circled the target, assessing results and instructing our planes by radio-telephone. The route taken was almost the same as in previous raids on Berlin, and a small force of Mosquitoes was sent over the capital to mislead the enemy.

The weather was worse than expected and landmarks were difficult to find, but it cleared towards Rügen Island and many crews punctually started their time and distance runs. There was more cloud over the target and the smoke-screen was working, but, says Harris, "the very careful planning of the attack ensured a good concentration of bombs on all the aiming points." The enemy was at first deceived by the feint on Berlin, but not for long enough. Most of our force got away, but the German fighters caught them during their return, and in the bright moonlight forty of our bombers were shot down.

★   ★   ★

The results were of capital importance. Although the physical damage was much less than we supposed, the raid had a far-reaching influence on events. All the constructional drawings just completed for issue to the workshops were burned, and the start of large-scale manufacture was considerably delayed. The parent factory at Peenemünde was hit, and the fear of attacks on factories producing the rocket elsewhere led the Germans to concentrate manufacture in underground works in the Hartz Mountains. All these changes caused serious delays in perfecting and producing the weapon. They also decided to shift their experimental activities to an establishment in Poland beyond the range of our bombers. There our Polish agents kept vigilant watch, and in the middle of January 1944 the new weapon was tried. They soon discovered its range and line of fire, but of course the rockets came down many miles apart from each other. German patrols always raced to where they fell and collected the fragments, but one day a rocket fell on the bank of the river Bug and did not explode. The Poles got there first, rolled it into the river, waited till the Germans had given up the search, and then salvaged and dismantled it under cover of darkness. This dangerous task accomplished, a Polish engineer was picked up by a Royal Air Force Dakota on the night of July 25, 1944, and flown to England with many technical documents and more than 100 lb. of essential parts of the new weapon. The gallant man returned to Poland, and was later caught by the Gestapo and executed in Warsaw on August 13, 1944.

*   *   *

The attack on Peenemünde, for which such sacrifices were made, therefore played an important and definite part in the general progress of the war. But for this raid and the subsequent attacks on the launching points in France, Hitler's bombardment of London by rockets might well have started early in 1944. In fact it was delayed until September. By that time the prepared launching sites in Northern France had been overrun by General Montgomery's forces. In consequence the projectiles had to be fired from improvised positions in Holland, nearly twice as far from the target of London, and with much less accuracy. By the autumn German communications became so congested by battle needs that the transport of rockets to the firing-point could no longer secure high priority.

In his book *Crusade in Europe* General Eisenhower expressed his opinion that the development and employment of the "V" weapons were greatly delayed by the bombing of the experimental plants at Peenemünde and other places where they were being manufactured. He goes so far as to say:

It seemed likely that if the German had succeeded in perfecting and using these new weapons six months earlier than he did our invasion of Europe would have proved exceedingly difficult, perhaps impossible. I feel sure that if they had succeeded in using these weapons over a six-months period, and particularly if they had made the Portsmouth-Southampton area one of their principal targets, "Overlord" might have been written off.

This is an overstatement. The average error of both these

weapons was over ten miles. Even if the Germans had been able
to maintain a rate of fire of 120 a day and if none whatever had
been shot down the effect would have been the equivalent of only
two or three one-ton bombs to a square mile per week. However, it shows that the military commanders considered it necessary to eliminate the menace of the "V" weapons, not only to
protect civilian life and property, but equally to prevent interference with our offensive operations.

★   ★   ★

In the early autumn it became clear that the Germans were
planning to attack us not only with rockets but also with pilotless
aircraft. On September 13, 1943, Mr. Sandys reported:

There is evidence that the enemy is considering using pilotless aircraft as a means of delivering bombs on London. Unless the aircraft
used are abnormally small or are capable of flying at an exceptional
height or speed, it should be possible to deal with them by means of
the fighter and anti-aircraft defences of this country. If these pilotless
aircraft should be capable of flying at such heights and speeds as to
render their interception impossible by air-defence methods they should
for all practical purposes be regarded as projectiles.
The counter-measures should be the same as for the long-range
rocket, namely, the destruction by bombing of the sources of manufacture and of the sites or airfields from which they are launched.

The state of our knowledge at that time was summed up in a
report, dated September 25, by Dr. R. V. Jones, the head of the
Air Ministry's Scientific Intelligence Branch:

Much information has been collected. Allowing for the inaccuracies
which often occur in individual accounts, they form a coherent picture which despite the bewildering effect of propaganda has but
one explanation: the Germans have been conducting an extensive
research into long-range rockets at Peenemünde. Their experiments
have naturally encountered difficulties, which may still be holding up
production. Although Hitler would press the rockets into service at the
earliest possible moment, that moment is probably still some months
ahead.
It is probable that the German Air Force has also been developing a
pilotless aircraft for long-range bombardment in competition with the
rocket, and it is very possible that the aircraft will arrive first.

Meanwhile it was observed that in Northern France a large

number of groups of curiously shaped structures were being erected. All were laid out after the same fashion, and most of them appeared to be directed on London. Each included one or more buildings shaped rather like a ski. We later discovered from air photographs that there were structures similar to these in the neighbourhood of Peenemünde, and one of the photographs revealed a minute aircraft close to an inclined ramp. From this it was deduced that the so-called "ski sites" in Northern France were probably designed to store, fill, and launch small unmanned aircraft or flying bombs.

★　★　★

It was not until late in the autumn that I burdened the President with our grave and prolonged preoccupations. The United States Staffs were kept constantly informed on the technical level, but at the end of October I cabled by our special personal contact:

Former Naval Person to President Roosevelt　　　　25 Oct 43

I ought to let you know that during the last six months evidence has continued to accumulate from many sources that the Germans are preparing an attack on England, particularly London, by means of very long-range rockets which may conceivably weigh sixty tons and carry an explosive charge of ten to twenty tons. For this reason we raided Peenemünde, which was their main experimental station. We also demolished Watten, near St. Omer, which was where a construction work was proceeding the purpose of which we could not define. There are at least seven such points in the Pas de Calais and the Cherbourg peninsula, and there may be a good many others which we have not detected.

2. Scientific opinion is divided as to the practicability of making rockets of this kind, but I am personally as yet unconvinced that they cannot be made. We are in close touch with your people, who are ahead of us in rocket impulsion, which they have studied to give aeroplanes a send-off, and all possible work is being done. The expert committee which is following this business thinks it possible that a heavy though premature and short-lived attack might be made in the middle of November, and that the main attack would be attempted in the New Year. It naturally pays the Germans to spread talk of new weapons to encourage their troops, their satellites, and neutrals, and it may well be that their bite will be found less bad than their bark.

3. Hitherto we have watched the unexplained constructions proceeding in the Pas de Calais area without (except at Watten) attacking

33 A "V2" on its transporter.
34 The launching of a "V2".

35 A ''Buzz-bomb'' photographed immediately after launching.
36 London: the results of a flying bomb explosion.

37 Farrington Market, London, after a "V1" fell on it.

38 Aerial view of a factory making aviation material at Reggio-Emilia.

39 A photograph taken from the same angle after an allied bombing raid.

40-41 ''Baltimores'' of the R.A.F. over Italy.

42 American "B-25 Mitchell" bombers making for Cassino.
43 Spitfires of the R.A.F. returning from a flight over the Italian beach-heads.

44 Loading a German Junkers 87.

them, in the hope of learning more about them. But now we have decided to demolish those we know of, which should be easy, as overwhelming fighter protection can be given to bombers. Your airmen are of course in every way ready to help. This may not however end the menace, as the country is full of woods and quarries, and slanting tunnels can easily be constructed in hillsides.

4. The case of Watten is interesting. We damaged it so severely that the Germans, after a meeting two days later, decided to abandon it altogether. There were 6,000 French workers upon it as forced labour. When they panicked at the attack a body of uniformed young Frenchmen who are used by the Germans to supervise them fired upon their countrymen with such brutality that a German officer actually shot one of these young swine. A week later the Germans seem to have reversed their previous decision and resumed the work. Three thousand more workmen have been brought back. The rest have gone to some of those other suspected places, thus confirming our views. We have an excellent system of Intelligence in this part of Northern France, and it is from these sources as well as from photographs and examination of prisoners that this story has been built up.

5. I am sending you by air courier the latest report upon the subject, as I thought you would like to know about it.

He replied after an interval:

President Roosevelt to Prime Minister   9 Nov 43

We too have received many reports of the German rocket activity. The only information recently coming to me which might be of value to you is a statement that factories manufacturing the rocket bomb are situated in Kaniafried, Richshafen, Miztgennerth, Berlin, Kugellagerwerke, Schweinfurt, Wiener Neustadt, and at an isolated factory on the left side of the road going from Vienna to Baden, just south of Vienna. Production is said to have been delayed owing to the death in the bombing of the experimental station at Peenemünde of Lieut.-General Shemiergembeinski, who was in charge. This came from an informer via Turkey.

*   *   *

The evidence and conflicting views both among the scientists and my colleagues on the Defence Committee continued to be so evenly balanced and confusing that I asked Sir Stafford Cripps, the Minister of Aircraft Production, with his special knowledge and judicial mind, to review all the information about the German long-range weapons and present a conclusion. On November 17 he made his report.

It would seem that the order of probability from the purely experimental point of view is:

1. Large glider bombs.
2. Pilotless aircraft.
3. Small long-range rockets.
4. Large long-range rockets.

The R.A.F. raid on Peenemünde was undoubtedly of the greatest value, and has set back the developments, whatever they may be, for the long-range offensive weapon.

There is no doubt that the Germans are doing their utmost to perfect some long-range weapon, and the new unexplained structures in Northern France are certainly most suspicious, unless we can assign some other use to them. Under these circumstances I feel we should make all reasonable preparations to cope with the consequences if and when the attack materialises, though there is no evidence of its materialisation before the New Year at the earliest.

We should at the same time maintain photographic cover, and destroy the sites whenever we get the opportunity to do so.

This certainly left much in doubt. On December 14 Air Marshal Bottomley, the Deputy Chief of the Air Staff, reported:

The "Large Sites" in Northern France (including three which have been attacked) are suspected to be connected with long-range rocket attack. One of these sites is protected by as many as fifty-six heavy and seventy-six light anti-aircraft guns.

Evidence is accumulating that the "ski sites" are designed to launch pilotless aircraft. The existence of sixty-nine "ski sites" has been confirmed by photographic reconnaissance, and it is expected that the number will eventually total approximately a hundred. If present rates of construction are maintained the work on some twenty sites should be completed by early January 1944, and the remainder by February. The launching points on the sites in the Pas de Calais and Somme-Seine areas are oriented on London, and those on some of the sites in the Cherbourg area on Bristol.

On December 18 Lord Cherwell, who had been in close touch with Dr. Jones throughout, sent me a report giving his ideas about the date and intensity of the attack which might be expected from the flying bombs. In his view the bombardment would not begin before April, and not more than a hundred a day would be dispatched after the first day or two; of these about twenty-five would get within ten miles of the aiming point. As this would only correspond to fifty to a hundred fatal casualties a day he deprecated large-scale panic measures of evacuation. He still discounted the probability of the use of large rockets. Even if they could be made, which seemed impossible with any existing technique, they would cost twenty or thirty times as many man-hours to produce as the flying bombs, without, in his view, being more efficient.

During the early months of 1944 we developed our plans for meeting the flying bomb attack. It was decided that the defences should be laid out in three zones—a balloon barrage on the out-skirts of London, beyond that a gun belt, and beyond that again an area in which the fighter aircraft would operate. Steps were also taken to hasten the supply from America of the electronic predictors and radio proximity fuzes, which, when the bombard-ment eventually started, made it possible for the gunners to take a heavy toll of the flying bombs.

Meanwhile the British and American Air Forces continued to bomb the hundred or so "ski sites" in Northern France. This was so effective that at the end of April aerial reconnaissance indicated that the enemy was giving up work on them. But our satisfaction was short-lived, for it was discovered that he was building instead modified sites which were much less elaborate and more carefully camouflaged and therefore harder to find and to hit. Wherever found these new sites were bombed. Many were destroyed, but about forty escaped damage or detection. It was from these that the attack was ultimately launched in June.

* * *

Nearly fifteen months passed between the minute which the Chiefs of Staff sent me in April 1943 and the actual attack in June 1944. Not a day was wasted. No care was lacking. Preparations involving many months to perfect were set on foot on a large and costly scale in good time. When at length the blow fell upon us we were able, as the next volume will describe, to ward it off, albeit with heavy loss in life and much damage to property, but without any effective hindrance to our war-making capacity or to the operations in France. The whole story may stand as an example of the efficiency of our governing machine, and of the foresight and vigilance of all connected with it.

CHAPTER XIV

DEADLOCK ON THE THIRD FRONT

Hitler Resolves to Fight South of Rome – The German Winter Line – Alexander's Army Weakened – My Telegram to Alexander of October 24, and His Reply – General Eisenhower's Conference of Commanders – He Endorses Alexander's Review of the Battle Situation in Italy – The Withdrawal of Landing-craft Deprives Our Armies of Flexibility – Fall in the Rate of Build-up – Survey of the Changed Situation – My Telegrams to General Marshall and the President – General Marshall's Reply – I Appeal for the Retention of More Landing-craft in the Mediterranean – Eisenhower Authorised to Retain an Extra Sixty-eight until December 15 – My Telegram to Our Ambassador in Moscow, November 9 – I Tell General Brooke of Our Need for the Polish Corps – Undue Demands of the Allied Strategic Air Force – The Eighth Army Crosses the Sangro River – The United States Fifth Army Approaches the German Main Positions at Cassino – Air Fighting – Reduction of German Air Force in Italy – Diversionary Value of the Third Front – A Summary.

*E*ARLY in October, on Kesselring's advice, Hitler changed his mind about his Italian strategy. Till then he had meant to withdraw his forces behind Rome and hold only Northern Italy. Now he ordered them to fight as far south as possible. The line selected, the so-called "Winterstellung", ran behind the river Sangro, on the Adriatic side, across the mountainous spine of Italy, to the mouth of the Garigliano on the west. The natural features of the country, its steep mountains and swift rivers, made this position, several miles in depth, immensely strong. After a year of almost continuous retreat in Africa, Sicily, and Italy the German troops were glad to turn about and fight.

Although the approach of winter would seriously impede our

actions, the main strategic decisions taken at Quebec were helped by the Germans committing themselves so deeply. The primacy accorded to our cross-Channel invasion made Italy henceforward a secondary theatre. That Hitler felt impelled to use so many troops to resist our advance favoured our major objective, but did not justify our making a failure of the Italian campaign.

The Fifth Army resumed their attacks on October 12, and after a ten days' struggle both its corps, the Xth British and VIth American, were well established across the river Volturno and ready to engage the enemy's next delaying position, a series of heights lying south of the river Garigliano. Another week of fighting was needed to eject the enemy from these, but in the first fortnight in November the Army came to grips with the forward defences of the "Winterstellung". On this front the Fifth Army, of six divisions, was faced by an equal number of Germans, who were fighting with their usual stubbornness. The first probing efforts at the German line met with little success. Our men had been fighting hard for two months, the weather was shocking, and the troops needed rest and re-grouping. Nevertheless the plans made at Quebec for a different situation were rigidly enforced and the Mediterranean was to be largely stripped of landing-craft.

Thus the position in Italy was changed greatly to our disadvantage. The Germans were strongly reinforced and ordered to resist instead of to withdraw. The Allies, on the contrary, were sending eight of their best divisions from Italy and the Mediterranean back to England for the cross-Channel attack in 1944. The four extra divisions I was gathering or had sent did not repair the loss. A deadlock supervened, and was not relieved during eight months of severe fighting, which will presently be recounted.

* * *

With these facts on my mind I telegraphed to General Alexander on October 24:

Naturally I am made anxious by the departure while your battle is on of our two fine divisions, 50th and 51st, in pursuance of Quebec decisions. I should like to have your feelings about the strength of your army for the tasks which lie immediately ahead. Has the Eighth Army yet pulled its tail up? You mentioned 24th as the date.

2. I am asking for a Combined Staffs Conference somewhere in

Africa about November 15. Anyhow, I shall be along your way about that time. I have much to tell you. Every good wish.

Alexander replied that the number of German divisions in Italy was naturally causing him some anxiety. Their effect would depend on how far the enemy could maintain strong forces south of Rome. Everything was being done to paralyse the German lines of communication by air action, and he was keen to build up our air forces in Italy. All this took time, labour, and material. The Eighth Army had wound up their tail and started their offensive, which was making satisfactory progress in its early stages. "I consider," he said, "that the situation requires very careful watching. I am glad to hear you are visiting us shortly, and will be very glad to see you."

★　　★　　★

On the same day General Eisenhower held a Commanders' Conference. He called upon Alexander to review the situation. Alexander's report was so serious that Eisenhower transmitted the entire text to the President and to me. He endorsed all that Alexander had said and described his statement as giving a clear and accurate picture.

PART I

1. (a) On September 9, the date of the launching of "Avalanche" and the announcement of the Italian armistice, the estimate of the general enemy situation was that two divisions were opposing the advance of the Eighth Army in Calabria; one division was in the heel of Italy; three divisions were in a position south of Rome and available to take action against the Allied landing in Salerno Bay; more than two divisions were in the neighbourhood of Rome and nine in the north of Italy. The Germans therefore had a total of some eighteen divisions at their disposal on the mainland. Of these it was considered that some would be engaged in Northern Italy to deal with the internal situation, which was expected to cause them considerable embarrassment.

(b) It was of course realised that our assaults near Salerno would prove hazardous in the face of German opposition, but it was thought that the Italian situation, coupled with the opportunity of landing light forces in the heel and our overwhelming air superiority, weighted the scales sufficiently in our favour, and the risks quite rightly were taken. Further, landing-craft were available in large numbers, and gave us liberty of manœuvre and flexibility in both build-up and mainten-

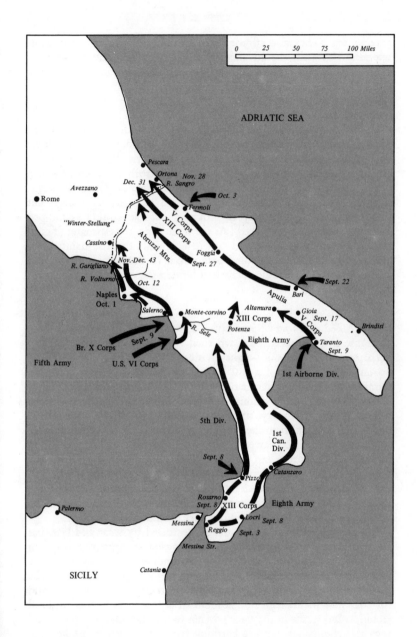

SOUTHERN ITALY: OPERATIONS, SEPT.—DEC. 1943

ance by sea. They also afforded the possibility of further amphibious operations to assist the advance by land. This flexibility proved invaluable, and was utilised fully by the Eighth Army in its operations along the coast of Calabria and by the Seventh Army in reinforcing the Salerno area with one division from Sicily in the critical early days of the battle.

(c) Although at that time it was known that craft were to be withdrawn during the winter, the number to be withdrawn and the dates of withdrawal were not established. Our plans then envisaged an estimated build-up of 1,300 vehicles a day from all Mediterranean ports. Such a figure meant that a total of twenty Allied divisions, together with the tactical air forces, could factually have been put intò Italy by the end of the year, provided that they could be equipped and their maintenance assured. At the same time, the estimates of craft available for the future allowed sufficient elasticity to assist maintenance and to provide for amphibious operations in conjunction with the land advance to Rome, should such steps be necessary.

PART II

2. (a) To-day the situation has changed greatly. In the south eleven Allied divisions oppose nine German, while farther north there are some fifteen more, a known total of twenty-four divisions, and perhaps as high as twenty-eight divisions. On the basis that there are no unforeseen causes of a still lower rate of build-up, the optimum number of formations at our disposal on the mainland will be: end of November, thirteen divisions; end of December, fourteen to fifteen divisions; end of January, sixteen to seventeen divisions. Our rate of build-up has fallen from the previous estimate of 1,300 vehicles a day to an estimated 2,000 a week, with a consequent delay in the calling forward of air forces and Army formations. The reduction in the build-up of ground forces has also been influenced by the decision to move the Strategic Air Force into the Foggia area as rapidly as possible rather than to wait for the capture of bases in the Rome area. The demands of the air forces should be met by the end of the year.

(b) The reduction in craft, already decreased by wear and tear, has been so serious as to preclude us from taking advantage, other than with minor forces, of the enemy's inherent weakness, which is the exposure of his two flanks to turning movements from the sea. The majority of such craft as are available are required for build-up and for coastwise maintenance on account of demolitions to road and rail facilities, and traffic in the ports, owing to the shortage of lighters and tugs and enemy sabotage to berthing facilities, which will take time to repair.

3. (a) An examination of the enemy position has shown that his

lines of communication enable him to build up in Italy, mainly in the north, to the order of sixty divisions, should they be available, and maintain them there in the winter months, despite our air superiority. The Germans clearly are trying to form a reserve by shortening their lines round the Fortress of Europe. Such a reserve could be employed in reinforcing further their armies in Italy.

(b) In comparison, the Allied position is less favourable. With the resources available no increase in rate of build-up can be made. A stabilised front south of Rome cannot be accepted, for the capital has a significance far greater than its strategic location, and sufficient depth must be gained before the Foggia airfields and the port of Naples can be regarded as secure. This being so, the seizure of a firm defensive base north of Rome becomes imperative. Moreover, we cannot afford to adopt a purely defensive rôle, for this would entail the surrender of the initiative to the Germans.

PART III

4. The obvious present German intention is to hold a line south of Rome, where the country favours defence and allows no scope to the deployment of our superiority in armour or artillery. Coming bad weather will limit the employment of our air forces, as indeed it has done already. Enemy troops may be tired, but they can be relieved by formations from the north. There are indications that this is being done now. We have neither the formations nor the shipping to enable us to do so. It would therefore appear that we are committed to a long and costly advance to Rome, a "slogging match", with our present slight superiority in formations on the battle-front offset by the enemy opportunity for relief; for without sufficient resources in craft no out-flanking amphibious operation of a size sufficient to speed up our rate of advance is possible. There is a danger that a successful conclusion of this "slogging match" might leave us north of Rome in such a state of exhaustion and weakness as not to be able to hold what we have gained, if the Germans bring down from the north fresh divisions for a counter-offensive. An enemy strike of this nature may not be fully neutralised by our air forces during the winter months; other-wise I should feel no concern. The German reinforcement of Italy appears greater than warranted by the internal situation or by purely defensive requirements. If the opportunity for an easy success occurs there is little doubt that it will be seized upon to counter the effects of a year of defeats on all fronts and to raise German morale prior to the campaigns of 1944. The effect in the Balkans and in France might be particularly to our disadvantage.

5. (a) In conclusion, the picture in September looked rosy, pro-vided the initial assault at Salerno was successful. The German divisions

in the north were about to become involved in difficult internal security problems. In the south the rate of build-up was believed to be such that, given no reinforcement by reserve German formations, we should have had twenty divisions opposed to probably his eighteen by the end of December, and our full air force requirements have been on the mainland. It was believed that sufficient craft would be, available to turn his sea flanks and maintain forces over the beaches, as might be necessary.

(b) To sum up: To-day the situation is that eleven Allied divisions are fighting a frontal battle in country favouring the defence against an immediate strength of nine German divisions, which can be reinforced at any moment. Our build-up has dwindled to a maximum of sixteen to seventeen divisions by the end of January against a present enemy strength of a certain twenty-four divisions, and our resources are not available for amphibious operations of much more than local character. We may be delayed south of Rome sufficiently long to enable the Germans to clear up the situation in Northern Italy and then reinforce their southern front. In this case the initiative might well pass to them.

This was indeed a masterly document, which touched all the gravest issues of our strategy.

*　　*　　*

I had already raised some of these issues with General Marshall.

Prime Minister to General Marshall (Washington)　　　　24 Oct 43
I hope the President will show you my long telegram to him about our much-needed meeting in Africa. Naturally I feel in my marrow the withdrawal of our 50th and 51st Divisions, our best, from the very edge of the Battle of Rome in the interests of distant "Overlord". We are carrying out our contract, but I pray God it does not cost us dear.

And I now telegraphed the President.

Former Naval Person to President Roosevelt　　　　26 Oct 43
You will have seen by now Eisenhower's [report] setting forth the condition into which we are sinking in Italy. We must not let this great Italian battle degenerate into a deadlock. At all costs we must win Rome and the airfields to the north of it. The fact that the enemy have diverted such powerful forces to this theatre vindicates our strategy. No one can doubt that by knocking out Italy we have enormously helped the Russian advance in the only way in which it

could have been helped at this time. I feel that Eisenhower and Alexander must have what they need to win the battle in Italy, no matter what effect is produced on subsequent operations.

I am so grieved to worry you with these matters while you are still suffering from influenza.

General Marshall replied on October 27 that he believed Eisenhower had adequate troops to fight in Italy without taking undue risks. His immediate problem was landing-craft, which would be examined. It seemed to him that in estimating the Italian situation the tremendous advantage of our overwhelming superiority in aircraft was almost ignored. Bad weather could not blot out for certain or for a long period the inevitable result of massed attack on enemy communications.

* * *

I now appealed to the President about the landing-craft in the Mediterranean.

Prime Minister to President Roosevelt   4 Nov 43
It is with very great regret that I must bring to your notice the increasing anxiety of His Majesty's Government about the withdrawal of landing-craft from the Mediterranean at this critical juncture. We now have before us General Eisenhower's forecast that he will not be able to occupy the line necessary to protect the Rome airfields before the end of January, or even February, if the present programme of withdrawals of landing-craft is rigidly adhered to. He further explains the costly and prolonged frontal attacks that will be necessary in order to achieve this disappointing result. We feel entitled to ask our American Allies to attach weight to our earnest representations in view of the very great preponderance of British troops deployed against the enemy in Italy, with proportionate losses, and also in view of the clear opinions of the United States Commander-in-Chief, under whom we serve.

2. Accordingly, the War Cabinet have formally desired me to ask that consideration shall be given by the United States Chiefs of Staff to the requests put forward by the British Chiefs of Staff. We very much regret that the urgency of the matter does not permit us to wait another three weeks until the next Staff Conference can be convened, as this would entail the departure or immobilisation meanwhile of the landing-craft, with grave injury to the Italian campaign.

3. I may mention that by various intense efforts we have every hope that an additional seventy-five tank landing-craft can be produced in the United Kingdom by the date fixed for "Overlord".

I was relieved to receive his reply.

President Roosevelt to Prime Minister   6 Nov 43
The Combined Chiefs of Staff to-day authorised Eisenhower to retain until December 15 sixty-eight L.S.T.s now scheduled for an early departure for the United Kingdom.
It seems to me that this action ought to meet his essential requirements.

I told Alexander at once. He answered:

General Alexander to Prime Minister   9 Nov 43
The retention of L.S.T.s will do a great deal to help my plans, and am most grateful for them. December 15 will not however allow me to carry out the whole of my plan, and I have explained this in telegram to C.I.G.S.

Prime Minister to General Alexander   9 Nov 43
You should make alternative campaign plans on the basis that the L.S.T.s stay on till January 15. I am pretty certain this will be agreed to at our Conference.

I also sent the following to our Ambassador in Moscow:

Prime Minister to Sir A. Clark Kerr   9 Nov 43
... The exceptionally good weather on the Russian front has carried with it heavy rains in Italy, and the frontal attacks we have had to make with forces which, though not very much stronger than those of the enemy, have been continuously active, have necessarily yielded slow progress.
My wish has always been to sustain and press to the utmost the campaign in Italy and to attract to that front and hold upon it as many divisions as possible. I am glad to say that agreement has been reached by the Combined Staffs that no more landing-craft shall be withdrawn until December 15. This will enable greater power to be put into the whole of our Italian operations. By new intense exertions at home I hope to make up by additional building of landing-craft for the delay in sending home the others.
Half the German strength is in Northern Italy and Istria, separated from our front by some 300 miles. It is from that half that the withdrawals back to South Russia have been made. They have been rendered possible, not by any inactivity on our fighting front, but by a diminution of the risks to internal security due to the passive attitude of the Italians in Northern Italy. We are in no doubt of the correctness of the estimate of German strength given by General Ismay. When he spoke there were six Panzer divisions there, half of them

fighting on our front. Deployed south of Rome there are now ten German divisions identified in action, against which we have twelve or thirteen of rather greater strength. This is not much of a preponderance for a continuous frontal attack in mountainous country.

To General Brooke I wrote:

Prime Minister to C.I.G.S. 16 Nov 43

It has now become urgent that Poles should enter the line. They have not done all these years, although an immense amount of preparation and material has been employed. Reinforcements also are urgently needed in Italy, and the Poles are scheduled to go next after the New Zealanders. This is not the time to make changes in their organisation. It is better to take the chance of two divisions becoming under strength. They would still be called the Polish Corps, and we must endeavour to find drafts from other quarters. . . .

Sooner than break up these organisations so laboriously formed in Persia, I would make an inroad on the Polish Armoured Division in Great Britain, which will not be engaged for some time to come. However, I believe that if Polish troops enter the line and are seen to be fighting the Germans it may be possible to obtain a further draft of Poles from Stalin, and I propose to try for this when we meet. The Soviet Government is inclined to be sceptical about this Polish Corps, and suspect that it is being held back and nursed so as to be employed against the Russians in defence of Polish rights. If however the Polish Corps enters the line against the Germans and begins to fight this view will be dissipated. Meanwhile I cannot approve any alteration in the existing unit.

* * *

I was increasingly disturbed by the great strain thrown on our limited shipping by the demands of the Allied Heavy Bomber Force, which was being built up on the Foggia airfields in order to attack industrial targets in Eastern Germany beyond the range of our home-based squadrons. It seemed to me that these demands were disproportionate and unrelated to the general situation at that time.

Prime Minister to General Ismay, for C.O.S. Committee 17 Nov 43

It is surely altogether wrong to build up the Strategic Air Force in Italy at the expense of the battle for Rome. The strategic bombing of Germany, however important, cannot take precedence over the battle, which must ever rank first in our thoughts. Major tactical needs must always have priority over strategic policy. I was not aware until recently that the build-up of the Army had been obstructed by the forward move of a mass of strategic air not connected with the battle. This is in fact a departure from all orthodox military doctrine, as well as seeming wrong from the point of view of common sense.

And a week later:

The monstrous block of air, in its eagerness to get ahead, has definitely hampered the operations of the Army.

*   *   *

The Eighth Army meanwhile had moved forward, and after a series of actions closed up to the river Sangro. Here four German divisions were installed. In order to retain the initiative it was General Alexander's intention that the Eighth Army should cross the river, break through the "Winterstellung" on this front, and then advance as far as the road Pescara–Avezzano, whence they would threaten Rome and endanger the communications of the enemy on the western coast. Bridgeheads were thrown across the river, but the main enemy defences lay on high ground beyond. Bad weather, with rain, mud, and swollen rivers, postponed the attack until November 28, but then the 78th, 8th Indian, and New Zealand Divisions, the last recently arrived, attacked and made good progress. After a week of heavy fighting they were established ten miles beyond the Sangro. By December 20 the Canadians had reached the outskirts of Ortone, but it was not until three days after Christmas, after very severe fighting, that the town was cleared of the enemy. This was the first big street-fighting battle, and from it many lessons were learned. But the enemy still held firm, and more reinforcements came to them from Northern Italy. Some more ground was gained during December by the Eighth Army, but no vital objectives were taken, and winter weather brought active operations to a close.

The U.S. Fifth Army, under General Clark, struggled on up the road towards Cassino, and attacked the foremost defences of the German main positions. The enemy were strongly posted on mountains overlooking the road on either side. The formidable Monte Cassino massif to the west was attacked by the Xth British and IInd U.S. Corps on December 2, and finally cleared a week later after a tough struggle. East of the road equally severe operations were carried out by the IInd and VIth U.S. Corps, the latter now including the 2nd Moroccan Division. It was not till the beginning of the New Year that the enemy were ejected and the Fifth Army fully aligned along the river Garigliano and its tributary, the Rapido, where it faced the heights of Cassino and the famous monastery.

In all these land operations the armies had been fully supported by our tactical air forces, while our Strategical Air Force had carried out a number of useful raids behind the enemy lines, notably on Turin, where an important ball-bearing plant was destroyed by American Fortresses. The German Air Force, on the other hand, put forth relatively little effort. By day fighter and fighter-bomber sorties were few. Half a dozen raids by their long-range heavy bombers on Naples had little effect, but a very damaging surprise attack on our crowded harbour of Bari on December 2 blew up an ammunition ship with a chance hit and caused the sinking of sixteen other ships and the loss of 30,000 tons of cargo.

The Germans hardly troubled to contest the mastery of the air that winter over Italy, and greatly reduced their air strength, as the following table shows:

GERMAN AIR FORCE STRENGTH

	July 1, 1943	Oct. 1, 1943	Jan. 1, 1944
Central Mediterranean	975	430	370

Our growing air offensive from England made the enemy withdraw all that could be spared from the Mediterranean and Russia. Every long-range bomber in Italy was taken away for "reprisals" against England, the "Little Blitz" of the following spring.

For reasons which have been explained I had called the Italian campaign the Third Front. It had attracted to itself twenty good German divisions. If the garrisons kept in the Balkans for fear of attack there are added, nearly forty divisions were retained facing the Allies in the Mediterranean. Our Second Front, North-West Europe, had not yet flared into battle, but its existence was real. About thirty enemy divisions was the least number ever opposite it, and this rose to sixty as the invasion loomed closer. Our strategic bombing from Britain forced the enemy to divert great numbers of men and masses of material to defend their homeland. These were not negligible contributions to the Russians on what they had every right to call the First Front.

★   ★   ★

I must end this chapter with a summary.

In this period in the war all the great strategic combinations of the Western Powers were restricted and distorted by the shortage of tank landing-craft for the transport, not so much of tanks, but of vehicles of all kinds. The letters "L.S.T." (Landing Ship, Tanks) are burnt in upon the minds of all those who dealt with military affairs in this period. We had invaded Italy in strong force. We had an army there which, if not supported, might be entirely cast away, giving Hitler the greatest triumph he had had since the fall of France. On the other hand, there could be no question of our not making the "Overlord" attack in 1944: The utmost I asked for was an easement, if necessary, of two months—*i.e.*, from some time in May 1944 to some time in July. This would meet the problem of the landing-craft. Instead of their having to return to England in the late autumn of 1943 before the winter gales, they could go in the early spring of 1944. If however the May date were insisted upon pedantically, and interpreted as May 1, the peril to the Allied Army in Italy seemed beyond remedy. If some of the landing-craft earmarked for "Overlord" were allowed to stay in the Mediterranean over the winter there would be no difficulty in making a success of the Italian campaign. There were masses of troops not in action in the Mediterranean: three or four French divisions, two or three American divisions, at least four (including the Poles) British or British-controlled divisions. The one thing that stood between these and effective operation in Italy was the L.S.T.s, and the main thing that stood between us and the L.S.T.s was the insistence upon an early date for their return to Britain.

The reader of the telegrams printed in this chapter must not be misled by a chance phrase here and there into thinking (*a*) that I wanted to abandon "Overlord", (*b*) that I wanted to deprive "Overlord" of vital forces, or (*c*) that I contemplated a campaign by armies operating in the Balkan peninsula. These are legends. Never had such a wish entered my mind. Give me the easement of six weeks or two months from May 1 in the date of "Overlord" and I could for several months use the landing-craft in the Mediterranean in order to bring really effective forces to bear in Italy, and thus not only take Rome, but draw off German divisions from either or both the Russian and Normandy fronts. All these matters had been discussed in Washington without regard to the limited character of the issues with which my argument was concerned.

As we shall see presently, in the end everything that I asked for was done. The landing-craft not only were made available for upkeep in the Mediterranean; they were even allowed a further latitude for the sake of the Anzio operation in January. This in no way prevented the successful launching of "Overlord" on June 6 with adequate forces. What happened however was that the long fight about trying to get these small easements and to prevent the scrapping of one vast front in order to conform to a rigid date upon the other led to prolonged, unsatisfactory operations in Italy.

CHAPTER XV

ARCTIC CONVOYS AGAIN

Suspension of the Convoys in March 1943 – Intense Struggle on the Eastern Front – The Soviet Summer Offensive – Battles of Kursk, Orel, and Kharkov – Retreat of the German Armies – Kiev Regained, November 6 – Molotov Asks for the Convoys to be Resumed – I Press the Admiralty to Comply – The "Tirpitz" Disabled – Hard Treatment of Our Personnel in North Russia – A List of Modest Requests – Mr. Eden Leaves for Moscow – Stalin's Answer to My Letter – I Report its Character to Mr. Eden and the President – I Refuse to Receive Stalin's Message from the Soviet Ambassador – The War Cabinet Endorses My Action – Mr. Eden's Account of His Discussion with Stalin and Molotov on October 21 – The Convoys are Resumed – The "Scharnhorst" Sunk by Admiral Fraser in the "Duke of York", December 25, 1943 – End of the "Tirpitz".

THE year 1942 had closed in Arctic waters with the spirited action by British destroyers escorting a convoy to North Russia. As recorded in a previous volume, this had led to a crisis in the German High Command and the dismissal of Admiral Raeder from control of naval affairs. Between January and March, in the remaining months of almost perpetual darkness, two more convoys, of forty-two ships and six ships sailing independently, set out on this hazardous voyage. Forty arrived. During the same period thirty-six ships were safely brought back from Russian ports and five were lost. The return of daylight made it easier for the enemy to attack the convoys. What was left of the German Fleet, including the *Tirpitz*, was now concentrated in Norwegian waters, and presented a formidable and continuing threat along a large part of the route. Furthermore, the Atlantic, as always, remained the decisive theatre in the war at sea, and in March 1943 the battle with the U-boats was moving to a violent crisis. The strain on our destroyers was more than we could bear. The March convoy had to be postponed, and in April the Admiralty proposed, and I agreed, that supplies to Russia by this route should be suspended till the autumn darkness.

*　　*　　*

This decision was taken with deep regret because of the tremendous battles on the Russian front which distinguished the campaign of 1943. After the spring thaw both sides gathered themselves for a momentous struggle. The Russians, both on land and in the air, had now the upper hand, and the Germans can have had few hopes of ultimate victory. Nevertheless they got their blow in first. The Russian salient at Kursk projected dangerously into the German front, and it was decided to pinch it out by simultaneous attacks from north and south. This was foreseen by the Russians, who had had full warning and were ready. In consequence, when the attack started on July 5 the Germans met an enemy strongly installed in well-prepared defences. The northern attack made some ground, but at the end of a fortnight it had been thrown back. In the south success at first was greater and the Germans bit fifteen miles into the Russian lines. Then major counter-attacks began, and by July 23 the Russian line was fully restored. The German offensive had completely failed. They gained no advantages to make up for their heavy losses, and the new "Tiger" tanks, on which they had counted for success, had been mauled by the Russian artillery.

The German Army had already been depleted by its previous campaigns in Russia and diluted by inclusion of its second-rate allies. A great part of its strength had been massed against Kursk at the expense of other sectors of the thousand-mile active front. Now, when the Russian blows began to fall, it was unable to parry them. While the Kursk battle was still raging and the German reserves had been deeply committed the first blow came on July 12 against the German salient around Orel. After intense artillery preparation the main Russian attack fell on the northern face of the salient, with subsidiary onslaughts in the east. Deep penetrations were soon made, and although the defenders fought stoutly their strong-points were in succession outflanked, surrounded, and reduced. Their counter-attacks were repulsed, and under the weight of superior numbers and material they were overborne. Orel fell on August 5, and by the 18th the whole salient to a depth of fifty miles had been cut out.

The second major Russian offensive opened on August 3, while the Orel attack was still at its height. This time it was the German salient around Kharkov that suffered. Kharkov was an important centre of communications, and barred the way to the Ukraine and the Donetz industrial basin. Its defences had been prepared with more than usual thoroughness. Again the major attacks fell on the northern face of the salient, one being directed due south against Kharkov itself, another thrusting south-westwards so as to threaten the whole German rear. Within forty-eight hours both of these had bitten deep, in places up to thirty miles, and Bielgorod had been taken. By August 11 Kharkov was threatened on three sides, a further attack from the east having been launched, while fifty miles to the north-west the Russians were advancing fast. On that day Hitler ordered that Kharkov was to be held at all costs. The German garrison stood to fight it out, and it was not till the 23rd that the whole town was in Russian hands.

These three immense battles of Kursk, Orel, and Kharkov, all within a space of two months, marked the ruin of the German army on the Eastern Front. Everywhere they had been outfought and overwhelmed. The Russian plan, vast though it was, never outran their resources. It was not only on land that the Russians proved their new superiority. In the air about 2,500 German aircraft were opposed by at least twice as many Russian planes, whose efficiency had been much improved. The German Air Force at this period of the war was at the peak of its strength, numbering about 6,000 aircraft in all. That less than half could be spared to support this crucial campaign is proof enough of the value to Russia of our operations in the Mediterranean and of the growing Allied bomber effort based on Britain. In fighter aircraft especially the Germans felt the pinch. Although inferior on the Eastern Front, yet in September they had to weaken it still more in order to defend themselves in the West, where by the winter nearly three-quarters of the total German fighter strength was deployed. The swift and overlapping Russian blows gave the Germans no opportunity to make the best use of their air resources. Air units were frequently moved from one battle area to another in order to meet a fresh crisis, and wherever they went, leaving a gap behind them, they found the Russian planes in overmastering strength.

In September the Germans were in retreat along the whole of their southern front, from opposite Moscow to the Black Sea. The Russians swung forward in full pursuit. At the northern hinge a Russian thrust from Viazma took Smolensk on September 25. No doubt the Germans hoped to stand on the Dnieper, the next great river line, but by early October the Russians were across it north of Kiev, and to the south at Pereyaslav and Kremenchug. Farther south again Dniepropetrovsk was taken on October 25. Only near the mouth of the river were the Germans still on the western bank of the Dnieper; all the rest had gone. The land approach to the Crimea, at Perekop, was captured by the Red Army, and the retreat of the strong German garrison in the Crimea was cut off. Kiev, outflanked on either side, fell on November 6, with many prisoners, and the Russians, driving forward, reached Korosten and Jitomir. But a strong armoured counter-attack on their flank drove them back, and the Germans recaptured the two towns. Here the front stabilised for the time being. In the north Gomel was taken at the end of November, and the upper reaches of the Dnieper crossed on each side of Mogilev.

By December, after a three months' pursuit, the German armies in Central and South Russia had been thrust back more than two hundred miles, and, failing to hold the Dnieper river line, lay open and vulnerable to a winter campaign in which, as they knew from bitter experience, their opponents excelled. Such was the grand Russian story of 1943.

★   ★   ★

It was natural that the Soviet Government should look reproachfully at the suspension of the convoys, for which their armies hungered. On the evening of September 21 M. Molotov sent for our Ambassador in Moscow and asked for the sailings to be resumed. He pointed out that the Italian Fleet had been eliminated and that the U-boats had abandoned the North Atlantic for the southern route. The Persian railway could not carry enough. For three months the Soviet Union had been undertaking a wide and most strenuous offensive, yet in 1943 they had

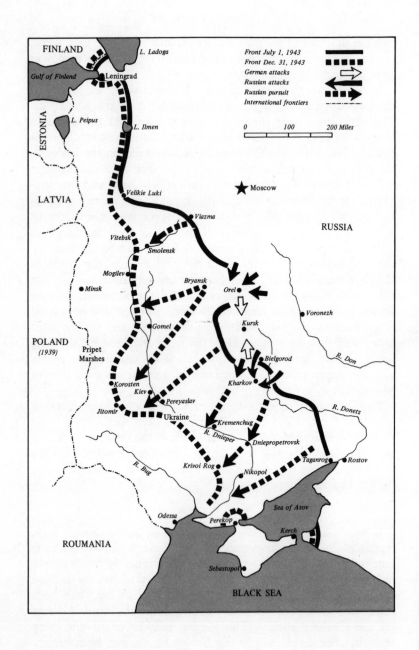

OPERATIONS IN RUSSIA, JULY—DEC. 1943

received less than a third of the previous year's supplies. The Soviet Government therefore "insisted" upon the urgent resumption of the convoys, and expected His Majesty's Government to take all necessary measures within the next few days.

Though there was much to be said in answer to all this, I raised the matter with the Admiralty and others on September 25.

Prime Minister to Foreign Secretary, Minister of Production,   25 Sept 43
Minister of War Transport, General Ismay, for C.O.S.
Committee, and Acting First Sea Lord

It is our duty if humanly possible to reopen these Arctic convoys, beginning in the latter part of November in accordance with the moon phase. We should try to run November, December, January, February, and March convoys, total five. Plans should be prepared by the Admiralty and the Ministry of War Transport. I understand that this is feasible.

Now that the Russians have asked for the reopening of these convoys we are entitled to make a very plain request to them for the better treatment of our personnel in North Russia.

The first reply from the Admiralty about the convoys was disappointing to me.

Prime Minister to Foreign Secretary, First Lord, General   27 Sept 43
Ismay, for C.O.S. Committee, and others concerned

CONVOYS TO NORTH RUSSIA

This is not satisfactory. Why cannot the November convoy be a full one? This also applies to the December 8 convoy. We must try to run at least five full convoys before "Overlord" operations start. I do not agree that the situation in the Atlantic or in the Mediterranean will be as strained as it was when we were running these convoys before. Naturally I am not going to make a solemn contract with Marshal Stalin, and we must safeguard ourselves against unforeseeable contingencies, but I consider that November, December, January, February, and March should each see a full-sized convoy dispatched.

I will have a Staff meeting on this subject at 10 p.m. on Tuesday night.

When we met on the night of the 29th to discuss the problem an agreeable new fact was before us. The *Tirpitz* had been disabled by the audacious and heroic attack of our midget submarines. Of six craft which took part two penetrated all the elaborate defences. Their commanding officers, Lieutenant

Cameron, R.N.R., and Lieutenant Place, R.N., rescued by the Germans, survived as prisoners of war, and received the Victoria Cross. Later air reconnaissance showed that the battleship was heavily damaged and would require refit in a dockyard before she could again be ready for action. The *Lützow* had already gone to the Baltic. Thus we had an easement, probably of some months, in the Arctic waters, and I was able to minute to the Foreign Secretary:

The resumption of the convoys question is practically settled in a favourable sense. Before I send my telegram to Stalin about it let me see your list of grievances about the treatment of our people in North Russia, so that I can combine the two to the best advantage. I should like to do the telegram to-night.

Mr. Eden's complaints were serious, and I accordingly sent the following telegram to Stalin:

Prime Minister to Premier Stalin   1 Oct 43
I have received your request for the reopening of the convoys to North Russia. I and all my colleagues are most anxious to help you and the valiant armies you lead to the utmost of our ability. I do not therefore reply to the various controversial points made in M. Molotov's communication. Since June 22, 1941, we have always done our best in spite of our own heavy burdens to help you defend your country against the cruel invasion of the Hitlerite gang, and we have never ceased to acknowledge and proclaim the great advantages that have come to us from the splendid victories you have won and from the deadly blows you have dealt the German armies.

2. For the last four days I have been working with the Admiralty to make a plan for sending a new series of convoys to North Russia. This entails very great difficulties. First the Battle of the Atlantic has begun again. The U-boats have set about us with a new kind of acoustic torpedo, which has proved effective against the escorting vessels when hunting U-boats. Secondly, we are at very full stretch in the Mediterranean, building up an army in Italy of about 600,000 men by the end of November, and also trying to take full advantage of the Italian collapse in the Ægean islands and the Balkan peninsula. Thirdly, we have to provide for our share of the war against Japan, in which the United States are greatly interested, and whose people would be offended if we were lukewarm.

3. Notwithstanding the above it is a very great pleasure to me to tell you that we are planning to sail a series of four convoys to North Russia in November, December, January, and February, each

of which will consist of approximately thirty-five ships, British and American. Convoys may be sailed in two halves to meet operational requirements. The first convoy will leave the United Kingdom about November 12, arriving North Russia ten days later; subsequent convoys at about twenty-eight-day intervals. We intend to withdraw as many as possible of the merchant vessels now in North Russia towards the end of October, and the remainder with returning convoy escorts.

To avoid new charges of breach of faith from the Soviet, if our efforts to help them proved vain, I inserted a safeguarding paragraph:

4. However, I must put it on record that this is no contract or bargain, but rather a declaration of our solemn and earnest resolve. On this basis I have ordered the necessary measures to be taken for the sending of these four convoys of thirty-five ships.

I then proceeded with our list of grievances about the treatment of our men in North Russia.

5. The Foreign Office and the Admiralty however request me to put before you for your personal attention, hoping indeed that your own eye may look at it, the following representations about the difficulties we have experienced in North Russia.

6. If we are to resume the convoys we shall have to reinforce our establishments in North Russia, which have been reduced in numbers since last March. The present numbers of naval personnel are below what is necessary, even for our present requirements, owing to men having to be sent home without relief. Your civil authorities have refused us all visas for men to go to North Russia, even to relieve those who are seriously overdue for relief. M. Molotov has pressed His Majesty's Government to agree that the number of British Service personnel in North Russia should not exceed that of the Soviet Service personnel and trade delegation in this country. We have been unable to accept this proposal, since their work is quite dissimilar and the number of men needed for war operations cannot be determined in such an unpractical way. Secondly, as we have already informed the Soviet Government, we must ask to be the judges of the personnel required to carry out operations for which we are responsible. Mr. Eden has already given his assurance that the greatest care will be taken to limit the numbers strictly to the minimum.

7. I must therefore ask you to agree to the immediate grant of visas for the additional personnel now required, and for your assurance that you will not in future withhold visas when we find it necessary to ask

for them in connection with the assistance that we are giving you in North Russia. I emphasise that of about one hundred and seventy naval personnel at present in the North over one hundred and fifty should have been relieved some months ago, but Soviet visas have been withheld. The state of health of these men, who are unaccustomed to the climatic and other conditions, makes it very necessary to relieve them without further delay.

8. We should also wish to send the small medical unit for Archangel to which your authorities agreed, but for which the necessary visas have not been granted. Please remember that we may have heavy casualties.

9. I must also ask your help in remedying the conditions under which our Service personnel and seamen at present find themselves in North Russia. These men are of course engaged in operations against the enemy in our joint interest, and chiefly to bring Allied supplies to your country. They are, I am sure you will admit, in a wholly different position from ordinary individuals proceeding to Russian territory. Yet they are subjected by your authorities to the following restrictions, which seem to me inappropriate for men sent by an ally to carry out operations of the greatest interest to the Soviet Union:

(a) No one may land from one of H.M. ships or from a British merchant ship except by a Soviet boat in the presence of a Soviet official and after examination of documents on each occasion.

(b) No one from a British warship is allowed to proceed alongside a British merchantman without the Soviet authorities being informed beforehand. This even applies to the British admiral in charge.

(c) British officers and men are required to obtain special passes before they can go from ship to shore or between two British shore stations. These passes are often much delayed, with consequent dislocation of the work in hand.

(d) No stores, luggage, or mail for this operational force may be landed except in the presence of a Soviet official, and numerous formalities are required for the shipment of all stores and mail.

(e) Private Service mail is subjected to censorship, although for an operational force of this kind censorship should, in our view, be left in the hands of British Service authorities.

10. The imposition of these restrictions makes an impression upon officers and men alike which is bad for Anglo-Soviet relations, and would be deeply injurious if Parliament got to hear of it. The cumulative effect of these formalities has been most hampering to the efficient performance of the men's duties, and on more than one

occasion to urgent and important operations. No such restrictions are placed upon Soviet personnel here.

11. We have already proposed to M. Molotov that as regards offences against Soviet law committed by personnel of the Services and of the ships of the convoys, they should be handed over to the British Service authorities to be dealt with. There have been a few such cases no doubt, partially at any rate due to the rigorous conditions of service in the North.

12. I trust indeed, M. Stalin, that you will find it possible to have these difficulties smoothed out in a friendly spirit, so that we may help each other, and the common cause, to the utmost of our strength.

These were modest requests considering the efforts we were now to make. No answer was received for nearly a fortnight.

* * *

As will be described in the next chapter, the Conference of the Foreign Secretaries of the three major Allies, long planned, was now due in Moscow. On October 9 Mr. Eden set out by air. His journey lay through Cairo and Teheran, where he had much business, and he did not reach Moscow till the morning of October 18. During his absence I took charge of the Foreign Office.

Prime Minister to Sir A. Clark Kerr (Moscow)   12 Oct 43

I have received no answer to my long telegram of October 1 about resuming the Arctic convoys. If the cycle of convoys is to begin on November 12 we must have an early reply to our requests about personnel. Several dozens of wireless operators and signals personnel, on whose work the safety of the convoys may well depend, are to leave the United Kingdom, together with about one hundred and fifty reliefs for men due to return home, by destroyers sailing from the United Kingdom on October 21. Pray therefore press for an answer. Meanwhile we are preparing the convoys in the hope that the Soviets still desire them.

Next day I received Stalin's answer.

Premier Stalin to Prime Minister   13 Oct 43

I received your message of October 1 informing me of the intention to send four convoys to the Soviet Union by the Northern route in November, December, January, and February. However, this communication loses its value by your statement that this intention to send Northern convoys to the U.S.S.R. is neither an obligation nor an agreement, but only a statement, which, as it may be understood, is one the British side can at any moment renounce regardless of any influence it may have on the Soviet armies at the front. I must say that I cannot agree with such a posing of the question. Supplies from the British Government to the U.S.S.R., armaments and other military goods, cannot be considered otherwise than as an obligation, which, by special agreement between our countries, the British Government undertook in respect of the U.S.S.R., which bears on its shoulders, already for the third year, the enormous burden of struggle with the common enemy of the Allies—Hitlerite Germany.

It is also impossible to disregard the fact that the Northern route is the shortest way which permits delivery of armaments supplied by the Allies within the shortest period to the Soviet-German front, and the realisation of the plan of supplies to the U.S.S.R. in appropriate volume is impossible without an adequate use of this way. As I already wrote to you earlier, and as experience has shown, delivery of armaments and military supplies to the U.S.S.R. through Persian ports cannot compensate in any way for those supplies which were not delivered by the Northern route.

By the way, for some reason or other there was a very considerable decrease in the delivery of military goods sent by the Northern route this year in comparison with those received last year; and this makes it impossible to fulfil the established [Soviet] plan of military supplies [to the armies] and is in contradiction to the corresponding Anglo-Soviet protocol for military supplies. Therefore, at the present time, when the forces of the Soviet Union are strained to the utmost to secure the needs of the front in the interests of success of the struggle against the main forces of our common enemy, it would be inadmissible to have the supplies of the Soviet armies depend on the arbitrary judgment of the British side. It is impossible to consider this posing of the question to be other than a refusal of the British Government to fulfil the obligations it undertook, and as a kind of threat addressed to the U.S.S.R.

2. Concerning your mention of controversial points allegedly contained in the statement of M. Molotov, I have to say that I do not find any foundation for such a remark. I consider the principle of reciprocity and equality proposed by the Soviet side for settlement of the visa question in respect of personnel of the military missions to be a correct and indeed a just one. The reference to the difference in the functions of the British and Soviet military missions, and that the numbers of the staff of the British military mission must be determined by the British Government only, I consider to be unconvincing. It has already been made clear in detail in the previous *aide-mémoires* of the People's Commissariat for Foreign Affairs on this question.

3. I do not see the necessity for increasing the number of British Service-men in the north of the U.S.S.R., since the great majority of British Service-men who are already there are not adequately employed, and for many months have been doomed to idleness, as has already been pointed out several times by the Soviet side. For example, it can be mentioned that, owing to its non-necessity, the question of the liquidation of the British port base in Archangel was put forward several times, and only now the British side have agreed to liquidate it. There are also regrettable facts of the inadmissible behaviour of individual British Service-men who attempted, in several cases, to recruit, by bribery, certain Soviet citizens for Intelligence purposes. Such instances, offensive to Soviet citizens, naturally gave rise to incidents which led to undesirable complications.

4. Concerning your mention of formalities and certain restrictions existing in Northern ports, it is necessary to have in view that such formalities and restrictions are unavoidable in zones near and at the front, if one does not forget the war situation which exists in the U.S.S.R. I may add that this applies equally to the British and other foreigners as well as to Soviet citizens. Nevertheless the Soviet authorities granted many privileges in this respect to the British Servicemen and seamen, about which the British Embassy was informed as long ago as last March. Thus your mention of many formalities and restrictions is based on inaccurate information.

Concerning the question of censorship and prosecution of British Service-men, I have no objection if the censorship of private mail for British personnel in Northern ports would be made by the British authorities themselves, on condition of reciprocity, and also if cases of small violations committed by British Service-men which did not involve court procedure would be given to the consideration of the appropriate military authorities.

*   *   *

Mr. Eden had now left Cairo for Teheran, on his way to Moscow, so I sent him the following:

Prime Minister to Foreign Secretary (Teheran)   15 Oct 43
This offensive reply has been received to our telegram about convoys. I send you the reply which I have drafted. As you will be on the spot, I leave it to you to handle as you see fit. I do not think we should give way about the naval reliefs and signalmen. It would be a great relief to be freed from the burden of these convoys and to bring our men home from North Russia. If this is what they really mean and want we ought to oblige them.

Here was my draft:

Prime Minister to Premier Stalin   15 Oct 43

It is impossible for His Majesty's Government to guarantee that the four convoys mentioned can be run irrespective of the military situation on the seas. Every effort and heavy loss and sacrifice would however be made to do so if the Soviet Government attaches importance to the receipt of their cargoes. I cannot undertake to do more than my best, and His Majesty's Government must remain the judge of whether any particular operation of war to be carried out by their forces is in fact practicable or not.

2. The running of these four convoys would be a very great burden to the Royal Navy, and involves the diversion of much-needed flotillas from the anti-U-boat war and from the escorting of troop and other important convoys. It also exposes the main units of the Fleet to serious risks. His Majesty's Government would be very glad to be relieved of the task of running the convoys if the Soviet Government do not attach importance to them.

3. In particular the refusal of the request of the British Government in respect of the reliefs and small increases in the few hundreds of British Service-men in the north of the U.S.S.R., and in particular the signals personnel, on which the safety of these convoys to some extent depends, raises an insuperable obstacle. His Majesty's Government would be very glad to withdraw the handfuls of Service personnel from North Russia, and will do so as soon as they are assured that it is not the desire of the Soviet Government to receive the convoys under the modest and reasonable conditions which the British Government consider necessary.

I commented to the President:

Former Naval Person to President Roosevelt   16 Oct 43

About Russian convoys. I have now received a telegram from U.J. which I think you will feel is not exactly all one might hope for from a gentleman for whose sake we are to make an inconvenient, extreme, and costly exertion. I have sent a suggested answer to Anthony for him to handle as he thinks best.

2. I think, or at least I hope, this message came from the machine rather than from Stalin, as it took twelve days to prepare. The Soviet machine is quite convinced it can get everything by bullying, and I am sure it is a matter of some importance to show that this is not necessarily always true.

Mr. Eden had now reached Moscow.

Prime Minister to Foreign Secretary   18 Oct 43

It is a very good thing you are on the spot to deal with the convoy question. I am seeing the Soviet Ambassador at 3 p.m. to-day, and propose to hand him back the offensive message from Stalin, saying that I do not wish to receive it, as the matter will be settled by you at Moscow. You should not hand in my suggested reply, or take it as anything more than a guide.

Further, the first convoy is assembling and leaves on November 12. The ships are being loaded, and I have not thought it right to interfere with this process, especially as it would involve the United States, who have sent their ships at our suggestion. I hope however that in personal contact with Stalin you may point out, first, the importance of these four convoys, with the 140 cargoes, and the efforts I have had to make to secure the necessary escorts; secondly, the small, petty mitigations we ask in the treatment of our men in North Russia; thirdly, our natural desire to be relieved of the burden of these convoys and to bring our people home from North Russia; fourthly, you could also disabuse his mind of the idea that any threat was intended by my declining to make an absolute contract or bargain; all I wished to do was to reserve the final right of judging whether the operation was militarily practicable or could be attempted, having regard to the general situation in the Atlantic, without being accused, as usual, of a breach of faith, and I must maintain this reservation. . . .

I feel so much for you in the bleak Conference, and wish I were with you. You may have full confidence in the strength of the British position on all these questions, and I have every hope that you will make them feel at once our desire for their friendship and our will-power on essentials. All good luck.

★ ★ ★

On the same day I asked the Soviet Ambassador to come to see me. As this was the first occasion on which I had met M. Gousev, who had succeeded Maisky, he gave me the greetings of Marshal Stalin and M. Molotov, and I told him of the good reputation he had made for himself with us in Canada. After these compliments we had a short discussion about the Moscow Conference and the Second Front. I explained to him that this kind of operation could not be undertaken on impulse, and that I was always ready to arrange for a meeting between British and Russian military experts, who would go into the facts and figures, upon which everything depended, and without which discussion was futile. I spoke to him earnestly about the great desire we had to work with Russia and to be friends with her, how we saw that she should have a great place in the world after the war, that we should welcome this, and that we would do our best also to make good relations between her and the United States. I further said how much I was looking forward to a meeting with Marshal Stalin if it could be arranged, and how important this meeting of the heads of the British, American, and Soviet Governments was to the future of the world.

I then turned to Stalin's telegram about the convoys. I said very briefly that I did not think this message would help the situation, that it had caused me a good deal of pain, that I feared any reply which I could send would only make things worse, that the Foreign Secretary was in Moscow and I had left it to him to settle the matter on the spot and that therefore I did not wish to receive the message. I then handed back to the Ambassador an envelope. Gousev opened the envelope to see what was inside it, and, recognising the message, said he had been instructed to deliver it to me. I then said, "I am not prepared to receive it," and got up to indicate in a friendly manner that our conversation was at an end. I moved to the door and opened it. We had a little talk in the doorway about his coming to luncheon in the near future and discussing with Mrs. Churchill some questions connected with her Russian fund, which I told him had now reached four million pounds. I did not give M. Gousev a chance of recurring to the question of the convoys or of trying to hand me back the envelope, and bowed him out.

The War Cabinet endorsed my refusal to receive Stalin's telegram. It was certainly an unusual diplomatic incident, and, as I learnt later, it impressed the Soviet Government. In fact, Molotov referred to it several times in conversation. Even before it could be reported to Moscow there were misgivings in Soviet circles. On October 19 Mr. Eden telegraphed that Molotov had called on him at the Embassy and said that his Government greatly valued the convoys and had sadly missed them. The Northern route was the shortest and quickest way of getting supplies to the front, where the Russians were going through a difficult time. The German winter defence line had to be broken. Molotov promised to speak to Stalin about it all and arrange a meeting.

Mr. Eden continued:

My attention has been drawn to the fate of two British merchant seamen recently given severe sentences for an assault in North Russia upon a local Communist leader. I am most reluctant, and the Ambassador agrees with me, to promise resumption of convoys unless these unfortunate British seamen are released and handed over to our naval authorities for removal. . . . I am convinced it would be utterly repugnant to you, as it is to me, to allow these men to languish in a Soviet gaol while we are accepting those risks to British seamen in future convoys. I shall try what I can do by personal appeal to Stalin or Molotov.

The important discussion took place on the 21st. Meanwhile, in order to strengthen Eden's hands, and at his suggestion, I suspended the sailing of the British destroyers, which was the first move in the resumption of the convoys.

Foreign Secretary to Prime Minister   22 Oct 43
I saw Stalin and Molotov last evening. His Majesty's Ambassador was with me, and the conversation, which roamed over a large variety of topics, lasted two and a quarter hours.

2. After some preliminary exchanges of greetings I raised the question of convoys. I said that I must explain how great a strain these convoys placed on the Royal Navy. The passage of each one was a major naval operation, which might require four cruisers and twelve destroyers for its immediate protection, in addition to which the entire Home Fleet would also have to come out to provide cover. To make available the necessary escorts we must reduce our naval strength in the Atlantic. Though it was true that anti-U-boat warfare was going better for us, this struggle was still a closely run thing. At this point I showed Stalin a chart of the number of U-boats in service over the past three years. This proved that the number was now still near its peak. The reason why we were not prepared to promise that we would carry out four convoys was that we did not wish to expose ourselves to reproach if, owing to some sudden development of the war, we could not in fact send all four. But it was our earnest desire to make these convoys available, and I told Stalin that you, who had yourself laboured hard to make the necessary arrangements, had now telegraphed me that you calculated that we should be able to send 130 to 140 cargoes in all, with about 860,000 tons of supplies. If the convoys were to be run we were anxious to start at once. We had made our naval dispositions on this basis, and we wished to avail ourselves of the period during which the *Tirpitz* was out of action. Our requirements in naval personnel had been reduced to what we considered the absolute minimum, and we must insist on that minimum. There were also certain minor requirements which, if general agreement were reached, I wished to put to Molotov.

3. Stalin, who had nodded agreement at my description of the U-boat warfare, said that his difference with you was not about the

difficulties of the operation, but as to whether we were bound to do it. You had implied that if we sailed any one of these convoys it would be as a gift. Stalin did not feel this was a true description of the position. On his understanding of it we were under an obligation to seek to deliver these goods. When he had sent his reply to you however you had been very much offended and would not accept his reply. I replied that we had never suggested that to send these convoys was an act of favour or charity. You had at all times been determined to make every effort to deliver these goods to our Ally, but for the reasons I had explained you could not pledge yourself to a series of operations which you might not be able to carry out. Stalin himself surely must have confidence in the good faith of his Ally, and therefore it was not surprising that you should have been hurt by the message. The Marshal said that this had not been intended.

4. After some further discussion Stalin said that he could not agree to increase the number of men. There were already many of our sailors in North Russian ports with nothing to do, and then they got into trouble with Russian sailors. The Russians might undertake such convoys themselves. I replied that this was not possible. He said that if only our people in North Russia had treated his people as equals none of these difficulties would have arisen, and that if our people would treat his people as equals we could have as much personnel as we liked. After some further argument it was decided that Molotov and I would meet to-morrow, when I would give him a list of our requirements and we would see whether we could reach agreement.

★ ★ ★

Thus it was arranged that the convoys should be resumed. The first started in November, and a second followed it in December. Between them they comprised seventy-two ships. All arrived safely, and at the same time return convoys of empty ships were successfully brought out.

The December outward-bound convoy was to bring about a gratifying naval engagement. The disablement of the *Tirpitz* had left the *Scharnhorst* the only heavy enemy ship in Northern Norway. She sallied forth from Alten Fiord with five destroyers on the evening of Christmas Day, 1943, to attack the convoy about fifty miles south of Bear Island. The reinforced convoy escort comprised fourteen destroyers, with a covering force of three cruisers. The Commander-in-Chief, Admiral Fraser, lay to the south-westward in his flagship, the *Duke of York*, with the cruiser *Jamaica* and four destroyers.

Twice the *Scharnhorst* tried to strike at the convoy. Each time she was intercepted and engaged by the escort cruisers and destroyers, and after indecisive fighting, in which both the *Scharnhorst* and the British cruiser *Norfolk* were hit, the Germans broke off the action and withdrew to the southward, shadowed and reported by our cruisers. The German destroyers were never seen and took no part. Meanwhile the Commander-in-Chief was approaching at his utmost speed through heavy seas. At 4.17 p.m., when the last of the Arctic twilight had long since gone, the *Duke of York* detected the enemy by Radar at about twenty-three miles. The *Scharnhorst* remained unaware of her approaching doom, until, at 4.50 p.m., the *Duke of York* opened fire at 12,000 yards with the aid of star-shell. At the same time Admiral Fraser sent his four destroyers in to attack when opportunity offered. One of these, the *Stord*, was manned by the Royal Norwegian Navy. The *Scharnhorst* was surprised, and turned away to the eastward. In a running fight she suffered several hits, but was able with her superior speed gradually to draw ahead. However, by 6.20 p.m. it became apparent that her speed was beginning to fall and our destroyers were able to close in on either flank. At about 7 p.m. they all pressed home their attacks. Four torpedoes struck. Only one destroyer was hit.

The *Scharnhorst* turned to drive off the destroyers, and thus the *Duke of York* was able to close rapidly to about 10,000 yards and reopen fire with crushing effect. In half an hour the unequal battle between a battleship and a wounded battle-cruiser was over, and the *Duke of York* left the cruisers and destroyers to complete the task. The *Scharnhorst* soon sank, and of her company of 1,970 officers and men, including Rear-Admiral Bey, we could only save thirty-six men.

Although the fate of the crippled *Tirpitz* was delayed for nearly a year, the sinking of the *Scharnhorst* not only removed the worst menace to our Arctic convoys, but gave new freedom to our Home Fleet. We no longer had to be prepared at our average moment against German heavy ships breaking out into the Atlantic at their selected moment. This was an important relief.

*   *   *

When in April 1944 there were signs that the *Tirpitz* had been repaired sufficiently to move for refit to a Baltic port aircraft from the carriers *Victorious* and *Furious* attacked her with heavy bombs, and she was once more immobilised. The Royal Air Force now took up the attack from a base in North Russia. They succeeded in causing further damage, which led to the *Tirpitz* being removed to Tromsö Fiord, which was two hundred miles nearer to Britain and within the extreme range of our home-based heavy bombers. The Germans had now abandoned hope of getting the ship home for repair and had written her off as a seagoing fighting unit. On November 12 twenty-nine specially fitted Lancasters of the Royal Air Force, including those of 617 Squadron, famous for the Möhne Dam exploit, struck the decisive blow, with bombs of twelve thousand pounds weight. They had to fly over 2,000 miles from their bases in Scotland, but the weather was clear and three bombs hit their target. The *Tirpitz* capsized at her moorings, more than half of her crew of 1,900 men being killed, at the cost of one bomber, whose crew survived.

All British heavy ships were now free to move to the Far East.

CHAPTER XVI

FOREIGN SECRETARIES' CONFERENCE
IN MOSCOW

Back to the Quebec Conference – Need of a Meeting of the Three Heads of Governments – Correspondence with Stalin – A Preliminary Conference of Foreign Ministers – My Note for Mr. Eden at this Conference, October 11 – The Meeting in Moscow, October 19 – The Soviet Proposals – Stalin Concentrates on the Cross-Channel Invasion – My Private Note to Mr. Eden, October 20 – The Question of Turkey and Sweden Joining in the War – Eisenhower and Alexander's Grave Report on the Battle in Italy – Further Discussion at the Kremlin – The Russians Press the Question of "Overlord" – A Friendly Atmosphere – Mr. Eden's Account – A Russian Share in the Italian Fleet Suggested – My Telegrams of October 29 on This – My Proposed Triple Declaration on German War Criminals Accepted – Important Achievements of the Conference.

RETROSPECT is now necessary to bring the course of diplomatic events into accord with the narrative. Ever since the Quebec Conference we had been making suggestions to Stalin for a triple meeting of the heads of Governments. Already at Quebec I had received the following reply from him:

Premier Stalin to Prime Minister (Quebec)   10 Aug 43
I have just returned from the front, and already had time to become familiar with the message of the British Government dated August 7.

1. I agree that a meeting of the heads of three Governments is absolutely desirable. Such a meeting must be realised at the first opportunity, having arranged with the President the place and the time of this meeting.

At the same time I ought to say that in the existing situation on the Soviet-German front I, to my regret, have no opportunity to absent myself and to leave the front even for one week. Although recently we have had several successes on the front, an extreme strain on the strength and exceptional watchfulness are required in regard to the new possible actions of the enemy from the Soviet troops and from the Soviet Command just now. In connection with this I have to visit the troops on that or other parts of our front more often than usual. In the circumstances at the present time I am not able to visit Scapa Flow or any other distant point for a meeting with you and the President.

Nevertheless, in order not to postpone an examination of the questions which interest our countries, it would be expedient to organise a meeting of the responsible representatives of our States, and we might come to an understanding in the nearest future concerning the place and date of such a meeting.

Moreover, it is necessary beforehand to agree on the scope of the questions to be discussed and the drafts of the proposals which have to be accepted. The meeting will hardly give any tangible result without that.

2. Taking this opportunity, I congratulate the British Government and the Anglo-American troops on the occasion of their most successful operations in Sicily, which have already caused the downfall of Mussolini and the break-up of his gang.

This was the first favourable mention from the Russian side of a meeting between the three Allies at any level. In passing this message to Mr. Eden for transmission to Moscow I said, "I was very glad to hear again from Bruin in the first person. Please forward him my reply, which is in the sense you desire."

After a discussion with the President we framed a joint message to Stalin.

Prime Minister and President (Quebec) to Premier Stalin   19 Aug 43

We have both arrived here with our Staffs, and will probably remain in conference for about ten days. We fully understand strong reasons which lead you to remain on battle-fronts, where your presence has been so fruitful of victory. Nevertheless we wish to emphasise once more importance of a meeting between all three of us. We do not feel that either Archangel or Astrakhan is suitable, but we are prepared ourselves, accompanied by suitable officers, to proceed to Fairbanks [in Alaska] in order to survey whole scene in common with you. The present seems to be a unique opportunity for making a rendezvous, and also a crucial point in the war. We earnestly hope that you will give this matter once more your consideration. The Prime Minister will remain on this side of the Atlantic for as long as may be necessary.

2. Should it prove impossible to arrange the much-needed meeting

of three heads of Governments we agree with you that a meeting on the Foreign Office level should take place in the near future. This meeting would be exploratory in character, as of course final decisions must be reserved to our respective Governments.

Stalin replied:

25 Aug 43

I have received your joint message of August 19.

I entirely share your opinion and that of Mr. Roosevelt about the importance of a meeting between the three of us. In this connection I beg you most earnestly to understand my position at this moment, when our armies are carrying on the struggle against the main forces of Hitler with the utmost strain, and when Hitler not only does not withdraw a single division from our front, but, on the contrary, has already succeeded in transporting, and continues to transport, fresh divisions to the Soviet-German front. At such a moment, in the opinion of all my colleagues, I cannot, without detriment to our military operations, leave the front for so distant a point as Fairbanks, although if the situation on our front were different Fairbanks undoubtedly would be very convenient as a place for our meeting, as I said before.

As regards a meeting of representatives of our States, and in particular of representatives in charge of foreign affairs, I share your opinion about the expediency of such a meeting in the near future. This meeting however ought not to have a purely exploratory character, but a practicable and preparatory character, in order that after that meeting has taken place our Governments are able to take definite decisions, on urgent questions. Therefore I consider it indispensable to revert to my proposal that it is necessary in advance to define the scope of the questions for discussion by the representatives of the three Powers, and to draft the proposals which ought to be discussed by them and presented to our Governments for final decision.

Prime Minister to Premier Stalin   5 Sept 43

The Conference of Foreign Ministers. I was glad to get your message of August 25, in which you agree to an early meeting of Soviet, United States, and British representatives in charge of foreign affairs. If M. Molotov comes we will send Mr. Eden.

2. The Conference even thus constituted could not of course supersede the authority of all Governments concerned. We are most anxious to know what your wishes are about the future, and will tell you our views so far as they are formed. After that the Governments will have to decide, and I hope that we may be able to meet personally somewhere. I would, if necessary, go to Moscow.

3. The political representatives might require to be assisted by military advisers. I would provide a general officer, Sir Hastings Ismay, who is my personal representative on the Chiefs of Staff Committee and conducts the Secretariat of the Ministry of Defence. He could supply the arguments and facts and figures on the military questions involved. I believe the United States would send an officer similarly qualified. This, I think, would be sufficient at this stage for the meeting of Foreign Ministers.

4. If however you wish to go in technical detail into the question of why we have not yet invaded France across the Channel and why we cannot do it sooner or in greater strength than is now proposed, I should welcome a separate technical mission of your generals and admirals coming to London or Washington, or both, when the fullest possible exposition of our thought, resources, and intentions could be laid before them and thrashed out. Indeed, I should be very glad that you should have this explanation, to which you have every right.

5. We are disposed to think that Britain, being a midway point, would be the most convenient place for the meeting, though it might be preferable to hold it outside of London. I have made this proposal to the President, but he has not given me a final decision upon it. If England were agreeable to you I should be glad of your support in the proposal.

6. I hope we can aim at assembling the Conference early in October.

Premier Stalin to Prime Minister   8 Sept 43
The time suggested by you for the meeting of the representatives of the three Governments—the beginning of October—is acceptable. As the meeting-place I propose Moscow. It is important to agree in advance on the agenda, and on the proposals concerning the decisions to be taken on the various questions of the agenda in which our Governments are interested. Now as before I believe that this is necessary for the success of the Conference, which ought to prepare the way for the subsequent agreed decisions of the Governments. I do not foresee any difficulty in coming to terms on other questions concerning the organisation of the meeting.

On the question of the personal meeting between the heads of the three Governments, I have written to the President that I have decided to bring about this meeting as soon as possible, that the time of the meeting suggested by the President—November, December—seems acceptable to me, but that the meeting-place should be selected in a country where all three States have their representatives—for example, in Persia. I made only one reservation—*i.e.*, that the exact moment of the meeting should be fixed in the light of the situation on the Soviet-German front, where more than five hundred divisions on

45 Kiev: the main street as it looked on the day the town was liberated.

47 Italian soldiers fighting in Russia had to wear German army uniform. They were also obliged to swear allegiance to the Fuehrer.

both sides are involved in the struggle.* This necessitates practically everyday control on the part of the High Command of the U.S.S.R.

On September 10 I answered Premier Stalin's proposal.

With regard to the meeting of Foreign Office representatives, we defer to your wishes that Moscow should be the scene. Accordingly our Foreign Secretary, Mr. Eden, will proceed thither at an early date in October. He will be attended by a suitable staff.

Agenda. His Majesty's Government declares itself willing to discuss any and every subject with its Russian and United States Allies. We will in a few days furnish you with our ideas. But we should particularly like to know what are the main points you have in mind.

This meeting of Foreign Office representatives seems to me a most important and necessary preliminary to the meeting of the three heads of Governments. I am pleased and relieved to feel that there is a good prospect of this taking place between November 15 and December 15. I have for months past informed you that I will come anywhere, at any time, at any risk, for such a meeting. I am therefore prepared to go to Teheran unless you can think of a better place in Persia. I should have preferred Cyprus or Khartoum, but I defer to your wishes. Marshal Stalin, I wish to tell you that on this meeting of the three of us, so greatly desired by all the United Nations, may depend not only the best and shortest method of finishing the war, but also those good arrangements for the future of the world which will enable the British, American, and Russian nations to render a lasting service to humanity.

★   ★   ★

Later, after my return from Quebec to London, I drafted for my colleagues a note upon the general points to be considered at the forthcoming Conference of Foreign Ministers, which had now been arranged.

NOTES BY THE PRIME MINISTER FOR FOREIGN SECRETARY AT THE FORTHCOMING MEETING
11 Oct 43

Great Britain seeks no territory or special advantage for herself as the outcome of the war, which she entered in pursuance of her obligations and in defence of public law.

2. We hold strongly to a system of a League of Nations, *which will include a Council of Europe, with an International Court and an armed Power capable of enforcing its decisions.*† During the Armistice period, which may be prolonged, we hold that the three Great Powers, the

---

* A Soviet division was equivalent to about a third of a British or United States division.
† Author's subsequent italics.

British Commonwealth and Empire, the United States, and the Union of Soviet Socialist Republics, with the addition of China, should remain united, well armed, and capable of enforcing the Armistice terms and of building up the permanent structure of peace throughout the globe.

3. We consider that States and nations that have been subjugated by Nazi or Fascist violence during the war should emerge at the Peace Conference with their full sovereign rights, and that all questions of final territorial transference must be settled at the peace table, due regard being paid to the interests of the populations affected.

4. We reaffirm the principles of the Atlantic Charter, noting that Russia's accession thereto is based upon the frontiers of June 22, 1941. We also take note of the historic frontiers of Russia before the two wars of aggression waged by Germany in 1914 and 1939.

5. We should welcome any agreement between Poland and Russia which, while securing a strong and independent Poland, afforded to Russia the security necessary for her western frontier.

6. We are resolved that Nazism and Fascism shall be extirpated in the aggressor countries where they have taken root, and that democratic Governments based upon the free expression of the people's will, obtained under conditions of reasonable tranquillity, shall be set up. This should not exclude measures of military diplomacy or relations with interim Governments which may come into being, so that our main objects may be achieved with the minimum of slaughter, especially to the forces of the Allies.

7. We repudiate all territorial expansion achieved by Germany or Italy during the Nazi or Fascist régimes, and further we consider that the future structure of Germany and the position of Prussia as a unit of the German State should be subject to an agreed policy among the three Great Powers of the West.

8. We are resolved to take all measures necessary to prevent the guilty Powers from becoming an armed menace to the peace of Europe, not only by disarmament, but by prolonged control of every form of warlike apparatus or organisation within their bounds.

9. We have no desire to keep any branch of the European family of nations in a condition of subjection or restriction, except as may be required by the general needs and safety of the world.

10. We proclaim our inflexible resolve to use the authority which victory will confer upon the three Great Powers in order to serve the general good and the cause of human progress.

*   *   *

The Conference of the three Foreign Ministers in Moscow now played an invaluable part in our complicated affairs. The President had hoped Mr. Hull, at his advanced age, could be spared the full journey to Moscow, and had asked for a rendezvous in London, but Stalin had refused this change. Mr. Hull however would not be deterred. It was a gallant enterprise for this veteran in his frail health to undertake this, his first journey by air.

Before the Conference met in Moscow there had been a considerable interchange of telegrams between the three Foreign Secretaries about the agenda. The Americans put forward four suggestions, including a four-Power declaration, upon the treatment of Germany and other enemy countries in Europe during the Armistice period, and so forth. We, for our part, put forward no less than twelve suggestions, including a common policy towards Turkey, a common policy in Persia, relations between the U.S.S.R. and Poland, and policy in relation to Poland generally. The Russians made one suggestion, and one suggestion only—"the consideration of measures to shorten the duration of the war against Germany and her allies in Europe." Although this was obviously a military rather than a political question, it was clear from the outset that they were not prepared to discuss anything else until it had been fully thrashed out. It was therefore thought advisable to include General Ismay in our delegation.

* * *

The first formal meeting of the Conference took place on the afternoon of October 19. M. Molotov, after a show of resistance, such as is put up by the Speaker of the House of Commons when he is escorted to the Chair, was elected chairman, to the obvious satisfaction of himself and his delegation. The agenda was then settled. These preliminaries concluded, Molotov handed round the following note of Soviet proposals:

1. That the Governments of Great Britain and the United States take in 1943 such urgent measures as will ensure the invasion of Northern France by Anglo-American armies, and, coupled with powerful blows of Soviet troops on the main German forces on the Soviet-German front, will radically undermine the military-strategical situation of Germany and bring about a decisive shortening of the duration of the war.

In this connection the Soviet Government deem it necessary to ascertain whether the statement made in early June 1943 by Mr. Churchill and Mr. Roosevelt to the effect that Anglo-American forces will undertake the invasion of Northern France in the spring of 1944 remains valid.

2. That the three Powers suggest to the Turkish Government that Turkey should immediately enter the war.

3. That the three Powers suggest to Sweden to place at the disposal of the Allies air bases for the struggle against Germany.

Molotov asked whether Mr. Hull and Mr. Eden would be prepared to discuss these proposals in a closely restricted meeting, after they had had time to study them. This was readily agreed.

Mr. Eden sent me an account of what had passed, and I sent him my views at once.

Prime Minister to Mr. Eden (Moscow)   20 Oct 43

Our present plans for 1944 seem open to very grave defects. We are to put fifteen American and twelve British divisions into France in May, and will have about six American and sixteen British or British-controlled divisions on the Italian front. Unless there is a German collapse, Hitler, lying in the centre of the best communications in the world, can concentrate at least forty to fifty divisions against either of these forces while holding the other. He could obtain all the necessary forces by cutting his losses in the Balkans and withdrawing to the Save and the Danube without necessarily weakening his Russian front. This is one of the most elementary war propositions. The disposition of our forces between the Italian and the Channel theatre has not been settled by strategic needs, but by the march of events, by shipping possibilities, and by arbitrary compromises between the British and Americans. Neither the force built up in Italy nor that which will be ready in May to cross the Channel is adequate for what is required, and only transferences of the order of seven or eight divisions can physically be made between them. I am determined that this situation shall be reviewed.

2. If it lay with me to decide, I would not withdraw any troops from the Mediterranean and would not debouch from the narrow leg of Italy into the valley of the Po, and would engage the enemy strongly on the narrower front while at the same time fomenting Balkan and Southern France disturbances. In the absence of a German collapse, I do not think we should cross the Channel with less than forty divisions available by the sixtieth day, and then only if the Italian front were in strong action with the enemy. I do not accept the American argument that our metropolitan Air Forces can flatten everything out in the battle zone or on its approaches. This has not been our present experience. All this is for your internal consumption, and not for deployment at this stage. It may show you however the

dangers of our being committed to a lawyer's bargain for "Overlord" in May, for the sake of which we may have to ruin the Italian front and Balkan possibilities and yet have insufficient forces to maintain ourselves after the thirtieth or fortieth day.

3. You should try to find out what the Russians really feel about the Balkans. Would they be attracted by the idea of our acting through the Ægean, involving Turkey in the war, and opening the Dardanelles and Bosphorus so that British naval forces and shipping could aid the Russian advance and so that we could ultimately give them our right hand along the Danube? How great an interest would they feel in our opening the Black Sea to Allied warships, supplies, and Allied military forces, including Turkish? Have they any interest in this right-handed evolution, or are they still set only on our attacking France?—observing that of course in any circumstances the steady building up of forces in England will hold large German forces in the West. It may be that for political reasons the Russians would not want us to develop a large-scale Balkan strategy. On the other hand, their desire that Turkey should enter the war shows their interest in the South-Eastern theatre.

4. I remain convinced of the great importance of our getting a foothold in the Ægean by taking Rhodes, re-taking Cos, and holding Leros, and building up an effective air and naval superiority in these waters. Do the Russians view with sympathy our effort to hold Leros and desire to take Rhodes? Do they understand the effect this has upon Turkey, and how it opens the possibility of a naval advance into the Black Sea? Again, all the above is simply for your inner thoughts.

★   ★   ★

On October 21 there was a session in Moscow to consider the Soviet proposals. Mr. Eden, Ambassador Sir Archibald Clark Kerr, Mr. Strang, and General Ismay represented the British, Mr. Hull, Ambassador Harriman, and Major-General Deane the Americans, M. Molotov, Marshal Voroshilov, M. Vyshinsky, and M. Litvinov the Russians. Ismay opened the meeting by a statement on behalf of both the British and American delegations, based on the Quebec decisions, in the course of which he emphasised the limiting conditions which governed the launching of the cross-Channel invasion.

In the discussion that followed our representatives made it absolutely clear that there had in fact been no change of plan on our part and that we intended to go ahead provided the conditions which we had laid down could be fulfilled. With this the Russians seemed content for the moment. Molotov said that the Soviet Government would study Ismay's statement in detail, and would wish to have a further discussion on it later in the Conference.

Mr. Eden then turned to the question of Turkey, and pointed out that we could not at present give the necessary effective support. The question of a joint approach to Turkey was deferred until later. The Russian proposal about Sweden was also mentioned. Sweden would clearly demand guarantees about Finland, a matter which the Russians were reluctant to discuss.

*   *   *

In the evening Eden called upon Stalin and for over two hours discussed a large variety of topics. First in importance, as we have seen, was the question of the Arctic convoys. The conversation then turned to the proposed meeting of the three heads of the Allied Governments. Stalin was insistent that this should take place at Teheran.

On the whole the conversation seemed to go well.

*   *   *

Mr. Eden had now received my telegram of October 20, and sent his comments. He said that the Russians were completely and blindly set on our invasion of Northern France. It was the one decision in which they took an absorbing interest. They asked again and again whether there had been any change in the understanding given to Stalin by the President and myself after the Washington Conference in May that we would invade in the early spring of 1944, and when the operation would start.

On the first point he had assured them that there had been no change, but had emphasised the three conditions which must be present to allow the expedition to be launched with any chance of success.* On the second point it was thought better not to give the actual date, but Mr. Eden assured them that all preparations were going forward to attack in the spring after the weather became favourable.

I replied by return:

Prime Minister to Foreign Secretary (Moscow)   23 Oct 43
If we force Turkey to enter the war she will insist on air support, etc., which could not be provided without detriment to our main operations in Italy. If however Turkey enters on her own initiative,

* See p. 69.

perhaps moving through a phase of non-belligerency, we should not have the same obligation, and yet great advantages might be reaped. Obviously timing is vital, and dependent upon what is the aggressive strength of the enemy in Bulgaria and Thrace. *The prize would be to get into the Black Sea with supplies for Russia, warships, and other forces. This is what I call 'giving Russia the right hand'.* Such a movement by Turkey is not impossible, especially if the Germans should begin to cut their losses in the Balkans and withdraw towards the Danube and the Save.

2. *Finland and Sweden.* It would be a great advantage to bring Sweden into the war. We do not think the Germans have the strength to undertake a heavy invasion of Sweden. We should gain a new country and a small but good army. Our gains in Norway would be far-reaching. Valuable facilities would be afforded to Russian air forces. For ourselves, we can do far better bombing of Germany from East Anglia, where we are mounted on a vast scale, than from Sweden, where everything would have to be improvised and imported by air. Our range from England over Germany is just as good as from Sweden. In fact, with present British facilities plus those we hope to acquire north of Rome there is no part of Germany we cannot reach with great weight.

3. Personally I should like to see Turkey come in on her own, and also Sweden. I do not think either of them would be overrun, and every new enemy helps Hitler's ruin. I suggest however that the first step is to find out what we and the Russians want and what will help both of us most in both quarters, and then as a second step go into ways and means immediately thereafter. Try this and let me know.

And two days later I added:

Prime Minister to Foreign Secretary   25 Oct 43
Further reflection confirms my view that we should not discourage the Russian desire that Turkey and Sweden should of their own volition become co-belligerents or actual allies. The Russians should not be put in the position of arguing for this and we of simply making difficulties. We should agree in principle and let the difficulties manifest themselves, as they will certainly do, in the discussion of ways and means. They may well be overcome or put in their proper place and proportion. Anyhow, we ought not to begin by crabbing everything.

*   *   *

The serious telegram, recorded in an earlier chapter, from General Eisenhower reporting General Alexander's appreciation

* Author's subsequent italics.

of the battle in Italy had now reached me.* I repeated it to Eden and asked him to show it to Stalin. I added:

26 Oct 43

The reason why we are getting into this jeopardy is because we are moving some of our best divisions and a large proportion of vital landing-craft from the Mediterranean in order to build up for "Overlord", seven months hence. This is what happens when battles are governed by lawyers' agreements made in all good faith months before, and persisted in without regard to the ever-changing fortunes of war. You should let him know, if you think fit, that I will not allow, while I am responsible, the great and fruitful campaign in Italy, which has already drawn heavy German reserves into action, to be cast away and end in a frightful disaster, for the sake of crossing the Channel in May. The battle must be nourished and fought out until it is won. We will do our very best for "Overlord", but it is no use planning for defeat in the field in order to give temporary political satisfaction.

2. It will therefore be necessary for you to make it clear that the assurances you have given about May "Overlord", subject to the specified conditions, must be modified by the exigencies of the battle in Italy. I am taking the matter up with President Roosevelt, but nothing will alter my determination not to throw away the battle in Italy at this juncture, so far as the King's armies are concerned. Eisenhower and Alexander must have what they need to win the battle, no matter what effect is produced on subsequent operations. This may certainly affect the date of "Overlord".

I concluded my comments on this subject three days later.

Prime Minister to Mr. Eden (Moscow)   29 Oct 43

There is of course no question of abandoning "Overlord", which will remain our principal operation for 1944. The retention of landing-craft in the Mediterranean in order not to lose the Battle of Rome may cause a slight delay, perhaps till July, as the smaller class of landing-craft cannot cross the Bay of Biscay in the winter months and would have to make the passage in the spring. The delay would however mean that the blow when struck would be with somewhat heavier forces, and also that the full bombing effort on Germany would not be damped down so soon. We are also ready at any time to push across and profit by a German collapse. These arguments may be of use to you in discussion.

*   *   *

* See pp. 216 ff.

In the evening our Ambassador and Ismay accompanied Mr. Eden to the Kremlin. Molotov was with Stalin. Eden opened the proceedings by handing Stalin the Russian text of Eisenhower's telegram about the situation in Italy. Stalin read it aloud to Molotov. When he had finished he showed no trace of disappointment, but said that according to Russian Intelligence there were twelve Anglo-American divisions fighting six German divisions south of Rome, and that there were a further six German divisions on the river Po. He admitted however that General Alexander was likely to have the better information. Mr. Eden said I was anxious that Stalin should have the latest account of the situation in Italy, and should know not only that I was anxious about it, but also that I was insistent that the battle in Italy should be nourished and fought out to victory whatever the implications on "Overlord". He added that the vitally important decisions now confronting the Allies made it all the more necessary that the three heads of Governments should meet as soon as possible.

Stalin observed with a smile that if there were not enough divisions a meeting of the heads of Governments could not create them. He then asked point-blank whether the telegram which he had just read meant a postponement of "Overlord". Eden replied that until it had been fully examined by the Combined Chiefs of Staff and decisions made about improving the position it was impossible to say, but the possibility must be faced. He quoted the passage in my telegram that we were determined to "do our very best for 'Overlord'", but that it was "no use planning for defeat in the field in order to give temporary political satisfaction". There were two difficulties: firstly, landing-craft, and, secondly, moving seven battle-tried divisions to the United Kingdom at the beginning of November for the spearhead of the "Overlord" assault. Perhaps the moving of some or all of them would now have to be postponed, but whether or not this would affect the date of "Overlord", and if so to what extent, it was impossible to say.

Stalin then turned to questions of general strategy. As he saw it, there were two courses open to us: to take up a defensive position north of Rome and use all the rest of our forces for "Overlord", or to push through Italy into Germany.

Mr. Eden said that the first alternative was what we had in

mind. There was no intention, so far as he knew, to go beyond the Pisa–Rimini line. This would give us depth north of Rome and air bases for bombing Southern Europe. Stalin clearly thought we were right, and said that it would be very difficult to get through the Alps, and that it would suit the Germans well to fight us there. After the capture of Rome British prestige would certainly be high enough to permit us to pass over to the defensive in Italy.

The discussion then turned to the other point of attack. Mr. Eden said that we might be able to stage a diversionary attack against Southern France synchronising with "Overlord". If we could secure a bridgehead with a couple of divisions it might be possible to use the French divisions which were being trained and equipped in North Africa. Stalin thought that this was a good idea, since the more we made Hitler disperse the better. These were the tactics he was employing on the Russian front But would there be enough landing-craft?

He then put the question, "Will the postponement of 'Overlord' be one month or two months?" Mr. Eden said that he could not possibly give an answer. All that he could state definitely was that we would do our very best to launch "Overlord" at the earliest possible moment at which it had a reasonable prospect of success, and that it was most desirable that the three heads of Governments should meet as soon as possible. Stalin entirely agreed, but said that there was some hesitation on the part of the President about going to Teheran. When Eden suggested Habbaniya both he and Molotov firmly refused. Stalin said that he himself could not go far away so long as there was an opportunity of continuing to damage Hitler's armies. The Germans had recently moved some tank divisions from France and Belgium to the Soviet front, but they were short of equipment and raw materials. It was essential to give Hitler no rest, and he volunteered that the Soviet armies would not have had the success that they had won if the Germans had been able to move from the West the forty divisions which were pinned there by the mere threat of our invasion. The Soviet fully understood this contribution to the cause.

Mr. Eden said that the Marshal well knew that the Prime Minister was just as keen on hurting Hitler as he was. Stalin fully acknowledged this, but added with a gust of laughter that

I had a tendency to take the easy road for myself and leave the difficult jobs to the Russians. Eden refused to agree, and mentioned the difficulties of naval operations and our recent heavy losses in destroyers. Stalin became serious again, and said that his people spoke little about naval operations, but realised how difficult they were.

"The whole talk," cabled Mr. Eden, "went off surprisingly well. Stalin seemed in excellent humour, and at no point in the evening was there any recrimination about the past or any disposition to ignore real difficulties that face us. This may only have been a first reaction and second thoughts may not be so good, but it is significant that he should have gone out of his way to acknowledge the contribution we were making by merely pinning forty German divisions in the West, and his sympathetic references to the difficulties of naval operations and to the necessity for landing-craft, etc., seemed to show that he no longer regards an overseas operation as a simple matter. It is clear however that he expects us to make every effort to stage 'Overlord' at the earliest possible moment, and the confidence he is placing in our word is to me most striking."

There had been many signs during the Conference that the Soviet Government sincerely desired permanent friendship with Britain and the United States. They had met us on a number of points, both large and small, about which we foresaw difficulties. Stalin had shown understanding of our problems, and so far there had been no unsatisfactory afterthoughts. "Molotov," said Mr. Eden, "has shown that spirit on many occasions, notably as chairman of our Conference to-day, when we had our final session on military matters. Though he was obviously disappointed at the outcome of what I had told him and Stalin last night, and at our failure wholly to endorse in a manner satisfactory to him Soviet proposals about Turkey and Sweden, he conducted our business with an evident desire to avoid embarrassment to either country. As an indication of goodwill I received a message from him to-night that our two imprisoned sailors have been pardoned.

"Russian representatives have given many other signs of an intention to open a new chapter. Your gesture in respect of convoys has made a deep impression. For the first time for many years Molotov and a number of his colleagues came to dinner at this Embassy to-night. Mikoyan, whose task it is to keep these people informed, was especially eloquent in his tributes to your personal share in the sailing of these convoys.

"In this atmosphere I would give much to be able to close the Conference with some tangible evidence of our goodwill. I am quite sure that if I could give them some encouraging message about their desire to have a small share of the Italian Fleet the psychological effect would be out of all proportion to the value of the ships, whatever that may be. The Ambassador and Harriman fully endorse this view. If it is impossible to give a specific reply before I leave it will be of the greatest help to me if I can at least tell M. Molotov that in principle we agree that the Soviet Government shall have a share of the captured Italian ships and that the proportion for which they ask is reasonable. Details can be worked out subsequently, including dates of delivery. If you can do this to help me I feel sure that the return will more than justify your gesture. I beg your aid."

I at once sent him the Cabinet view about the Italian Fleet.

Prime Minister to Secretary of State   29 Oct 43

. . . In principle we willingly admit the Russians' right to a share in the Italian Fleet. We had however thought that this Fleet would play its part against Japan, and we had been planning to tropicalise the *Littorios* and some other units for this later phase of the war. If Russia would like to have a squadron in being in the Pacific that would be a very considerable event, and we should like to discuss this project when we meet. . . .

5. At present the only place where Italian ships could be handed over to the Russians would be Archangel and Murmansk. The Italian warships are quite unsuited for working in Arctic waters, and would need several months of dockyard work first. We should also have to be careful lest the immediate transfer to the Russians would have an ill-effect on Italian co-operation. It is important for Italy to have her flag on the sea against Germany. We do not want to provoke a refusal by the Italians to carry on the important work they are doing for us in Taranto dockyard. One cannot be absolutely sure that they would not scuttle some of the ships they brought out from the German clutches if they thought they were to be handed over to foreign crews. They are doing a good deal for us at the present time. Italian submarines are carrying supplies to Leros. Italian destroyers, of which there are only seven good ones, are escorting local convoys. Their cruisers are transporting troops and supplies. We should therefore in

any case have to ensure against publicity until we could take steps to counter these ill-effects. Once distribution of the Italian Fleet begins, the French, the Yugoslavs, and the Greeks would put in their claims, which are pretty good.

6. For all these reasons it would be better to put off this question till "Eureka" [Teheran].

7. It is quite true that we have gained some Italian merchant tonnage, but the amount is actually less than what we have to provide for the minimum requirements of conquered and Italian territory, so that we are actually down on the balance, especially as most of these Italian ships are not fit for anything more than local traffic.

8. Has Mr. Hull referred this request to his Government? It would be essential that we should be agreed. I should like best of all to talk over all this at "Eureka", if that ever comes off.

And later the same day:

Provided the Americans agree, you may tell Molotov that in principle we agree that the Soviet Government shall have a share of the captured Italian ships and that the proportion for which they ask is reasonable. I am presuming the battleship for which they ask is not a *Littorio*. Details and dates of delivery must be settled with regard to operations and not losing Italian aid by precipitate publicity. This is very important. Of course we are looking forward to using the very newest vessels of this Fleet in the war against Japan, and the Russians will surely understand that we ought not to prejudice that. We also feel we [the British] ought to have the two *Littorios* after the war, first, because of the overwhelming share we have had in the whole war against Italy, secondly, because of our heavy naval losses in capital units, and, thirdly, because we have suspended the long-term building of battleships already sanctioned by Parliament in order to concentrate on the current needs of the war.

2. Most especially secret and for your own thought and perhaps fly-throwing: if it were decided that on the defeat of Hitler Russia would play her part against Japan a great design might come into being, as a part of which the fitting out under the Soviet flag and manning with Russian sailors of a substantial naval force at some Pacific base in our possession and the participation of this force of surface ships in the final phase of the war might come into view. However, I hope that the consent I have sent you in the first lines of this telegram will meet your difficulties.

★   ★   ★

I had drafted a proposed declaration on German war criminals as a basis of discussion at the forthcoming meeting of the three heads of Governments.

Prime Minister to President Roosevelt and Premier Stalin   12 Oct 43

Would you very kindly consider whether something like the following might not be issued over our three signatures:

"Great Britain, the United States, and the Soviet Union [in whatever order is thought convenient, we being quite ready to be last] have received from many quarters evidence of the atrocities, massacres, and cold-blooded mass-executions which are being perpetrated by the Hitlerite forces in the many countries they have overrun and from which they are now being steadily expelled. The brutalities of the Nazi domination are no new thing, and all peoples or territories in their grip have suffered from the worst forms of government by terror. What is new is that many of these territories are now being redeemed by the advancing armies of the liberating Powers, and that in their desperation the recoiling Hitlerites and Huns are redoubling their ruthless cruelties.

"Accordingly the aforesaid three Allied Powers, speaking in the interest of the thirty-two United Nations, hereby solemnly declare, and give full warning of their declaration, as follows:

"At the time of the granting of any armistice to any Government which may be set up in Germany those German officers and men and members of the Nazi Party who have been responsible for or have taken a consenting part in the above atrocities, massacres, and executions will be sent back to the countries in which their abominable deeds were done in order that they may be judged and punished according to the laws of these liberated countries and the free Governments which will be erected therein. Lists will be compiled in all possible detail from all these countries, having regard especially to the invaded parts of Russia, to Poland and Czechoslovakia, to Yugoslavia, Greece, including Crete and other islands, to Norway, Denmark, the Netherlands, Belgium, Luxembourg, France, and Italy. Thus Germans who take part in the wholesale shootings of Italian officers or in the execution of French, Dutch, Belgian, or Norwegian hostages, or of Cretan peasants, or who have shared in the slaughters inflicted on the people of Poland or in the territories of the Soviet Republic, which are now being swept clear of the enemy, will know that they will be brought back, regardless of expense, to the scene of their crimes and judged on the spot by the peoples whom they have outraged. Let those who have hitherto not imbrued their hands with innocent blood beware lest they join the ranks of the guilty, for most assuredly the three Allied Powers will pursue them to the uttermost ends of the earth, and will deliver them to their accusers in order that justice may be done.

"The above declaration is without prejudice to the case of the major criminals, whose offences have no particular geographical localisation.

"Roosevelt
Stalin
Churchill"

If this, or something like this (and I am not particular about the wording), were put over our three signatures it would, I believe, make some of these villains shy of being mixed up in butcheries now that they know they are going to be beat. We know, for instance, that our threats of reprisals about Poland have brought about a mitigation of the severities being inflicted on the people there. There is no doubt that the use of the terror-weapon by the enemy imposes an additional burden on our armies. Lots of Germans may develop moral scruples if they know they are going to be brought back and judged in the country, and perhaps the very place, where their cruel deeds were done. I strongly commend to you the principle of the localisation of judgment as likely to exert a deterrent effect on enemy terrorism. The British Cabinet endorse this principle and policy.

The declaration was accepted and endorsed, with a few verbal changes.

*   *   *

The three Foreign Ministers had met regularly every day, and covered an immense amount of ground. Their agreements were recorded in a secret protocol, drawn up on November 3. The importance of these lay in the additional machinery of co-operation which was now to be set up. It was agreed to establish a European Advisory Committee in London to begin work on the problems which would arise in Germany and on the Continent when the Hitler régime neared collapse. It was this body which drew up the initial plans for dividing Germany into zones of occupation, an arrangement which caused grave problems later. Of this more in due course. For Italian affairs another Advisory Council was to be constituted, to include a Russian representative. There was to be an exchange of information on any peace-feelers put out by the Axis satellites. The Americans were anxious that a Four-Power Declaration, to include China, pledging themselves to a united conduct of the war "against those Axis Powers with which they are respectively at war", should be signed at this Moscow meeting. This was achieved on October 30. Finally, a protocol agreeing on joint action between Russia and Great Britain in regard to Turkey was drafted by Mr. Eden and signed on November 2.

We had every reason to be content with these results. There had been a smoothing of many points of friction, practical steps for further co-operation had been taken, the way had been prepared for an early meeting of the heads of the three major Allied Governments, and the mounting deadlock in our working with the Soviet Union had in part been removed.

Those who took part in the Conference sensed a far more friendly atmosphere, both on and off duty, than had ever existed before. One of the best-known Russian painters was commissioned by his Government to do a conversation piece of the Conference, and he had made preliminary sketches of various members of the British and American delegations. It is not known whether the picture was ever completed, but it has not yet seen the light of day.

CHAPTER XVII

ADVENT OF THE TRIPLE MEETING
THE HIGH COMMANDS

Urgency of Choosing a Supreme Commander for "Overlord" – We Favour the Choice of Marshall – My Correspondence with Roosevelt – The President's Delay in Deciding – His Desire for a Supreme Commander to Control Both Western Theatres – I Disagree with this Suggestion – Need to Arrange for a Meeting of the Three Powers – My Telegram to Stalin of September 25, and His Reply – Difficulties of Agreement Upon a Suitable Place for the Meeting – Roosevelt's Suggestions – Stalin Will Come Only to Teheran – Roosevelt's Disappointment – Constitutional Difficulties Invoked – I Seek a Preliminary Anglo-American Discussion – My Telegram to the President of October 23 – His Proposal to Invite Generalissimo Chiang Kai-shek – His Suggestion for Including the Russians in the Preliminary Meeting – I Argue Against This – Agreement for a Meeting – The Russians Decline to Confer with the Chinese Government at this Stage.

THE selection of a Supreme Commander for "Overlord", our cross-Channel entry into Europe in 1944, was urgent. This of course affected in the most direct manner the military conduct of the war, and raised a number of personal issues of importance and delicacy. At the Quebec Conference I had agreed with the President that "Overlord" should fall to an American officer, and had so informed General Brooke, to whom I had previously offered the task. I understood from the President that he would choose General Marshall, and this was entirely satisfactory to us. However, in the interval between Quebec and our meeting in Cairo I became conscious that the President had not finally made up his mind about Marshall. None of the other arrangements could of course be made before the main decision had been taken. Meanwhile rumour became rife in the American Press, and there was the prospect of Parliamentary reactions in London. Admiral Leahy in his book* mentions some of the American cross-currents. "The public," he writes, "assumed that Roosevelt would name Marshall as Supreme Commander. There was vehement objection to such a move in the Press. Opponents charged that Marshall was being given 'Dutch promotion'; that Roosevelt planned to take him out of a big job and put him into a small job; that it was a plot against Marshall. At the other extreme there were reports that the American Joint Chiefs considered the post of Supreme Command promotion and were jealous of Marshall."

This question was discussed between us at some length. I was anxious to emphasise the status of General Marshall in every way, provided that the authority of the Joint and Combined Chiefs of Staff was not impaired. I cabled Hopkins in this sense at the end of September.

Prime Minister to Mr. Harry Hopkins   26 Sept 43
There is a lot of talk in the papers about Marshall becoming Supreme Commander-in-Chief over all the forces in the West. What I understood from our talks was that he would command the operation "Overlord". He would not however be only a theatre commander. He might have the same sort of general outlook with us on the whole war against Germany, in addition to his specific command, as Dill has on the Combined Chiefs of Staff Committee in Washington over the whole field. We should be very glad for him to sit with our Chiefs of Staff frequently and to have the whole scene laid before him. But I made it clear that our Chiefs of Staff would more often have to sit together to consider our position from the British point of view, just as your Chiefs of Staff sit together in Washington. It would not fall to him to give decisions outside the sphere of "Overlord". The control of all our combined operations and world strategy must rest with the Combined Chiefs of Staff in Washington, under the final direction of the heads of Governments. Please let me know whether there is anything wrong with this.

A few days later I addressed myself to the President.

                                                           1 Oct 43
I am somewhat worried by the way in which our great changes in the High Commands are being broken to the public. So far nothing

* *I Was There* (Gollancz), p. 227.

has been said here, but almost every day some statement is made in the United States about Marshall, and I shall certainly be asked questions when Parliament meets on Tuesday, the 12th. Moreover, it would be difficult for me if Marshall's appointment to the Chief Command in Britain were to be announced apart from Alexander's succession in the Mediterranean. Rumour runs riot, and is fed by carefully balanced and guarded statements, such as that made by Stimson reported in to-day's papers. An impression of mystery and of something to be concealed is given. This is a fine field for malicious people. All this would be blown away by publication of the clear-cut decisions to which we have come. In all the circumstances I hope you will see your way to a simultaneous announcement by us both of the changes, coupled with a statement that they will be brought into effect as soon as convenient to the military situation.

2. Will you also consider my difficulties in the consequential appointments. For instance, I understood that Marshall would like Montgomery for Deputy, or, alternatively, to command under him the British expeditionary armies in "Overlord". This would entail my clearing the Home Command here, now held by General Paget. An opportunity is now open for this, as General Pownall, who was formerly Commander-in-Chief Iraq and Persia, goes with Mountbatten to India as Chief of Staff, and I can post Paget to Iraq and Persia. It is difficult and also harmful to leave these commands vacant for long.

3. Some of the United States papers seem to have begun attacking Mountbatten bitterly, and he has been affected by accounts telegraphed here describing him as "the British princeling and glamour boy who has ousted the proved veteran MacArthur from his rightful sphere", or words to that effect. The prominence given to the Indian Front command by these controversies is of course leading the Japanese to reinforce in that quarter, and intelligence to this effect has already been received. We are told that a large number of correspondents are proceeding or trying to proceed from the United States to Delhi, and that expectation is rife of an early beginning of the campaign. On the other hand, the floods and the monsoon rains will of course prevent any decisive action till the New Year. But this cannot be stated publicly without relieving any anxieties of the Japanese. The prospect of having a formidable band of correspondents champing their bits in Delhi is not a pleasant one, and it would help our fighting chances if everything possible could be done to damp down controversy and publicity in this area.

4. In these circumstances a plain statement of what we have settled for all theatres, including commanders, their Chiefs of Staff, and one

or two of the principal officers, all brought out together, would in my opinion be a great advantage. I could, if you desire, draft such a statement and submit it to you.

The President replied:

President Roosevelt to Prime Minister   5 Oct 43

The newspapers here, beginning with the Hearst-McCormick crowd, had a field day over General Marshall's duties. The drums were beaten rather loudly by the rest of the Press for a few days, but it is pretty much of a dead cat now. It seems to me that if we are forced into making public statements about our military commands we will find ourselves with the newspapers running the war. I therefore hope that nothing will be said about the business until it is actually accomplished. It may be that the situation, other than newspaper criticism by our political enemies, will warrant a joint announcement sooner than I have anticipated, but at the moment I earnestly urge that we say nothing. I agree with you that at the appropriate time we must make an overall statement relative to commands, and I fully appreciate your position at home, but I do not think that the difficulties about secondary commands throughout the world are adequate reasons for making the major announcement in regard to Marshall.

I will do what I can about Mountbatten, because I realise that some of our Press have been treating him very badly, although, on the whole, he has come out of it very well. Certainly American public opinion thoroughly approves of his appointment. I agree with you that we should not permit any undue optimism about this [Burma] campaign either at home or abroad. Nevertheless there is a very proper feeling that Mountbatten will prosecute vigorously anything he is assigned to do.

I hope very much that you will agree that statement about Marshall need not be made at present.

I found the delay in the American decision embarrassing, and on October 17 I cabled to the President, "It seems to me that it is becoming very necessary to have a decision about the High Commands. Unless there is a German collapse, the campaign of 1944 will be far the most dangerous we have undertaken, and personally I am more anxious about its success than I was about 1941, 1942, or 1943."

Nearly a fortnight passed before I received an answer, and then it was indeterminate.

President Roosevelt to Prime Minister   30 Oct 43

Preparations for "Overlord" seem to have reached a stage from which progress is difficult unless and until the Commander is appointed. As you know, I cannot make Marshall available immediately. I am none the less anxious that preparations proceed on schedule agreed at "Quadrant", with target date May 1. I suggest you may care to consider the early appointment of British Deputy Supreme Commander for "Overlord", who, in receipt of precisely the same measure of support as will eventually be accorded to Marshall, could well carry the work forward. If I may make proposal, I suggest appointment of Dill, Portal, or Brooke.

★   ★   ★

By the beginning of November we became aware that the President himself and his advisers desired that the Supreme Commander of "Overlord" should also command the Mediterranean, and that the President's idea was that Marshall should command both theatres, and play them in one with another. I presumed that this would be from a headquarters at Gibraltar. I thought it necessary to make the British position clear without delay. As the matter was not suited at this stage for a direct interchange between me and the President, I thought it better to tell Field-Marshal Sir John Dill to talk about it to Admiral Leahy, the chairman of the American Chiefs of Staff Committee.

Prime Minister to Field-Marshal Dill (Washington)   8 Nov 43
You should leave Admiral Leahy in no doubt that we should never be able to agree to the proposal of putting the "Overlord" and Mediterranean commands under an American Commander-in-Chief. Such an arrangement would not be conformable to the principle of equal status which must be maintained among the great Allies. I cannot accept a combination of the two commands under one Commander-in-Chief. This would place him above the Combined Chiefs of Staff, and would also affect the constitutional control of the movements of forces by the President as United States Commander-in-Chief and by the Prime Minister acting on behalf of the War Cabinet. I should certainly never be able to accept responsibility for such an arrangement. Hitherto we have successfully prevented any carping here at the fact that we have been fighting and sustaining casualties in Tunis, Sicily, and Italy on something like a two-and-a-half-to-one basis, although we are serving loyally under a United States general. If I were to attempt to propose anything such as is suggested above there would be an explosion. However, this will not occur while I hold my present office. You may at your discretion impart the above to Mr. Hopkins.

The next day Dill saw Leahy, and made my attitude towards

the unification of the "Overlord" and Mediterranean commands quite clear. Leahy, though personally disappointed, accepted the position, saying, "If that is the opinion of the Prime Minister there is nothing more to be said about it." Dill also saw Hopkins, whom he reported as similarly "disappointed". "At any rate," said Dill, "Hopkins and Leahy know how useless it would be to return to the charge, and I hope they won't."

* * *

I had hardly got home after my visits to the Citadel, the White House, and Hyde Park during the Quebec Conference, already described, when I turned again to the theme of a meeting of the three heads of Governments which logically followed the Anglo-American conversations. In principle there was general agreement that this was urgent and imperative, but no one who did not live through it can measure the worries and complications which attended the fixing of the time, place, and conditions of this, the first conference of what were then called the Big Three. I give a full account here, because the tale is at least a diplomatic curiosity.

I addressed myself first to Stalin, who, I knew, favoured the idea of a rendezvous at Teheran.

Prime Minister to Premier Stalin   25 Sept 43
I have been pondering about our meeting of heads of Governments at Teheran. Good arrangements must be made for security in this somewhat loosely controlled area. Accordingly I suggest for your consideration that I make preparations at Cairo in regard to accommodation, security, etc., which are bound to be noticed in spite of all praiseworthy efforts to keep them secret. Then perhaps only two or three days before our meeting we should throw a British and a Russian brigade around a suitable area in Teheran, including the airfield, and keep an absolute cordon till we have finished our talks. . . . Thus we shall have an effective blind for the world Press, and also for any unpleasant people who might not be as fond of us as they ought.

2. I suggest also that we use the expression "Cairo Three" instead of Teheran, which should be buried, and also that the code-name for the operation should be "Eureka", which I believe is Ancient Greek. If you have other ideas let me know, and we can then put them to the President. I have not said anything to him about this aspect yet.

Stalin's reply was direct and positive.

Premier Stalin to Premier Churchill   3 Oct 43

I have no objection to the diversionary preparations which you intend to carry out in Cairo. Regarding your proposal to throw British and Russian brigades into the region of "Cairo Three" several days before our meeting in that city, I find this measure inexpedient, as it would cause an unnecessary sensation and would decamouflage the preparations. I suggest that each of us should take with him a sufficient police guard. In my opinion this would be enough to secure our safety. . . .

In fact a complete cordon was established, and the military and police forces used, especially by the Russians, were numbered by thousands.

* * *

As I could not be sure whether the President would be allowed by his security advisers to go to Teheran, I suggested alternatives. One of these was a desert encampment around the Air Force Training School at Habbaniya, which had made so brilliant a defence in 1941. Here we should have been absolutely by ourselves and in perfect security, and the President would have had no difficulty in flying thither in a few hours from Cairo. I therefore telegraphed this proposal to him.

Former Naval Person to President Roosevelt   14 Oct 43

I have a new idea about "Eureka", which I have asked Anthony [then on his way to Moscow] to try on Uncle Joe for subsequent submission to you if U.J. agrees. There is a place in the desert which I now call "Cyprus", but whose real name is Habbaniya. This would be a much easier journey for you from Cairo than "Cairo Three", and very little longer for U.J. We could put up three encampments and live comfortably in perfect seclusion and security. I am going into details on the chance of agreement in the trinity. See also, meanwhile, St. Matthew, chapter xvii, verse 4.

President Roosevelt to Prime Minister   15 Oct 43

I have finally sent the following telegram to Uncle Joe, and I think your idea is an excellent one. St. Peter sometimes had real inspirations. I like the idea of three tabernacles. We can add one later for your old friend Chiang.

"The problem of my going to Teheran is becoming so acute that I feel I should tell you frankly that, for constitutional reasons, I cannot take the risk. The Congress will be in session. New laws and resolutions must be acted on by me after their receipt, and must be returned to the Congress physically before ten days have elapsed. None of this can be done by radio or cable. Teheran is too far to be sure that the requirements are fulfilled. The possibility of delay in getting over the mountains—first east-bound and then west-bound—is insurmountable. We know from experience that planes in either direction are often held up for three or four days. . . .

"In many ways Cairo is attractive, and I understand there are a hotel and some villas out near the Pyramids which could be completely segregated.

"Asmara, the former Italian capital of Eritrea, is said to have excellent buildings, and a landing-field good at all times.

"Then there is the possibility of meeting at some port in the Eastern Mediterranean, each one of us to have a ship. . . . Another suggestion is in the neighbourhood of Baghdad. . . .

"In any event, I think the Press should be entirely banished, and the whole place surrounded by a cordon so that we would not be disturbed in any way.

"I am placing a very great importance on the personal and intimate conversations which you and Churchill and I will have, for on them the hope of the future world will greatly depend.

"Your continuing initiative along your whole front heartens all of us."

Prime Minister to President Roosevelt   16 Oct 43
I entirely agree with the telegram you have sent to U.J. about "Eureka". Let me know what he replies.

Stalin was however adamant on Teheran.

President Roosevelt to Prime Minister   21 Oct 43
Last night I received the following from U.J.:

". . . Unfortunately, not one of the places proposed instead of Teheran by you for the meeting is suitable to me. It became clear during the operations of the Soviet forces in the summer and fall of this year that the summer campaign may overgrow into a winter one and that our troops can continue their offensive operations against the German Army. It is considered by all my colleagues that these operations demand my personal contact with the command and daily guidance on the part of the Supreme Command. Conditions are better in Teheran, because wire telegraph and telephone communications with Moscow exist there. This cannot be said about the other locations. My colleagues insist on Teheran as the place of the meeting for this reason.

"I accept your suggestion of November 20 or 25 as a possible date for the Conference, and I also agree that representatives of the Press should be excluded from the meeting. I hope that a great deal of good will be accomplished by the direct participation in the Moscow meeting of Mr. Hull, who has arrived safely in Moscow."

The President had replied at once:

I am deeply disappointed in your message received to-day in regard to our meeting. I fully understand your reason for requiring daily guidance on the part of the Supreme Command, and your personal contact with the command, which is bringing such outstanding results. . . .

I wish you would realise that there are other vital matters which, in this constitutional American Government, represent fixed obligations on my part which I cannot change. Our Constitution calls for action by the President on legislation within ten days of the passage of such legislation. That means that the President must receive and return to the Congress with his written approval or his veto physical documents in that period. I cannot act by cable or radio, as I have told you before. The trouble with Teheran is the simple fact that the approaches to that city over the mountains often make flying an impossibility for several days at a time. This is a double risk—first, for the plane delivering documents from Washington, and, second, for the plane returning these documents to the Congress. I regret to say that, as head of the nation, it is impossible for me to go to a place where I cannot fulfil my constitutional obligations. I can assume the flying risks for documents up to and including the low country as far as the Persian Gulf, through a relay system of planes, but I cannot assume the delays attending flights in both directions into the saucer over the mountains in which Teheran lies. Therefore, with much regret I must tell you that I cannot go to Teheran, and in this my Cabinet members and the legislative leaders are in complete agreement.

The President suggested Basra.

I am not in any way considering the fact that from United States territory I would have to travel 6,000 miles, and you would only have to travel 600 miles from Russian territory. I would gladly go ten times the distance to meet you were it not for the fact that I must carry on a constitutional Government more than one hundred and fifty years old. . . . I am begging you to remember that I also have a great obligation to the American Government and to maintain the full American war effort.

As I have said to you before, I regard the meeting of the three of us as of the greatest possible importance, not only to our peoples as of to-day, but also to our peoples in relation to a peaceful world for generations to come. It would be regarded as a tragedy by future generations if you and I and Mr. Churchill failed to-day because of a few hundred miles. . . .

Mr. Eden was still in Moscow, and was doing all he could to extract from Stalin an agreed place and time of meeting which would satisfy the President. It was clear that Stalin would insist on Teheran as the place of meeting, and, although it was yet by no means certain that the President would be induced to go there, I began to consider the planning of such a meeting.

* * *

Several serious aspects of the impending Conference absorbed my mind. I thought it most important that the British and American Staffs, and above them the President and I, should reach a general agreement on the policy of "Overlord" and its impingement on the Mediterranean. The whole armed strength overseas of our two countries was involved, and the British forces were to be equal at the outset of "Overlord", twice as strong as the Americans in Italy, and three times as numerous in the rest of the Mediterranean. Surely we ought to reach some solid understanding before inviting the Soviet representatives, either political or military, to join us.

I therefore suggested such a plan to the President.

President Roosevelt to Prime Minister 22 Oct 43
. . . There should be sufficient time allowed to analyse the results of the current Moscow Conference, and also I think the subsequent Conference we have in mind. For us to stage a meeting while the Moscow Conference is in progress, or at least before its results can be carefully considered, probably would have unfavourable results in Russia.

2. Combined planning teams are now planning an overall plan for the defeat of Japan. It is important that this work be completed and that the respective Chiefs of Staff have an opportunity to study it before a general meeting.

3. Certain outline plans from Eisenhower and commanders in the Pacific covering operations approved at Quebec are to be submitted on November 1, and these should receive some consideration before we arrive at the moment for a combined meeting. . . .

The President thus appeared to favour the idea, but not the timing. There was emerging a strong current of opinion in American Government circles which seemed to wish to win

Russian confidence even at the expense of co-ordinating the Anglo-American war effort. I therefore returned to the charge. I felt it of the utmost importance that we should meet the Russians with a clear and united view both on the outstanding problems of "Overlord" and upon the question of the High Commands.

Former Naval Person to President Roosevelt   23 Oct 43
   The Russians ought not to be vexed if the Americans and British closely concert the very great operations they have in hand for 1944 on fronts where no Russian troops will be present. Nor do I think we ought to meet Stalin, if ever the meeting can be arranged, without being agreed about Anglo-American operations as such.

   2. I would be content with November 15 if this is the earliest date for your Staffs. I thought the Staffs would work together for a few days before you and I arrive, say 18th or 19th, and we could then go on together to "Eureka". I do not yet know whether it is to be November 20 or 25. I had not imagined that "Eureka" would take more than three or four days or that large technical staffs would take part in it.

   3. November 15 would be ninety days from the beginning of our Conference at Quebec. In these ninety days events of first magnitude have occurred. Mussolini has fallen; Italy has surrendered; her Fleet has come over; we have successfully invaded Italy, and are marching on Rome with good prospects of success. The Germans are gathering up to twenty-five or more divisions in Italy and the Po valley. All these are new facts.

   4. . . . The date of "Overlord" itself was fixed by splitting the difference between the American and British view. It is arguable that neither the forces building up in Italy nor those available for a May "Overlord" are strong enough for the tasks set them.

   5. The British Staffs and my colleagues and I all think this position requires to be reviewed, and that the commanders for both our fronts should be named and should be present. In pursuance of the Quebec decisions we have already prepared two of our best divisions, the 50th and the 51st, now in Sicily, for transfer to England. Thus they can play no part in the Italian battle to which they stood so near, but will not come into action again for seven months, and then only if certain hypothetical conditions are fulfilled. Early in November a decision must be taken about moving landing-craft from the Mediterranean to "Overlord". This will cripple Mediterranean operations without the said craft influencing events elsewhere for many months. We stand by what was agreed at Quebec, but we do not feel that such agreement

should be interpreted rigidly and without review in the swiftly changing situations of war.

6. Personally I feel that if we make serious mistakes in the campaign of 1944 we might give Hitler the chance of a startling come-back. Prisoner German General von Thoma was overheard saying, "Our only hope is that they come where we can use the Army upon them." All this shows the need for the greatest care and foresight in our arrangements, the most accurate timing between the two theatres, and the need to gather the greatest possible forces for both operations, particularly "Overlord". I do not doubt our ability in the conditions laid down to get ashore and deploy. I am however deeply concerned with the build-up and with the situation which may arise between the thirtieth and sixtieth days. I feel sure that the vast movement of American personnel into the United Kingdom and the fighting composition of the units requires to be searchingly examined by the commander who will execute "Overlord".

I wish to have both the High Commands settled in a manner agreeable to our two countries, and then the secondary commands, which are of very high importance, can be decided. I repeat I have the greatest confidence in General Marshall, and that if he is in charge of "Overlord" we British will aid him with every scrap of life and strength we have. My dear friend, this is much the greatest thing we have ever attempted, and I am not satisfied that we have yet taken the measures necessary to give it the best chance of success. I feel very much in the dark at present, and unable to think or act in the forward manner which is needed. For these reasons I desire an early conference.

7. All that you say about the plans for Eisenhower and the commanders in the Pacific which are due to be submitted on November 1 would harmonise with a meeting on November 15 at latest. I do not know how long you consider is required for the long-term overall plan for the defeat of Japan to be completed by the combined planners and studied by our respective Chiefs of Staff. I do not consider that the more urgent decisions to which I have referred above ought to be held up for this long-term view of the war against Japan, which nevertheless should be pressed forward with all energy.

8. I hope you will consider that these reasons for [an Anglo-American] meeting are solid. We cannot decide finally until an answer is received from U.J. Should the Teheran meeting not be possible it makes it all the more necessary that we should meet in the light of the information now being received from the Moscow Conference [of Foreign Secretaries]. I am expecting Anthony to start home before the end of the month, and am ready myself to move any day after the first week in November.

9. You will, I am sure, share my relief that Leros has so far managed to hold out. "The dogs eat of the crumbs which fall from their masters' table."

★   ★   ★

Before the President replied to this proposal he sent me the following message, which showed that he was not yet decided to accept the idea of going to Teheran.

President Roosevelt to Prime Minister   25 Oct 43
It is a nuisenza to have the influenza. McIntire says I need a sea voyage.
No word from Uncle J. yet.
If he is adamant what would you think of you and me meeting with small staffs in North Africa, or even at the Pyramids, and toward the close of our talks getting the Generalissimo [Chiang Kai-shek] to join us for two or three days? At the same time we could ask Uncle J. to send Molotov to the meeting with you and me. Our people propose November 20.

Two days later he sent me his comments on my idea of a preliminary meeting of the Combined Chiefs of Staff.

President Roosevelt to Prime Minister   27 Oct 43
The present Moscow Conference appears to be a genuine beginning of British-Russian-United States collaboration, which should lead to the early defeat of Hitler. . . .

He suggested sending Stalin the following:

Heretofore we have informed you of the results of our combined British-American military Staff Conferences. You may feel that it would be better to have a Russian military representative sit in at such meetings to listen to the discussions regarding British-American operations and take note of the decisions. He would be free to make such comments and proposals as you might desire. This arrangement would afford you and your staff an intimate and prompt report of these meetings. . . .

The suggestion of including the Russians in such a meeting filled me with alarm.

Former Naval Person to President Roosevelt   27 Oct 43
Like you I rejoice in the good progress made at Moscow, and I greatly hope we may arrange "Eureka".
2. I deprecate the idea of inviting a Russian military representative to sit in at the meetings of our Joint Staffs. Unless he understood and

spoke English the delays would be intolerable. I do not know of any really high officer of the Russian Army who can speak English. Such a representative would have no authority or power to speak except as instructed. He would simply bay for an earlier Second Front and block all other discussions. Considering they tell us nothing of their own movements, I do not think we should open this door to them, as it would probably mean that they would want to have observers at all future meetings and all discussions between us would be paralysed. We shall very soon have six or seven hundred thousand British and American troops and airmen in Italy, and we are planning the great operation of "Overlord". There will not be a Russian soldier in any of these. On the other hand, all our fortunes depend upon them.

I regard our right to sit together on the movements of our own two forces as fundamental and vital. Hitherto we have prospered wonderfully, but I now feel that the year 1944 is loaded with danger. Great differences may develop between us and we may take the wrong turning. Or, again, we may make compromises and fall between two stools. The only hope is the intimacy and friendship which has been established between us and between our High Staffs. If that were broken I should despair of the immediate future. . . . I need scarcely say the British Chiefs of Staff fully share these views. I must add that I am more anxious about the campaign of 1944 than about any other in which I have been involved.

★　★　★

The President was still unsure about going to Teheran, and strong pressure was being brought to bear on him in American political circles and his position under the United States Constitution was invoked. I fully appreciated his difficulties.

Prime Minister to President Roosevelt　　　　　　30 Oct 43

I will meet you in Cairo on the 20th as you suggest, and will, if you will allow me, assume responsibility for making all arrangements for your general security and comfort which would fall upon us as the Occupying Power. Casey has been lent a beautiful villa, which I have seen myself, and am sure would be in every way suitable for you. It is a mile or two from the Pyramids, and surrounded by woods affording complete seclusion. It can be reached from the airfield in twenty minutes without going through any towns. The whole area can be easily cordoned off by British troops. There are some very interesting excursions into the desert which we could make together. I have no doubt Casey would be delighted to place the villa at your disposal. I should probably myself stay at the British Embassy in Cairo, which is perhaps twenty minutes away, but it may be that arrangements could be made for us both to be in the Pyramids area. I believe your Mr. Kirk also has a very fine house. Every facility exists in Cairo for the full Staffs to be accommodated and to meet for business, and they can easily come out to your villa whenever desired. If you like this plan, which, knowing the lay-out, I consider far the best, I will immediately make all preparations, and perhaps you would send an officer to make sure everything is arranged to your liking. . . .

Our plans now began to take shape.

President Roosevelt to Prime Minister   31 Oct 43
Hull's departure from Moscow has meant two days' delay in his getting home. It is essential I see him before I myself leave, as you can readily understand. I had hoped to get three days in North Africa before reaching Cairo. I can however do some of the North African and Italian business on the way back. Therefore I still hope to arrive Cairo by the 20th by flying there directly I reach the harbour. But if wind and weather are bad I might not make Cairo until the 22nd. I think my ship will take me to Oran.

Ever so many thanks for offering to make arrangements at Cairo, which we accept with pleasure. If any hitch develops there we can of course meet in Alexandria, the Staff living ashore and we on our respective ships.

I am wiring Generalissimo [Chiang Kai-shek] to prepare to meet us in the general neighbourhood of Cairo about November 25.

Prime Minister to President   31 Oct 43
Everything will be ready for Operation Sextant* from 20th onwards, and Colonel Warden will await Admiral Q and also Celestes†
at rendezvous. No difficulty about accommodation for Staffs.

Eden told me that there was no question of being able to move Stalin from the Teheran proposal. I made therefore every effort to smooth the way.

Prime Minister to General Ismay (Moscow)   1 Nov 43
Reason which prevents triple meeting at "Cairo Three" [Teheran] is said to be possible interruptions of flying over the mountains between Cairo and "Cairo Three", thus putting Admiral Q [President Roosevelt] constitutionally out of touch for transmission of documents. Pray probe the weather facts on the spot, and also let me know whether there is a road from Teheran into Syria, and how long a motor-car would take to travel it with dispatches, which could be brought on by air once south of the mountains. If I could convince Admiral Q

* Our code-name for the Conference between Britain, the United States, and China.
† "Your humble servant, yourself, and the Generalissimo respectively."

that there would be no interruption in the movement of dispatches our original plan might again be valid.

I now tried a last expedient, namely, that the President and I should meet at Oran in our respective battleships, and that the two Staffs should have a preliminary consultation of four days at Malta. This failed, but the President decided to start in his battleship. He now proposed that the Combined Chiefs of Staff should meet in Cairo before any contact was made with the Russians or the Chinese, whose presence in Cairo had been so strongly urged by him. But the first possible date for a meeting of the Combined Chiefs of Staff would be November 22. The Americans were proposing that the Chinese delegation should arrive on that day, and their presence would inevitably lead to their being drawn into our discussions. I further learned indirectly that the President was simultaneously inviting Molotov to Cairo. I therefore sent the following messages to the President:

Prime Minister to President Roosevelt   11 Nov 43
There seems to have been a most unfortunate misunderstanding. I thought from your telegram that the British and American Staffs would have "many meetings" before being joined by the Russians or Chinese. But now I hear from Ambassador Clark Kerr that on November 9 the United States Ambassador at Moscow delivered a message from you to Stalin inviting Monsieur Molotov to go to Cairo on November 22 with a military representative. November 22 is however the first day on which the Staffs can meet. I ask therefore that the date of the arrival of Molotov and his military representative shall be postponed till November 25 at the earliest.

2. I am very glad to hear also from Ambassador Clark Kerr that you contemplate going on November 26 to Teheran. I rather wish you had been able to let me know direct.

I wished the proceedings to take three stages: first, a broad Anglo-American agreement at Cairo; secondly, a Supreme Conference between the three heads of the Governments of the three major Powers at Teheran; and, thirdly, on returning to Cairo, the discussion of what was purely Anglo-American business about the war in the Indian theatre and the Indian Ocean, which was certainly urgent. I did not want the short time we had at our disposal to be absorbed in what were after all comparatively minor matters, when the decision involving the course of the whole war demanded at least provisional settlement. It seemed also unsuitable that the Soviets should be formally brought into conference with the Chinese Government when they had not declared war against Japan.

"It is very difficult," I wrote to Stalin on the 11th, "to settle things by triangular correspondence, especially when people are moving by sea and air." Some of the difficulties, happily, cancelled each other out.

President Roosevelt to Prime Minister   12 Nov 43

I have just heard that Uncle J. will come to Teheran. . . . I wired him at once that I had arranged the constitutional matter here, and therefore that I could go to Teheran for a short meeting with him, and told him I was very happy. Even then I was in doubt as to whether he would go through with his former offer to go to Teheran. His latest message has clinched the matter, and I think that now there is no question that you and I can meet him there between the 27th and the 30th. Thus endeth a very difficult situation, and I think we can be happy.

In regard to Cairo, I have held all along, as I know you have, that it would be a terrible mistake if Uncle J. thought we had ganged up on him on military action. During the preliminary meetings in Cairo the Combined Staffs will, as you know, be in the planning stage. That is all. It will not hurt you or me if Molotov and a Russian military representative are in Cairo too. They will not feel that they are being given the "run around". They will have no Staff and no Planners. Let us take them in on the high spots.

It is only five hours ago that I received Uncle J.'s telegram confirming Teheran. Undoubtedly Molotov and the military representative will return there with us between the 27th and the 30th, and when and after we have completed our talk with Uncle J. they will return with us to Cairo, possibly adding other military staff to the one representative accompanying Molotov on the first trip.

I think it essential that this schedule be carried out. I can assure you there will be no difficulties.

I am just off. Happy landing to us both.

Prime Minister to President Roosevelt   12 Nov 43

I am very pleased that you have managed to arrange the constitutional matter and that our meeting is now definitely arranged. That is a great step forward.

2. The Chiefs of Staff are however very apprehensive about the arrangements which you have settled for military conversations, and I share their misgivings. I thought from your message that the British and American Staffs would have "many meetings" before being joined

by the Russians or Chinese. I still regard this as absolutely essential in view of the serious questions which have to be settled. There is no objection to you and me seeing Molotov before our meeting with U.J., but the presence of a Soviet military observer so early in the Conference may cause grave embarrassment. His Majesty's Government cannot abandon their rights to full and frank discussions with you and your officers about the vital business of our intermingled armies. A Soviet observer cannot possibly be admitted to the intimate conversations which our own Chiefs of Staff must have, and his exclusion may easily cause offence. None of these objections would have applied to the formal Triple Staff Conference which I suggested should take place in due course.

In the end this danger was removed by the President's invitation to Chiang Kai-shek. Nothing would induce Stalin to compromise his relations with the Japanese by entering a four-Power conference with their three enemies. All question of Soviet representatives coming to Cairo was thus negatived. This was in itself a great relief. It was obtained however at a serious inconvenience and subsequent cost.

Premier Stalin to Premier Churchill   12 Nov 43
Although I wrote to the President that M. Molotov would come to Cairo on November 22, now I must say however that for certain reasons of serious character M. Molotov, to my regret, cannot come to Cairo. He will be able to come to Teheran at the end of November, and will arrive there together with me. Several military men will also accompany me.

It stands to reason that a meeting of the heads of only three Governments must take place at Teheran as it had been agreed. There should be absolutely excluded the participation of the representatives of any other Powers.

I wish success to your meeting with the Chinese concerning the Far Eastern affairs.

It was in this manner that our arrangements took final shape, and we started on our journeys.

APPENDICES

APPENDICES

APPENDIX A

LIST OF ABBREVIATIONS

A.A. guns	Anti-aircraft guns, or ack-ack guns
A.D.G.B.	Air Defence of Great Britain
A.F.V.s	Armoured fighting vehicles
A.T. rifles	Anti-tank rifles
A.T.S.	(Women's) Auxiliary Territorial Service
C.A.S.	Chief of the Air Staff
C.I.G.S.	Chief of the Imperial General Staff
C.-in-C.	Commander-in-Chief
C.O.S.	Chiefs of Staff
F.O.	Foreign Office
G.H.Q.	General Headquarters
G.O.C.	General Officer Commanding
H.M.G.	His Majesty's Government
M.A.P.	Ministry of Aircraft Production
M.E.W.	Ministry of Economic Warfare
M.O.I.	Ministry of Information
M. OF L.	Ministry of Labour
M. OF S.	Ministry of Supply
P.M.	Prime Minister
V.C.A.S.	Vice-Chief of the Air Staff
V.C.I.G.S.	Vice-Chief of the Imperial General Staff
V.C.N.S.	Vice-Chief of the Naval Staff
W.A.A.F.	Women's Auxiliary Air Force
W.R.N.S.	Women's Royal Naval Service ("Wrens")

APPENDIX B
LIST OF CODE-NAMES

ACCOLADE: Operations in the Ægean.

ADMIRAL Q: President Roosevelt.

ANAKIM: Recapture of Burma.

ANVIL: Allied landings in the South of France, 1944.

AVALANCHE: Amphibious assault on Naples (Salerno).

BAYTOWN: Attack across the Straits of Messina.

BOMBARDON: Steel outer breakwater used in artificial harbours

BUCCANEER: Operation against the Andaman Islands.

CAIRO THREE: The Teheran Conference, 1943.

CALIPH: Operation to assist "Overlord" by an invasion of Southern and Central France.

COLONEL WARDEN: The Prime Minister.

CULVERIN: Operations against Northern Sumatra.

EUREKA: The Teheran Conference, 1943.

GEE: Radar aid to bomber navigation.

GOOSEBERRY: Breakwater used in artificial harbours.

HABAKKUK: Floating seadrome made of ice.

HERCULES: The capture of Rhodes.

HUSKY: The capture of Sicily.

JUPITER: Operations in Northern Norway.

LILO: Breakwater used in artificial harbours

MULBERRY: Artificial harbour.

OBOE: Blind-bombing device.

OVERLORD: The liberation of France in 1944.

PENITENT: Operations against the Dalmatian coast.

PHŒNIX: Concrete caisson used in artificial harbours.

PIGSTICK: Landings behind the Japanese positions south of Mayu peninsula, on the Arakan coast of Burma.

PLOUGH FORCE: Special Combined Operations Force.

PLUTO: Oil pipe-line across the English Channel.

POINT-BLANK: Directive issued by the Combined Chiefs of Staff amending the Casablanca decisions.

QUADRANT: The Quebec Conference, 1943.

ROUND-UP: Plan for liberation of France in 1943.

SATURN: Establishment of an Allied force in Turkey in 1943.

SEXTANT: The Cairo Conference, 1943.

SHINGLE: Amphibious operation south of Rome at Anzio.

SLEDGEHAMMER: Plan for attack on Brest or Cherbourg in 1942.

STRANGLE: Air attack on railway lines in Northern Italy.

TENTACLE: Floating airfield, constructed mainly of concrete.

TORCH: Allied invasion of French North Africa in 1942.

TRIDENT: The Washington Conference, 1943.

TUBE ALLOYS: Atom bomb research.

WHALE: Floating pier used in artificial harbours.

WINDOW: Tinfoil strips used to confuse German Radar.

ZIP: Signal used by Commanders-in-Chief to denote the start of an operation.

APPENDIX C

PRIME MINISTER'S PERSONAL MINUTES AND TELEGRAMS

JUNE–OCTOBER 1943

JUNE

Prime Minister to Minister of War Transport and   6 June 43
First Sea Lord

I should be obliged if you would let me have a note on the ships that have passed through the Mediterranean in the different convoys, the character of the cargoes, and what stores have been carried for the British Red Cross to Russia.

Let me also know what is proposed in the future.

Prime Minister to Secretary of State for Air and   8 June 43
Minister of Home Security

Please let me have a report setting out what is being done to protect our reservoirs from attacks like those we have made recently in Germany [on the Möhne Dam].

Prime Minister to Lord Cherwell   10 June 43

POST-WAR CIVIL AVIATION

A Preliminary Note

My ideas about post-war civil aviation are based on the principle of "a fair field and no favour". All the airports of the world should be open to the through traffic of all nations (except the guilty nations) on the payment of reasonable expenses for maintenance and service. No country would however have *the right* to operate an air company, State or private, inside the territory of another. If possible no subsidies should be paid by any Governments. If the traffic proved unremunerative the necessary support should be given on a schedule agreed by the countries concerned, and in part on the basis of air mail contracts. Subject to the above, any company or corporation, State, or individual would be free to operate throughout the world.

2. After the war it is proposed that a World Organisation responsible for maintaining peace should be set up. Air-power resulting from civil aviation would necessarily be subject to the control of this body. A sub-committee of the World Council or sub-committees of the Continental councils (if any) would regulate disputes and supervise

or control quasi-military developments and implications. Subject to this, nations would be encouraged and afforded all facilities to render the best service from the point of view of safety, comfort, and speed of which they were capable.

3. The difficulty of getting agreement among the Dominions at this stage should not prevent the formulation of British policy after consultation with them. At the same time it is of the utmost importance and urgency to ascertain the views and wishes of the United States. Everything will be much easier if agreement is reached with them. . . .

Prime Minister to Major Morton   11 June 43
What is the truth about the tales I hear of applications by various bodies for the leading captured generals to visit some of our education centres and generally to be taken about the country to see things? There was an idea, for instance, that [the Italian] General Jesse should visit Eton. I should be opposed to any of this nonsense. These generals are not to be moved out of their places of internment without my being informed beforehand in each case.

Prime Minister to Sir Edward Bridges   13 June 43
Please draft for me a further warning to all Ministers, high officials, Parliamentary Private Secretaries, etc., about speaking with extreme caution and reticence to foreign [neutral] diplomatic representatives in this country. Although these are very often quite friendly and sincerely wish us to win the war, they do not hesitate to magnify their own positions with their Governments by reporting anything they can pick up, and the Governments may trade this to the enemy in return for other items. Only those who have the duty and authority, either general or special, to impart information should discuss war matters with them or in their presence.

2. Even general war matters and items appearing in the newspapers should not be discussed, because confirmation of these is obtained by these foreigners when they come into contact with persons who have secret knowledge. Lunches and dinners of an informal character with members of the diplomatic staffs should be avoided. You should be consulted in any particular case, and you have my authority to advise. Personal intimacy with foreigners should be reduced to a minimum.

Prime Minister to First Lord   13 June 43
Admiral Cunningham expressed the opinion to me that our light naval craft could have achieved even more in the Mediterranean if the engines of the motor torpedo-boats had been more reliable. Let me have a report on this, and let me know whether this is a local problem connected with the maintenance of these craft or whether there is a basic weakness in the design.

Prime Minister to Foreign Secretary and   13 June 43
Minister of Information

I have read the report on German morale in Tunisia. It is hardly possible to pay a higher tribute to the fighting qualities of the German soldier, and the introduction of words like "brutish" in no way detracts from the formidable impression this account gives. Their "extraordinary stupidity" certainly does not extend to the use of their arms or to their seizing of tactical opportunities.

Prime Minister to General Ismay and   15 June 43
Sir Edward Bridges

Will you please make the following terminology effective in all British official correspondence:

For "aeroplane" the word "aircraft" should be used; for "aerodrome" either "airfield" or "airport". The expression "airdrome" should not be used by us.

It is a good thing to have a rule and stick to it.

Prime Minister to Minister of Aircraft Production   15 June 43
[Sir Stafford Cripps]

I am very pleased to see that you are keeping so well up to your programme. You are quite right about the harm that is done by over-calling the hand. Promises which cannot be fulfilled lead to a large waste of effort by the Air Ministry in training, buildings, etc., quite apart from the effect on your own factories.

What I am not quite clear about is your labour situation. I note that you have received a very much smaller quota than was allocated to you. Had you discounted this when you made the programme, or does the fact that you could fulfil it mean that efficiency has increased beyond your expectations? These matters will all have to be considered most carefully in view of the constantly increasing labour stringency. You certainly seem to have received a smaller fraction than any other department so far.

I approve of your list of aircraft with special priorities. As you say, anything that can be done to exceed the programme would be particularly valuable for these types.

I am very pleased that you are pushing ahead with new types of fighters. I am particularly interested in the jet-propelled type of aircraft, of which you showed me a model the other day. Please report progress from time to time, and let me know when we may expect these machines to become available for operations.

Prime Minister to Director of Military Intelligence   15 June 43

What is your present most detailed estimate of the strength in Sicily? First, the Germans: we know the strength in detail of the division which is forming. It is under 7,000. What oddments are there, including air groundsmen? What reinforcements have reached them, or are on the way?

Secondly, give me an analysis of the Italians there. There was a story about eighty-four battalions for coastal garrison purposes; also, another estimate said seven or eight divisions. How are they divided? The easy surrender of the 15,000 men on Pantelleria and the four or five thousand on Lampedusa shows the temper of these Italian masses.

Prime Minister to Chief of the Air Staff   16 June 43

The air forces in Egypt, etc., are very large indeed. Pray let me know how they are to play their part in the next few months. They seem to be doing very little at present. What state of preparation have the plans for reinforcing Turkey reached? What proportion of the air forces in Egypt, etc., are employed in helping in Sicily? We cannot afford to have any part of the Air Force standing idle.

Prime Minister to General Ismay   17 June 43

I am strongly of the opinion that wound stripes should be issued as in the last war. Pray bring this to the notice of the three departments. The War Office are of course the principal party concerned. I wish to make a submission to the King by Monday. The matter must have been previously considered. Let me have any papers on the subject. There must be no further delay in this, on account of the "Purple Hearts" which the Americans are giving to their own soldiers and are distressed not to give to ours.

2. The second question is the issue of chevrons for every year of service abroad, which I think also would be greatly appreciated by the soldiers.

Prime Minister to General Ismay, for C.O.S. Committee   17 June 43

I am anxious about deception plans for Sicily, and therefore asked last night for a special report. The newspapers all seem to be pointing to Sicily, and, to judge by the maps and cartoons that are published in so many organs here, and, I have no doubt, in the United States, this objective would seem to be proclaimed and common property.

2. Safety lies in multiplication and confusion of objectives. A helpful note seems to have been struck this morning in some papers in saying that we have sufficient forces to attack several objectives at once. This should be stressed. Mr. Bracken is seeing the Press representatives this afternoon. Also, surely Greece requires some prominence?

Prime Minister to General Ismay, for C.O.S. Committee   18 June 43

Why cannot we fit some of these Fijian Commandos into the Burma fighting or elsewhere?

Prime Minister to Chief of the Air Staff   19 June 43

I quite understand the relief given to Takoradi by the new route through Casablanca, and by the opening of the Mediterranean. Indeed, the time has come to consider economies of personnel on the Takoradi route, and I shall be glad to receive your proposals to this end.

Prime Minister to Secretary of State for India   20 June 43

I entirely agree with the Deputy Prime Minister that the pay of the Indian Army should be increased. Broadly speaking, I should make a 25 per cent. reduction in the numbers and spread the saving over the pay of the rest.

Prime Minister to Lord President   20 June 43

Would it not be well to instruct the Minister of Works and Buildings to use his compulsory powers for land acquisition and to build these 3,000 cottages [for agricultural labourers] exactly as if they were airfields or war factories, and to fit them in as best possible with the necessary war requirements, assigning them a reasonable priority? To ask local authorities all over the country, unarmed with the necessary powers, to get a move on in respect of this handful of cottages and to make their way through the inevitable correspondence with all the public departments engaged in war activities would lead to an immense amount of futile effort. It seems to me that everybody is being disturbed and that we are becoming involved in discredit through this comparatively small job. Broadly speaking, my view is, either do it or don't do it.

Prime Minister to Brigadier Jacob   22 June 43

Please make out the table about the coast defences of Tripoli, showing the contrast between the pre-war estimates and what was actually found. Naturally, as the war progressed we learnt through frequent contacts more about the defence armaments of Tripoli. We shall now however be attacking a number of new places with which we have not been in contact, and for these the inflated pre-war estimates may exercise an undue influence. This was the whole point of my inquiry.

Prime Minister to C.I.G.S.   25 June 43

What is the position about the increased proportion of rifle strength in an infantry battalion? It was agreed that it should be increased by thirty-six, and I hoped that it might be by seventy-two.

Prime Minister to Secretary of State for War   26 June 43

I am glad to see that large receipts of .300 ball ammunition are expected by the end of July. In view of these, and having regard to the existing stocks, it should be possible to make extra issnes to the

Home Guard for training at once, so as to take advantage of the remaining summer months.

Prime Minister to Chiefs of Staff Committee   30 June 43

I note that 95 per cent. of the Army and R.A.F. vehicles shipped in May to theatres other than North Africa were boxed. This is most satisfactory, and a considerable contribution to the war effort.

I trust you will aim at a similarly high standard in the remaining theatres. Every month gained in getting adequate assembly plant running is a real saving.*

Prime Minister to Minister of Production and   30 June 43
President of the Board of Trade

I am still anxious about the leather position. Are you satisfied that there will not be a run on the shops when the new ration books become valid? Cannot anything be done to ease the shoe repair position?

In view of the seriousness of the civilian situation, could any relief be obtained from the Services, either in boots or in leather? I note that stocks of boots for the 2½ million men in the Army are higher than civilian stocks for 14 million men.

What are you doing about the long-term outlook? Would it not be desirable to work out with the Americans a picture of world supply and demand over, say, the next twelve months?

Prime Minister to C.I.G.S.   30 June 43

I understand that seventy-five cargo ships are said to be required to carry the equipment of the British troops who will return from North Africa in the winter. This presumably means that they will bring back most of their vehicles with them.

As we are still sending out considerable numbers of vehicles to North Africa, could we not make a saving of shipping in both directions if the returning divisions left most of their vehicles in Africa and were given new ones in England?

JULY

Prime Minister to General Ismay, for C.O.S. Committee   2 July 43

The North African Headquarters seem to be getting more than ever "sicklied o'er with the pale cast of thought". It is quite right for Planning Staffs to explore mentally all possible hypotheses, but happily human affairs are simpler than that.

2. We must first fight the battle which is in the hands of Alexander and Montgomery. Supposing that all goes well, or that there is even

---

* See Book VIII, pp. 379, 384, 396.

a collapse, the next step will show itself quite clearly. If, on the other hand, we do not succeed in Sicily no question of the next step arises.

3. We cannot allow the Americans to prevent our powerful armies from having full employment. Their Staffs seem now to be wriggling away to [the idea of] Sardinia. We must stiffen them all up and allow no weakness. I trust the Chiefs of Staff will once again prevent through the Combined Chiefs of Staff this weak shuffling away from the issue.

4. Above all we must preserve to ourselves the full power to judge and launch once we know what Sicily tastes like.

5. I should be very glad to discuss this with you this afternoon at 3 p.m. I do not like the present attitude. Strong guidance must be given.

Prime Minister to Lord Cherwell   3 July 43
MAN-POWER

Please divide the subject into seven or eight main claimants—Army, Navy, Air, Ministry of Aircraft Production, etc. How many did they have, and what did they ask for in the January review? What did they get, and how many have they got now? How many more are they asking for now?

It is on this table that I propose to work.

Let me have it to-night.

Prime Minister to Lord President and Sir E. Bridges   3 July 43

What is the exact situation now about these cottages for agricultural labourers? Who is in charge of building them, and when are they going to get built? The Minister of Works and Buildings led me to understand that he has the whole matter in his hands now. Is this so?

Prime Minister to Lord President   5 July 43

You may remember my note last December about the increase in short-term sickness, shown in figures compiled by the Government Actuary.

It is disquieting to find that the rising trend has continued during the winter. The addition thus revealed to the numbers normally kept away from work by sickness is quite an appreciable fraction of our total labour force; and the effect on the war effort is the same if a large proportion of them are war-weary rather than genuinely ill.

Prime Minister to Secretary of State for Air and   5 July 43
Chief of the Air Staff

In view of all the assurances given about the comparative impotence of enemy bombing, I am of the opinion that the time has come to review the question of the black-out so far as night work in industrial establishments is concerned.

APPENDIX C

The need for saving labour in every direction in order to speed up
the aircraft programme makes it indispensable that night work is not
hampered by black-out restrictions.

I should like an assurance that the Air Ministry is not insisting on
any restrictions of this character which hamper production.

Prime Minister to Secretary of State for War 5 July 43

I am glad to note that your requirements of crude rubber are no
higher than in 1942, and that the Army is helping to conserve our
supplies of vital raw materials. Since the number of Army vehicles will
be greater this year the result is satisfactory.

Prime Minister to Minister of Economic Warfare 5 July 43

I do not view the situation in France as you do, and I do not agree
with your sweeping generalisations, taken from much too narrow a
base. If the [French] Liberation Committee so conduct themselves as
to win the confidence of the British and United States Governments,
we could no doubt transfer to them the responsibility of financing the
Resistance movements in France. It is however the Committee, and
not General de Gaulle, with whom we should work. We are now
endeavouring to build up the collective and impersonal strength of the
Committee and to elevate the civilian influences as much as possible.

Prime Minister to Sir Edward Bridges 11 July 43

I am very much interested in the question of Basic English. The
widespread use of this would be a gain to us far more durable and
fruitful than the annexation of great provinces. It would also fit in
with my ideas of closer union with the United States by making it
even more worth while to belong to the English-speaking club.

2. I propose to raise this to-morrow at the Cabinet with a view to
setting up a committee of Ministers to examine the matter, and, if the
result is favourable, to advise how best to proceed. The Minister of
Information, the Colonial Secretary, the President of the Board of
Education, and perhaps Mr. Law, representing the Foreign Office,
would all seem suitable.

3. I contemplate that the B.B.C. should teach Basic English every
day as part of their propaganda, and generally make a big push to
propagate this method of interchange of thought.

4. Let me know your ideas about the committee, and put the matter
on the agenda for to-morrow.

Prime Minister to Foreign Secretary 11 July 43

About King Peter's marriage, we should recur to first principles.
The whole tradition of military Europe has been in favour of *les noces
de guerre*, and nothing could be more natural and nothing could be

297

more becoming than that a young king should marry a highly suitable princess on the eve of his departure for the war. Thus he has a chance of perpetuating his dynasty, and anyhow of giving effect to those primary instincts to which the humblest of human beings have a right.

2. Against this we have some tale, which I disbelieve of a martial race, that the Serb principle is that no one must get married in wartime. *Prima facie* this would seem to condone extra-marital relations. Then a bundle of Ministers that has been flung out of Yugoslavia are rolling over each other to obtain the shadow offices of an *émigré* Government. Some are in favour of the marriage, some are not. The King and the Princess are strongly in favour of it, and in my view in this tangle they are the only ones whose opinions should weigh with us.

3. The Foreign Office should discard eighteenth-century politics and take a simple and straightforward view. Let us tell the King and tell his Ministers we think the marriage should take place, and if the King is worthy of his hazardous throne we may leave the rest to him.

4. I may add that I am prepared to go into action in the House of Commons or on any democratic platform in Great Britain or the United States on the principles set forth above; and I think the Cabinet ought to have a chance of expressing its own views. We might be back in the refinements of Louis XIV instead of the lusty squalor of the twentieth century. Are we not fighting this war for liberty and democracy? My advice to the King, if you wish me to see him, will be to go to the nearest Registry Office and take a chance. So what?

Prime Minister to Secretary of State for Air and   12 July 43
Chief of the Air Staff

AIRCRAFT FOR AUSTRALIA

It is of high importance for the future of the British Commonwealth and Empire that we should be represented in the defence of Australia and the war in the Pacific. From this point of view the single squadron of the Royal Air Force which we have sent has played a part out of all proportion to the size of the unit. The fact that Australia has over here 8,100 Australian air crews, including some of their very best airmen, and the share they have taken in the Empire Training Scheme, certainly leaves us heavily in their debt so far as the air is concerned.

2. It is not merely a question of Spitfires or other fighter aircraft, but of British squadrons capable of doing full justice to the Royal Air Force. I should therefore like to send three Spitfire fighter squadrons to Australia during the present year, and persuade the Americans to give us the fighter aircraft they would otherwise have sent to Australia. I have little doubt that I can explain all this quite satisfactorily to the President. You will note however that I am not proposing to mount Australian airmen on British machines, but to send complete British

units. I note from my last return that you have 945 more fighter pilots on effective strength than fighter machines serviceable, and therefore it seems to me that forty or fifty could easily be spared out of these. It is my duty to preserve goodwill between the Mother Country and this vast continent of Australia, inhabited by six million people of our race and tongue.

3. Pray let me have your comments and proposals.

(*Action this Day.*)
Prime Minister to General Ismay, for C.O.S. Committee   13 July 43
The time has come to bring the Polish troops from Persia into the Mediterranean theatre. Politically this is highly desirable, as the men wish to fight, and once engaged will worry less about their own affairs, which are tragic. The whole corps should move from Persia to Port Said and Alexandria. The intention is to use them in Italy.

2. We have five months in hand to use all our strength against Italy. Let me have a list of the British-controlled [Allied] troops available which are not yet committed to the Sicilian battle and are capable of active field operations.

Prime Minister to First Sea Lord   13 July 43
I am shocked to see the destruction of the *Duchess of York* convoy. Will you let me have a copy of the signal from the C.-in-C. Mediterranean about ten days ago, warning us of the "intolerable" (I think that was the word) dangers of the air attack on this route too near the Spanish coast? The loss of these large ships will spoil our monthly record, which anyhow is burdened with operational casualties. Pray let me know what will be done to avoid this form of air attack in the future. Surely it is worth while going farther out beyond the range of Focke-Wulfs.

2. I see that *Port Fairy* was damaged west of Cape St. Vincent. Where did the aircraft come from, and how far out was she? If the enemy could reach her why could not Gibraltar air give her protection?

Prime Minister to Sir Edward Bridges   14 July 43
The Public Relations Officers are becoming a scandal, and the whole system requires searching scrutiny and drastic pruning. Pray advise me how to proceed. A small Cabinet committee with a suitable reference would seem to be indicated.

(*Action this Day.*)
Prime Minister to Secretary of State for War and   16 July 43
C.I.G.S.
I learn with great concern from C.I.G.S. that our 1st Armoured Division, a unit of exceptional quality and experience, on which years of training have been lavished, is now being used to guard prisoners

of war. As an emergency measure for, say, a month this might be
tolerated. It must now immediately be brought to an end. Rifle-
armed formations, not incorporated in divisional units, to the number
of at least 10,000 must be sent to North Africa either from this country
or the Delta to guard prisoners. Lord Leathers should regard the
shipping for any from this country as a high priority.

2. At the earliest moment the 1st Armoured Division is to be reconstituted with its vehicles and brought up to full strength. The
necessary training to restore its efficiency cannot be delayed. Let me
have a programme and time-table. I understand that C.I.G.S. has
already protested to General Eisenhower. Let me know exactly what
happened, and what the answer was.

3. Are there any more units in this condition? Let me have a list of
all divisional and separate brigade formations (a) in North-West Africa
and (b) in the Middle East, stating the condition of each and the task
on which it is employed. What is the state of the South African
Division? What has happened to the 201st Guards Brigade? Where
is the 7th Armoured Division? Where is the 4th Indian Division? Is
the New Zealand Division progressing to schedule? What stage has
been reached in the movement of the Polish Division to Syria? How
far are these divisions complete and equipped?

Prime Minister to Chief of the Air Staff   16 July 43
I still do not understand why it is necessary to have 2,946 crews
on effective strength [in Fighter Command] in order to man 1,732
serviceable aircraft, or indeed a total initial equipment of 1,966.

See how different are the figures of Bomber Command, who are
far more heavily engaged than the fighters, and who have only 1,353
crews to an initial establishment of 1,072 aircraft, and only 1,095 crews
operational for 1,039 aircraft serviceable.

The losses in Fighter Command are not comparable to those endured
by the bombers, and yet it has this enormous surplus of crews. How
far does this personnel surplus extend into the ground staff?

Prime Minister to Lord President of the Council   17 July 43
I have promised Lord Winterton a further communication about
the building of the agricultural cottages. I now feel however that as
I should like him to have a fuller explanation of the position than
could conveniently be contained in a letter it would be helpful if you
could see Lord Winterton yourself.*

(*Action this Day.*)
Prime Minister to C.I.G.S.   19 July 43
I do not feel very comfortable about the strength of the Dover

* See minute of July 3 to Lord President.

Garrison, which I visited on Saturday. There is only one battalion in Dover, and another at St. Margaret's Bay. These can be reinforced by a brigade after some hours. There are of course plenty of troops farther back.

2. There is of course no question of invasion, but when I asked General Swayne what would happen if three or four thousand Storm Troopers of the Commando type came across one night he was not able to give me a very reassuring answer. He said they would certainly get ashore, but would be turned out afterwards, and he also emphasised the shortness of the warning that would be received. This is not good enough. Dover is so near that perhaps half an hour is all the notice you would get by Radar. I do not think the Germans are likely to try, but it would be a tremendous score if they did have possession of part of Dover for even three or four hours. It would produce an effect on public opinion ten times as bad as the *Scharnhorst* and *Gneisenau* incident.

3. I should be much against locking up too many troops even at this point on the coast, but it seems to me we have gone to the other extreme and are exposing ourselves to what might be a most vexatious affront. In my opinion, at least another brigade should be actually in the coast defences or the strong-points, and available for immediate action should a landing be attempted. We should all look very silly if some of our valuable guns were blown up.

Pray go into this matter anew.

Prime Minister to Secretary of State for War and   19 July 43
Minister of Information

In difficult cases about releases from military service it is important that the rules should not be broken or relaxed. Nevertheless the Secretary of State has a discretionary power, where the public service may be advantaged, to make exceptions in respect of high-class personnel whose contributions to the war effort may be greater in their civilian employment. In using this discretion he would naturally have regard to the fact that only a very small part of the Army is engaged in actual fighting, and that many transferences from civil life to the Army merely involve a change of non-combatant job.

2. It is the duty of Ministers to settle such matters by personal arrangement, and not to let them come to a point where either departmental antagonisms arise on small points or I am called upon to intervene.

Prime Minister to Minister of Information   19 July 43

I saw again yesterday the two American Army films *Divide and Conquer* and *The Battle of Britain*. I think they are the best propaganda yet seen in this country. Moreover, they teach people about what happened in 1940, which few realised completely at the time and which is already beginning to fade in memory. I consider that these films should have the widest possible showing. Is there any difficulty in our picture-houses taking them? What terms, broadly, would you arrange with them? If there is any monopolistic refusal do not hesitate to come to me. I would ask for legislation if necessary.

2. Where are the other four films? Two have certainly been mentioned by name. I wish to see them. Why is there this long delay? Are the film companies making underground resistance? Please let me have a report on these second two films. What is holding them up?

3. As you know, I am willing to make a short statement introducing the films and praising the attitude of the Americans. But I wish to see the other two films first. I take much interest in this business, and I hope you will press it forward strongly. ·

Prime Minister to Chief of the Air Staff   21 July 43
I am disposed to sanction this proposal of the Secretary for Petroleum. You know I attach the greatest importance to the creation of a sufficiency of landing-grounds specially adapted to meet fog conditions. I hope this is fully realised.

Prime Minister to First Lord   23 July 43
I think it is rather a pregnant fact that out of 45,000 officers and ratings [in the Fleet Air Arm], of whom over 4,000 are officers, only thirty should have been killed, are missing, or have been taken prisoners during the three months ending April 30. I am very glad of course that they have not suffered, but the whole question of the scale of the Fleet Air Arm is raised by this clear proof of how very rarely it is brought into contact with the enemy. When such immense demands are made upon us by the Fleet Air Arm in respect of men and machines, one is bound, however ungrateful the task may seem, to scrutinise its actual employment against the enemy. I am sure it is not the fault of the officers and men that they have not had more opportunity, and it may be the period in question was exceptional. We cannot however keep such a large mass of high-class personnel of the highest fighting quality in a condition of non-activity so far as actual contact with the enemy is concerned.

Pray give this matter your careful consideration, because I shall be returning to it in the near future.

Prime Minister to General Ismay, for C.O.S. Committee   24 July 43
See now how all these difficulties [in Burma] are mounting up, and what a vast expenditure of force is required for these trumpery gains. All the commanders on the spot seem to be competing with one

another to magnify their demands and the obstacles they have to overcome.

2. All this shows how necessary it is to decide on a commander. I still consider he should be a determined and competent soldier, in the prime of life, and with the latest experience in the field. General Oliver Leese is, I believe, the right man, and as soon as the fighting in Sicily is over he should come back to this country for consultation. I consider Wingate should command the army against Burma. He is a man of genius and audacity, and has rightly been discerned by all eyes as a figure quite above the ordinary level. The expression "the Clive of Burma" has already gained currency. There is no doubt that in the welter of inefficiency and lassitude which has characterised our operations on the Indian front this man, his force and his achievements, stand out, and no mere question of seniority must obstruct the advance of real personalities to their proper stations in war. He too should come home for discussion here at an early date.

Prime Minister to General Ismay, for C.O.S. Committee　　25 July 43

See the various telegrams about the ill-treatment of our people in North Russia. The only way to deal with this kind of thing is for ostentatious preparations to be made to withdraw the whole of our personnel without saying anything to the Russian authorities. Let a plan be made for this. As soon as the local Russians see that we are off they will report to Moscow, and will of course realise that the departure of our personnel means the end of the Arctic convoys. If anything will bring them to their senses this will. If not, anyway we had better be out of it, as it only causes friction. Experience has taught me that it is not worth while arguing with Soviet people. One simply has to confront them with the new fact and await their reactions.

Prime Minister to C.I.G.S.　　25 July 43

I am obliged to you for reviewing the strength of the Dover Garrison. I had not taken into consideration the important forces mentioned by you. Are you sure that all these, especially the Royal Navy and Royal Air Force, are organised for immediate action at the shortest notice? Of course it could only be by night.

The possibility I had in mind was a smash-and-grab raid by about 2,000 Storm Troopers brought across in fast motor-boats. Provided you are satisfied that there is no danger of this, that the cliffs are unscalable and that the landing-points and defences are adequately garrisoned, I am content.*

Prime Minister to General Ismay, for C.O.S. Committee　　26 July 43

It is vital and urgent to appoint a young, competent soldier, well

* See minute of July 19 to C.I.G.S.

trained in war, to become Supreme Commander [in the Burma theatre], and to re-examine the whole problem of the war on this front so as to infuse vigour and audacity into the operations.

2. I know the Chiefs of Staff fully realise what a foolish thing it now looks to go and concentrate precious resources from the Mediterranean in order to attack the one speck of land in the whole of this theatre, namely, Akyab, which the enemy are making a kind of Gibraltar and are capable of reinforcing up to an entire Japanese division. For this petty purpose, now rightly stripped of its consequential attempt upon Rangoon, we are to utilise the whole amphibious resources available in the Bay of Bengal for the whole of the year 1944. Even Ramree is to be left over until after the 1944 monsoon. A more silly way of waging war by a nation possessing overwhelming sea-power and air-power can hardly be conceived, and I should certainly not be prepared to take responsibility for such a waste of effort, and above all of time.

3. The proper course for the campaign of 1944 is as follows:

(a) Maximum air aid to China; improvement of the air route and protection of the airfields.

(b) Maximum pressure by operations similar to those conducted by General Wingate in Assam, and, wherever [else] contact can be made on land, with the Japanese forces.

(c) The far-flung amphibious operation hitherto called "Second Anakim", which can be launched in regions where fighting is not interrupted by the monsoon season and where our naval and air powers can be brought into the fullest play. It is on this that the most urgent and intense study should now be concentrated by the Staffs.

4. The matter must now be brought up before the Defence Committee, in order that their views in principle may be ascertained before our Conference at Quebec.

Prime Minister to President of the Board of Trade 26 July 43

I am told that in spite of contributions from civilian supplies there is at present a shortage of playing-cards for use by the forces and workers in industry. The importance of providing amusement for the forces in their leisure hours and in long periods of waiting and monotony in out-of-the-way places, and for the sailors penned up in their ships for months together, cannot be overstated. Nothing is more handy, more portable, or more capable of prolonged usage than a pack of cards.

Let me have a report on this subject, and show me how you can remedy this deficiency. It ought to mean only a microscopic drain on our resources to make a few hundred thousand packs.

Prime Minister to Secretary of State for War (to see)   26 July 43
and C.I.G.S.

I am willing not to send a personal telegram to Eisenhower on the state of the 1st Armoured Division in order that he may not think you were pressing me to do so. However, I can only agree to this if prompt and drastic action is taken, for I am determined that this fine unit shall be immediately brought to the highest state of efficiency and equipment. We shall need it all the more if large distances have to be covered rapidly in Italy, and especially if our front broadens out into the northern part of Italy and the valley of the Po.

2. Will you therefore inform General Eisenhower that I am deeply concerned in this matter, and procure a prompt and satisfactory settlement with him.

3. Will you also give me a programme of the re-equipment of the division, and thereafter let me have reports fortnightly on the progress made towards its becoming in all ways fit for action.*

Prime Minister to Minister of Agriculture   30 July 43

I shall be much obliged if you will give me a brief report on the harvest, both hay and corn.

Prime Minister to Colonel Price   31 July 43

I do not consider that the date 1948 should now be mentioned as the hypothetical date for the ending of the war with Japan. This matter can be discussed between us during our Conference at Quebec and on the way to it. . . . Obviously the long-term projects of the Admiralty must be before us at the time of taking any such decisions.

Prime Minister to Minister of Aircraft Production   31 July 43

I am concerned that you hold out such slender hopes of our getting jet-propelled aircraft soon. I have heard that there is considerable diffusion of effort, and that even the air frames, which should not present any difficulty, are apt to be behindhand.

Would it not be a good thing to examine the numerous engines which it seems are under development and to concentrate our efforts on the two or three [types] which we may hope to get into production quickly? There are numerous reports of German jet-propelled aircraft, and we cannot afford to be left behind.

AUGUST

Prime Minister to President of the Board of Trade   1 Aug 43

Thank you for your note about shortages of playing-cards. What happened to the 1,950,000 produced over and above the 1,300,000 issued in the last twelve months?

* See minute of July 16 to Secretary of State for War.

2. As to the future twelve months, the demands appear to be well under 2,000,000 packs, against which you propose to make 2,250,000 packs. I should be very willing to support you in getting the twenty more workers and hundred tons of paper necessary to make an additional million, but first I must know what has happened to the 1,950,000 surplus in the last twelve months, and, secondly, what is the reserve you consider necessary to have "in hand for emergency". The important thing is to have the cards freely forthcoming when called for, and although the soldiers should have priority civilian workers need them too.*

Prime Minister to First Sea Lord　　　　　　　　　　1 Aug 43
I have suggested to the President that we issue from Hyde Park during "Quadrant" our monthly statement about the anti-U-boat warfare. This will mean it will come out on the 13th or 14th, instead of on the 10th.

2. I am anxious to strike a strong and heavy blow this time on German hopes, and I should like to press the President to agree to the following items:

  (a) In the first half of 1942 1.6 ships; in the second half of 1942 .8 of a ship; in the first half of 1943 .4 of a ship.
  (b) In the ninety-two days of May, June, and July eighty-seven, or whatever is the figure, U-boats are known to have been destroyed, in addition to the many which have been damaged.
  (c) The losses of Allied merchant shipping all over the world were greater in July than in June, which was a record month, but they are substantially less than the average of, say, the period January 1942 to June 1943, inclusive, or January 1943 to June 1943, inclusive, whichever you like. The operational losses in the capture of Sicily do not exceed, say, 70,000 tons.
  (d) During the present year—i.e., to the end of July—the new ships completed by the United States, Great Britain, and Canada exceeded all sinkings in the shipping of the United Nations by upwards of, say, three million tons—i.e., the nearest million under the true figure.

Pray let these points be considered before we leave, so that I can discuss the whole matter with the President.
P.S. How many of them were sunk by the British?

Prime Minister to General Ismay　　　　　　　　　　2 Aug 43
Make sure that no code-names are approved without my seeing them first.

* See minute of July 26 to President of the Board of Trade.

Prime Minister to C.I.G.S. 2 Aug 43
Eisenhower's telegram about relief of the 1st Armoured Division
from garrison duties.

1. Please let me know what can be done, consulting Lord Leathers
about shipping, to meet the further requirements of guards for prisoners
of war.*

2. I do not understand why it was necessary to strip all other
armoured units in the Middle East in order to provide the very
limited armoured forces taking part in "Husky". Let me have a
report showing the exact number of tanks held by each of the various
units in Africa, and also the last tank report, which showed, I think,
nearly 3,000 tanks in possession of Middle East Command.

3. We should not hesitate to take Shermans from a British armoured
division in this country to send out at once by special ships in order to
get the 1st Armoured Division rapidly re-equipped.

4. Let me also have a return showing the number of tanks available
in Great Britain, and the number expected from America and from
supply in the next three months.

Prime Minister to C.I.G.S. 2 Aug 43
I am counting on you to make sure that these prime units of our
Army which we have had so much trouble and delay in making are
not melted down into slush by uncomprehending hands.

We are getting a mass of tanks of all kinds in the Middle East, and
also at the same time a litter of bits and pieces of personnel, where once
stood perfectly organised veteran armoured divisions and brigades.

Nothing must stand in the way of rehabilitation.

Prime Minister to Lord President of the Council 2 Aug 43
I am much obliged to you for all the trouble you have taken, and
I welcome the further inquiries you are to make into the Army Bureau
of Current Affairs.

Every effort should be used to prevent extra time, money, and
military personnel being absorbed in these activities, which, although
admirable in themselves, must not be allowed unduly to cumber the
military machine and increase the heavy disproportion of non-
combatant services. Above all, no man fit to fight should be drawn
into this organisation, and the utmost vigilance must be used to correct the tendency of all such bodies to magnify themselves and their
numbers.

Prime Minister to Minister of Aircraft Production 3 Aug 43
The fall in engine production is very painful. I quite realise that it

* See minutes of July 16 and 26.

is the holiday season, but the fall in new production seems to have been much greater this year than last.

Prime Minister to Deputy Prime Minister   6 Aug 43

Your committee on Air Force establishments should certainly probe the enormous surpluses of crews compared with serviceable aircraft in the fighter squadrons.* 3,038 crews are maintained to man 1,725 aircraft. The reason given is that they have to be standing about waiting to take off at any moment, but this reason is good only over certain areas and under certain conditions. The fighter aircraft have not had heavy losses since the Battle of Britain, and it looks to me as if substantial economies could be made here. One wonders whether everything is on a similarly lavish scale. Bomber Command, although in far more continuous heavy action, works on a much smaller margin. Coastal Command are however remarkably well supplied with surplus crews. Here however the need to have as many aircraft as possible out on the long patrols is paramount, and may be only satisfiable by practical duplication of crews. This, I repeat, does not apply to fighter aircraft.

2. Another point which requires searching is the accumulation of Hurricanes and Spitfires at Takoradi. In the latest return, dated July 30, there are 183, of which forty-three are Spitfires. Considering that this route is falling into abeyance on account of a much better route becoming open through the Mediterranean, we should scrutinise narrowly the personnel employed on the route, as well as this habit of keeping a mass of invaluable aircraft additional to all Middle East reserves in the tank at Takoradi.

Prime Minister to Foreign Secretary   6 Aug 43

I do not think that the Russians have any anxieties about the rearmament of Turkey on its present scale. The Russians' preponderance of strength is so great that the trifling improvements we are making in the Turkish forces need not, and I believe will not, disturb them.

2. No doubt they would be annoyed by Turkey complicating the situation in the Balkans without doing anything effective to help Russia defeat Germany.

3. Obviously however the Russians will not remain contented with the present state of the Straits, and I do not suppose they have forgotten that we offered them Constantinople in the earlier part of the late war. Turkey's greatest safety lies in the active association with the United Nations. As you know, the time may come very soon when we shall ask her to admit our air squadrons and certain other forces to protect them in order to bomb Ploesti and gradually secure the control of the

* See minute of July 16 to Chief of the Air Staff.

Straits and the Black Sea. There is not much basis of real conversation with Russia about Turkey till we know what line Turkey takes.

Prime Minister to General Ismay 8 Aug 43

I have crossed out on the attached paper many unsuitable names. Operations in which large numbers of men may lose their lives ought not to be described by code-words which imply a boastful and over-confident sentiment, such as "Triumphant", or, conversely, which are calculated to invest the plan with an air of despondency, such as "Woebetide", "Massacre", "Jumble", "Trouble", "Fidget", "Flimsy", "Pathetic", and "Jaundice". They ought not to be names of a frivolous character, such as "Bunnyhug", "Billingsgate", "Aperitif", and "Ballyhoo". They should not be ordinary words often used in other connections, such as "Flood", "Smooth", "Sudden", "Supreme", "Fullforce", and "Fullspeed". Names of living people—Ministers or commanders—should be avoided; *e.g.*, "Bracken."

2. After all, the world is wide, and intelligent thought will readily supply an unlimited number of well-sounding names which do not suggest the character of the operation or disparage it in any way and do not enable some widow or mother to say that her son was killed in an operation called "Bunnyhug" or "Ballyhoo".

3. Proper names are good in this field. The heroes of antiquity, figures from Greek and Roman mythology, the constellations and stars, famous racehorses, names of British and American war heroes, could be used, provided they fall within the rules above. There are no doubt many other themes that could be suggested.

4. Care should be taken in all this process. An efficient and a successful administration manifests itself equally in small as in great matters.*

Prime Minister to General Ismay, for C.O.S. Committee 10 Aug 43

Please see this telegram.† There is no objection to the employment of Commandos, which are in fact regular troops of the highest order and the only ones we are likely to be able to spare for the Balkans this year. Fully accredited British military or diplomatic officers can of course accompany the Commandos to negotiate any surrender that may be asked for. The Middle East Commanders-in-Chief must not be encouraged to take conventional reactionary views.

Prime Minister to Minister of Production and 11 Aug 43
Minister of Supply

I am shocked at the appallingly low output of thirty-nine tanks for

* See minute of August 2 to General Ismay.
† From Middle East Defence Committee, deprecating the employment of Commandos in the Dodecanese, etc., as the Italians and Germans were unlikely to surrender to them.

the week ending July 31. I do not feel that the explanation of summer holidays is sufficient, and I shall be glad if you will let me have a full report. How does this figure compare with forecasts, and are your forecasts being realised, especially in the modern type of tanks? I shall require to be fully convinced on this matter, which has an important bearing on our policy regarding acceptance of American tanks.

Prime Minister to Foreign Secretary   14 Aug 43
All this is quite true, but it might better have been left unsaid. The displacement of Ribbentrop by von Papen would be a milestone of importance, and would probably lead to further disintegration in the Nazi machine. There is no need for us to discourage this process by continually uttering the slogan "Unconditional Surrender". As long as we do not have to commit ourselves to dealing with any particular new figure or new Government our advantage is clear. We certainly do not want, if we can help it, to get them all fused together in a solid desperate block for whom there is no hope. I am sure you will agree with me that a gradual break-up in Germany must mean a weakening of their resistance, and consequently the saving of hundreds of thousands of British and American lives.

Prime Minister to First Sea Lord   15 Aug 43
I hope you will consider whether it is not possible to arrest the traffic in the Cape area by turning your ships into Simonstown and Kilindini until the anti-U-boat reinforcements now on the way have arrived. I have asked Lord Leathers to give me the proportion of ships sunk to the total sailed. Nineteen is however a very heavy loss on a small and severely rationed traffic.

SEPTEMBER

Prime Minister (Washington) to Sir Ronald Campbell   13 Sept 43
I have drafted the following message, as you desire, for our Consuls in the Middle West.

Before sending it out you should consult Mr. Harry Hopkins privately as to whether he thinks it would be a suitable intervention for me to make.

"British Consuls in the Middle West should let everyone there know how much we in Britain admire and value the tremendous war effort made by so many of these States, which, though a thousand miles from the sea, are making their weight tell on all the battle-fronts and hastening the triumph of the good cause.

"I wish indeed I could have come to some of these great cities to

APPENDIX C

express myself our British thanks for the splendid exertions which are being made."

Prime Minister to Mr. President   13 Sept 43
CIVIL AVIATION

I have told our Government that you made no objection when I said that we intended to hold a preliminary Commonwealth meeting in London or Canada, and that this would be only to focus our own British Commonwealth ideas for subsequent discussion with the United States Government.

2. I said that, about the proposed International Conference, you thought it might wait till the matter had been discussed at the forthcoming tripartite Anglo-Soviet-American meetings.

3. I mentioned that your preliminary view comprised the following:
(i) There should be private ownership.
(ii) Key points should be available for international use on a reciprocal basis.
(iii) Internal traffic should be reserved to internal companies.
(iv) Government support may be required on an international basis for certain non-paying routes.

Prime Minister to Lord President of the Council   16 Sept 43

The Italians have not been able to comply with the conditions specified in General Eisenhower's broadcast of July 29, and in my view we may therefore consider our hands free in the matter. We should proceed with all arrangements now made for the further importation of Italian prisoners. Where are the great mass that we have taken? Over 250,000 were captured by General Wavell alone. It would be rather difficult to move to England men taken after the armistice, who in many cases have done their best to help us or have not resisted at all, but we have these larger pools to draw on, and work in the United Kingdom is more important than in India or South Africa. There should be a certain amount of return shipping from India. The War Office should supply the exact location of all Italian prisoners belonging to us, wherever they may be.

2. An arrangement could no doubt be made with the Badoglio Government, whom we have many ways of helping, in respect of further supplies of Italian labour. As a result of an arrangement with the Italian Government by which we get more labour, I see no reason why the status of Italian prisoners now in Great Britain should not be modified and they be placed on the basis of civilian Pioneer Corps internees, or something like that. I certainly look

311

forward to getting 100,000 more Italians into England for work purposes during 1944.

Prime Minister to First Lord and V.C.N.S.   26 Sept 43

What is being done to equip our submarines with an acoustic torpedo for their own defence when submerged and attacked by enemy anti-submarine craft?

Prime Minister to Minister of Food and   27 Sept 43
Minister of War Transport

I think we should certainly use some of the shipping space in vessels returning from North Africa for bringing over oranges and lemons from the Mediterranean area to this country. Pray consult together and let me have a note setting out what is being done and what is possible.

Prime Minister to First Lord   27 Sept 43

Please see that Lord Cherwell is kept informed about the German glider bomb, and also about the foxing devices, so that he can keep me in touch with all developments.

Prime Minister to Minister of War Transport   29 Sept 43

It is indispensable to diminish the queues for the buses and provide a better service for workers returning home, especially in the London area. This is certainly possible in view of the greatly improved oil position. Pray make proposals for immediate action in good time before the winter comes. You should aim at a 25 per cent. increase in the evening services. War efficiency is lost when people are tired out before they get home.

Prime Minister to C.I.G.S.   30 Sept 43

Let me have a short return of the present garrison at Cyprus. They ought to be able to find seven or eight thousand men in case the opportunity comes for an unopposed re-entry into Greece. There would be no question of occupying the country, but only giving a political support to a lawful restored Government.

Prime Minister to President of the Board of Trade and   30 Sept 43
Minister of Food

It seems clear that there may be a world shortage of many important foodstuffs after the liberation of Europe. I am anxious lest we should be committed to any estimates of relief requirements, which might prejudice our own supplies, before the Cabinet has had an opportunity of discussing the whole question.

Pray let me have a note on this as soon as possible.

OCTOBER

Prime Minister to Admiral Mountbatten, and to　　　　　　　2 Oct 43
General Ismay, for C.O.S. Committee

It seems to me that this draft Order of the Day would be a very good text for Admiral Mountbatten to use when visiting detachments of his forces. I deprecate however at this stage any general publication of such a document. The only consequence of it will be to draw more Japanese to this theatre. I cannot too strongly emphasise the importance of damping down all publicity about this theatre for at least three months. If it is communicated to any portion of the troops the strictest censorship should be used to prevent it being printed either in the Indian or world Press. I shall myself be referring to the South-East Asia theatre when I next speak in the House of Commons, in terms like these:

"The climatic conditions, the famine and the floods, have greatly set back all possibilities in this theatre. The new Commander-in-Chief will require to survey the whole situation on the spot and to visit many parts of the great regions with which he is concerned. Further prolonged periods of training are necessary for the troops. It would be very foolish to base expectations of large-scale action upon the fact that a new Commander-in-Chief has been appointed and that the Command is undergoing a very complete reorganisation."

This is much the best way to get through these next three or four months. It need in no way prevent the animation of the Army by visits of Admiral Mountbatten to the various widely separated centres of the Command or his infusing into all officers and men the sense of great days coming. The opposite impression should however be given to the world public and to the enemy.

> The sower went forth sowing,
> The seed in secret slept
> Through months of faith and patience,
> Till out the red blade leapt.

Prime Minister to Secretary of State for India　　　　　　　3 Oct 43

Basic English

I was shocked to find on my return to this country that the Cabinet committee appointed on July 12, 1943, had never once met. You volunteered to undertake this task, and I certainly thought you would be admirably qualified for it. Pray let me have a report of your progress up to date.

I have received a letter from Mr. Ogden suggesting that a special investigator should be sent to spend a week with him to learn all about Basic English, and I think it would be very wise to accept this invitation, so that your committee can be advised on details at an early date. The matter has become of great importance, as Premier Stalin is also interested. If you feel the pressure of your other duties is too heavy on you I will myself take on the duty of presiding over the committee, but I hope you will be able to relieve me of this.*

Prime Minister to First Lord   4 Oct 43
I should be obliged if you would let Lord Cherwell make me a short report on acoustic homing torpedoes, as he will be able to explain them to me very briefly.†

Prime Minister to Minister of War Transport   4 Oct 43
Surely we ought to get hold of this 24,000-ton ship [Italian merchant ship *Saturnia*] and put her on the Atlantic route at the earliest moment for the build-up for "Overlord".

Prime Minister to Minister of Labour and   6 Oct 43
National Service
I am glad to see you have managed to get 17,800 new workers into M.A.P.'s labour force in August, apart from increases in the additional work done for M.A.P. in other factories. If you can keep up this excellent rate we should achieve the target set on July 23 by the end of the year.

Prime Minister to Chief of the Air Staff   6 Oct 43
Recent evidence shows that the Germans are working hard on jet-propelled aircraft, and accentuates the need for the utmost pressure to be put on their development here.

Prime Minister to Foreign Secretary   6 Oct 43
It should be remembered that the reason why we sheered off making this agreement about the western frontiers of Russia and substituted the Twenty Years Treaty was the perfectly clear menace of very considerable division of opinion in the House of Commons. I know of no reason for supposing that this same opposition might not manifest itself again, perhaps in an even stronger form. The opponents would have the advantage of invoking very large principles against us.

At a Peace Conference the position can be viewed as a whole, and adjustments in one direction balanced by those in another. There is therefore the greatest need to reserve territorial questions for the general settlement. This is even more true of the United States' position, especially in an election year. It would be well therefore to have the American attitude clearly deployed before we adopt a new position in advance of the Twenty Years Treaty.

* See minute of July 11 to Sir Edward Bridges.
† See minute of September 26.

2. I think we should do everything in our power to persuade the Poles to agree with the Russians about their eastern frontier, in return for gains in East Prussia and Silesia. We could certainly promise to use our influence in this respect.

Prime Minister to Chief of the Air Staff   7 Oct 43

FOG DISPERSAL

Lord Cherwell tells me he had seen the installation working at Graveley, although not in fog, and that he was much impressed by it. Although it burns several tons of oil per minute, this will probably be improved. If the installations allow us to operate on nights which have hitherto been barred because there is a risk of fog a lot will be gained even if the burners never have to be turned on. And of course the saving of bombers, if and when fog occurs, is worth many tons of oil, of which we now happily have a good stock.

I hope that the rate of progress with the installations will be maintained and that all eight will be operational by December.

Prime Minister to Foreign Secretary and   7 Oct 43
Minister of War Transport

What is this report from Washington so widely quoted in to-day's newspapers, on the Allied shipping position, stating that at least 2,500,000 Americans can be sent over here before Christmas and that the invasion of the Continent can be advanced by at least six months? This nonsense is said to emanate from the Senate Sub-Committee on War Mobilisation.

I shall certainly be asked questions about this when the House meets.

Prime Minister to Secretary of State for War   11 Oct 43
and C.I.G.S.

Confusion is caused by the attempt to calculate Allied and enemy strength in "divisions". The word "division" is no common standard. For instance, the establishment of a German standard division is 20,000. The average standard strength on the Russian front is probably not more than 7,000 or 8,000. We had a case the other day of a German division of no more than 1,800 infantry and eighteen guns. What is the establishment and strength of the Russian divisions opposite to them? Let me have a list of the German divisions south of Rome, showing their estimated battle strength. What are the estimated battle strengths of all British divisions in Italy and in North Africa in men and guns, including anti-tank and anti-aircraft? What is the believed strength of the United States divisions in Italy and in Africa? What is the strength of each British division in the Expeditionary Force—*i.e.*, the number of men who will actually go overseas as a unit?

It is said that a British division with its share of corps troops and L. of C. is 42,000, yet when they are moved abroad 15,000 seems to be the maximum. I have been told that the United States divisions being built up for "Overlord" have an overall strength of 51,000. How many of these per division will actually proceed overseas?

2. A report showing the effective strengths of all divisions in the West should be prepared, and I should like to have this return kept up to date every month, according to the best information or estimates possible.

3. Let me have the best analysis you can make of the British forces in Italy, showing the number of divisions and their battle strengths, and also, separately, the ration strength of the British army now landed in Italy.

Prime Minister to Minister of War Transport 11 Oct 43
Let me have a report on bus queues in London and other great cities, and what measures you are taking to reduce them.*

Prime Minister to Minister of Production 12 Oct 43
I recently invited Lord Cherwell to inquire into and report on the relative efficiency of the high explosives used by the German and British forces respectively. A copy of his preliminary report is attached.

The Chiefs of Staff strongly recommend that we should change over to aluminised explosives without waiting for the result of further trials. I agree. Pray let me have a report of what this change will involve in the course of the next week.

The question of how this state of affairs has been allowed to arise should be the subject of an inquiry held under the authority of the Minister of Defence. Pray propose three members, with reference. The whole matter is to be kept most secret.

Prime Minister to Foreign Office, Lord President of the 13 Oct 43
Council, and Chancellor of the Exchequer
Field-Marshal Smuts tells me that he has about 80,000 Italian prisoners in South Africa, and that he would be very glad to let us have a large number of them—he mentioned up to 40,000—for work in the United Kingdom.

This seems to me very important, and should be considered.†

Prime Minister to Brigadier Jacob 16 Oct 43
Let me have the most detailed analysis possible, without undue delay, of the base troops [in Egypt], amounting to 241,000. What are they the base of now the war has moved away from the Middle East and

* See minutes of September 29 and October 16.
† See minute of September 16 to Lord President.

the armies remain based on North-West Africa to a large extent? It seems to me that this figure of 241,000 men, including 116,000 British, requires most searching examination, and I propose that a special committee shall be appointed on that subject. Let me first of all however have the facts immediately available.

Prime Minister to Minister of War Transport   16 Oct 43
BUS QUEUES
I am glad you are taking steps to improve the position. In the London Passenger Transport Board region about $5\frac{1}{2}$ million bus journeys are made daily. An extra minute wasted per journey every day is equivalent to 10,000 persons working a nine-hour day over the year in this area alone.*

PLANS FOR THE TRANSITION PERIOD
23 Oct 43
At their meeting on October 21 the War Cabinet approved generally the line of approach set out in my memorandum of October 19, and I undertook to circulate a further note setting out the procedure for ensuring the completion of plans for the transition period.

I

2. The first step is to obtain a list of all the action which has to be taken, the schemes which must be prepared, and the administrative arrangements which must be planned and organised in advance, so that when hostilities with Germany cease the country as a whole will find that the new emergency has been foreseen and the necessary preliminary action has been taken.

3. For this purpose each department is called upon to submit to the Secretary of the War Cabinet not later than November 10 a schedule showing all the action which they will have to take and the measures required,

  (a) in the period immediately after hostilities with Germany end;
  (b) so far as can reasonably be foreseen, during the rest of the transition period, which may be taken as a working basis as two years from the defeat of Germany.

4. The returns should cover all matters for which each department is primarily responsible. There are however numerous questions of common concern to many departments which have been remitted for examination to special organisations or committees. In these cases returns should be submitted by the head of the organisation or the chairman of the committee concerned.

* See minutes of September 29 and October 11.

5. The returns should include the following particulars:

(a) The state of preparedness of the schemes—*i.e.*, whether they are ready now or how long they will take to complete.

(b) Points of principle on which decisions are necessary before further work can be carried out.

(c) Whether legislation by statute, Order in Council, or Defence Regulation is called for, whether such legislation has been prepared, and whether it needs to be enacted before the defeat of Germany.

6. An important part of the plan will be a careful survey of the whole field of legislation (including Defence Regulations and other subordinate legislation) to determine which war-time powers must be retained and which can be dispensed with in the transitional period. This examination is already being carried out by the committee on emergency legislation, under the chairmanship of Sir Claud Schuster.

II

7. The second stage will be for a general survey to be framed showing the whole range of preparations for the transition period. At this stage we must make sure that there are no gaps or contradictions between the different parts of the plan. I will myself supervise this process.

8. While the transition from peace to war differs in many respects from the transition from war to peace, and War Book procedure is not altogether appropriate, it will probably be convenient that all departments should have a copy of this survey to assist them in understanding how their preparations fit in with the general scheme.

An officer of high rank should be designated in each department who should be personally responsible for seeing that the schedule of the preparations for which his department is primarily responsible is kept continuously up to date.

III

9. The third stage will be to make sure that the whole scheme is brought to a state of readiness and is so maintained. It may be found, in the first instance, that preparatory action on a number of important matters is being delayed because decisions have not been reached on points of principle. I propose, when the general plan has been drawn up, to preside over a series of meetings at which the various parts will be reviewed, and decisions thereafter obtained from the War Cabinet on any matters which hamper the progress of preparations.*

* See Chapter IX, pp. 151-2

Prime Minister to Home Secretary   24 Oct 43

Once we are sure that we have a plan for food, work, and homes ready in case Hitler collapses it will be quite possible to refine it.

Prime Minister to Brigadier Hollis, for C.O.S. Committee   24 Oct 43

This paper about directives to Supreme Commanders looks very simple from a distance and appeals to the American sense of logic. However, in practice it is found not sufficient for a Government to give a general a directive to beat the enemy and wait to see what happens. The matter is much more complicated. The general may well be below the level of his task, and has often been found so. A definite measure of guidance and control is required from the Staffs and from the high Government authorities. It would not be in accordance with the British view that any such element should be ruled out.

Prime Minister to First Lord   24 Oct 43

I do not consider you have any right to strike off these forty vessels from the escort and fleet destroyer strength. They may, if you will, be left unmanned in material reserve and only brought out in case of serious emergency.

It is quite impossible for us to take up so much of the war effort of the country in building up such enormous new programmes if you do not make full use of your material. Considering that you are now building destroyers which take two years to build, we must consider whether these older ones cannot be repaired and kept going. This failure, coupled with the immense demands for aircraft-carriers, causes me a great deal of concern now that the Italian Fleet and the German Navy are practically extinct. Future naval programmes must be subjected to a very strict scrutiny, not only by me but by the War Cabinet.

Prime Minister to Brigadier Hollis   27 Oct 43

Why has it been decided to abandon the rubber Lilo? Let me have photographs showing the cruciform Lilo, and explain how it produces the desired effect. It seems to me that a complete change of plan has been made.

What is the difference between this concrete and steel structure and ordinary breakwaters? What time would it take to put down? How many ships would it require to carry, and so on?

It would be a pity to spoil a promising plan by magnifying the demands on material and labour to an excessive degree.

Prime Minister to Chancellor of the Duchy of Lancaster   27 Oct 43

I am not in favour of the appointment to high military rank of, or of the wearing of uniform by, civilians holding civilian or quasi-civilian posts unless this is clearly necessary to the successful perform-ance of their duties. In this light, pray inquire into the principles adopted in the Security Service for gazetting its officers to commissions and as regards their wearing uniform. Let me have a short report.

Prime Minister to Brigadier Hollis   31 Oct 43
    Let me have a return showing the present development of the British forces for "Overlord"; also a statement of what formations will be left here at home apart from the above.

APPENDIX D

MONTHLY TOTALS OF SHIPPING LOSSES, BRITISH, ALLIED, AND NEUTRAL, BY ENEMY ACTION

MONTH	BRITISH		ALLIED		NEUTRAL		TOTAL	
	No. of Ships	Gross Tons	No. of Ships	Gross Tons	No. of Ships	Gross Tons	No. of Ships	Gross Tons
January 1943	19	98,096	24	143,358	7	19,905	50	261,359
February	29	166,947	39	232,235	5	3,880	73	403,062
March	62	384,914	53	303,284	5	5,191	120	693,389
April	33	194,252	27	137,081	4	13,347	64	344,680
May	31	146,496	26	151,299	1	1,633	58	299,428
June	12	44,975	13	75,854	3	2,996	28	123,825
July	30	187,759	26	166,231	5	11,408	61	365,398
August	14	62,900	9	56,578	2	323	25	119,801
September	12	60,541	15	94,010	2	1,868	29	156,419
October	11	57,565	17	81,631	1	665	29	139,861
November	15	61,593	12	82,696	2	102	29	144,391
December	10	55,611	21	112,913	—	—	31	168,524
TOTALS	278	1,521,649	282	1,637,170	37	61,318	597	3,220,137
January 1944	16	67,112	9	62,115	1	1,408	26	130,635
February	12	63,411	8	53,244	3	200	23	116,855
March	10	49,637	14	104,964	1	3,359	25	157,960
April	3	21,439	10	60,933	—	—	13	82,372
May	5	27,297	—	—	—	—	5	27,297
TOTALS	46	228,896	41	281,256	5	4,967	92	515,119

APPENDIX E

SUMMARY OF
ORDER OF BATTLE, GERMAN AND ITALIAN
DIVISIONS, ON SEPTEMBER 8, 1943*

(Source: *Come Arrivammo all'Armistizio*, by General Francesco Rossi)

Divisions marked with a "dagger" are recorded as being weak or of low category.

	Italian	*German*
North Italy	5 infantry †5 infantry	6⅓ infantry 2 motor and armoured
Central Italy	3 infantry 2 motor and armoured †2 infantry	2 motor and armoured
Southern Italy	3 infantry †1 infantry	2 infantry 4 motor and armoured
Sardinia	4 infantry	1 motor
Southern France	4 infantry (under relief by German troops, strength unknown, from Rundstedt's command)	
Corsica	2 infantry	⅓ infantry
Slovenia, Croatia, Dalmatia	8 infantry	9 infantry 6 brigades (Croat Alpine troops)
Herzegovina, Montenegro	6 infantry	2 infantry 1 motor and armoured 2 brigades (Croat Alpine troops)

* See Chapter VIII.

Albania	5 infantry 1 motor	Nil (but a call on 2 German and 2 Bulgarian divisions in Serbia and Macedonia)
Greece	7 infantry	6 infantry 1 armoured
Crete	1 infantry	1 infantry
Ægean	2 infantry	1 infantry with A.F.V.s

TOTALS

	Italian	German
Italian mainland	21 divisions, of which 8 are weak or of low category	$16\frac{1}{3}$
Sardinia	4	1
"Overseas"	36	$21\frac{1}{3}$
GRAND TOTALS	61 Italian divisions, of which 8 are weak or of low category	$38\frac{2}{3}$ German divisions

---

GERMAN DISPOSITIONS IN DETAIL, SEPTEMBER 8, 1943

ARMY GROUP – ROMMEL

Northern Italy	24 Armd. Div. Hitler S.S. Armd. Div. }	*Area* Parma–Bologna
	44 Inf. Div. One inf. bde. }	Alto Adige
	71 Inf. Div.	Tarvisio–Piedicolle–Postumia
	65 Inf. Div. 76 Inf. Div. 94 Inf. Div. 305 Inf. Div. }	Sestri Levante–Val Taro– Pontremoli–Apuania

GERMAN SOUTHERN COMMAND – KESSELRING

Central Italy	3 Pz. Gr. Mot./Armd. 2 Pz. Gr. Parachute	Lake Bolsena– Viterbo
Southern Italy	15 Inf. Div. H. Goering Armd. Div. 16 Armd. Div. 1 Parachute Div. 26 Armd. Div. 29 Pz. Gr. Mot. Div.	Formia Naples Salerno Puglia Basilicata Calabria Calabria
Sardinia	90 Inf. Mot. Div.	
Corsica	One brigade "Reich Fuehrer", Mot./Armd.	

GERMAN SOUTH-EAST COMMAND – LOHR

Slovenia, Croatia,
  Dalmatia
	114 Inf. Div.
	373 (German–Croat) Inf.
	  Div.
		} Bihac

	187 Inf. Div. 369 (German–Croat) Inf. Div. 173 Inf. Div.	} Sava
	Two (?) inf. divs. One S.S. div.	} Zagreb
	One (Croat) Mtn. Div. Six (Croat) Mtn. Bdes.	} Various

Herzegovina,
  Montenegro
	Prinz Eugen S.S. Mot./Armd.
	  Div.
	118 (?108) Inf. Div.
	297 Inf. Div.
	Two (Croat) Mtn. Bdes.
		Mostar
		
		Prijepolie Plevlja
		Ibar Valley
		Various

Greece	One Mtn. Div. One L. of C. div. One inf. div. 104 Inf. Div. 11 Inf. Div. 117 Inf. Div. One armd. div.	Janina Salonica Larissa Agrinion Piræus } Peloponnese
Crete	22 Inf. Div.	
Rhodes	One 55 mot./armd. div.	

INDEX

"Accolade", Operation, 74, 191, 288
Acquarone, Duke of, 40, 46
"Admiral Q", 288
Admiralty, War Room map of "Husky" in, 31; proposes suspension of Arctic convoys, 220; and resumption of convoys, 233; construction programme of, 319
Adriatic Sea, help to Balkan peninsula across, 53-4, 74, 114; Germany fears attack in, 196. *See also* Dalmatia
Ægean, effect of Italian surrender on, 55; projected operations in, 74, 118, 181-2, 186, 192, 255; fate of Italian troops in, 170, 180; chance of gaining command of, 180-1; Wilson's action in, 184-5; Hitler urged to evacuate, 184-5; Roosevelt on follow-through of action in, 190-1; enemy forces diverted to, 193, 196, 199; forced abandonment of, 194, 198-9; evacuating troops from islands of, 194-5, 198; German losses in, 199; enemy divisions in, September 8, 1943, 323. *See also* Dodecanese; Rhodes
Agricultural cottages, 294, 296, 300
Airborne troops, Allied, in Italy, 129. *See also* British Airborne Division
Aircraft production, U.S., 11, 298; labour for, 292, 314; black-out hampers, 297
Aircraft-carriers, merchant, 11; escort, 11; Nimitz asks for British, 18, 20; construction of new Royal Navy, 319
Airfield(s), floating, 69; need for, in invasion of Italy, 85; near Rome, plan to land troops on, 97-100; in New Guinea, 122; near Naples, 133; in Cos, 185; fog dispersal on, 302, 315
Air raids, on Italy, 35, 41, 45, 50; on Peenemünde, 206-8; German, on Bari, 225; on England, 225
Ajaccio, 163
Akyab, failure at, 70-1; attempt to capture, 78-9, 304
Albania, aid for, 53; fate of Italian troops in, 170; enemy divisions in, September 8, 1943, 323
Alexander, Rt. Hon. A. V., First Lord of Admiralty (Viscount, of Hillsborough), minutes to, 177, 291, 302, 312, 314, 319; mentioned, 145

Alexander, Field-Marshal Sir Harold (Viscount, of Tunis), in command in Sicily, 25-6, 31, 95; reports on progress in Sicily, 37-8; minutes, etc., to, 86, 95, 117, 127, 130, 134-5, 194, 215, 222, 287-316; army of, in Italy, 86-7; asked to advance date of "Avalanche", 95-6; minutes, etc., from, 96, 99, 128-31; 222; as Eisenhower's Deputy, 111; on progress in Italy, 117; bold stroke at Taranto, 125-6, 135; at Salerno, 128-31; at signing of Italian armistice, 173; and operations in Ægean, 191, 193-4; reports on conditions in Italy, 216-20, 257-9; wants more landing-craft, 219-220, 222; plans of, in the Italian campaign, 224; provisionally chosen to command in Mediterranean, 269
Alexandria, 281
Algiers, de Gaulle and Giraud meet in, 153; French Committee of National Liberation in, 154
Allied Inter-Service Staff, plan "Overlord", 65
Altavilla, 130
Alten Fiord, 244
Aluetta, 131
Aluminised explosives, 316
Ambrosio, General, 40; plans arrest of Mussolini, 41, 46; at meeting with Hitler, 44; requests return of Italian divisions, 90
Amery, Rt. Hon. L. S., minutes to, 294, 313
Ammunition, for Home Guard, 294-5
Amphibious load-carrier (D.U.K.W.), 26
Amphibious operations, preparations for, 24, 28-9, 31, 139; vehicles for, 26; importance of weather in, 31-2; Combined Operations Organisation and, 64-65; against Akyab, 71, 79, 304; on Italian coast, 218-19; "Second Anakim", 304. *See also* "Overlord"
"Anakim", Operation, 288; "Second Anakim", 304
Anatolia, Allies seek air bases in, 194-5
Ancona, 136
Anderson, Rt. Hon. Sir John, Chancellor of Exchequer, 144-5; minutes to, as Lord President of Council, 294, 296, 300,

307, 311; minutes to, as Chancellor, 316

Anti-aircraft protection, of rocket and flying-bomb sites, 212; of London from flying bombs, 213

"Anvil", Operation, 77, 288

Arakan, corps defeated in, 70-1

Archangel, medical unit for, 236; liquidation of British base at, 239

Arctic convoys, Royal Navy's work in, 18, 243; postponement of, 228-9; Molotov insists on resumption of, 232-233; arrangements to restart, 233-5, 241, 243; number and treatment of personnel of, in Russia, 234-9, 241, 243-4, 303; Stalin's offensive letter on, 237-42; Molotov on value of, 242; Eden's interview with Stalin on, 243-4; resumption of, 244-5, 261-2

Army Bureau of Current Affairs, 307

Arnold, General H. H. (U.S.), tests Pykrete, 81; at Anglo-U.S. Conference at White House, 118, 122; on Allied Air Force in Italy, 122

Asmara, 274

Atlantic, Battle of, 6-15

Atlantic Convoy Conference, 6

Atlantic Ocean, victory over U-boats in, 4, 9-11; pooling of Allied resources in, 6, 8; air gap in North, 8; U-boats in South, 10, 232, 310; U-boat battle starts in, 228-9, 234

Atomic bomb, German researches into, 204

Attlee, Rt. Hon. Clement R., Deputy Prime Minister, Mountbatten's appointment referred to, 73, 79; telegrams to, from Quebec, 79, 83-4; and rebuilding of House of Commons, 150; minutes to, 308, 316; mentioned, 294

Auchinleck, Field-Marshal Sir Claude, 126

Augusta, 26, 33

Australia, MacArthur in, 16; Japanese threat to, 16; aircraft for, 298-9

Australian Army, in New Guinea, 21

Australian Navy, 15

"Avalanche", Operation, 36-7, 85; scale of, 86; need to advance date of, 95-6; imminence of, 98-9; shipping for, 116; build-up after, 117, 189; launching of, 124-5; complaint of delay in launching, 138-9; air superiority during, 216. See also Salerno

Avellino, 129, 131

Ayeta, Marquis D', 89-90

Azores, as naval and air base, 77, 146-148

Badoglio, Marshal, appointed head of the State by King Emmanuel, 41, 47-9; negotiates for armistice, 52, 89-98; Government of, attitude of Allies to, 59, 140-1, 143, 167-9, 171-5, 178-9; proposes to join Allies against Germany, 92; means open to, of hampering Germans, 93, 95; and proclamation of armistice, 100; escapes to Brindisi, 100-101; signs long-term armistice, 172-3; Sforza willing to co-operate with, 175-176

Baghdad, 274

Balkans, hopeful situation in, 34-5; Italian troops in, 41, 50, 53, 54, 93, 95, 170-1; effect of surrender of Italy on, 51, 54-5, 121; German divisions in, 53-4, 225; extent of Allied help to, 74, 77, 113-14, 121, 187; Smuts advises invasion of, 114; effect of successful Ægean action on, 187, 190; possible Allied strategy in, 255; effects of Germans leaving, 254, 257

Bari, airborne division at, 133; Alexander's H.Q. at, 135; enemy air attack on, 225

Basic English, 297, 313-14

Basra, 275

Battipaglia, 125, 130

Battle of Britain, The, film, 301-2

Battleships, disposal of Italian, 177, 263; Britain suspends building, 263

"Baytown", Operation, 86, 288

B.B.C., and Basic English, 297

Beirut, disturbances in, 165

Bengal, Bay of, preparations for amphibious operations in, 304

Bergamini, Admiral, 102

Berio, Signor, peace overtures of, 90-2

Bevin, Rt. Hon. Ernest, minute to, 314

Bey, Rear-Admiral, 245

Bielgorod, 230

Biscay, Bay of, air offensive against U-boats in, 9-10

Bismarck Archipelago, 16

Bismarck Sea, Japanese convoy destroyed in, 21

Black Sea, opening route to, for supplies to Russia, 114, 255, 257

Black-outs, 296-7

Boisson, M., 154-5

"Bombardon" breakwaters, 68, 288

Bomber Command, raids Peenemünde, 206-8; proportion of crews to aircraft in, 300, 308

Bottomley, Air Chief Marshal Sir N.H., 212

Bracken, Rt. Hon. Brendan, at Quebec, 74; minutes to, 292, 301; Minister of Information, 293

Breakwaters, for "Overlord" landings, 66-68, 319; floating, schemes for, 68

Brest, 66

Bridges, Sir Edward, minutes to, 291-2, 296-7, 299

Brindisi, Italian King and Government at, 101, 104; landing of Allied troops at, 131

British Airborne Division, in Sicily, 28, 32-3; at Taranto, 118, 126, 131; in Italy, 133

British Armoured Division, re-forming of, 86-7, 300, 307; in Italy, 129-31; used for guarding prisoners, 177, 299-300, 305, 307

British Army, in North Africa, size of, 24-25; in Sicily, 25; in Italy, reinforcements for, 87, 129; in Italy, 125, 133, 215, 316; strength of divisions in, 315-16. *See also* Eighth Army; Fifth Army

British Commonwealth, Smuts on danger to, of Russian diplomatic mastery, 112-113; discussion by, on civil aviation, 311

Broadhurst, Air Vice-Marshal Sir H., 26

Brooke, Field-Marshal Sir Alan (Viscount Alanbrooke), Chief of Imperial General Staff, disappointed at not being given command of "Overlord", 76, 267; reforms armoured divisions, 86-7; at Lake of Snows, 105-6; minutes to, 223, 294-5, 299-300, 303, 305, 307, 312, 315; Roosevelt suggests that he should be Deputy Supreme Commander, 271. *See also* Chiefs of Staff

Bruneval, Commando raid on, 64; German construction at, 205

"Buccaneer", Operation, 288

Bulgaria, behaviour in 1918, 50-1; effect of collapse of Italy on, 54, 121, 187

Buna, New Guinea, 21

Burma, Wingate's theory on fighting in, 62; failure in, 70, 302; attack on Japan through, 77-9; improved communications needed in Upper, 79; floods in, 80, 269; plans for campaign in, 113, 115; U.S. Press gives prominence to coming campaign in, 269-70; question of command in, 303-4

Bus queues, 312, 316-17

Cadogan, Rt. Hon. Sir Alexander, in Washington, 84

Cairo, diversionary preparations at, before Teheran meeting, 272-3

Cairo Conferences, difficulties over arrangements for, 279-84

Calabria, descents on coast of, 85; progress through, 86, 117, 218; German troops in, 216

Caltagirone, 33

Cameron, Lieutenant Donald, R.N.R., 234

Campbell, Rt. Hon. Sir Ronald, Ambassador at Lisbon, 88-9; minute to, 310

Canada, takes joint responsibility for North Atlantic convoys, 7; work on Pykrete in, 69; Churchill greeted in, 72; Churchill sworn Privy Counsellor of Cabinet of, 106; his broadcast to, 107-9; war contributions of, 107-8

Canadian Air Force, in Battle of Atlantic, 8

Canadian Army, in Sicily, 28, 37; protects Britain, 107; in Italy, 116, 131, 224

Canberra, H.M.A.S., loss of, 17, 20

Cape Orlando, 37

Careless talk, precautions against, 291

Caroline Islands, Japanese base in, 16, 113

Carton de Wiart, Lieut.-General Sir Adrian, liaison officer with Chiang Kai-shek, 84; accompanies Italian emissary to Lisbon, 96-7

Casablanca, 294

Casablanca Conference, Sicilian campaign decided upon by, 23; "Overlord" planning arranged at, 65

Casey, Rt. Hon. R. G., Minister of State Resident in Middle East, 132; Cairo villa of, 280

Cassino, Monastery Hill at, 224-5, 308

Castellano, General, proposes Italian cooperation against Germans, 92; discussions on peace terms with, 94-8; signs armistice, 99

Castelrossa island, 184

Catania, 26, 33, 37-8

Catapult-aircraft merchant ships, 11

Catroux, General Georges, on French Committee of National Liberation, 154-155, 160; in Levant, 165

Caviglia, Marshal, 101

Centuripe, 37

Cephalonia, 170

Cesaro, 37

Cherbourg, objective in "Overlord", 66; flying-bomb launching sites near, 210, 212

Cherwell, Lord, on danger from rockets, 206, 212-13; on aluminised explosives, 316; minutes to, 290, 296; and glider

INDEX

bombs, 312; Paymaster-General, 314; on fog dispersal apparatus, 315

Chevrons for service abroad, 293

Chiang Kai-shek, Generalissimo, British liaison officer with, 84; at Cairo Conference, 279, 281, 284

Chiefs of Staff, consultations with, on way to Quebec, 63, 69-70; Mountbatten a member of, 64, 81; and South-East Asia Command, 70-1, 77, 80; minutes to, 79, 295 (see also Ismay, Lord); demand Britain's fair share in assault on Japan, 81; report on long-range rocket danger, 201-2; Supreme Commander and, 268; desire review of Quebec decisions, 277; apprehensive of arrangements for Cairo Conference, 283; on use of aluminised explosives, 316

Chiefs of Staff, U.S., propose one overall Supreme Commander, 271-2

China, assault on Japan through, 77; land and air communications with, 82, 113, 304; to sign Four-Power Declaration, 265

Churchill, Mary, with Mr. Churchill to Quebec, 63; at Hyde Park, 73; speaks to American W.A.C.s, 107; adventure of, on Renown, 132

Churchill, Mrs., accompanies husband to Quebec, 63, 72-3; at Lake of Snows, 106-107; Russian Relief Fund of, 242

Churchill, Major Randolph, at Salerno with Commandos, 132

Churchill, Rt. Hon. Winston S., correspondence with Roosevelt, 18, 42, 51-52, 54-60, 73, 89, 92, 107, 133, 154-7, 159-62, 164, 167-9, 172-9, 186-92, 194, 210-11, 220-2, 240, 268-70, 273-4, 276-283, 311; stresses need for attack on Italy, 34-5, 74; correspondence with Smuts, 34, 112-16; on consequences of Italian collapse, 50-55; recognises Badoglio Government, 52, 59, 140-1, 167-9, 171, 174-6, 178; Atlantic crossing, autumn 1943, 63-71; correspondence with George VI, 72; visits President, 73, 109-10, 117, 126; correspondence with Stalin, 73, 98-9, 171, 234-40, 247-51, 272-3, 284; and leadership of "Overlord", 76, 267-71; Far Eastern strategy of, 78-9, 304; takes holiday after Quebec Conference, 84, 105-7; broadcasts in Quebec, 84, 105-9; broadcasts at Harvard, 84, 110-111; increases strenght of army to attack Italy, 86-7; on opening negotiations with Italy, 92-5;

urges action in Eastern Mediterranean, 101, 181, 186-92, 255; on treatment of Italian Fleet, 102-3; at Anglo-U.S. Conference at White House, 118-19, 122-3; returns home on Renown, 126; message to Alexander about Salerno, 127; on proportion of effort in Mediterranean, 134; criticisms of, on conduct of war, 138; speech of, after Quebec Conference and fall of Italy, 138-44; speech of, on mining industry, 148-9; memorandum of, on post-war tasks, 154; invites French Committee to lunch, 154; and de Gaulle, 154-65; his interview with Sforza, 176; on uses for Italian ships, 177, 262-3; prepares to fly to Tunis, 188-9, 191; on withdrawal of landing-craft needed in Italy, 221, 226-7, 258; on re-opening of Arctic convoys, 233-7, 243, 261-2; seeks to avoid charge of breach of faith from Russia, 235, 240-241, 243-4; refuses to receive offensive letter from Stalin, 241-2, 244; seeks to arrange meeting of Big Three, 247-51, 272 et seq.; notes of, for Moscow Conference of Foreign Secretaries, 251-2; on disposition of Allied and enemy forces at "Overlord", 254-5; on entry of Turkey into war, 256-7; on entry of Sweden into war, 257; on necessity of sustaining campaign in Italy, 258-9; Stalin on, 260-1; on Russian claim to Italian ships, 262-3; on war criminals, 263-5; presses for choice of Supreme Commander, 267-71, 277-8; rejects idea of one command for Mediterranean and "Overlord", 271-2; suggests Anglo-U.S. meeting before Teheran Conference, 276-9; anxiety of, for 1944 campaign, 278, 280; deprecates presence of Russians at Combined Chiefs of Staff meetings, 279-80, 283-4; differs from Roosevelt as to proceedings at Cairo, 282-4; personal minutes and telegrams of, 290 et seq.; on King Peter's marriage, 297-8; on U.S. propaganda films, 301-2; plans of, for post-war transition period, 317-18

Ciano, Count, 46

Civil aviation, post-war, Churchill's views on, 290; Roosevelt's views on, 310

Clark, General Mark (U.S.), commands Fifth Army in Italy, 124-5, 224; congratulations to, 131; Darlan's agreement with, 153-4

Clarke, Colonel Frank W., 105-6

Coal-mining situation, 148-9

Coastal Command, chief of, 6; no similar organisation in the U.S., 7; H$_2$S apparatus used by, 8; work of long-range aircraft of, 11; proportion of crews to aircraft in, 308

Co-belligerency, explanation of Italian, 174

Code-names, list of, 288; P.M. to approve, 306; unsuitable examples, 309

"Colonel Warden", 73, 107, 288

Combined Chiefs of Staff, and Operation "Husky", 24; disagreement among, on invasion of Italy, 36-7, 296; directive on Italian situation for, 54; report on "Overlord", 75; on Italian campaign, 76-7, 85; and S.E.A.C., 77, 80, 82; discuss British share in assault on Japan, 80-2; final report of, at Québec, 82-3; approve action in Dodecanese, 102, 182, 186, 188; Churchill praises, 111; meetings of, with Churchill, at White House, 118-19, 122-3; order from, prevents capture of Rhodes, 181; Churchill seeks to arrange meeting of, 215, 276-8; authorise retention of L.S.T.s in Italy, 222; Supreme Commander and, 268, 271; Roosevelt suggests Russian representative at meetings of, 279-80, 283-4

"Combined Commanders", 65

Combined Operations Organisation, 64

Commando troops, in Sicily, 28, 33; cross-Channel raids of, 64; at Salerno, 125, 132; in Italy, 133; in Balkans, 309; Fijian, 293; German, danger of raids on Dover, 301, 303

Commons, House of, criticism in, of conduct of the war, 138-41; rebuilding of the Chamber, 149; size and shape of, 150

Communism, in Italy, 89

Communists, British, and Second Front, 140

Coningham, Air Vice-Marshal Sir A., 26, 135

Convoys, protection of, in North Atlantic, 8-11; for Operation "Husky", 31-2; lost off coast of Spain, 299; lost in South Atlantic, 310

Cooper, Rt. Hon. Sir Alfred Duff, minute to, 319

Coral Sea, Japanese seek mastery of, 16

Corfu, 52, 170

Corsica, Eisenhower advocates landing in, 23; surrender of, 53, 57; question of occupation of, 77, 85, 134; French troops

for, 121, 131; fall of, 135, 137; incidents between French and Free French in, 163; enemy divisions in, September 8, 1943, 322, 324

Cos, strategic value of, 180, 185; British occupation and loss of, 184-7, 194-5, 255

Crete, Italian troops in, 181, 185; Hitler urged to evacuate, 184-5; enemy divisions in, September 8, 1943, 323-4

Crimea, 232

Cripps, Right Hon. Sir Stafford, reports on information about "V" weapons, 211-12; minutes to, 292, 305, 307

"Culverin", Operation, 78-80, 288

Cunningham, Admiral of the Fleet Sir Andrew (Viscount Cunningham of Hyndhope), in naval command at "Torch", 6; in naval command in Sicily, 25; on passage of convoys to Sicily, 31-2; reports surrender of Italian Fleet, 102; minutes to, 103, 128; lands troops at Taranto, 126; sends battleships to Salerno, 128; becomes First Sea Lord, 145; on M.T.B. engines, 291; on danger from air attacks off Spain, 299; mentioned, 124. See also Chiefs of Staff

Cunningham, Admiral of the Fleet Sir John, in command Mediterranean, 145; minute to, 177; and operation in Ægean, 193-4

Curtin, Rt. Hon. John, 80

Cyprus, as site of Big Three meeting, 251; garrison at, and Greece, 312

Dalmatia, ports of, 121; fate of Italian troops in, 170

Dalton, Rt. Hon. Hugh, minutes to, 295, 304-5, 312

Davidson, Major-General F. H. N., Director of Military Intelligence, minute to, 292

Deane, Major-General J. R., 255

Defence Committee, and rocket danger, 204-6, 211; and Far Eastern policy, 304

Demobilisation, preparation of scheme for, 151

Dempsey, General Sir M. C., in Sicily, 28

Destroyers, on Arctic convoy work, 228-9; laying up old, and building new, 319

Dieppe raid, 64

Dill, Field-Marshal Sir John, at White House Conferences, 118, 122; and Com-

bined Chiefs of Staff, 268; minute to, 271-2; mentioned, 271
Divide and Conquer, film, 301-2
Divisions, strength of, 315-16
Dnieper, river, 231
Dniepropetrovsk, 231
Dodecanese, Italian bases in, 52, 101-2, 185; plans for operations in, 121, 181-2; Hitler insists on retaining, 184; British successes in, 185; Churchill urges action in, 187; British evacuate islands of, 194, 198-9; use of Commandos in, 309
Doenitz, Admiral, U-boat offensive of, 7-8, 11; on improved U-boat, 15
Dominions, British, and civil aviation, 291
Dover, protection of, 301, 303
Duchess of York convoy, loss of, 299
Duke of York, H.M.S., sinks *Scharnhorst*, 244-5
D.U.K.W., 26
Duncan, Rt. Hon. Sir Andrew, minute to, 309
Dutch East Indies, 78, 113

Eastern Fleet, reduced to convoy protection, 15; aircraft-carrier taken from, 18; addition to, from Mediterranean, 119
Eastern Front, German defeats on, 229-32; Stalin unable to leave, for long, 247-51, 260, 274; German tank divisions moved to, 260. *See also* Russia
Eden, Rt. Hon. Anthony, Foreign Secretary, Churchill's letters, minutes, etc., to, 59, 91, 198, 239-40, 248, 254, 256-7, 292, 297, 308, 310, 314-15; Mountbatten's appointment referred to, 73; at Quebec, 74, 80, 84, 93; work of, in relations with French Committee, 80, 83; and Italian peace moves, 89-92; letters, etc., from, 91-2, 242-3; on powers vested in de Gaulle, 158; and situation in Ægean, 193-4, 198; and resumption of Arctic convoys, 233-4, 239, 241, 243-4; at Conference of Foreign Secretaries, 237, 240-1, 249, 251, 254-6, 261-2, 278; his talks with Stalin, 243-4, 256, 259-61, 276; on friendly atmosphere in Moscow, 261-2
Eder Dam, destruction of, 63
Egypt, defence of, from Rhodes, 180; British troops sent to Eisenhower from, 199; R.A.F. in, 293; base troops in, 316-17
Eighth Army, in North Africa, 24; in Sicily, 25-6, 28, 33, 38; enters Italy, 99;

116-17; seeks to link up with Fifth, 125, 129-30, 136; joins Fifth, 130-1; in Italy, 131, 134-6, 215-16, 224. *See also* British Army
Eisenhower, General Dwight, is opposed to Sicilian landing, 23-4; Supreme Commander of "Husky", 24-5, 56; in Malta, 31; and question of Italian invasion, 34, 36, 85-6, 137; broadcast of, to Italy, 55-7, 91; Churchill's letters, etc., to, 56, 131, 133-5, 186; armistice terms in hands of, 57-8; in "Combined Commanders", 65; instructed to negotiate with Italy, 94-5; proclamation of armistice by, 94, 100, 124-5; Zanussi sent to, 96-7; plans to land airborne troops at Rome, 97-8; Allied staff of, 111; minute from, 134; on Middle East offensive, 134; and French Committee, 154-7, 160; directive to, on Italian situation, 169; at signing of Italian armistice, 172-3; and Italian co-belligerency, 174, 176; instructed to press Italy to declare war, 177-8; and Badoglio Government, 179; Middle East forces at disposal of, 184, 195, 199; fails to give assistance to Ægean action, 184, 188, 195, 199-200; asked to consider Rhodes operation, 191-2; on "V" weapons, 208; Alexander's report to, 216, 220; landing-craft for, 221-2; protest to, on use of Armoured Division, 300, 305; mentioned, 221, 276, 278
Emergency Legislation, Committee on, 318
Empire Air Training Organisation, 107, 298
English Channel, U-boats intended for, 15; tides of, 67; weather of, 67
Enna, 33
Enterprise, U.S.S., 18
Etna, Mount, 33, 37-8
"Eureka", Operation, 263, 272, 288
Europe, Council of, 251
European Advisory Committee, 265
Evatt, Rt. Hon. H. V., 80
Evill, Air Chief Marshal Sir Douglas, 203

Fairbanks, Alaska, 248-9
Far East, U.S. regains mastery in, 15-22; discussion at Quebec on strategy in, 77-82; projected British action in, 113, 115. *See also* Pacific Ocean; South-East Asia Command
Farinacci, Signor, 95

Fascism, German need for revival of, 49-50; gives place to Bolshevism, 89; attempted revival of, 103, 169-70

Fascist Grand Council, convening of, 41; Mussolini defeated at, 45-7, 89

Feltre, Hitler and Mussolini at, 44-5

Fifth Army, Anglo-U.S., at Salerno, 124-125, 127-31; Alexander with, 128-31; reinforcements for, 129; Eighth joins, 130, 136; in Italy, 131, 215, 224; takes Naples, 135. *See also* British Army; United States Army

Fighter Command, surplus crews of, 300, 308

Fijian Commandos, 293

Films, U.S. Army, 301-2

Finland, Swedish need for guarantees on, 256

First Army, 25

Fleet Air Arm, 302

Flying bombs (pilotless aircraft), launching sites for, 203, 205, 208, 210-13; construction of, 204, 209; Britain's danger from, 205-6, 212; counter-measures to, 209, 213; raids on sites, 213

Fog dispersal installation, 302, 315

Foggia, airfields at, 85, 131, 133, 136; moving Strategic Air Force to, 218, 223; insecure position at, 219

Food shortage, post-war, 312

Foreign Secretaries Conference, Moscow, Eden on journey to, 193-4, 237, 239; suggestions for, 248-9; arrangements for, 249-53; military advisers at, 250; agenda for, 250-1, 253; sessions of, 253-256, 262; friendly atmosphere at, 261-2, 266; results of, 265-6, 279; need for Anglo-U.S. meeting after, 276, 278

Formidable, H.M.S., 18

Four-Power Declaration, signed at Moscow, 265

Four Years Plan, for post-war period, 152

France, Commando raids on, 64; choice of site for invasion landings, 65-6; projected landing in Southern, 77, 113, 260; German troops moved to Italy from, 109; de Gaullist movement in, 153; need for strong, 159; launching sites of flying bombs in, 203, 205, 208, 210-13; air reconnaissance of North-West, 203-4; forced labour in, 211; British Intelligence in, 211; launching sites of rockets in, 212; financing resistance in, 297; German and Italian divisions in South, September 8, 1943, 322. *See also* "Anvil"; "Overlord"

Fraser, Admiral of the Fleet Sir B. A. (Baron Fraser of North Cape), narrow escape of, 84; offered post of First Sea Lord, 145; sinks *Scharnhorst*, 146, 244-5

Free French, de Gaulle and, 154-5; in Corsica, 163; administration of, in Syria, 164-5

French Army, and conquest of Corsica, 121, 137, 163; Giraud and de Gaulle dispute command of, 155-7; must be subject to Eisenhower's direction, 156; U.S. arming of, 157, 160-1; Churchill wishes to see the new Army, 164; proposed attack by, in Southern France, 260

French Committee of National Liberation, question of "recognition" of, 80, 83, 155, 158-62; formation of, 154; dissension in, 155, 157, 163; and question of command of Army, 155-7; British relations with, 158-9, 164-5, 297; need for unity in, 160-1; recognition of, 162-163; Giraud resigns from, 163; Churchill hopes to visit, 164; action taken by, in Levant, 164-5

French Consultative Assembly, 163

Furious, H.M.S., 246

Garda, Lake, Fascist Government set up by, 104, 170

"Garibaldi Divisions", in Montenegro, 170

Garigliano, river, 214-15; Fifth Army on, 225

Gaulle, General de, U.S. hostility to, 80, 155-6, 158-9; difficult relations with, 153-65, 157-8; prestige of, 153; in Committee of National Liberation, 154, 158-60, 162; struggle for power between Giraud and, 153-5, 157, 163-4; sole President of French National Committee, 164-5; and French action in Levant, 165; mentioned, 297

Gaullist Committee in London, 154, 158-159; criticism of American policy, 158

"Gee" device for guiding bombers, 288

Gela, 26, 33

General Election, post-war, 152

Genoa, Italian Fleet sails from, to surrender at Malta, 102

George VI, King of England, informed of arrangements made at Quebec, 72-3

Georges, General, on French Committee of National Liberation, 154-5, 160

Gerbini airfields, 26, 33

German Air Force, in Sicily, 23, 28, 33; needed reduction in fighter strength of, before "Overlord", 69; drawn to Italy from Russian front, 109; at Salerno, 125; in Dodecanese, 187, 199; raids Naples and Bari, 225; reduced in Italy, 225; Russian superiority over, 230, 232; weakness of, in fighters, 230

German Army, in Sicily, 23, 28, 33, 35, 38, 56, 292; unpopularity of, in Sicily, 28-9; escapes from Sicily, 38, 85; fatal dispersion of, 48-9; to meet invading armies, 49, 69-70, 254; in Italy, demand for surrender of, 53; in Balkans, 53-4, 121, 225, 322-4; in Italy, disposition of, 85, 96, 120, 216; reinforcements for, 86, 97, 109, 122, 192, 219, 224; near Rome, 89, 216; occupies Rome, 100-1, 117-18; retreats in South Italy, 117; at Salerno, 125; makes stand in Italy, 136, 190, 192, 194, 214-15, 219; in Rhodes, 182, 184; strength of, in Italy, 216, 218-220, 222-3; in North Italy, 216, 220, 222; withdrawn from Italy to Russian front, 222; Russian victories over, 229-232; fighting qualities of, 292; strength of divisions in, 315; order of battle, September 8, 1943, 322-4

German Navy, concentrates against Arctic convoys, 228

German Parachute Division, in Sicily, 33; rescues Mussolini, 103; in Italy, 125; takes Cos, 185; in Leros, 196

Germany, deceived as to Allied objective in Mediterranean, 31; air attacks on, from Italian bases, 36, 53, 223; ill-treatment of Italy by, 43, 53; new weapons of, 44, 125, 142-3, 201-13; unable to spare divisions from Russian front, 44, 49; combined bomber offensive against, 75, 225, 230; Italy afraid to break with, 89-90, 97-8; Italy's desire to fight against, 92-5; Allies' aims regarding, 141-2; Italy declares war on, 173-4; Churchill on post-war plans for, 252-3, 265; satellite States of, post-war treatment, 252; completely within range of British aircraft, 257; warning to, on fate of war criminals, 264-5; hope of break-up within, 310

Ghormley, Vice-Admiral R.L. (U.S.), 16, 18
Gibraltar, 271
Gibson, Wing-Commander Guy, 63
Gioja, 133
Giraud, General Henri, de Gaulle and, 153-155, 157, 163-4; threatens to resign, 155;

in United States, 160-1; resignation of, 163

Glider bombs, German, 125, 128, 143, 212, 312

Goebbels, Joseph, on Mussolini, 170
Goering, Hermann, 49
Gomel, 231
"Gooseberry" blockships, 68, 288
Gort, Field-Marshal Viscount, 173
Gousev, M., Soviet Ambassador, 240-2
Graf Zeppelin, the, 18
Grandi, Dino, at Grand Council meeting, 45-6; not acceptable in Badoglio Government, 176
Graveley, fog dispersal apparatus at, 315
Great Britain, pools Atlantic resources with U.S., 8; takes joint responsibility for North Atlantic convoys, 8; disagrees with U.S. on invasion of Italy, 34-7; not given fair share of credit, 42; demands full share in assault on Japan, 80-2; Italian peace proposals to, 88-98; unity of, with U.S., 110-11, 115, 136; at end of man-power resources, 115; impending attack on, by new weapons, 142-3; need to prepare for peace in, 151-2; relations of, with French Committee, 158-9, 164-5; Italian prisoners of war in, 177, 311-12; "Little Blitz" on, 225; war aims of, 251-2; agenda of, for Moscow Conference, 253; attitude of, to Poland, 314; in post-war transition period, 317-18

Great Powers, importance of meetings between heads of, 242; post-war duties of, 251-2; fixing a meeting of heads of, 272 et seq. See Teheran Conference

Greece, aid for, 53; British troops to keep order in, 312; enemy divisions in, September 8, 1943, 323-4

Greek Navy, in Ægean campaign, 198
Grigg, Rt. Hon. Sir James, minutes to, 294, 297, 299, 301, 305, 315
Guadalcanal, 16-17, 20
Guariglia, Signor, 89-90

"Habakkuk", floating airfield, 69, 288
Habbaniya, as meeting-place for Big Three, 260, 273
Halifax, North Atlantic convoy protection commanded from, 7; Churchill welcomed in, 72
Halsey, Admiral W. F. (U.S.), asks for carriers, 18; reports conquest of Guadalcanal, 20; advances in Solomons, 22

Harbours, artificial, for "Overlord" landings, 66-70

Harriman, Averell, at White House Conference, 122; at Moscow Conference, 255; on Italian ships for Russia, 262

Harris, Marshal of the Royal Air Force Sir A. T., raids Peenemünde, 206-7

Hartz Mountains, rockets made in, 207

Harvard University, gives Churchill degree, 84; speech at, 110-11

"Heavy water", 204

Helleu, M., 164

"Hercules", Operation, 288

Hewitt, Admiral H. K. (U.S.), 25

Hitler, Adolf, on H_2S apparatus, 9; discusses conditions in Sicily, 29-30; meets Mussolini, 44-5, 49, 169-70; crowning strategic error of, 48-9; and Italian crisis, 49-50; holds on to Ægean, 184-5; secret weapons of, 201-13; inspects Peenemünde, 204; orders stand south of Rome, 214; orders holding of Kharkov, 230

Hoare, Rt. Hon. Sir Samuel (Viscount Templewood), Italian approach to, 92, 94

Hollis, Lieut.-General Sir L. C., minutes to, 319-20

Home Fleet, aircraft-carrier needs of, 18; and Arctic convoys, 243; and sinking of Scharnhorst, 244-5

Hopkins, Harry L., at Quebec, 74; illness of, 110; at White House Conference, 122; cable to, on Commander for "Overlord", 268; told of objection to one command for Mediterranean and "Overlord", 271-2; mentioned, 310

Hornet, H.M.S., 17

Horton, Admiral Sir Max, 6

Housing, of agricultural workers, 294, 296, 300

Hube, General, 35

Hudson, Rt. Hon. R. S., minute to, 305

Hughes-Hallett, Rear-Admiral J., 66

Hull, Cordell, and "recognition" of French Committee, 80, 83, 162; at Moscow Conference of Foreign Secretaries, 253-255, 263, 275, 281

Hungary, effect of collapse of Italy on, 54, 121, 187

Hurricane fighter-bombers, at Takoradi, 308

"Husky", Operation, 23-4, 288; preparations for, 24-6, 28-31; British command of, 25; U-boats sink ships for, 31, 306; importance of weather to, 31-2; tanks for, 307. See also Sicily

Hyde Park, President's home, 107, 126

Iceland, Liberators based in, 8

Illustrious, H.M.S., 18

India, "Husky" shipping and aircraft for, 34, 36-7; and command in Burma, 70; assault shipping sent to, 181; U.S. Press correspondents in, 269; Italian prisoners in, 311

Indian Army, in Italy, 87, 131, 224; trained for capture of Rhodes, 181, 184, 186; increased pay for, 294

Indian Ocean, U-boats in, 10; British Fleet in, 52, 119

Indomitable, H.M.S., 18

Irwin, Major-General N. M. S., 70

Ismay, General Sir Hastings (Baron), minutes to, for C.O.S. Committee, 79, 181, 223, 233, 293, 295, 302-3, 309, 313; at White House Conferences, 118, 122; reports on long-range rocket construction, 201-2; at Conference of Foreign Secretaries, 250, 253, 255-6; at Kremlin, 259; minutes to, 281, 292-3, 306, 309

Italia, the, 102

Italian Advisory Council, 265

Italian Air Force, after armistice, 94-5, 136

Italian Army, in Sicily, 23, 28-9, 35, 38, 293; in Balkans, 41, 50, 53-4, 93, 95, 114, 170-1, 322-3; gathered near Rome, 89, 98; demoralisation in, 100; valuable equipment of, 101; in action against Germans, 120; joins Resistance movement, 166; in Rhodes, submits to Germans, 182, 184; order of battle, September 8, 1943, 322-3

Italian Fleet, U-boat losses in, 10; strength of, 23; Germans plan seizure of, 50; advantages of surrender of, 52, 74, 119; Allies ask for surrender of, 93-4; surrender of, 101-3, 118, 167, 171; question of manning, 120; question of uses for, 177, 262-3; Russia asks for ships from, 262-3

Italy, best preliminary to invasion of, 23-24; question of invasion of, 33-7, 74, 76-7; air attacks on, 35, 41, 45, 50; likelihood of collapse of, 35-6, 50-1, 74-5; air attacks on Germany from, 36, 53, 223; blames Mussolini, 40, 47; Allied appeal to people of, 41-4, 51; Great Britain's part in campaign against, 42; seeks to come out of war, 44-5, 49, 89-90; Mussolini's achievements in, 48; German reaction to crisis in, 49-50, 90; discussion of terms for, 51-5, 56-60; question of recognition of Badoglio Government of, 52, 59, 140-1, 143, 167-

169, 171, 174; Allied prisoners of war in, 53, 55-6, 93-4, 166-7; clashes in, between Germans and Italians, 53, 94, 101, 119; Eisenhower's broadcast to, 55-6; surrender of ports and airfields of, 58; armistice terms for, 57-60, 88, 94-5; Churchill's plan for attack in, 74, 77; plan of attack on, 85-7; Fascist-Quisling Government in, 86, 95, 103-4, 143; peace overtures from, 88-98, 110; afraid to break with Germany, 89-90, 97-8; turns from Fascism to Communism, 89; desires to fight Germany, 92-5, 168-9; means of helping Allies suggested to, 93, 95, proclamation of armistice by, 94, 97, 100, 124; must work her passage, 94, 119, 168; danger of anarchy in, 95; signs armistice, 97, 99, 110; virtually under German occupation, 97, 109; Allied landings in, 116-18; Resistance movement in, 103, 166-7; Allied military government in, 104, 168-9; campaign in, 113-14, 120, 134, 214-27; Smuts on action in, 114; build-up of Allied troops in, 117, 189, 192, 218, 220, 223; question of fortified line in, 120; Allied air superiority in, 122, 216, 221; proportion of effort needed for build-up of troops in, 134; Third Front in, 134-5; cause of delay in invasion of, 138-9; question of treachery of, 141; sufferings of, 141, 441; civil war in, 143, 166; political intrigues in, 167-8; free to choose own form of government, 168-9, 171, 174; co-belligerency of, 168-9, 171, 174; Control Commission in, 168-9, 171; King's broadcast to people of, 167-8, 171-3; free to declare war on Germany, 168-9, 171-2; broad-based Government for, 168, 171, 176, 178-9; signs longterm armistice, 171-3; declares war on Germany, 173-4, 176-8; influence of situation in, on operations in Ægean, 188-90, 192-4; landing-craft needed for, 188-9, 215, 218-22, 226, 258, 277; results of campaign in, 199; Allies at disadvantage in, 215-21; withdrawal of troops from, for "Overlord", 215, 220, 254, 258-9, 277; establishing Strategic Air Force in, 218, 223; bad weather in, 219, 222, 224; reduction of German air strength in, 225; campaign in, in relation to "Overlord", 254-5, 258-9, 276-8; Stalin informed of conditions in, 259-60;

alternative courses open to Allies in, 259-60; value to "Overlord" of campaign in, 277-8; troops available for, 299; Armoured Division for, 305; unable to comply with conditions as to prisoners, 311; enemy divisions in, September 8, 1943, 322-4

Jacob, Hon. Major-General Sir E. I. C., minutes to, 294, 316
Jamaica, H.M.S., 244
Japan, U.S. bears brunt of war on, 15; British High Command against, 70; discussions on offensive against, 77-80, 82; attack on, by sea, 78; British share in assault on, 80-2; probable duration of war with, 82, 152, 305; Churchill seeks to send ships against, 119; Italian ships for war on, 262-3; question of Russia joining war against, 263; planning for defeat of, 276, 278
Japanese Marines, in New Guinea, 21
Japanese Navy, in New Guinea operations, 16, 21; in operations off Guadalcanal and the Solomons, 16-20; losses in, 20
Jellicoe, Major the Earl, 182
Jesse, General, 291
Jet-propelled aircraft, British, 292, 305; German, 305, 314
Jones, Dr. R. V., 209, 212
"Jupiter", Operation, 288

Keitel, Field-Marshal, 29, 90
Kerr, Rt. Hon. Sir Archibald Clark, Ambassador to Russia, minutes to, 222, 237; present at Eden's talks with Stalin, 242-3, 259; at Moscow Conference, 255; on Italian ships for Russia, 262; mentioned, 282
Kesselring, Field-Marshal von, in Italy, 85, 130; stands south of Rome, 214
Keyes, Admiral of the Fleet Sir Roger (Baron), 64
Kharkow, 109, 230
Khartoum, as place of Big Three meeting, 251
Kiev, 231
King, Fleet Admiral E. J. (U.S.), Atlantic Convoy Conference under, 6; plans oc-

INDEX

INDEX

cupation of Solomons, 16; seeks priority for Pacific war, 17; and aircraft-carrier exchange, 20; at Anglo-U.S. Conference at White House, 118, 122

King, Rt. Hon. W. L. Mackenzie, and Quebec Conference, 61, 83; Churchill made Privy Counsellor of the Canadian Cabinet at instance of, 106

Kirk, A. C., U.S. Ambassador to Egypt, 280

Korosten, 231

Kremenchug, 231

Kursk, 229-30

La Maddalena, 103

Lae, destruction of reinforcements for, 21; Japanese garrison at, 22; U.S. Army near, 122

Lampedusa, capture of, 30-1, 293

Lancaster bombers, sink *Tirpitz*, 246

Landing-craft, for Sicily landing, 26; for Italian landing, 74, 139, 216, 218; sent from Middle East to India, 181, 189; needed for taking Rhodes, 186, 188-9; needed for Italy but allotted to "Overlord", 188-9, 215, 218-22, 226, 258, 277; manufacture of, 221-2; continuous problem of shortage of, 226

Landing-ships, tank (L.S.T.), 26, 222, 226. *See also* Landing-craft

Laycock, Major-General R. E., at Salerno, 132

Leahy, Fleet Admiral W. D. (U.S.), at White House Conferences, 118, 122; on choice of Commander for "Overlord", 268; told of objection to one command for Mediterranean and "Overlord", 271-272

Leather shortage, 295

Leathers, Lord, minutes to, 290, 312, 314-317; mentioned, 300, 307, 310

Lebanon, independence of, 164; action of French in, 164-5

Leese, Lieut.-General Sir Oliver, in Sicily, 28; and Burma command, 303

Leghorn-Ancona line, 74

Leros, strategic value of, 180, 187, 255; British occupation of, 184-7, 193, 279; loss of, 192, 194-8; Italians in, 194; German attacks on, 195

Liberator aircraft, V.L.R., in U-boat warfare, 7

Licata, 26, 32

"Lilo" breakwater, 68, 288, 319

Lingayen Gulf, death of General Lumsden at, 84

Linnell, Air Marshal Sir Francis, 193

Linosa, capture of, 30

Lisbon, Italian peace overtures at, 88-90; negotiations with Italy at, 93-5

Littorios, the, British claim to, 177, 263; for Pacific war, 177, 262

Litvinov, M., 255

Liverpool, North Atlantic convoy protection commanded from, 7

Lloyd, Rt. Hon. Geoffrey, Secretary for Petroleum, 302

Locri, 117

London, Hitler orders construction of rockets for attack on, 205; flying bombs prepared for, 209; preparations to meet the attack, 213; reducing bus queues in, 312, 316-17

Lumsden, Major-General Sir Herbert, 84

Lützow, the, in Baltic, 234

Lyster, Admiral Sir Lumley, 20

Lyttelton, Captain the Rt. Hon. Oliver, Minister of Production, minutes to, 295, 309, 316

MacArthur, General D. (U.S.), commands in South-West Pacific, 15-16; seeks priority for Pacific theatre, 17; advances in New Guinea, 22; British liaison officer on staff of, 80, 84

McLean, Lieut.-General K. G., 67

Macmillan, Rt. Hon. Harold, and French Committee, 155-7, 160; minutes to, 156, 162-4, 172, 178; and signing of Italian long-term armistice, 172

Madrid, Italian peace overtures in, 92

Malta, Eisenhower's H.Q. at, 31; Italian Fleet at, 102-3; Randolph Churchill at, 132; signing of Italian surrender at, 173; Combined Chiefs of Staff to meet at, 282

Mandalay, 79

Man-power, Britain at end of resources for, 115; use of Italian, 176-7, 311-12, 316; in aircraft production, 292, 314; minute on, 296

Markham valley, 122

Marseilles, 77

Marshall, General G. C. (U.S.), in North Africa, 34, 188-9; approves Mountbatten's appointment, 79; at Anglo-U.S. Conference at White House, 118, 122; on battle for Naples, 122; minute to,

220; on situation in Italy, 221; for Supreme Command of "Overlord", 267-71, 278; mentioned, 117

Massigli, M., 160

Mediterranean, Allied mastery of, 4; U-boats sunk in, 10; Allied forces in area of, 25, 34, 75, 114, 226; German aircraft sent to, 31; effect in, of surrender of Italian Fleet, 74; British Commander in, 76, 269, 271; plans to take Italian bases in Eastern, 101-2, 181-2; Smuts advocates transferring Second Front to, 116; proportions of effort in, 134; Roosevelt's attitude to operations in, 190-1; troops and equipment for "Overlord" withdrawn from, 215, 220-1, 277; German strength in, 225; in relation to "Overlord", 254-5, 258-9, 276-8; suggested single command for "Overlord" and, 271-2. *See also* Ægean; Dodecanese

Mediterranean Commission, French not represented on, 162

Merchant aircraft-carrier (M.A.C. ship), 11

Merchant ships, losses of, to U-boats, 4, 7-10, 12-14, 306; aircraft-carrying, 11; Italian, 57, 94, 263, 314

Messina, 26, 35; ferries at, 29, 31; German reinforcements at, 33; capture of, 38

Messina, Straits of, Germans escape across, 38, 85; British attack across, 85-6, 99, 116-17

Middle East, convoys through Mediterranean to, 4; use of forces in, 121, 300

Middle East Command, plans campaign in Ægean, 181; ordered to send shipping to India, 181, 189-90; stripping of, for Eisenhower, 184, 192, 195, 199; Air Forces of, needed in Dodecanese, 187, 195-6; tanks in possession of, 307

Mikoyan, M., 261

Milan, Communist demonstrations in, 89

Military service, releases from, 301

Mogilev, 232

Möhne Dam, destruction of, 63

Molotov, Vyacheslav, asks for resumption of Arctic convoys, 232, 234; demands limitation of British Service personnel in North Russia, 235; on value of Arctic convoys, 242; present at Eden's talks with Stalin, 243-4, 259; at Conference of Foreign Secretaries, 249, 253-6, 261; elected chairman, 253; conciliatory attitude of, 261; and Cairo Conference, 279, 282-4

Monnet, M., 160

Montecorvino airfield, 85, 125

Montenegro, "Garibaldi Divisions" in, 170

Montgomery, Field-Marshal Sir Bernard (Viscount), in Sicily, 25-6; brings Eighth Army up to link with Fifth at Salerno, 125, 130, 134-6; minute to, 135; minute from, 136; position of, in "Overlord", 269

Moore, Admiral Sir H. R., minute to, 312

Morgan, Lieut.-General Sir F. E., goes to Quebec, 62; "Cossac", 65; plan of, for "Overlord", 75

Moroccan division, in Italy, 224

Morrison, Rt. Hon. Herbert S., and London's danger from rockets, 206; minutes to, as Minister of Home Security, 290, 319

Morton, Major Sir Desmond, 291

Moscow, Conference of Foreign Secretaries in, 237, 241, 247-66

Mosquito aircraft, over Berlin, 207

Mountbatten, Vice-Admiral Lord Louis (Earl), Chief of Combined Operations, 64-6; minutes to, 66, 313; for S.E. Asia Command, 70, 73, 79, 109, 115, 313; demonstrates strength of Pykrete, 81; U.S. Press criticisms of, 269-70

"Mulberry" harbours, 66-8, 288

Murphy, Robert, and French Committee, 155, 157, 160

Mussolini, Benito, difficult position of, 30, 40-1; fall of, 37, 40-9; blamed for war, 40, 43, 47; convenes Grand Council, 41; meets Hitler, 44-5, 169-70; sees the King, 45-7; defeated at Grand Council, 45-6; arrest of, 46-8; achievements of, 48; fatal mistake of, 48; plan to rescue, 49, 103, 143; Allies seek surrender of, 51, 54; consequences of fall of, 52-5; need to decide fate of, 54; "Hundred Days" of, 104, 170; Goebbels on, 170

Naples, plan to attack, 34-7, 74, 85, 131; Allied air attacks on, 35; attack on, nearly a failure, 37; repairs to port of, 87, 117, 133; battle for, 122; capture of, 133, 135; German air attacks on, 225

National Coalition Government, unswayed by agitation, 140; and coal industry, 148-9

Nationalisation issue, 148

Nazism, fight against, 142, 252; punishment of atrocities of, 264-5

Nelson, H.M.S., Italian armistice signed aboard, 173

Netherlands, rockets fired from, 208
Neurath, Herr von, on conditions in Sicily, 29-30
New Britain, 123
New Guinea, Japanese action in, 16, 21; MacArthur advances in, 22, 122
New Mexico, U.S.S., 84
New Zealand Army, in Italy, 87, 223-4
New Zealand Navy, 15
Newfoundland, Liberators based in, 8
Niagara Falls, 73
Nimitz, Admiral C. W. (U.S.), in control, North, Central, and South Pacific, 15; seeks priority for Pacific theatre, 17; asks for aircraft-carriers, 18
Noble, Admiral Sir Percy, head of Naval Mission in Washington, 6
Nogues, General, 154
Normandy, chosen as site for landings, 65-66
North Africa, British naval responsibility in landing on, 18; campaign in, 108; Vichy administrators in, 154; French Committee of National Liberation in, 154-64; transporting Italian prisoners from, 177; shipment of Army equipment from, 295; guards for Italian prisoners in, 300
North Atlantic convoys, Britain and Canada assume responsibility for, 7; come through safety, 8-11
Northern convoys—*see* Arctic convoys
Norway, German ships in waters of North, 228, 244
Norwegian Navy, 245
Novorossisk, 128

"Oboe" blind-bombing device, 288
Ogden, C. K., 313
Oil, improved position regarding, 312; consumption of fog dispersal installation, 315
Oran, 281-2
Orel, 109, 229-30
Ortone, 224
"Overlord", Operation, landing-carft and troops moved from Mediterranean for, 34, 36, 74, 188-9, 215, 218-22, 226, 254, 258-9, 277; discussed at Quebec, 62, 68, 75-6; discussed on Atlantic crossing, 64, 67-71; organisation to prepare plan for, 64-5; choice of site for, 65-6; synthetic harbours for, 66-70; scale of, 69, 254; necessary conditions

for, 69-70, 75, 113, 255-6; C.O.S. report on approved plan for, 75; need for initial strength in, 76, 254, 278; choice of Supreme Commander for, 76, 267-71, 277-8; gathering of army for, 114-15, 140, 215, 220, 320; Smuts suggests abandonment of, 116; Churchill seeks use of landing-craft from build-up for, 188-90, 226-7, 277; danger of rockets to, 208-9; helped by Hitler's strategy in Italy, 215; date of, 226-7, 253-5, 258-60, 277; disposition of Allied forces at, 254; Allied air forces in, 254; in relation to campaign in Mediterranean, 254-5, 258-9, 276-8; suggested single command for Mediterranean and, 271-2. *See also* Second Front

Pachino, 26, 33
Pacific Fleet, U.S., short of aircraft-carriers, 18; British ships for, 22, 119; Italian ships for, 177, 262-3
Pacific Ocean, U.S. regain control of, 15; offensive in South-West, 16-22; British aircraft-carriers for, 18, 20; U.S. victories in South, 122-3; suggested Russian squadron for, 262-3
Paget, General Sir Bernard, in Home Command, 269
Palermo, 26, 35
Pantelleria, capture of, 30, 293
Papen, Herr von, 310
Partisans, Balkan, Italian troops join, 170. *See* Yugoslavia
Pas de Calais, considered as site for "Overlord" landing, 65; flying-bomb launching sites in, 210, 212
Pathfinders, 207
Patton, General G. S. (U.S.), in Sicily, 25, 26, 35, 37
"Pay-as-you-earn", 144
Pearl Harbour, Nimitz's headquarters at, 15, 20
Pennemünde, experimental station at, 201, 209; air reconnaissance of, 202-3; raid on, 203-4, 206-8, 210-12; Hitler inspects, 204; flying-bomb sites at, 210
"Penitent", Operation, 288
Perekop, 231
Pereyaslav, 231
Persia, supplies to Russia through, 231, 238; as venue for Big Three meeting, 250-1. *See also* Teheran Conference

Pescara, 136
Peter II, King of Yugoslavia, marriage of, 297-8
Petralia, 33
Pevensey, 204
Peyrouton, M., 154
Philippine Islands, 16; attack on Japan through, 78
"Phoenix" structures, 68, 288
"Pigstick", Operation, 288
Pilotless aircraft—see Flying bombs
Pizzo, 117
Place, Lieutenant B. C. G., R.N., 234
Playing-cards, shortage of, 304-6
Ploesti, 308
"Plough Force", 288
"Pluto", 288
Poland, rocket experimental works in, 207-8; services of British agents in, 207-208; post-war adjustments to frontiers of, 252, 315
Poling, 204
Polish Armoured Division, 223
Polish Corps, in Syria, 34; in Italy, 87, 223; to leave Persia, 299-300
Ponza, 103
Port Fairy, s.s., 299
Port Moresby, Japanese objective, 16, 21
Portal, Marshal of the Royal Air Force Sir Charles (Viscount), Chief of Air Staff, on Italian-based raids on Germany, 36; at Lake of Snows, 105-6; suggested for Supreme Command, 271; minutes to, 293-4, 296, 298, 300, 302, 314-15. See also Chiefs of Staff
Portal, Viscount, and agricultural cottages, 294, 296
Porto Empedocle, 33
Portugal, grants bases in Azores, 146-8
Potenza, 131
Pound, Admiral of the Fleet Sir Dudley, First Sea Lord, and Sicilian landings, 32; illness of, 106, 118, 128; resignation of, 118, 145; death of, 146; minutes to, 290, 299, 306, 310; mentioned, 20
Pownall, Lieut.-General Sir H. R., 269
Press, criticism of conduct of the war in, 139; discussion of command of "Overlord" in U.S., 268-70; attacks on Mountbatten in U.S., 269-70; excluded from Teheran Conference, 274; proclaims Sicily as next objective, 293
Price, Lieut.-Colonel C. R., 305
Prisoners of war, in Italian hands, 53, 55-57, 93-4; Italian, release of, 55-6, 91; Italian help given to Allied, 166-7; use of Italian, in Britain, 177, 311, 316; Armoured Division used to guard, 177, 299-300, 307; alteration in status of Italian, 311
Prussia, militarism of, 141-2; plans for postwar treatment of, 252
Public Relations Officers, 299
Pyke, Mr., 69
Pykrete, 69, 81

"Quadrant", 62, 72-87, 288. See Quebec Conference
Quebec, Churchill broadcasts in, 84, 105-9; mentioned, 106
Quebec Conference, 61, 74-83; Churchill's staff for, 62-3; voyage to, 63-4, 68-71, 90-1; arrangements for housing the Conference, 72-3; "Overlord" plan approved at, 75; question of Supreme Commander raised at, 77, 267; amusing incident at, 80-1; decisions arrived at, 82-3, 94, 182; Smuts on results of, 113-114; question of recognition of French Committee discussed at, 162; attempt at, to arrange meeting of Big Three, 247-250; decisions made at, invalidated by subsequent events, 277
Queen Mary, 62-3

Rabaul, Japanese base at, 16; U.S. threat to, 22
Radar, short-wave, defeats U-boats, 8; U.S. production of, 11; in detection of long-range rockets, 204-5
Radio-controlled bombs, German, 125
Raeder, Admiral, 228
Ragusa, 28
Ramsay, Admiral Sir B. H., and "Husky", 25
Randazzo, 37
Ranger, U.S. aircraft-carrier, 18, 20
Rangers, U.S., at Salerno, 125
Rangoon, 79, 304
Reconstruction, Ministry of, 152
Reggio, 116-17, 136
Renown, H.M.S., Churchill's return home in, 126, 128-9, 132-3
Republican-Fascist Government, Mussolini's, 170-1
Resistance movement, in Italy, 103, 166-7; in Balkans, 121; Italians join, in Balkans, 170; in France, financing of, 297. See also Partisans

Rhodes, plans for operations against, 74, 101-2, 118, 121, 181-2, 186; proportion of troops needed for, 134; strategic value of, 180, 186; too strong to attack, 182, 184; shipping needs for attack on, 186-90; Churchill urges importance of attack on, 186-7, 189, 191-2, 195, 255; Roosevelt on attack on, 190; Wilson's planned attack on, 192-3; deferment of attack on, 194; German division on, September 8, 1943, 324

Ribbentrop, Herr von, meets Italian Foreign Minister, 89-90; mentioned, 310

Rifle strength in infantry battalion, 294

Riviera, Italian forces on, to be withdrawn, 53

Roatta, General, 29-30

Rockets, fired from aircraft, at U-boats, 8; Churchill gives warning of V2, 142; reports of German construction of, 201-205, 210-11; Hitler orders enormous quantities of, 205; London's danger from, 205-6, 210, 213; effect of Peenemünde raid on use of, 207-8, 211; experimental, salvaged by British agents, 208; Eisenhower on menace of, 208; sites of factories making, 211; launching sites of, 212

Roma, the, 102

Rome, air raids on, 35, 45; leaflets dropped on, 44; German occupation of, 49, 95, 100-1, 104, 117; Allies seek to capture airfields near, 76, 85; German troops near, 85, 89; danger of delay in liberating, 86, 95; Italians desire landing north of, 96-7; plan to land airborne troops at, 97-100, 117; General Taylor in, 99-100; Committee of Liberation in, 103; question of making open city of, 173; reconstruction of Government to take place after occupation, 178-9; German stand south of, 190, 192, 194, 214; Allied need for, 219-20; Allied advance to, 224; policy after capture of, 259-60

Rommel, Marshal, 29, 85

Roosevelt, President Franklin D., correspondence with Churchill, 18, 42, 51-52, 54-60, 73, 89, 92, 107, 133, 154-7, 159-62, 164, 167-9, 172-9, 186-92, 194, 210-11, 220-2, 240, 268-70, 273-4, 276-283, 311; and attack on Italy, 34; message of, to Italian people, 42-3; on terms for Italy, 51, 55-8, 60; suggests Quebec Conference, 61; arrangements made for, at Quebec, 72-3; Churchill visits, 73, 109-10, 117, 126; at Quebec,

74, 107 n.; and leadership of "Overlord", 76, 267-71; Far Eastern strategy of, 77-8; approves Mountbatten's appointment, 79; mistrusts de Gaulle, 80, 154-7; offended at Russian message, 83-4; on opening negotiations with Italy, 93-5; at Anglo-U.S. Conference at White House, 118-19, 122; on "recognition" of French Committee of National Liberation, 160-2; on recognition of Badoglio Government, 169, 174-6; approves co-belligerency declaration, 174-175; on Sforza, 175-6; attitude of, to Eastern Mediterranean operations, 188, 190, 192; told of menace of rockets on London, 210-11; joint message of, to Stalin, on Big Three meeting, 248-9; against Teheran as meeting-place, 260, 273-6, 279-81; signs declaration on war criminals, 264-5; wishes to combine Mediterranean Command with "Overlord", 271; correspondence with Stalin, on meetingplace for Big Three, 274-5, 283; anxiety of, to placate Russia, 276, 283; on Anglo-U.S. meeting before Teheran, 276, 279; suggests Russian representative at Combined Chiefs of Staff meetings, 279-80; differs from Churchill as to proceedings at Cairo, 282-4; and monthly reports on U-boat warfare, 306; and post-war civil aviation, 311

Rosarno, 117

Rossi, General Francesco, 322

Roumania, effect of collapse of Italy on, 54, 121, 187

"Round-up", Operation, 288

Rowan, Leslie, 133

Royal Air Force, part of, in Battle of Atlantic, 8-11; in Sicily, 25-6, 28, 38; in Italy, 37, 129, 133, 135-6; destruction of Möhne and Eder Dams by, 63; Peenemünde raid of, 206-8; raids "ski sites", 210-11, 213; sinks Tirpitz, 245-6; squadrons for Australia, 298-9; Australian air crews in, 298. See also Bomber Command; Coastal Command; Fighter Command; Strategic Air Force

Royal Navy, aircraft-carrier position in, 18; in invasion of Sicily, 25, 38; in invasion of Italy, 37, 125-6, 128, 130; effect of surrender of Italian Fleet on, 52; meets Italian Fleet, 102; in Taranto harbour, 126; question of accession to, of Italian ships, 177; helps in Ægean operations, 185, 195-6; losses of, in

Ægean, 198; midget submarines of, disable *Tirpitz*, 233-4; and Arctic convoy work, 228-9, 243; M.T.B.s of, 291; construction programme of, in relation to laying up vessels, 319
Rubber, Army requirements, 297
Russia, not included in the Quebec discussions, 82; increasing bearishness of, 83-4; urges Second Front, 108, 135; victories of, 109, 229-32; Smuts on disproportionate share of, in land warfare, 112-13; opening Black Sea route to, 114, 181, 238, 242, 255, 257; hopes for post-war relations with, 115; Italian campaign an aid to, 128, 220, 225; and French Committee, 159-60; withdrawal of German troops from Italy to, 222; sceptical of Polish Corps, 223; suspension of Arctic convoys to, 228-9; insists on resumption of convoys, 232-233, 237-9; number and treatment of British personnel in North, 234-9, 241, 243-4, 303; British seamen arrested in, 242-3, 261; R.A.F. attacks *Tirpitz* from, 246; post-war consideration of frontiers of, 252, 314; relations between Poland and, 252-3; agenda of, for Moscow Conference, 253; aided by threat of Second Front, 260-1; asks for share of Italian Fleet, 262-3; friendly attitude in, 266; Red Cross supplies to, 290; attitude of, to rearmed Turkey, 308
Russian Air Force, superiority of, over German, 230, 232
Russian Army, victories of, 109, 128, 229-232; strength of divisions in, 315
Russian Navy, question of Pacific squadron, 262-3
Russian Relief Fund, 242
Rye, 204

St. Nazaire raid, 64
Salamaua, 22, 122
Salazar, Dr., 147
Salerno, landing at, 35, 85-6, 124-5; airfields near, 85; battle of, 125-31, 216, 218; reinforcements for, 125, 129-31; naval bombardment at, 125, 128; Spitfires operating from, 129; complaints about delay in landing at, 138-9. *See also* "Avalanche"
Salo, Republic of, 170
Samos, British occupation of, 184-5, 193; German attacks on, 195; garrison of, sent to Leros, 196; evacuation of, 198

Sandys, Right Hon. Duncan, investigates reports on long-range rockets and flying bombs, 202-5, 209
Sangro river, 214, 224
Saratoga, U.S.S., 17
Sardinia, Eisenhower advocates landing in, 23; air attacks on, 31; question of seizing, 34, 52, 77, 85, 121, 131, 296; capture of, 135, 137, 171; enemy divisions in, September 8, 1943, 322-4
"Saturn", Operation, 288
Saturnia, the, 314
Scharnhorst, the, sinking of, 146, 244-5
"Schnorkel" device, 15
Schuster, Sir Claud (Baron), 318
Second Front, command of sea essential for, 4; U-boats prepared against, 15; German troops to meet threat of, 49, 260-1; Russian urgency on question of, 108, 253, 256; demands for, 140; rockets as weapons against, 204, 208-9; British readiness to discuss, with Russian experts, 241, 250; discussed at Moscow Conference, 253-6. *See also* "Overlord"
Selborne, Earl of (Viscount Wolmer), minute to, 297
Seventh Army, U.S., in Sicily, 25-6, 28, 33, 35, 37-8; in Italy, 218
"Sextant", Operation, 281, 288
Sforza, Count, 168; agrees to work with King and Badoglio, 175-6
Shemiergembeinski, Lieut.-General, 211
"Shingle", Operation, 288
Shipbuilding, U.S. programme of, 4, 11; Canadian, 107-8
Shipping, effect of opening Mediterranean on, 4; stringency in Mediterranean, 115-6, 125; stringency in Far East, 115; for carrying Italian prisoners from Africa, 177; sent to India from Middle East, 181-2; great demands on, 234; for Arctic convoys, 234-5; lost to aircraft off Spain, 299; losses in South Atlantic, 310; Washington report on, 315; monthly totals of losses, 321
Sicily, decision to invade, 23-4; ports and airfields of, 26, 33; plan of attack on, 26-8; enemy strength in, 28, 38, 292-3; assembling troops and equipment for, 28-9, 31; unpopularity of German troops in, 29-30; air attacks on, 31; discussions on operation to follow invasion, 33-7, 295-6; invasion of, 32-3, 35, 37-9, 56-57, 108; casualties in, 39; Hitler on defence of, 44-5; return of Italian prisoners taken in, 55-6; importance of destruction

of German divisions in, 56-7; limited range of air cover from, 85, 125; Alexander congratulated on conquest of, 95; Italian armistice signed in, 97, 99; disengaging landing-craft from beaches of, 139; Stalin's congratulations on conquest of, 248; deception plans for, 293. *See also* "Husky"

Sinclair, Rt. Hon. Sir Archibald, minutes to, 290, 296, 298

"Ski sites", bombing of, 210, 212-13

"Sledgehammer", Operation, 289

Slessor, Air Chief Marshal Sir J. C., chief of Coastal Command, 6

Smith, Lieut.-General Bedell (U.S.), negotiates with Italian emissary, 95-7; at signing of armistice, 99, 173

Smolensk, 231

Smuts, Field-Marshal Rt. Hon. J. C., letters to, on invasion of Italy, 34, 114-116; on disappointing progress of Allies, 112-14; recommended to Eisenhower, 132; offers Italian prisoners to Britain, 316

Solomon Islands, Japanese plan to seize, 16; U.S. attack, 16; naval actions off, 17-20; U.S. advance in, 22; Japanese defeat in, 123

Soong, Dr. T. V., in Quebec, 80, 83

South Africa, Italian prisoners in, 311, 316

South African Armoured Division, 300

South Dakota, U.S.S., 18

South-East Asia Command, 70-1; Mountbatten to command, 70, 73, 79, 82-3, 109; approved at Quebec, 77, 82; Viceroy told of, 82-3; need to damp down publicity on, 313

Spaatz, General C. A. (U.S.), 26

Spain, convoy lost off, 299

Spears, Major-General Sir Edward, 164

Special Air Service Regiment, 132, 182

Speer, Dr., on V2 rockets, 205

Spezia, Italian Fleet sails from, to surrender, 102

Spitfires, for Australia, 298; at Takoradi, 308

Stalin, Generalissimo, correspondence with Churchill, 73, 98-9, 171, 234-40, 247-251, 272-3, 284; on Italian overtures, 83; bearishness of, 83-4; kept informed of Italian situation, 83, 98-9, 171, 259-60; on value of Italian campaign, 128; agrees to recognition of Badoglio Government, 167, 171, 173, 177; approves co-belligerency declaration, 174-5; offensive letter

of, on the resumption of convoys, 237-42; Churchill's attempts to arrange meeting with, 242, 247-51; Eden's talks with, 243-4, 256, 259-61; unable to go far from Russia, 247-9; on Conference of Foreign Secretaries, 248-50; insists on Teheran as place of meeting, 256, 272-4, 276, 279, 281; on alternative courses open in Italy, 259-60; friendly and sympathetic attitude of, 261; signs declaration on war criminals, 264-5; correspondence of, with Roosevelt, on meetingplace for Big Three, 274-5; confirms Teheran arrangements, 283; on Cairo Conference, 284; interested in Basic English, 314

Stirling, Lieut.-Colonel David, 182

Stord, the, 245

Strang, Sir William, 255

"Strangle", Operation, 289

Strategic Air Force, in Italy, demands of, obstruct build-up of Army, 218, 223-4; raids Turin, 225

Strong, Major-General K. W. D., opens negotiations with Italy, 93-4

Submarines, midget, disable *Tirpitz*, 233-234; acoustic torpedoes for, 312. *See also* U-boats

Sumatra, need to seize tip of, 78-9. *See also* "Culverin"

Surrender, Instrument of, for Italy, 58, 60, 168

Suvla Bay, 126, 127

Swayne, Lieut.-General Sir John, 301

Sweden, Russia suggests approach to, for air bases, 254, 256, 261; advantages to be gained from entry of, into war, 257

Swingate, 204

Syfret, Admiral Sir Neville, 118

Syracuse, 26, 33, 99

Syria, 164-5

Tactical air forces, in Italy, 218, 225

Taganrog, 109

Takoradi, economies in personnel at, 294; aircraft accumulating at, 308

Tangier, Italian peace moves in, 90-2

Tanks, in Mediterranean area, 307; fall in output of, 309

Taranto, plan to take, 85, 117-18; Italian squadron sails from, to surrender, 102; Navy lands airborne troops at, 125-6; British troops near, 131; value of port of, 135; base at, 136; attitude of dockyard workers in, 262

Taylor, General Maxwell D. (U.S.), 99-100

Tedder, Marshal of the Royal Air Force Sir A. W. (Baron), in command of Air in Sicily, 25-6, 31

Teheran Conference, difficulties in arranging, 247-51, 256, 260, 272 *et seq.*; Roosevelt against location of, 260, 273-6; Italian Fleet discussed at, 263; war criminals to be discussed at, 263-5; cordon round area of, 272-3; Anglo-U.S. meeting preliminary to, 279-84; venue finally settled, 283

"Tentacle", floating airfield, 289

Termoli, 133, 136

Third Front, 134-5, 140, 225

Thoma, General von, 49, 278

Tirpitz, the, threatens Arctic convoys, 228; disabled by midget submarines, 233-4, 243; sunk, 245-6

Tito, Marshal, "Garibaldi Divisions" of, 170

"Torch", Operation, 17, 289; British naval responsibilities in, 18; an American expedition, 24-5

Torpedoes, acoustic, 312; acoustic homing, 314

Toulon, Italian forces in, 53; question of attack near, 77

"Trident" Conference, 34-5, 75, 289

Tripoli, coast defences of, 294

Troina, 37

Tromsö Fiord, 246

"Tube Alloys", 144, 289

Tulagi, Japanese hold, 16

Tunis, Churchill proposes to go to, 188-9, 191; conference in, and Ægean campaign, 191-3

Tunisia, campaign in, 25-6; return of Italian prisoners taken in, 55-6; de Gaullist movement in, 153; German morale in, 292

Turin, Communist demonstrations in, 89; air raid on, 225

Turkey, question of putting pressure on, to enter war, 54, 114, 256-7; effect of Italian capitulation on, 121; effect of events in Ægean on, 181, 187, 255; need for air bases in, 193-5, 308; value to Allies of participation of, in war, 257; Russia seeks three-Power approach to, 254, 256-7, 261; and German strength in Balkans, 257; joint Anglo-Russian action regarding, 266; British plans to establish air force in, 293; arms for, Russia and, 308

Twenty Years Treaty with Russia, 314

U-boats, victory over, 4, 11-15; shipping losses to, 4, 7, 12-14, 306; rise and decline of fleet of, 5, 7-10, 243; means taken to combat, 7-11; in South Atlantic, 10, 232, 310; new type of, 15; sink ships gathering for "Husky", 31, 306; crisis in battle with, 228-9; acoustic torpedo of, 234; joint statements on warfare against, 306

Unconditional surrender, Italian, 51, 56, 91-2, 94-5, 98-9, 173

Unicorn, H.M.S., 18

United States, shipbuilding programme of, 4, 11; pools Atlantic resources with Britain, 6, 8; aircraft production of, 11, 298; bears brunt of war against Japan, 15; increasing strength of, 22; misgivings in, on extending Mediterranean campaign, 34-7; does not give Britain fair share of credit, 42; seeks to separate Italian people from Government, 51; given leadership of "Overlord", 76; feeling about de Gaulle in, 80, 155-6, 158-9; Churchill in, 109-10, 117; unity of, with Britain, 110-11, 115, 136; hampers Italian campaign, 137; attitude to French Committee of National Liberation in, 159-62; Sforza in, 175; agenda of, for Moscow Conference, 253; and Russian share in Italian Fleet, 262-3; and post-war civil aviation, 291; message to Consuls in Middle West, 310; and question of Russian frontiers, 314

United States Air Force, "sea frontiers" of, 7; part of, in Battle of Atlantic, 7-11; in Sicily, 25-6, 28, 38; bombs Rome, 35; bombers of, withdrawn from Mediterranean, 36; successes of, in South Pacific, 122; raids "ski sites", 213

United States Airborne Division, in Sicily, 28, 32; plans to land at Rome, 97-100, 117; in Italy, 130

United States Army, on Guadalcanal, 20; in New Guinea, 21; in North-West Africa, 24-5; in Sicily, 25; in invasion of France, 76, 115; assembling in Britain, 115, 140; in Italy, 124-5, 129-131, 133, 215; strength of divisions in, 315-16. *See also* Fifth Army

United States Marines, on Guadalcanal, 16-17, 20

United States Navy, convoy escort duties of, 8; regains superiority in Pacific, 15; surprised off Guadalcanal, 16-17; engagements of, off Solomons, 17-20; losses in, 20; part of, in attack on Japan, 78

"V" weapons—see Flying bombs; Rockets
Vaagsö raid, 64
Valiant, H.M.S., 102, 128
Vehicles, boxing of, 295
Ventnor, 204
Victor Emmanuel, King of Italy, dismisses Mussolini, 41, 45-7; called upon to assume responsibilities, 45-6; Churchill's message to, 56; attitude of Allies to, 59, 140-1, 143, 167-9, 171-2; 178; seeks peace, 89; escapes to Brindisi, 100-1; broadcast of, to Italian people, 167-8, 171-3; to form broadbased, anti-Fascist Government, 168, 171, 176, 178-9; Sforza willing to co-operate with, 175-6
Victorious, H.M.S., 18, 20, 246
Volturno, river, 136, 215
Voroshilov, Marshal, 255
Vyshinsky, M., 255

Walker, Captain F. J., R.N., 11
War Cabinet, approves directive on Italy, 54; on armistice terms for Italy, 56; telegram to, 83; asks that landing-craft be left in Italy, 221; agrees to transference of Italian ships to Russia, 262; and plans for transition period, 317-18
War criminals, drafted declaration on, 263-5
War damage insurance, 144
Warspite, H.M.S., meets Italian Fleet, on the way to surrender, 102; disabled at Battle of Salerno, 128
Washington, Atlantic Convoy Conference in, 6, 7; Churchill in, 84, 109-10, 117-118
Washington Conference, 34, 181
Wasp, H.M.S., 17

Watten, German constructions at, 205; raid on, 210-11
Wavell, Field-Marshal Sir A. P. (Earl), Viceroy of India, told of S.E.A.C., 82-3; prisoners taken by, 311
"Whale" floating piers, 289
White House, Washington, Churchill at, 109, 118, 122; conference with President at, 118-22; Churchill presides at conference at, 122-3
Whiteley, Lieut.-General Sir J.F.M., 86-7, 199
Wilson, General Sir Henry Maitland, minutes to, 101, 191, 195, 198; plans operations in Dodecanese, 121, 181-2, 186, 192; instructions to, regarding Levant, 165, 194; deprived of needful shipping, 181-2, 184-6; minutes from, 184, 192, 196; action taken by, 184; shipping needs of, 186; mentioned, 25, 74
"Window" device, 289
Wingate, Major-General O. C., 62, 73; at Quebec Conference, 63, 71; plans of, for Burma campaign, 78-9, 115; Churchill on his qualities, 303
Wingate, Mrs., 63
"Winterstellung", the, 214-15; breaking through, 224
Winterton, Earl, 300
Wood, Rt. Hon. Sir Kingsley, Chancellor of Exchequer, death of, 144
Woolton, Lord, Minister of Reconstruction, 152; minute to, 312
World Organisation, and civil aviation, 290
Wound stripes, 293

Yugoslavia, Allied aid for, 53; fate of Italian troops in, 170; enemy divisions in, September 8, 1943, 322, 324
Yunnan, 79

Zanussi, General, 96-7
Zionists, 62
"Zip", 289

SOURCES OF THE ILLUSTRATIONS

1 German mine-layers. (Atlantic)
2 A German aircraft and a destroyer coordinating an attack on a British submarine. (Presse-Bild Zentrale)
3 The sinking of a submarine: an explosive charge hits the submarine as, damaged, it surfaces. (War Museum)
4 An attack on a British convoy bound for Russia. (War Museum)
5 The British destroyer "Bittern" on fire. (War Museum)
6 Russian motor torpedo boats ready to depart. (Novosti, Moscow)
7 Sicily: the invasion fleet. (War Museum)
8 Infantry reach the beaches after debarking from landing craft. (War Museum)
9 Light equipment and shells pass from hand to hand. (French Documentation)
10-11 Heavy equipment being landed. (War Museum)
12 Troops at work making landing-areas on the sand. (War Museum)
13 The arrival of the Highland Division. (War Museum)
14 Officers go from one ship to another by the hazardous means of a breeches-bouy. (War Museum)
15 Maybe the enemy is just behind the wave. (War Museum)
16 Street fighting in Acireale on road to Messina. (American Cultural Centre)
17 The victors of the deserts fighting in different conditions: the invasion of a mountainous region. (War Museum)
18 Devasted streets in Pantelleria. (War Museum)
19 The landings South of Rome. (War Museum)
20 Under enemy fire. (War Museum)
21 Fording a river under fire. (War Museum)
22 British soldiers crouching in a bomb crater before the assault; burning fuel stores can be seen in front of them. (War Museum)
23 In the villages, each house contains an enemy soldier. (French Documentation)
24 German soldiers at the Nettuno front. (German photo, B.N. Prints)
25 German prisoners. (French Documentation)
26 American prisoners. (German photo, B.N. Prints)
27 Sir Winston Churchill reviews the Highlanders. (Keystone)
28 The Quebec Conference: front row: Mackenzie King, Roosevelt and Churchill; back row: Admirals and Generals Arnold, Portal, Brooke, King, Dill, Pound, Leahy. (War Museum)
29 Nikita Khruchev as an officer of the Red Army. (Novosti, Moscow)
30 Sir Winston and Lady Churchill aboard the "Queen Mary". (War Museum)

31 Sir Winston at Whitehall making his "V" for victory sign to the crowd. (War Museum)

32 The German General, Guderian. (Army Cinematographic Service)

33 A "V2" on its transporter. (War Museum)

34 The launching of a "V2". (War Museum)

35 A "Buzz-bomb" photographed immediately after launching. (War Museum)

36 London: the results of a flying bomb explosion. (War Museum)

37 Farrington Market, London, after a "V1" fell on it. (Radio-Times, London)

38 Aerial view of a factory making aviation material at Reggio-Emilia. (War Museum)

39 A photograph taken from the same angle after an allied bombing raid. (War Museum)

40-41 "Baltimores" of the R.A.F. over Italy. (War Museum)

42 American "B-25 Mitchell" bombers making for Cassino. (French Documentation)

43 Spitfires of the R.A.F. returning from a flight over the Italian beach-heads. (War Museum)

44 Loading a German Junkers 87. (Weltbild)

45 Kiev: the main street as it looked on the day the town was liberated. (Novosti, Moscow)

46 "Halt"! A German soldier on the Russian front. (Scherl)

47 Italian soldiers fighting in Russia had to wear German army uniforms. They were also obliged to swear allegiance to the Fuehrer. (Fulgur)

48-49 Fighting in Zhitomir which was taken, lost and then retaken by the Germans. (48: Transocean—49: Trampus)